*NAPOLEON'S SATELLITE
KINGDOMS*: MANAGING
CONQUERED PEOPLES

NAPOLEON'S SATELLITE KINGDOMS:

Managing Conquered Peoples

by Owen Connelly

ROBERT E. KRIEGER PUBLISHING COMPANY
MALABAR, FLORIDA
1990

Original Edition 1965
Reprint Edition 1990 with updated bibliography

Printed and Published by
ROBERT E. KRIEGER PUBLISHING COMPANY, INC.
KRIEGER DRIVE
MALABAR, FLORIDA 32950

Library of Congress Cataloging-in-Publication Data

Connelly, Owen, 1929-
    [Napoleon's satellite kingdoms]
    Napoleon's satellite kingdoms: Managing conquered peoples / Owen
Connelly.
        p.   cm.
    Reprint. Originally published: Napoleon's satellite kingdoms. New
York : Free Press, c1965.
    Includes bibliographical references.
    ISBN 0-89464-416-5
    1. Frances—History—Consulate and Empire, 1799–1815. 2. Europe—
History—1789–1815. 3. Napoleon I, Emperor of the French,
1769–1821—Influence. 4. Bonapartism. I. Title.
    DC202,C6   1990
    940.2'7—dc20   89-19917
                                                                          CIP

10 9 8 7 6 5 4 3 2

". . . through this village I saw him ride,
followed by kings."
                              —*Pierre-Jean de Béranger*
                                    (1780–1857)

FOREWORD

This book is a fascinating essay on a historical subject of contemporary relevance: the government of conquered peoples by an imperial power. The author might have drawn his data from the government of satellite countries by imperial communist Russia or from the management of outlying areas by the imperial United States. However, he describes, and describes very well, the handling of conquered peoples by the imperial France of Napoleon.

When in 1792 and 1793 French armies of the French Revolution began to invade the neighboring lands of Belgium, Holland, Germany, and Italy, nothing in the experience of Frenchmen had prepared them for the problem of introducing radically different institutions to peoples who were perhaps reluctant to receive them. When the French monarchy of the old regime had annexed a contiguous province, such as ducal Lorraine, there was little fundamental difference between the institutions of unreformed France and unreformed Lorraine. Besides, the French monarchy already tolerated so many provincial variations of customary law and privilege that the addition of a few more was not considered serious. The new province was usually allowed to retain most of its local laws and customs, while the top-level French administrative institutions were introduced above them. But revolutionary France differed profoundly from her neighbors. When the Revolutionary

(vii)

armies moved into the advance, into the Low Countries and the Rhineland and over the Alps into Italy, the changing French leadership faced the problem not only of whether these recently conquered regions should be retained but also whether the new French institutions should be introduced and if so, how. At first, French leadership was largely unconscious of the intricacies of the latter problem. They felt, why, of course! all the subject peoples will want liberty. Gradually, however, civil servants, generals, and ministers who were operating in the conquered areas became aware of the complexities of governing conquered populations. Individually, several of the administrators moved from naïveté to sophistication with regard to the government of conquered peoples, while French policy, which they helped to form, also evolved toward maturity.

The evolution of Napoleon Bonaparte's views on this question after he assumed command of the French Army of Italy in 1796 was part of the broader evolution of French policy, while his handling of conquered peoples after 1805 was its culmination. One element of his imperial policy was to commission his relatives as administrators of conquered areas. From 1805 to 1807 he made his step-son Eugène the viceroy of the Kingdom of Italy, his brother Joseph the king of Naples, his brother Louis the king of Holland, and his brother Jérôme the king of Westphalia. Later, in 1808, he appointed his brother Joseph king of Spain and his brother-in-law Joachim Murat king of Naples. Professor Connelly's volume tells what became of these kingdoms and their rulers and Napoleon from 1805 to 1815.

Professor Connelly of the University of North Carolina at Greensboro is one of the best-qualified scholars in the country to prepare this work. Through prolonged research into the history of Joseph as king of Spain, he gained insights into Napoleon's methods of managing a conquered people Through extensive reading he was able to extend these insights to the other satellite kingdoms. The result is a volume scholarly in content and filled with human interest. I consider it a privilege to recommend it to your attention.

Harold T. Parker

Duke University

PREFACE

This book deals with the Napoleonic kingdoms of Italy, Naples, Holland, Westphalia, and Spain. These five form a category among states of the Grand Empire in that each was (1) of sufficient size, population, and wealth to be a kingdom, (2) subject to more direct control by the emperor than allied kingdoms, like Saxony and Bavaria, and (3) governed by a member of Napoleon's own dynasty. The rulers were Eugène de Beauharnais, Napoleon's stepson (Italy), Joseph Bonaparte, his elder brother (Naples, then Spain), Marshal Joachim Murat and wife Caroline Bonaparte, the emperor's sister (Naples), Louis Bonaparte, his brother (Holland), and Jérôme Bonaparte, his youngest brother (Westphalia).

My object has been to produce a work of synthesis based largely on the findings of specialists on individual states or geographic areas of the Grand Empire and printed primary sources. If it has been done properly, such a book should be useful. Nothing satisfactory has been written in any language to fill the gap between general histories, which perforce devote little space to the kingdoms, and the special studies and monographs, which are too detailed for most readers. Even the great multivolume histories, excellent but antiquated, give short shrift to the puppet states. The biographies and collective biographies are of some use in studying the rulers, but give only scattered and unreliable information on the kingdoms. In all categories much material is unavailable in English.

I acknowledge my great debt to my good friend Professor Herbert H. Rowen of Rutgers, who asked me to write this book and subsequently, with humor and good will, gave me honest advice; Mr. Peter Quennell, a "man of letters" in the great English tradition, and Mr. Alan Hodge, co-editors of *History Today*, who generously promoted my early work; Professor Harold T. Parker of Duke University, a selfless teacher and consummate scholar, who shared with me his insights on Napoleonic history; Professors Carl H. Pegg and George V. Taylor of the University of North Carolina, who taught me the historian's craft and much of humility; Professors Theodore Ropp and Joel Colton of Duke University, my friends and counselors; Chancellor Otis A. Singletary, Dean Mereb E. Mossman, and Professor Richard Bardolph of the University of North Carolina at Greensboro, who personally encouraged me and did much to facilitate my work; Mr. Elvin Strowd and Mr. Charles Adams of the Duke and University of North Carolina at Greensboro libraries respectively and their staffs, who have been consistently helpful; and my loyal girl-friday, Miss Karen Whitley. I express my sincere gratitude also to the Research Council of the University of North Carolina at Greensboro, which helped defray the cost of producing the manuscript of this book.

Regarding the 1990 Reprint Edition, I am most grateful to The Institute for Advanced Study, at Princeton, and its Director, Dr. Marvin L. Goldberger, for allowing me to revise the Bibliography (among other projects) during the Fall of 1989, and to my many helpful friends at Princeton, especially Professors Peter Paret and R. R. Palmer. I also thank the University of South Carolina for giving me leave to take up membership at the Institute. Finally, I must express my appreciation to Mr. Robert E. Krieger, President of Krieger Publishing, who, of course, made the reprint possible, and Ms. Marie Bowles, his efficient and personable Production Manager, who saw the book through to completion.

Owen Connelly

1. For full bibliography see pp. 347–74.

CONTENTS

LIST OF MAPS

An Introduction:
SOME QUESTIONS

In late September 1812 smoke still rose above Moscow. For days the Grande Armée had done nothing more glorious than fight fires. Unable to make the Russians either negotiate or fight, Napoleon pondered retreat. Awaiting his orders were soldiers made morose and short-tempered by the ominous atmosphere, hunger, cold, and inactivity, cheered only by the thought of saving the loot which burdened their knapsacks, saddlebags, caissons, wagons, and carriages. Ready to march also were the French of the Moscow community—men, women, and children—who knew they would be massacred if the army left without them.

In Spain at the same moment a similar group crowded Valencia, recovering from a retreat. King Joseph Bonaparte had lost Madrid to Wellington. With part of his army he had shepherded hundreds of French and Spanish civilians across the blistering plains of La Mancha. Guerrillas had pursued him all the way, butchering his stragglers. His Spanish guard had deserted, silently, a few at a time. His courtiers and their ladies, fainting in the heat, carping at the soldiers, their sullen faces condemning him, had put his patience to a bitter test. But the king was recovering his spirits. Wellington, he said, had struck before his forces were assembled. He was assembling them. Meanwhile he and his splendid court took in the sights of the city.

In Westphalia, King Jérôme Bonaparte, sent home from the Grande Armée in July for disobedience, was dividing his time among three mistresses—two German and one Polish. His devoted queen, Catherine of Württemberg, sedulously avoided noticing her "Frifi's" adventures, but his people did not. His kingdom was peaceful and he was supplying fresh troops to Napoleon. His people did not hate him, or fail to see that he controlled his government and army well. But his playboy's reputation overshadowed his virtues.

In Austria Louis Bonaparte, who had abdicated the throne of Holland in 1810, was in self-imposed exile. Neurotic and partially paralyzed, he swilled medicines, immersed himself in mineral baths, and wrote. In the fall of 1812 he was fretting over the poor reception of his novel, *Marie, ou les peines d'amour,* sure that its bad reviews had been ordered by his brother.

Joachim Murat, king of Naples, and Eugène de Beauharnais, viceroy of Italy, were with Napoleon. Both had fought valiantly in the campaign, but Murat's morale had begun to deteriorate. He was afraid Queen Caroline Bonaparte, regent in his absence, would usurp his power, and he was sure she was unfaithful. Moreover he had become very attached to his crown, and keeping it was more important to him than Napoleon's fate. He had begun complaining of illness and asking to go home. Before many weeks he would desert the Grande Armée. Alone among the satellite rulers, Eugène seemed fully dependable. In Moscow he remained, as he had always been, efficient, loyal, uncomplaining, ready to accept new responsibility. He gave Napoleon honest advice, when asked, and tried to keep up the emperor's spirits by arranging entertainments and playing cards with him.

Of the 611,000[1] men in the Grande Armée only some 17,000 were Westphalians, 27,000 Italians, and 5,000 Neapolitans. In Spain an almost solidly French army of 250,000 kept Joseph on his throne. In the balance therefore, the kingdoms absorbed many more troops than they supplied.

In Spain Joseph's budget had never balanced, and his government and armies had drained the imperial treasury of almost a billion francs in gold. The finances of Naples were in reasonable order, and those of Italy in excellent condition. Both, however, had depended heavily on the sale of confiscated and crown properties. Neither had supplied money to France (except through unfavorable trade agreements), and Naples had absorbed small sums for the maintenance of French troops. Westphalia's budget had never balanced. To build an army and maintain French troops in his

1. This figure includes 300,000 French of whom 100,000 were from newly annexed foreign departments; 180,000 Germans including 30,000 Austrians and 20,000 Prussians; 9,000 Swiss; 90,000 Poles and Lithuanians; 32,000 Italians, Neapolitans, and Illyrians.

kingdom, Jérôme had added 150,000,000 francs to the national debt and sold virtually all crown and confiscated properties.

Spain was in open rebellion. In the other kingdoms, especially since 1811, the people had become steadily more restive and resentful over conscription, war taxes, and the unemployment, dislocations, inflation, and shortages caused principally by the Continental System and the subordination of the satellites' economies to the needs of France. Nationalism, for some years the virus of the intelligentsia in Germany and the Italian peninsula, was beginning to infect the masses. The consolidation of small states into kingdoms had given large populations common resentments. Naples and Spain could have been broken down into small administrative units, and the states which composed Westphalia and Italy governed separately or broken down further. In this case resentments would still have been present, but unity of sentiment and purpose harder to achieve.

From the foregoing one might conclude that the creation of satellite kingdoms had been a mistake. Was it? Why did Napoleon create them? Were they part of a master plan, a "Grand Design?" If so what was it? If the kingdoms weakened the empire, did they benefit their peoples in any way? Which successes and failures should be charged to the rulers, and which to Napoleon? Did the emperor choose his rulers badly or did he drive them into failure or disloyalty, or in Louis's case, abdication? What is the historical importance of the kingdoms, individually and collectively?

These are questions which we shall try to answer after we have studied the kingdoms and related their histories to that of the empire.

and silver epaulets gleaming, plumes flying; turbaned Egyptian Mamelukes in colorful silks, scimitars unsheathed; French, Swiss, Poles, Germans, Italians. To the front marched the eagle bearers, trumpeters, drummers. The spectacle was irresistible, and so was Napoleon. Smiling and affable, attended by local clergy and officials, he harangued the crowds in their native tongue (which he spoke better than French). By the time he reached Milan for the coronation, the throngs were huge and enthusiastic.

Napoleo Rex Totius Italiae read the inscription on a medal cast at Milan: *Napoleon King of All Italy*. With the Iron Crown Napoleon had taken the title of the medieval kings who had worn it.[3] For the imperial coronation, the previous December, the supposed crown, sword, and regalia of Charlemagne had been brought to Paris from Aachen (Aix-la-Chapelle). Both coronations had been affronts to the Austrian Holy Roman Emperor, by tradition successor to Charlemagne, and to legitimate monarchs generally. The Frankish chieftain had conquered Lombardy, then the ancient Saxon kingdom between the Rhine and the Elbe. Napoleon's troops were already in Hanover, on the Elbe. By virtue of his victories over Austria and her allies in 1800 he had remade the map of Germany.[4] Now he seemed to claim the right to remake that of Italy. The establishment of the first satellite kingdom pushed Europe much closer to general war.

THE COALITION FORMS

England was already at war with France. The Peace of Amiens, signed in 1802, had lasted barely a year. Napoleon seemed to have regarded it as an armistice to be used to maximum advantage. He denied French markets to the British, limited those of Spain, the Batavian (Dutch) Republic, and their colonies, and menaced those of Portugal, Germany, and the Baltic. He attempted to revive the French Empire in Louisiana and the West Indies. Through Spain, his ally, he hoped to control the eastern Mediterranean. He moved

3. The Iron Crown is actually a heavy oval band of gold. Its name derives from the iron plate it contains, which was by tradition made from one of the nails of the cross of Christ.
4. By the *Reichsdeputationshauptschluss* of 1803, nominally a solution dictated by a commission of the Holy Roman Empire (*Reichsdeputation*), but heavily influenced by Napoleon.

to deny England bases in the central Mediterranean by dominating Italy and the islands. In 1802 he annexed Piedmont and Elba, forced the Ligurian Republic (Genoa) into closer relations with France, installed a French administration in Parma-Piacenza, converted Tuscany into a puppet kingdom, and became president of the Italian Republic. He pressed for an alliance with the Neapolitan Bourbons, which would give him southern Italy and Sicily. Turkey opened the straits to France, and Napoleon's agents worked feverishly in Egypt, the Balkans, Greece, and the Ionian Islands. If all his schemes worked, and the British evacuated Malta, as agreed at Amiens, the Mediterranean would be his. Two imperialisms clashed, and the British could not stand by and let Napoleon win. They held fast to Malta, and in May 1803 again went to war with France.

Napoleon responded by throwing French troops into Hanover, property of the British king, closing Dutch and Spanish ports to British ships, and augmenting his garrisons in Italy.[5] In 1804 French troops invaded neutral German territory, and seized the duke d'Enghien, last scion of the Condés, first Princes of the Blood in France. Napoleon had him shot for treason, a warning to the Bourbons and a challenge to all legitimate monarchs. He went on to make himself emperor. At Boulogne he assembled an army for what was loudly touted as an invasion of England. Ships, barges, and boats, some from as far away as Genoa, collected in the channel ports. Dutch, Spanish, and Italian warships augmented the French fleet.

Probably at the beginning Napoleon did mean to invade England. But by early 1805 he surely knew that a new continental war was imminent. Russia allied with England in April. Austria was arming. Naples, though still bargaining with France, was obviously under British influence, and was negotiating with Russia. Austria and Naples were outraged when Napoleon assumed the crown of Italy. Mounting an invasion of England, even if successful, might only lead to disaster on the continent.

After his coronation in Milan, Napoleon waited only to introduce his viceroy, Eugène, to the Italian parliament (June 7, 1805).

5. The Batavian Republic declared war on England in 1803; Spain in 1804.

He then made a beeline for the quadrilateral fortresses, which guarded Italy against Austria. His visit to the most important one, Mantua, occupied three days. His was no routine visit; he expected war.

From Mantua the emperor moved via Bologna and Parma to Genoa. By prearrangement the city fathers of Genoa waited on the emperor and begged that the city be annexed to France. Napoleon benevolently acceded to their request. Oddly enough, the addition of Genoa to France finally decided Austria for war. In August she adhered to the Anglo-Russian treaty of April 1805.

NAPOLEON PREPARES TO STRIKE

On July 18 the emperor was in Paris; on August 3, after two weeks of frenzied work in the capital, in Boulogne. During the next month he continued to play the game of preparing for the invasion of England. His correspondence reveals that his eyes were elsewhere. Marshal Masséna was dispatched to command the army of Italy for Eugène, who was considered too inexperienced. General Gouvion Saint-Cyr was given command of an army cantoned in the north Italian states with orders to be ready to invade Naples "before 15 September." In the Rhineland, depots were stocked and garrisons consolidated into marching units.

It is sometimes said that Austria caught Napoleon off balance in 1805. The opposite was true. The correct estimate of the two time factors was essential for Austrian success: that required for Russian troops to reinforce the Austrians, and that required for the Grande Armée to move from Boulogne to Germany. The first was calculated correctly. But the second was underestimated by three weeks.

While Napoleon prepared to strike at Austria, he professed all too publicly that the descent on England would begin shortly —when Admiral de Villeneuve's fleet appeared in the channel. Villeneuve did not arrive, and Napoleon blamed him for the failure of the enterprise. But his arrival probably would have changed nothing. When on August 22 the emperor wrote Villeneuve ". . . enter the channel. England is ours. . . ." troops were already leaving the coast for Germany. On August 24 the entire Grande Armée was ordered to march for the Rhine. Embittered by

Napoleon's reproaches, Villeneuve, who had taken refuge at Cádiz, proved his courage by sailing the French and Spanish fleets to suicide at Trafalgar (October 1805).[6] The consequences were grave, but long in becoming apparent. For the moment French victories in Germany held the world's attention.

THE CAMPAIGN OF 1805

At the end of September most of the Grande Armée was in Germany—over 200,000 men, shortly joined by 100,000 more from Bavaria, Württemberg, Baden, and some of the lesser German states. The corps commanders were already famous men whose names would become legend: Bernadotte, Ney, Lannes, Marmont, Davout, and Soult. Ahead of the cavalry rode the flamboyant Gascon Murat, marshal and prince, later to be king of Naples.

Screened by their gaudy cavalry, the infantry streamed in long columns along the shadowed roads of the Schwarzwald and the lanes of the farm country to the north. The soldiers' average height was five feet; their uniforms dust-covered and rumpled, their faces pinched from the strain of forced march and lack of sleep. Their equipment was light: a musket, a blanket roll high on the shoulders with the shako, which burdened the head during the march, hanging from it, and a cartridge box riding in the small of the back. Individually they were not impressive, but they were the finest foot-soldiers in Europe. Their discipline, though flippantly French, was real. They still retained some of the fervor of the republican armies, but especially they had confidence in their leadership. Most were vague even on where they would fight or against whom, but they were sure they would win. Behind them was a man they believed could not lose, a little man in a worn green coat riding somewhere behind his little infantry. He was the emperor now, but he still knew how to fight.

The army was first directed on Ulm, where it was expected to follow the Danube toward Vienna. About October 7, however,

6. During the summer Villeneuve had decoyed Lord Nelson's fleet to the West Indies and dashed back to cover the invasion. But Nelson had sent a fast ship to alert the admiralty, and Villeneuve found the channel covered. In mid-August he entered Cadiz. He was not killed at Trafalgar, but captured. Returned to France by an exchange of prisoners in 1806, he killed himself.

Napoleon heard that General Mack's Austrians were at Ulm, and put his troops in a wide sweeping movement toward Donauworth, which would plunge them into the Austrian rear. Mack heard of this and moved north to counterattack, but was driven back into Ulm, was surrounded, and on October 20 was forced to surrender. Giving the enemy no time to recover, Napoleon pushed his forces through Bavaria toward the Austrian frontier. The Archduke Ferdinand, over-all Austrian commander in Germany, retreated into Bohemia. A Russian army under Kutuzov, which had come up to reinforce him, fled into Moravia. The Grande Armée marched on to Vienna.

In Italy, meanwhile, Masséna and Eugène were faced by the Archduke Charles, whose army outnumbered theirs (50,000 to 40,000). Napoleon, however, had kept the promise he had made Eugène in August: "I will lead the enemy in such a dance that he will not bother you in Italy." After an indecisive battle at Caldiero, the Archduke Charles got news of French victories in Germany and withdrew rapidly north.

On November 13 Murat's cavalry seized the Vienna bridges and scattered the remaining defenders. The army passed on into Moravia. Napoleon established headquarters briefly in the Schönbrunn Palace, then moved up to Brünn, close behind his advance corps. The Austrian Emperor Francis had meanwhile joined Czar Alexander at Olmütz, fifty miles away. Their combined forces, 86,000, commanded by Alexander, were mostly Russian. The Archduke Ferdinand was in Prague; the Archduke Charles in Hungary. Alexander might have waited for their arrival, but his men needed food. Rather than retreat into unforaged country, he advanced, and to his delight, the French fell back. He decided they were retreating on Vienna, and marched southwest to cut them off. Napoleon was expecting him, however. His army (73,000 on the spot) had concentrated behind the Goldbach Brook, near the village of Austerlitz. On December 2, scorning the advice of Kutuzov and the Austrian generals, Alexander attacked. Still determined to block the Vienna road, he massed half his army against Napoleon's right (south) flank. It stalled miserably in the half-frozen marshes of the Goldbach, its movement disorganized by fog and smoke, its men dying before the fire of Davout's infantry and artillery bombs, which shattered trees and sent the lethal fragments flying. The other half of the allied army, extended north over a five-mile front, became Napoleon's target. Soult's corps crashed through the center and attacked south. Lannes and Bernadotte routed the northernmost elements. Murat's cavalry rode between and charged to the pursuit. When the unusually bright "Sun of Austerlitz" finally set, the allied army was totally destroyed. Snow fell on the fleeing remnants, which were so scattered that the French could distinguish no main line of retreat. Though only 2,000 French had been killed in the battle, the campaign was over.

Disgusted with Alexander's precipitous actions, Austria signed an armistice on December 6. Alexander, equally disgusted with the Austrians, simply withdrew to the north. By the Treaty of Pressburg (December 26, 1805), Austria lost Venice, Istria, and Dalmatia, all shortly ceded to the Kingdom of Italy. The Austrian Tyrol went to Bavaria, and small territories in southern Germany to Bavaria, Württemberg, and Baden.[7] Austria was excluded from Italy, and the Holy Roman Empire was dead. The Austrian emperor's role in Germany was now assumed by the emperor of the French. The balance of Austrian against Prussian power could no longer be used to benefit France. Ultimately neither Austria nor Prussia could gain anything but by fighting Napoleon to the death.

Pressburg may have been a point of no return for Napoleon. Talleyrand advised the emperor to placate Austria by freeing Venetia, neutralizing the Kingdom of Italy, leaving her Adriatic possessions intact, and promising her territory in the Balkans. Napoleon declined, probably because he was weary of alliances and balances and saw no possibility of European peace except through one-power domination.[8]

7. The dukes of Bavaria and Württemberg were recognized as kings.
8. Or perhaps he saw himself as a "New Alexander," and the Italian and Adriatic territories as bases for eastern conquest. This thesis was thoroughly exploited by Emile Bourgeois in his *Manuel historique de politique étrangère,* 4 vols. (1892–1926). Fugier calls Talleyrand's proposals "morally reprehensible," that is, not made in Napoleon's interest but to build the minister's influence with Austria (Fugier, *Napoléon et l'Italie,* pp. 188–189).

Two More Satellite Kingdoms

In January 1806 Venice and the Istrian and Dalmatian territories were annexed to the Kingdom of Italy. A French army was already marching into Naples to establish a second satellite kingdom. In nominal command, seconded by Masséna and Gouvion Saint-Cyr, was Joseph Bonaparte, Napoleon's elder brother. Thirty-eight, taller than Napoleon, slender, handsome, charming, he had been detached with some difficulty from Paris society and the pleasures of his country estate, Mortefontaine. "The dynasty of Naples has ceased to reign . . ." Napoleon had proclaimed in December 1805. He had designated Joseph to be king, threatening him with destitution if he refused. "Those who do not rise with me will no longer be members of my family." At the same time he guaranteed Joseph's rights in the imperial succession; the attitude of the powers no longer mattered.

The behavior of the Neapolitan Bourbons in 1805 had been the essence of duplicity. After signing a treaty of neutrality with France in September, they allowed British and Russian troops to land at Naples in November. Alquier, the French ambassador, watched the landing through his telescope, then with mock indignation took down the arms of the embassy and hied himself to Rome. The allied sympathies of the royal family had been no secret. The real ruler, Queen Marie Caroline, a sister of Marie Antoinette, considered Napoleon merely a crowned Jacobin. She had a loathing for him approaching mania, and a marvelous gift for expressing it: "That ferocious animal, that ferocious beast . . . that Corsican bastard, that *parvenu,* that dog!"

Unhappily for the queen, the allied expedition departed soon after the news of Austerlitz arrived. She simultaneously damned her allies for deserting her and vowed to the French that they had landed by surprise. Her minister to France, Gallo, was told to beg peace of "the emperor of all Europe." Cardinal Ruffo pled her case to Alquier, Cardinal Fesch (Napoleon's uncle and ambassador to Rome), and Marshal Masséna, and started for Paris to see Talleyrand, but was turned back. Swallowing her pride, the queen personally wrote to Napoleon, but it was useless. ". . . I will finally punish that whore," the emperor had written Talleyrand.

As French troops neared Naples, the queen tried to organize popular resistance, but the people did not respond. In 1799 the *lazzaroni* had helped overthrow the short-lived Parthenopean Republic[9] and restore the Bourbons. The queen had rewarded them with vicious repression. They liked King Ferdinand, called affectionately "The Nose," but they knew Marie Caroline controlled him. For her they would do nothing. Her final appeal, in the form of a pilgrimage on foot to the Church of Saint Anne, yielded nothing but blank stares. Ferdinand, no man for heroics, had withdrawn to Sicily on January 21, and attended the theater at Palermo the same evening. The queen followed on February 11.

The French advance on Naples, says Rambaud, was a "*promenade militaire.*" Joseph's troops entered the capital on February 14. It had rained steadily during the march, and the men's uniforms were wet and muddy, but their spirits were high. Accompanied by a horde of camp followers, they swung along with loaves of bread stuck on their bayonets and wine bottles protruding from their knapsacks. The city fathers happily welcomed the French. The merchants had feared only one thing: that the *lazzaroni* would run wild and destroy their property before the troops arrived. Joseph arrived on February 15 and the next day attended a Te Deum celebrating his entry; the clergy was not hostile either.

Neapolitan armies withdrew rapidly from the peninsula. Only the fortress of Gaeta held out. Its commander, a little potbellied man with a drooping cavalry moustache, was the prince of Hesse-Philippsthal, one of the top international soldiers of the day. "Gaeta is not Ulm! Hesse is not Mack!" he howled at the French from his ramparts. It was only after Hesse was wounded and evacuated to Sicily in July that the fortress surrendered. While he held out the British landed an expedition and drove the French from the southern coast, but they retained only Reggio and Scilla. While French sieges reduced these fortresses, Joseph set about organizing the second of the satellite kingdoms.

9. From Parthenope, the name of the ancient city on the site of which Naples (*neapolis, new city*) had been constructed.

Napoleon in 1805 had deposed the directory of the Batavian Republic and installed a single executive, the grand pensionary. In that office he placed Rutger Jan Schimmelpenninck, former ambassador to France, and a Dutch patriot, but one whom Napoleon thought realistic enough to cooperate with him. The grand pensionary's government was exemplary; it came closer to balancing the budget than any since the Revolution; it made internal reforms and improved the dikes. But it was not sufficiently slavish for Napoleon's tastes. Schimmelpenninck continually agitated for the reduction of the number of French troops his government supported and the size of the navy the emperor required he maintain. He favored opening trade with the English, which, he argued, would make the Dutch economy boom, and supply him with revenues adequate to meet Napoleon's demands. The emperor, however, was possessed with the idea that he could bankrupt the English by denying them continental markets. (This fixation would shortly produce the Continental System.)

During the winter of 1805–1806 Schimmelpenninck began to go blind. Napoleon determined not to replace him. His first impulse was to annex "Holland,"[10] which he regarded as properly part of France, since it contained the mouths of the Schelde, Meuse, and Rhine, so essential to French commerce. But Prussia was opposed to such a move, and the emperor was attempting to keep her neutral. Frederick William had been allowed to occupy Hanover, but was not sure Napoleon would let him keep it. Annexation of Holland might push him into war. The emperor decided to compromise, and create a satellite kingdom, nominally independent, under his brother Louis; thereby he hoped to have all the advantages of annexation without the formality.

Louis, twenty-seven, was the only brother trained for the army. The boy Louis had shown military aptitude, but the man was softheaded, a dreamer, and afflicted with all sorts of ills, real and

10. The Netherlands were and are often referred to as "Holland," but Holland was only one of nine provinces. The others were Zeeland, Utrecht, Overijssel, Gelderland, Drenthe, Groningen, Friesland, and Brabant. The republic reduced administrative divisions to eight by consolidating Overijssel and Drenthe into one department.

imaginary. His army career had been punctuated by falls off horses (and even out of carriages), repeated medical treatments, and long sojourns at mineral baths. His marriage to Hortense, warm-blooded daughter of Josephine, was so unhappy that they rarely lived together. They nevertheless had two children, both boys, who were heirs presumptive to the imperial throne.[11]

During the campaign of 1805 Louis, constable of the Empire, had commanded the Army of the North, formed hastily in November to guard against a threatened British invasion of the Lowlands. By December 18, however, when Louis belatedly arrived at his headquarters in Nijmwegen, the British had heard of Auster-litz, and all danger was past. The French press, however, styled Louis the savior of Holland, and Napoleon ordered him to remain there, hoping he would win a measure of popularity. To the emperor's great irritation, the grand constable instead gave his command to General Leland and withdrew. Nevertheless the program for making Louis king of Holland continued.

On January 6, 1806, Talleyrand notified Schimmelpenninck that the Dutch government must be reformed to provide for a permanent, orderly succession of executives. In mid-March Admiral Verhuel, Dutch ambassador in Paris, was handed a draft constitution for a monarchal government which in April was submitted to a Great Committee at the Hague.[12] The committee tried to negotiate with Napoleon, but to no avail. No arguments, the emperor had already written Talleyrand, ". . . that or annexation." On May 3 the Great Committee yielded. Schimmelpenninck alone refused to submit, and proudly went into retirement. The rest was a performance staged to soften the effect of Napoleon's actions on the Dutch (and European) public, and save face for their representatives. On June 5 delegates of the Great Committee petitioned Napoleon to make Louis king of Holland, and the same day he was so proclaimed.

On June 23 the king entered his capital. Napoleon had intended that he appear surrounded by French troops, to impress the people with the power of France. Louis, however, dismissed

11. See footnote 2, p. 2.
12. The committee comprised ministers, councilors of state, and the legislature, which had only seventeen members.

his French troops at Huis-ten-Bosch, where he delayed a number of days. When he entered the Hague he was escorted by Dutch troops and accompanied only by Dutch officials. "From the moment I set foot on Dutch soil I became Dutch," he declared to the legislature. Unfortunately for himself Louis meant it. He fell very quickly and willingly under the influence of Dutch councilors and in spite of florid professions of loyalty to Napoleon, was soon as recalcitrant as Schimmelpenninck. But for better or worse the third of the satellite kingdoms had been created.

Again War, and a Fourth Satellite

WAR ON PRUSSIA AND RUSSIA

The death of William Pitt, on January 23, 1806, put the British government under Grenville and Fox. The new government began negotiations with France, and brought in the Russians. For recognizing Napoleon's system (with some alterations), the British demanded that Hanover be returned, which meant that Napoleon would have to compensate Prussia elsewhere. And all that the French could offer the czar was a free hand in the Near East, which he doubted Napoleon would sincerely give. Nevertheless for a time general peace seemed vaguely possible. Prussia in 1805 had given Neuchâtel and Ansbach in exchange for Hanover, but in February 1806 Napoleon, renouncing his earlier bargain, had demanded and gotten Cleves also. Frederick William's pride was hurt. At his court intellectuals such as Johannes von Müller, Schleiermacher, and von Homboldt were encouraging him to stand up to Napoleon. So were military men who did not appreciate that Prussian military capacity had deteriorated markedly since the time of Frederick the Great. During the summer of 1806 Napoleon created the Confederation of the Rhine, which gave the death blow to Prussia's plan for a north German confederation. Almost simultaneously false news arrived that Prussia would lose Hanover, with compensation uncertain.

Frederick William decided on war. The czar, encouraged by Prussia's decision and enraged by the efforts of Napoleon's agents to incite Turkey to attack Russia, also was ready to fight. And after the death of Fox in September 1806, the British broke off negotiations with France, which were stalled anyway over the question of compensation for the Neapolitan Bourbons.[13]

Prussian armies, mobilized in August, were already in motion, hoping to strike before Napoleon was ready. As usual, however, he was well prepared. A considerable portion of the Grande Armée was still in Germany and the Rhineland. Alerted September 5, the army had concentrated and was on the march in less than two weeks. The Prussians should have waited for Russian troops. Without them they had little chance, especially since their commanders, the duke of Brunswick and Prince Hohenlohe, were ancient believers in obsolete tactics, and violently jealous of each other. Plunging into the Confederation of the Rhine they suddenly realized that the enemy was both alerted and numerically superior. Desperately, they tried to fall back to the Elbe, but the Grande Armée cut south of them, then north along the Saale. On October 14 they found their line of retreat blocked, and were crushed in the twin battles of Jena and Auerstädt.

On October 27 the French entered Berlin. Prussia's client states, Brunswick and Hesse-Cassel, were occupied. Saxony, initially allied with Prussia, went over to the French on December 11.[14] Russia remained to be defeated, but unless the British landed an expedition, she was alone. Moreover Turkey, urged on by Napoleon's ambassador, General Sébastiani, had opened a second front against Russia.

The French pushed into East Prussia and Poland. The Russians, however, proved elusive foes, and no major battles ensued. On February 8 Napoleon, though momentarily outmanned and outgunned, attacked an army under Bennigsen. But though the French won the day and inflicted 30,000 casualties, Bennigsen withdrew undefeated, and Napoleon lost 25,000 men. The emperor, worried over the effect on his allies, and the French, of a

13. It is possible that both Napoleon and the allies were merely buying time through these negotiations—Napoleon to reorganize Germany and Holland, the British and Russians to prepare for a continuation of the war and to bring over Prussia.

14. Napoleon made the duke of Saxony a king, and also ruler of the Grand Duchy of Warsaw, created from Prussia's Polish provinces.

long campaign, pressed for victory, but was forced to fight a war of maneuver.

Then Bennigsen blundered. Coming up to Friedland on June 13 with 60,000 men, he saw beyond the Alle River a lone French corps, under Lannes. During the night his men laboriously crossed over four small bridges. On June 14 he attacked. At Eylau Napoleon had been notified, however, and after routing all available forces toward Friedland, rode ahead hell-for-leather to direct the battle. Bennigsen had his back to the river, and could not withdraw under fire. While Lannes held the Russians at bay, Napoleon, riding about in high excitement, funneled reinforcements into the lines as they arrived. In late afternoon the French, now 80,000 strong, moved forward, driving the Russians into the river. As at Austerlitz, the victory was total. The campaign was over.

WESTPHALIA

On July 7 peace was made at Tilsit. Russia and Prussia recognized Italy, Holland, and Naples, and agreed to the formation of a fourth kingdom, Westphalia, in central Germany. Westphalia comprised essentially Hesse-Cassel and Brunswick, whose rulers were deposed for having fought with Prussia, Prussian territory west of the Elbe, and part of Hanover. Its capital at Cassel was in the basin of the Weser; its territory stretched to the Elbe. In the heart of old Germany, the Saxony of Charlemagne's time, it was a French Imperial March with the guns of Fortress Magdeburg trained on Prussia.

Into this kingdom the emperor proposed to send the prodigal of the Bonaparte family, twenty-two-year-old Jérôme. After leaving school, he had spent three gay and insubordinate years in the navy, and then had taken two years' unauthorized leave in the United States, where he married Baltimore's reigning beauty, Elizabeth Patterson, and fathered a son. Returning to face Napoleon in 1805, he agreed to an annulment of his marriage, returned briefly to the navy, and then marched with the Grande Armée during 1806–1807. As general of a division of Bavarians and Württembergers, he proved a good leader, though he saw only minor action in Silesia. In August 1807 he wed Catherine of Württemberg, whose father Napoleon had elevated from duke to king in

1805. Jérôme and Catherine entered Cassel on December 7, 1807. The fourth of the satellite kingdoms had been a reality since September, however, having been governed by a trio of capable French administrators, Siméon, Beugnot, and Jollivet.

At the end of 1807 Napoleon's empire, though slightly larger, matched in startling degree that held by Charlemagne a thousand years before. In the north his puppet states stretched from the Channel coast to the Elbe, in central Germany beyond the Oder-Neisse, and in south Germany beyond the Inn. In Italy he held all the territory Charlemagne had dominated, save that still ruled by the Pope—and Naples in addition. Only on the Iberian peninsula did his empire fail to match that of the Frankish king. Napoleon had no Spanish March, but he was bent upon acquiring one, and more.

Spain: An Angry Fifth Satellite

Spain had since 1795 been allied with France. The architect of this alliance, Manuel de Godoy, was first minister of Spain, a post he had acquired by taking as mistress his queen, the much older Maria Luisa. The king of Spain, Charles IV, was in 1807 a doddering old man—mild, trusting, a lover of the countryside, and given to spells of insanity. The crown prince, Ferdinand, a slippery and devious character, plotted endlessly to seize the throne.

Spain had been a poor ally. Napoleon had hoped to make her the pivot of his Mediterranean policy, and through her to control the Bourbons of Naples-Sicily. But Marie Caroline's overweening aversion to Napoleon and respect for British sea power had offset any inclination she might have had to follow the policies of her relatives in Madrid. The Spanish had not stopped Portugal from trading with the English, as Napoleon had directed. Worse, Spain traded with them herself, allowing English vessels to enter Iberian ports with forged papers and under neutral flags. In 1803 Charles IV had promised Napoleon a war contribution of 6,000,000 francs a year, which had not been paid. He had supplied thirty antiquated and rotten ships which had been shot to pieces at Trafalgar. The few troops he sent to Napoleon had proved unreliable.

Neither Spain nor Portugal was strong, but either might invite the English to land on the peninsula. As matters stood Iberia endangered the empire, denied it her riches, fouled Napoleon's system, and offended his sense of order. He needed no excuse to seize Portugal, for centuries linked with England. As for the Spanish, why should they not be grateful if he removed the sick and ineffective Bourbons? Finally, Spain had seemed ready to betray him in 1806.

In October of that year, shortly before the battle of Jena, Napoleon received news that Godoy had issued a grandiose proclamation asking for unity against "The Enemy" and ordered mobilization. After Jena and Auerstädt, Godoy had stopped preparations, and with magnificent *sang-froid* stated that "The Enemy" had been Portugal. Napoleon, with war enough for the moment, let the matter drop. But after Tilsit he was ready to act.

By promising Godoy a kingdom in south Portugal, Napoleon secured the Treaty of Fontainebleau (October 27, 1807) which allowed him to send 28,000 troops through Spain to Portugal, and to establish a reserve of 40,000 at Bayonne. The reserve, as Godoy well knew, was the advance guard of the French Army of Spain. Before the treaty was formally signed, Napoleon's invasion armies were on the march. Junot took Lisbon on November 29, 1807, and shortly thereafter other corps were inching into Spain. In March 1808 Marshal Murat, "Lieutenant of the Emperor in Spain," assumed command of the French army, which then numbered 100,000, and pushed on toward Madrid.

Before Murat reached the capital, however, the Spanish crown prince deposed his father and proclaimed himself Ferdinand VII. To Napoleon's delight, both the old and new kings sued for his favor, Ferdinand begging to marry a Bonaparte princess. Murat, after occupying Madrid, dispatched the entire royal family to Bayonne "for talks." Once the Bourbons were in France, Napoleon forced all of them, kings and possible successors, to renounce claim to the throne (May 10).

Murat had not sent the Bourbons off without difficulty. On May 2 Madrid had exploded in a furious popular uprising. The marshal had been prepared for trouble, however, and his troops and cannon had made short work of the mobs. At the end of May Spain showed few signs of further resistance. But a pattern had been set in Madrid. Men had fought French soldiers with sticks and rocks; snipers had fired from rooftops; women had poured boiling water and filth from balconies. As it would prove, the "whiff of grapeshot" would not suffice for Spain. But Napoleon saw Madrid's Dos de Mayo as a feeble, ill-armed, ill-planned, short-lived uprising and continued with his plans to install a Bonaparte dynasty in Spain. This may well have been the greatest mistake of his career.

To rule Spain Napoleon called Joseph Bonaparte from Naples. As deftly as he had sent the Italian *consulta* to Lyons, Murat arranged for a Spanish junta to meet at Bayonne. It swiftly approved a constitution supplied by Napoleon. Joseph arrived at Bayonne on June 7, and on July 7 was crowned in elaborate ceremonies presided over by the archbishop of Burgos. On the following day he crossed the Bidassoa and began his journey to Madrid. Meanwhile on May 28, Marshal Murat, due in no small part to the agitation of his ambitious wife, Caroline Bonaparte, had been designated king of Naples. The system of satellite kingdoms was complete.

Take for your motto also France before Everything.

—NAPOLEON TO EUGÈNE

chapter two

THE KINGDOM OF ITALY

Eugène and Italy: Origins

EUGÈNE DE BEAUHARNAIS

During 1809 Eugène de Beauharnais, already a successful viceroy, made himself a hero at Raab and Wagram, and was joyfully embraced by Napoleon at Vienna, and proclaimed his "true son." Summoned to Paris at the end of the year, he expected to be rewarded for his services with the crown of Italy. Instead he found that his mother was to be divorced by the emperor and that Italy would go to the son Napoleon expected by his second marriage. Eugène went before the senate. In the white and gold uniform of a French prince, the Grand Cross of the Legion of Honor about his neck, the muscular cavalryman of twenty-eight had a truly royal presence. The senators, standing, applauded the man and his reputation, resumed their seats, and waited. Rumor had it he would approve the divorce and make it easy for them to assent. Would he? "My mother, my sister and I," said Eugène, ". . . owe everything to the Emperor. He has been a true father to us; he will find us, at all times, devoted children and submissive subjects. It is for the good of France that [the emperor] . . . have direct descendants, who will be our guarantee of everything. . ." So it was with Eugène. Loyalty was foremost among his virtues.

Eugène de Beauharnais, as viceroy of Italy styled Eugène Napoleon, was the son of the Viscount Alexandre de Beauharnais, scion of old French nobility. His mother, born Joséphine Tascher de Pagerie in Martinique, had status sufficient to marry the viscount. Alexandre went to the guillotine during the Terror;

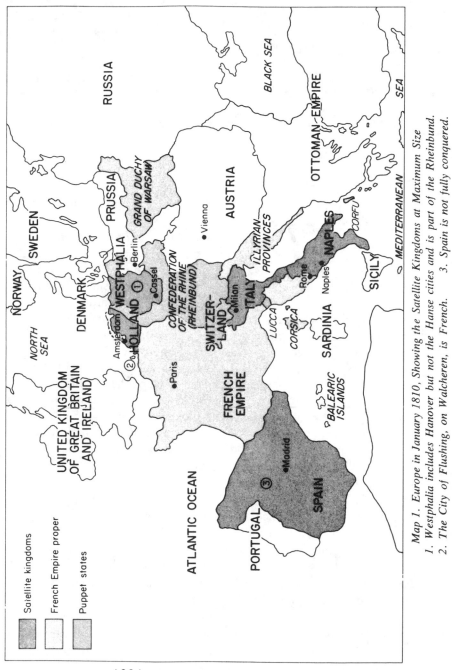

Map 1. *Europe in January 1810, Showing the Satellite Kingdoms at Maximum Size*
1. *Westphalia includes Hanover but not the Hanse cities and is part of the Rheinbund.*
2. *The City of Flushing, on Walcheren, is French.*   3. *Spain is not fully conquered.*

(20)

Joséphine survived and married Napoleon. The viscount was a talented soldier, politician, intellectual, and writer. His portraits show a handsome aristocrat, almost a type—fine-featured, stylishly haughty, hair silvered in lieu of a wig. Before marriage his affairs had been legion, and his vows did not change him. Aside from his erotic pursuits, he absented himself for months on private or official business. After the birth of Eugène in 1781, the winsome Joséphine reacted to Alexandre's neglect with such abandon that, when Hortense was born in 1783, he denied paternity. She sued successfully for separation.

In 1789 Alexandre was elected to the Estates General; in 1791 he was president of the Constituent Assembly and a key figure in the government during Louis XVI's ill-fated "flight to Varennes." Elected to the Convention in 1792, he shed his title and became a *Montagnard*. In 1793 he commanded the Army of the Rhine, then became minister of war. But the French republican armies lost initially, and ex-nobles were always suspect. Alexandre was retired, then arrested. Joséphine all the while was at Croissy and intermittently at Paris, an apolitical socialite, but also of the old order, and suspect. She too was arrested, and she and Alexandre, like characters in a Stendhal novel, found themselves together in the Prison des Carmes. There they lived as man and wife until Alexandre was sent to the guillotine in 1794. Joséphine was saved by the fall of Robespierre and released through the influence of Tallien, who also rescued Joséphine's friend Thérésa Cabarrus, later the scandalous Madame Tallien.

Eugène had since age five been in various schools, the last at Cherbourg. In 1795 Joséphine brought him to the Scottish *lycée* at Saint-Germain. He was now fourteen, tall and strong, with the grace of his father and the dark coloration of his mother. In October 1795 he and his mother met Napoleon.

General Bonaparte, whose cannon on October 5 broke the Paris mob and saved the Convention, ordered the people disarmed. According to his story, Eugène came to him and with youthful dignity asked to be allowed to retain his father's sword. Struck by the composure and good looks of the boy, he gave it to him. The following day Joséphine came to convey her thanks and so met Napoleon. Actually Napoleon and Joséphine probably met at the salon of Madame Tallien. They were married in March 1796, and Napoleon, doubtless because of Joséphine's influence with the Director Barras, shortly took command of the Army of Italy.

In June 1797 Eugène, aged fifteen, was made a sublieutenant of hussars and joined Napoleon at Mombello to enjoy the aftermath of his victories over Austria. In 1798 he was General Bonaparte's aide-de-camp in Egypt, and returned with him to France (August 1799), when Napoleon left his blockaded army to help overthrow the Directory. During the previous year, Joséphine had renewed her affair with the perfumed and elegant Hippolyte Charles, who also had consoled her during the Italian campaign. Napoleon might have broken with her but for the pleas of Eugène, who had earned his respect and who was mature enough to have discussed Napoleon's own love affairs with him. During the *coup d'état* of 18 Brumaire (November 19, 1799), Eugène, just turned eighteen, was largely innocent of the intrigue. But he did carry messages for Napoleon, announce his arrival to the senate, and accompany him to Saint-Cloud, where the legislative bodies were bullied into submission.

France was hard pressed by the Second Coalition. In the spring of 1800 First Consul Bonaparte struck through the Alps, taking the Austrians in Italy by surprise. With him was Eugène, now captain of cavalry in the Consular Guard, forerunner of the legendary Imperial Guard. At Marengo, though half his men fell, he led charge after charge. Wrote Napoleon to Joséphine: "He has covered himself with glory. . . . He should become one of the Great Captains of Europe."

The years of the Consulate were hectic for Napoleon, but not for Joséphine, Eugène, and Hortense. They spent weeks on end in the country at Malmaison, playing games on the lawns, fishing in the disciplined little streams, and riding to the hounds. Occasionally, in the evenings, they received droves of guests from Paris, and saw command performances by the opera or theater companies. More often they played cards, read, or talked. Sometimes the family, supported by Joséphine's ladies in waiting, staged amateur productions. Napoleon, when present, most often requested *The Barber of Seville,* with Eugène and Hortense singing the leading roles.

The peaceful routine was broken by the onset of a new war in 1803, and the family in-fighting and new duties that accompanied the establishment of the empire in 1804. Napoleon, appalled at the prideful bickering of the Bonapartes, was grateful for the quiet cooperation of the Beauharnais. At the coronation Eugène marched in the emperor's suite, and after the eligible Bonapartes refused the Italian crown, Napoleon picked him to be viceroy.[1] To assure the Italians that their ruler was no mere prefect, Eugène was named prince of France, and called by Napoleon before the senate "the child of our adoption."

The spring of 1805 Eugène, as commander of the Imperial Guard, preceded Napoleon to Milan. Though he was not yet officially designated viceroy, rumors were flying, and he was received rather coldly. The Milanese were not hostile, merely a little stunned at the seemingly sudden political changes. Marescalchi, Italian ambassador in Paris, wrote the emperor that only his presence would win over the Milanese. As we have noted, Napoleon responded by conducting a veritable political campaign in Italy. On May 9 he entered Milan through the Porta Ticinese amid a cacophony of church bells, blaring bugles, beating drums, applause, and cheers. To all appearances, Italians were won over not merely by his power, and the matchless parade which accompanied him; they were captivated by the man, and convinced, as many would believe to the end, that he was good for Italy.

Counting the time before and after his coronation, Napoleon spent a month in Milan. He organized Eugène's government, selected his key ministers, and did not depart until the parliament had met. Aware of Eugène's inexperience, he wanted to give him the best possible opportunity for success.

Italy: the Background

Italy had risen with Napoleon and its political institutions changed with his changing ideas and opportunities. In 1796 the conquering General Bonaparte arrived breathing enthusiasm for republican institutions and was received by progressive Italians

1. See p. 2.

as a liberator. In the course of 1796–1797 the more radical liberals, such as Antonio Ranza and Salfi, were driven into the background. The Cisalpine Republic was dominated by moderate liberals, largely Milanese.[2] Prominent among these were the statesmen-politicians Francesco Melzi d'Eril, Aldini, Serbelloni, Marescalchi, Verri, and Parini. They had been encouraged by the French Revolution, but were also heirs of the liberalism of the Holy Roman Emperors Joseph II and Leopold II, who had greatly influenced Italian thought. Many of the professors at the great universities of Pavia, Bologna, and Padua were also liberals and reformers. Among the clergy there was still a Jansenist element, which influenced and cooperated with the liberals, and whose ideas Rome considered as dangerous as Jacobinism.

Most liberals were more attached to French ideas than to France; most dreamed of independence from all the great powers, a minority of Italian unification. Their quarrels with the French Directory were many. But the destruction of the republic by the Second Coalition (1799), and its restoration (1800) by Napoleon convinced the majority that only under French auspices would they have even a measure of independence. Napoleon again became "Bonaparte *liberatore*." The Cisalpine was more amenable to his control.

By the treaty of Lunéville (1801) the Adige was made the boundary of the republic and from Piedmont Napoleon ceded Novara and the entrances to the Simplon Pass. Napoleon sent to Milan Pierre Louis Roederer, a multitalented bureaucrat, who would later hold, among others, posts in Naples and the Grand Duchy of Berg. With his help, and consultations with Napoleon, the Italian Bonapartists produced a constitution which renamed the Cisalpine the Republic of Italy, and increased the power of the executive and reduced that of the parliament. As previously noted, the *consulta* of Lyons, dominated by Melzi, Paradisi, Marescalchi,

2. In May 1796 Napoleon organized the Duchy of Milan (Lombardy) under a civil government dominated by the French military, the "Congregation of State," sometimes called the Lombard Republic. In December 1796 delegates from the Duchy of Modena (Modena and Reggio), and the Papal states of Ferrara and Bologna formed the Cispadane Republic south of the Po. In 1797 Lombardy was designated the Cisalpine Republic, and in the course of the year Napoleon added to it the Cispadane Republic, Mantua, Romagna, part of Venetia, to give it a frontier on the Adige and the Valtelline.

and their faction approved the constitution and made Napoleon president.[3]

Napoleon put the Italian government in the hands of his vice-president, Count Francesco Melzi d'Eril. Of an illustrious Milanese family, Melzi had served Austria on the administrative council of Milan, held diplomatic posts, and traveled extensively in France, England, Portugal, and Spain. He was aristocratic, a lover of music and art, a gourmet, and brilliant conversationalist in Italian, French, Spanish, or German. But in spite of his background and tastes Melzi was a leftist liberal, a republican, and violently anti-clerical. In 1796 he had been one of the first to welcome Napoleon.

In 1802 Melzi instituted laws regulating church affairs which outraged the Pope. He relented long enough to negotiate a con-cordat with Rome (1803), but interpreted it so broadly that the Pope never ratified it. He made progress in breaking down pro-vincialism and class distinctions by making talent the sole criterion for administrative appointment. *Laissez-faire* was his rule in eco-nomics, and he began a concerted attack on provincial, city, and guild privileges. He created a Ministry of Public Instruction, an Institute on the French model, and pushed Jansenist professors into chairs of religion and philosophy at the universities. He began the reorganization of the Italian army, which in 1805 numbered 23,000, at least on paper.

Liberal government in the Italian Republic progressively came more to resemble enlightened monarchy of the eighteenth century than the constitutional-representative systems propounded, if not always applied, by the various French Revolutionary govern-ments. Napoleon was becoming more authoritarian. In Italy as in France, democracy came to mean "careers open to talent," not popular participation in government. The Bonapartists who re-tained influence were those amenable to discipline, either from self-interest, disillusionment with representative processes, or in-bred lack of faith in them. The enlightened could not allow rights, law, parliamentary bodies to impede "progress."

Italian liberals, inclined to distrust the unwashed masses, were

3. See pp. 1–2.

not much offended by authoritarian liberalism. They were alarmed, however, when it excluded from voice and influence increasing numbers of themselves. They objected even more to progressive subordination of Italian to French interests. The more radical of them went into exile. Some joined the Freemasons, which cooperated with the government until 1813 but had a radical wing, or became members of the more secret Carbonari, Guelphs, or Adelfi, which worked for Italian independence and unification. Some liberals retired in despair. Those who retained influence surrendered to the French (as did Marescalchi), or worked *with* the French, but *for* "Italy." For the liberals lost, however, the government gained great numbers of the old aristocracy and formerly apolitical bourgeoisie. And the people were generally satisfied with Napoleonic government.

Melzi himself had his troubles. Italian to the core, he tried to maintain maximum independence within the scope of Napoleon's directives. He attempted doggedly but without success to establish Italian diplomats in the major European courts. Italy continued to be represented by Napoleon's ministers, and even the Italian ambassador in Paris, Marescalchi, did little more than transmit directives. Melzi, though a friend of enlightened authority, retained a belief in personal freedom, especially of expression. This brought him into conflict with Murat, commander of occupation troops, meddler in politics, and self-appointed censor.

Melzi and Murat became political rivals, the more slavish Bonapartists following the marshal. Their conflict climaxed in the "Ceroni Affair" of 1803. Captain Ceroni, an ardent democrat, composed a poem reproaching the French for abandoning Revolutionary ideals. Melzi suppressed the poem, but only gave the author a reprimand. Murat angrily notified Napoleon, who supported his commander's view. Ceroni lost his rank and was imprisoned. Melzi's enthusiasm began to fade.

In 1804 Napoleon's confidence in him was shaken by the revelation that he had been in correspondence with an Austrian diplomat, Baron Moll, though nothing treasonable was uncovered. With the creation of the kingdom, Melzi was "kicked upstairs." Made duke of Lodi, senator, and keeper of the seals, given the

Grand Cordon of the Legion of Honor, he was nevertheless removed from executive position in the government.

Melzi's last important service to Napoleon was in the conversion of the republic into the kingdom. Typically, he did his best for Italy. In May 1804 he called a *consulta* to Milan which framed a constitution for a monarchy totally separate from France. His candidate for the throne was Joseph Bonaparte, a liberal who, as Napoleon's elder brother, got a certain deference from him. If the constitution had been accepted, Italy would have had its own diplomatic corps and French troops would have withdrawn from the kingdom. But even if Joseph took the crown, Napoleon envisioned no such independence for Italy. He rejected Melzi's constitution and threatened to annex Italy to France. Marescalchi, thoroughly intimidated, recommended that Italy accept whatever Napoleon offered; anything was better than annexation. Melzi, Paradisi, Giuseppe Luosi, Diego Guicciardini, and others went to Paris to negotiate. When in January 1805 Joseph refused the crown, their hopes waned. In February they accepted a constitution presented by the emperor, and in March 1805 a *consulta* at Milan approved their action.

When Eugène took control of Italy, the country had a nine-year history of French domination. Italians were accustomed to the presence of French troops and to progressive government which limited individual freedom. Italy's liberals had adjusted to French control, each in his own way. Her more prominent artists, poets, and writers, like Canova, Foscolo, and Monti, if they had private reservations, publicly glorified Napoleon with the abandon of lovers. Italian industry and agriculture, though under some strictures, had already adjusted to close ties with France; Italian businessmen were generally prospering. The nobility had long accepted posts in the civil and military service, and had adjusted to the increasing prominence of the middle class and intelligentsia. The basic structures of the administration and judiciary were established; ministries were in operation. Some ministers, like Prina in finance, would continue in office. Churchmen, though still stubborn and sometimes troublesome, had been brought to rein by Melzi. Perhaps most important, the people were easily adaptable to French-style government. Their culture more nearly resembled that of France than that of any other kingdom Napoleon established. Their differences in character, customs, and education, for example, their clannishness, city-state loyalties, and greater religiosity, were well understood by the Corsican-born French emperor. The way was prepared for Eugène, and his chances for success excellent.

To the native talent available, Napoleon added a "French cabinet." Abrial, a former judge and French minister of police, was his legal adviser; General of Artillery Anthoulard, councilor for military affairs; and Lagarde, who in the words of Napoleon was ". . . a man who has played many roles . . . in sum, a man of the Police." Finally, Étienne Méjean, lawyer, journalist, bureaucrat, and manipulator of people, who became Eugène's confidant, adviser, and troubleshooter.

Eugène and Napoleon

THE EARLY YEARS

Napoleon was immensely fond of Eugène, and took pride in the latter's record, particularly as a soldier. But the viceroy was not yet twenty-four and had no governmental experience; and the emperor, anxious for his success, tried initially to control his every decision and even his behavior. Before he left Milan he dictated a thick sheaf of instructions: ". . . glory in being French," but persuade the Italians you love them. "Cultivate their language . . . honor them . . . approve what they approve and love what they love." "Speak as little as possible [in Council]: you are not well enough educated. . ." "Don't imitate my conduct altogether; be more reserved." "Listen. . . silence often produces the same effect as science." "Don't encourage spies." "Spend time with the army, you know about that." "See your ministers twice a week. . ." ". . . the discovery of a dishonest bookkeeper is a victory for the administration."

Eugène was told to write Napoleon daily, and in the beginning he did, even summarizing police reports, including murders, robberies, and wife-beatings. As he traveled, the emperor kept firing back instructions. Attend drill every day. Imitate the Great Elector of Prussia—don't neglect details. Change departmental administrations on July 1. Get a breakdown of the revenue of each department. Police thugs cost 700,000 francs a year; reduce it to 200,000. Consult Paradisi on organizing the administration of roads and bridges.

Behind the instructions came angry reprimands, to which Eugène replied with apologies. But within weeks he began to exercise his own judgment, which proved good. He presided forcefully in the council of state, and got his way, on one occasion keeping the members in their seats until hunger and natural needs drove them to approve his decrees. In July the parliament became recalcitrant, and he dismissed it. Napoleon approved the action, but was angry because Eugène had acted without permission. "If Milan were on fire" wrote Duroc for the emperor, "you should let Milan burn and wait [for instructions]." Do nothing without imperial authority ". . . even if the moon is about to fall on Milan," wrote Napoleon personally. The viceroy's authority increased as he proved his ability, but in the beginning he was only a magnificent prefect.

In war also Eugène was initially ruled unqualified. Masséna was sent to command the Army of Italy in 1805. Eugène objected, but all he got from Napoleon was advice to cooperate with the marshal and learn. He wrote Joséphine and his sister Hortense, hoping they could sway the emperor, but to no avail. Since Masséna did not arrive until mid-September, however, it fell to Eugène to organize the army of 40,000 French and Italians. On this the emperor gave him orders in detail on everything from the armaments and munitions needed in the Quadrilateral forts to the words he should use in informing Italy the war had begun. The viceroy did well. In the emperor's letters, which seldom gave praise, the words "I approve . . ." appear frequently. And Masséna too got his instructions. Napoleon, familiar with every foot of ground on the Adige frontier, and apprised by Eugène of the exact composition of the Army of Italy, prompted him constantly. "If I were in Italy, I would form my army into six divisions . . ." ran an early letter. As it happened the campaign was short. Masséna fought the Archduke Charles at Caldiero, then pursued him into Hungary. Eugène occupied Venice with the troops remaining to him, and sent reinforcements to Saint-

Cyr, who was preparing to march on Naples. After Austerlitz (December 2, 1805) Eugène's chief task was organizing administrations for Venetia, Istria, and Dalmatia, ceded by Austria at Pressburg (December 26, 1805) and transferred to Italy in January 1806.[4] In January Masséna was shifted to the Army of Naples, which included a corps of Eugène's Italians under Lechi.

The great events of 1805 did produce a vice-queen for Italy. Since July 1804 Napoleon had tried to arrange a marriage for Eugène with Augusta, daughter of the elector of Bavaria, Max Joseph, but the elector had been noncommittal. He wavered also over fighting for Napoleon in 1805, but finally did. Napoleon, as he passed through Munich in October, personally discussed the marriage with the elector. In December, the same courier who notified the elector of the victory of Austerlitz carried a message regarding the marriage. Within days Napoleon's marshal of the palace, Duroc, arrived to press for an answer. Until this time Max Joseph had been reluctant to establish family ties with the "upstart" Bonapartes. More opposed than the elector was his second wife, Augusta's stepmother, born princess of Baden, who had reputedly loved the duc d'Enghien, whom Napoleon had executed. Augusta shared her fear and loathing of the emperor, and moreover was already engaged to Prince Charles of Baden. But Duroc brought Max Joseph confirmation that, by the peace treaty being negotiated at Pressburg, Austria would recognize him as king, and Bavaria would be expanded. The French emperor was both his benefactor and the possessor of terrible power. He could no longer refuse.

Napoleon arrived in Munich to celebrate New Year's Day, 1806. Heralds, escorted by cavalry, toured the city proclaiming the kingship of Max Joseph. In overpowering numbers, French and Bavarian troops escorted to the Frauenkirche Bavarian cannon and flags captured in previous wars by the Austrians. The emperor had meanwhile met Augusta. To her amazement, the ogre she expected had a brilliant smile that gave his face a boyish cast, and was

4. Venetia was fully absorbed into the Kingdom of Italy. For Istria and Dalmatia Eugène furnished only civil officials for Marshal Marmont, who was the real ruler. In 1809 Istria and Dalmatia became part of the Illyrian Provinces, and Italy was compensated from Papal territory.

slightly ill-at-ease. He was so obviously charmed with her that she could not help but like him. And he behaved as if she could still refuse, speaking of Eugène's looks and merits and hinting that their children would be kings of Italy.

Augusta was seventeen, slender and graceful, with a very full figure which was devastatingly revealed by the styles of the day. Her dark hair and eyes matched a flawless, glowing, olive complexion. Napoleon was so pleased with the marriage he had arranged between "models of their sex" that he delayed his departure from Munich to participate in the wedding. Eugène was tall, with thinning hair and a drooping cavalry moustache which made him seem older than twenty-four. But he had the catlike grace of an athlete and horseman, dark aristocratic features, and a love for fun which endeared him to his intimates. Ordered up from Italy, he appeared in Munich on January 10, 1806, and went directly to the emperor, who fussed over his appearance and had him prepared by his own valet to meet the king and queen of Bavaria and Augusta. He was introduced the same day, and he and Augusta liked each other immediately. They were married on January 14 by the prince primate of Germany in the presence of Napoleon, Joséphine, and the Bavarian monarchs. To all appearances they came to love each other; their marriage was a happy one.

Their relations with the emperor would be marred, however, by the question of the Italian crown. During the marriage negotiations, Napoleon had promised Gravenreuth, Max Joseph's representative, that Eugène would have it "at the general peace." But the marriage contract, drawn up by Talleyrand and Maret, guaranteed the viceroy only suitable estates and income. In 1806 Napoleon did, however, adopt Eugène formally, which seemed to put him in line for the throne. But he was destined not to get it, and Augusta would come to feel that her children had been disinherited.

In late January Eugène and Augusta entered Venice. Cheered by crowds along the canals, they toured the city in a gondola decorated with multicolored plumes and flowers, serenaded by water-borne musicians, and accompanied by a myriad of other boats. A few days later they entered Milan, through triumphal arches, in the midst of a military parade. At La Scala an allegoric cantata was performed in their honor. The court at Milan had been quite somber during Eugène's bachelor days. Visitors found a shocking absence of scandal about which to prattle. Now it took on the pleasant, homey, atmosphere of a German ducal court. Whenever possible Eugène and Augusta fled Milan for the quiet country atmosphere of Monza. Napoleon, remembering Augusta's beauty, half-expected her to be bored even in Milan. In the early days he wrote to Eugène cautioning him to keep her entertained. But he finally accepted that Augusta was content as a wife and mother, and that Eugène was happy with her.

During the 1806–1807 campaign Eugène sent Italian troops to the Grande Armée but was given no command himself. To his requests for action Napoleon consistently replied that he was needed in Italy. Troubles were multiplying on the Italian peninsula because of the hardened attitude of the Pope. During the 1805 campaign Pius VII, hoping to remain neutral, had given permission for French troops to pass through his territory to Naples. To his outrage they had left a garrison at Ancona. To Napoleon, neutrality was only a word; he kept Ancona, and considered objection treasonable. "For the Pope, I am Charlemagne . . ." he wrote Cardinal Fesch. Pius VII, at the same time, was being advised to resist. Men like Di Pietro, Roverella, and Antonelli had gained influence; moderates like Cardinal Consalvi were out. In June 1806 the Pope issued the bull *Non Possumus* asserting his independence of all political control.

Napoleon was too busy to react. But after Tilsit (July 1807) he turned to the problem of the Papacy with his usual vigor. He instructed Eugène to convey a courteous warning to the Pope. Rome, said Napoleon, had been preaching rebellion for two years. "There remains only [the alternative] for me to cut the Holy Father's hair and put him in a monastery." As the emperor had expected, Eugène's warning got a hostile response. In November the emperor arrived in Milan to plan moves against the Papacy and inspect the defenses of the Kingdom of Italy against Austria, in case she reacted. He conferred with Eugène, Joseph, king of Naples, and Lucien, who was living in Rome. Public attention was concentrated on the installation of Eugène as prince of Venice, done to placate Max Joseph, who had arrived to demand the crown of Italy for Eugène. But quietly it was arranged for an army of French and Italians to occupy the Papal States. In February 1808, after Napoleon had returned to Paris, the army marched; in April 1808 Urbino, Macerata, Ancona, and Camerino were annexed to the Kingdom of Italy. For the moment disposition of the city of Rome remained uncertain. The Pope confined himself to the Papal Palace with nothing to cheer him but the warm regard of the Roman populace and its passive hostility to the French.

During the Austrian campaign of 1809, Napoleon by imperial decree annexed Rome to France, granted the Pope two million francs a year, and declared his palace inviolate. Pius replied with the bull *Quum Memoranda,* excommunicating Napoleon, though without mentioning his name. When in late May news of the bull reached the emperor, he had suffered defeats in Austria. "The Pope is a furious madman who must be locked up!" he raged. Napoleon was under great stress and may not have meant the words as an order. But at Rome they were so interpreted by Generals Miollis and Radet. They seized Pius and sent him a prisoner to Savona; he would remain there and at Fontainebleau until January 1814. Though the Pope's temporal power seemed at an end, nothing could have improved it more than imprisonment. Resentment over Napoleon's actions swept Catholic Europe and especially affected events in Spain, as we shall note presently.

EUGÈNE EMERGES AS A COMMANDER

Austria was humiliated by the Treaty of Pressburg and the creation of the Confederation of the Rhine (*Rheinbund*), which prompted Francis II to abandon in 1806 the now meaningless title of Holy Roman Emperor. After Tilsit Vienna thronged with disgruntled refugees from Germany, vocal in their hatred of Napoleon. Many, like Friedrich von Gentz, were possessed by a new nationalism which encouraged Germans to resist Napoleon as a people, ignoring provincial differences and old loyalties.[5] A war party formed in Vienna around Count Stadion, von Gentz, Baldacci, Baron Hormayr, and the empress, Maria Ludovica d'Este. In 1809, taking advantage of Napoleon's involvement in Spain,[6] the

5. One cannot ignore that the basic appeal was to *racial* unity, or that much was said of German superiority, whatever the terms used.
6. The war in Spain will be treated at length in Chapter 7.

Archduke Ferdinand proclaimed a war of German liberation, and in March the Austrian army invaded Germany. But in January Napoleon had given command of the armies in Spain to his brother Joseph and hurried to Paris. When the Austrians marched Napoleon was prepared. The *Rheinbund* was loyal to France, and Russia and Prussia were neutral. Austria fought alone; her great appeal to the Germans had brought only small bands of freebooters to her side. As in 1805, the Grande Armée swept across southern Germany, occupied Vienna, and prepared to cross the Danube.

In Italy Eugène assembled an army of 37,000 Italians and 15,000 French. He was given command partly because of his maturity and dependable performance as viceroy, and partly because men such as Ney, Junot, and Soult were needed in Spain. Eugène, perhaps overanxious to please, did poorly at first. The Archduke John came down through the Alps with 65,000 men. Eugène, who had detached men to protect the Tyrol, had only 45,000, but he disdained withdrawing to the Quadrilateral, or the line of the Adige. Instead he deployed his troops in northeastern Venetia, at Sacile. On April 16 the Austrians appeared before he was ready, and he might still have retreated, but he was too proud. Riding about frantically, leading men into position personally, disdaining danger to himself, he made himself a hero his men could remember, but his army was shattered. The Army of Italy withdrew in confusion to the Piave, then the Adige. With blunt honesty Eugène wrote Napoleon: "I have fought a battle . . . I have lost." Luckily for the viceroy, the Archduke John pursued with less and less enthusiasm as news from Germany reached him.

Napoleon gave Eugène little sympathy. He complained, with some justice, of the lateness and lack of detail in the viceroy's reports. (The emperor heard of Sacile nine days after the battle, and had no complete report until May 10.) "I made a mistake in giving you command . . ." he wrote ". . . I should have sent you Masséna . . . if the circumstances become pressing you should call the King of Naples [Murat] to the army . . ."

But Eugène stubbornly refused to call on Murat, and military developments allowed him to justify his faith in himself. The Archduke John responded to Napoleon's successes in Germany by ending his campaign in Italy and marching to join Austrian forces north of the Danube; Eugène pursued. At the crossings of the Piave and Tagliamento, he inflicted heavy losses on the Austrians, which improved the morale of the Italian army. The archduke had expected to be reinforced in Styria by an army of Hungarians and Croatians under Jelačić. Eugène, making for Leoben, got between the Austrians and Jelačić, turned on the latter at Sankt Michael, and defeated him decisively. The Archduke John passed Gratz and moved into Hungary.

The viceroy placed 15,000 of his men under General (later Marshal) Macdonald to watch the Archduke John, turned the bulk of his army toward Vienna, and made junction with the Grande Armée. Napoleon had failed in his first attempt to cross the Danube (battles of Aspern and Essling, May 21–22), and was reorganizing on the island of Lobau. Cheered by Eugène's success, the emperor was unrestrained in his praise of the Italians and their commander. "Soldiers of the Army of Italy," ran his proclamation of May 27, "you have gloriously fulfilled my orders . . . [and joined] the Grande Armée . . . the Austrian Army . . . which intended to smash my Iron Crown, is dispersed, beaten, destroyed . . . Dio me la diede, guai a chi la tocca!"[7] Read the thirteenth bulletin of the Grande Armée: "The Viceroy displayed during the whole campaign a *sang-froid* and perception which marks a Great Captain."

Victory still depended, however, on crossing the Danube and defeating the main Austrian army of the Archduke Charles. To insure success the Archduke John had to be prevented from joining Charles. Eugène, his army reinforced to 45,000 (including Macdonald), was given the task.

John had followed the Raab River, which flows into the Danube southeast of Pressburg, and was within sixty miles of the main Austrian army. Macdonald had impeded his march, however, and on June 14 Eugène overtook him south of the town of Raab. The archduke had 50,000 men, but they were hungry and exhausted, and his defensive position, with his back to the river, was poor. Aided by the deadly artillery fire of General Sorbier,[8] the Army of Italy attacked. Thrown back, Eugène rode among his

7. "God has given it to me, let him who touches it beware."
8. Later commander of the artillery of the Imperial Guard.

infantry, driving them back into line, and the Austrians began to give ground. At the head of his cavalry, Eugène delivered the *coup de grâce*. The archduke retreated south, leaving on the field 3,000 dead to Eugène's 900. It was a great victory, and fought on the anniversaries of Marengo and Friedland, as Napoleon noted in his nineteenth bulletin. Eugène had proved himself, and so crippled John's army that the Army of Italy could join Napoleon for the final campaign against the Archduke Charles.

At Wagram (July 5–6) the Army of Italy occupied the center of the line. Repulsed on July 5, Eugène staunchly held his position on July 6, while Macdonald (his subordinate) with three corps smashed the Austrian line. The viceroy had received his accolades for Raab, however. It was Macdonald whom Napoleon made the hero of his twenty-fifth bulletin and shortly marshal of the empire.

Eugène stayed briefly with the emperor at Schönbrunn, and was then given the task of pacifying the Tyrol. Incited by the Archduke John and the Baron Hormayr, the Tyroleans, under Andreas Hofer, had risen against Bavaria, to which their states had been added by Napoleon in 1805. Impelled by centuries-old emotional ties to the Austrian emperors, whom they saw as God's appointees, the sturdy mountaineers had bested all comers. They had surprised French, Bavarian, and Italian units, sent boulders crashing from mountain tops like the artillery of the gods, and once captured a whole division en route from Italy. But now they alone fought on. Eugène respected the valiant Andreas Hofer and sympathized with the Tyroleans' resentment over having been arbitrarily given to Bavaria. But Napoleon would not allow them to defy him, and Eugène did his duty. He tried first to convince Hofer that his cause was hopeless. But the Tyrolean chief, vowing that the Virgin Mary would sustain him, would not surrender unless Bavarian troops withdrew. The viceroy reluctantly gave the order for an all-out campaign. Hofer's forces were decimated and driven into the mountains, where most of them laid down their arms. Hofer was betrayed for a price, transported in chains to Mantua, where, despite Eugène's objections, Napoleon had him executed.

Saddened by his experience in the Tyrol, but wearing the laurels of Raab and Wagram and now unquestionably a man worthy of viceroyalty and command, Eugène returned to an expanded kingdom in November. At Schönbrunn Napoleon had taken Istria and Dalmatia from his kingdom, but he was compensated with part of the Tyrol.

THE DIVORCE AND ITALY

Shortly after returning to Milan, Eugène was summoned to Paris. After the fatherly affection and praise Napoleon had given him in Vienna, he felt certain that the emperor intended to proclaim him king of Italy. When he arrived in Paris (December 1809), however, he found that Napoleon intended to divorce Joséphine and marry the Archduchess Marie Louise of Austria.

Eugène had been adopted with the specific condition that he and his heirs would succeed in Italy if Napoleon had no natural and legitimate heirs. The emperor was remarrying specifically in the hope of producing a son. Further, he was convinced he could, for he had fathered illegitimate children in 1806 and 1807, and had learned at Schönbrunn that Madame Walewska was with child.[9] Eugène's hope of inheriting the Italian crown was exploded, and Napoleon left no doubt of it. In January 1810 (two months before his marriage) he reserved Italy for his second son. Eugène and Augusta were guaranteed only a principality in Italy with an income of a million francs a year, or an estate in France with an equivalent income. Eugène would remain viceroy, however, until the anticipated second son was eighteen.[10]

Joséphine had determined to oppose the divorce unless Napoleon gave Eugène the crown of Italy, but Eugène dissuaded her. He knew that the emperor would have his way and preferred dignified acquiescence. In the end, he felt, they would only get what Napoleon granted; concessions forced from him would probably be renounced. Moreover Eugène appreciated that, without Napoleon, he would be nothing. The viceroy not only consented to the divorce, but announced it to the senate and presented Napoleon's "official

9. The news of Walewska's pregnancy was decisive, for he did not doubt her faithfulness to him, whereas that of Élénore Denuelle, mother of Léon, born 1806, and the actress Pellapra, who gave him a daughter, was questionable.

10. Napoleon, who delighted in financial calculations, had estimated the viceroy's income for twenty years at 30,000,000 francs, to which he added 10,-000,000 interest. This, said he, was Eugene's in addition to the estate and income guaranteed thereafter. Well-invested, 40,000,000 should bring 300–400,000 a year, he thought.

demand" for the hand of Marie Louise to Prince Schwarzenberg, representing the Austrian emperor.

Augusta, who had pictured Eugène not only as future king, but possibly emperor, was for a time almost inconsolable. She felt her husband had been "destituted" because of the emperor's jealousy of him, and her children disinherited. (She had two girls, would have two more girls and two boys.) She was never completely reconciled with Napoleon, for whom she had earlier shown great affection. She came to Paris in March at Eugène's request, but went straight to Malmaison to console Joséphine and did not leave until commanded to join the emperor's suite at Compiègne. Augusta and Eugène attended the civil and religious ceremonies (April 1–2), but both spent much time with Joséphine, and when they returned to Italy in July she accompanied them as far as Geneva.

While Eugène was in Paris, a Swedish delegation asked Napoleon to choose a successor to the failing King Charles XIII. The crown was offered to Eugène, but he declined. The viceroy preferred to retain his rights in the French succession, however diminished. Though brave in battle, Eugène shrank from political adventure. He was at heart a traditionalist, French to the core, and could not face going to an altogether foreign country and changing his religion (Sweden was Lutheran). Eugène was bound by ideals of service carried down through his father's family and strengthened by his military training. Going off to Sweden was too radical a step for him. He was comfortable as Napoleon's loyal subordinate; he would so remain to the end. His temperament and concept of honor required it.

On March 20, 1811, Napoleon's son was born. All Paris got drunk on the emperor's wine while the cannon boomed, the church bells rang, the semaphore telegraph wagged out the news to Brussels, Antwerp, Lyons, Strasbourg, and Milan, and Madame Blanchard in her balloon ascended from the Place du Carrousel to carry the news to the world.[11] Eugène had attended the (privately) nervous emperor during the days before the birth, and stood by in the empress's antechamber during the final hours.

11. She came down with a ferocious bump only sixty miles from Paris and the world had to do without her notification.

Internal Affairs

GOVERNMENT AND ADMINISTRATION

Eugène's government comprised men of all classes and provinces. Among the grand officers of the realm were Melzi, keeper of the seals, created duke of Lodi by Napoleon, and the Count Caprara, grand equerry, who was of old nobility. The ministry was composed at its core of ex-Jacobins who had gradually gone conservative. Giuseppe Prina, a Piedmontese of Novara, held the portfolio of finance. Ferdinando Marescalchi, of Bologna, was both minister of foreign affairs and ambassador to Paris. Antonio Aldini, another Bolognese, was secretary of state and intermediary with Napoleon at Paris. Giovanni Paradisi, of Modena, was minister of roads and waterways, and after 1807 also president of the senate. With them worked moderates and men of the old regime, some of whom had also served the republic. The minister of justice was Giuseppe Luosi, a brilliant lawyer famed for his elegance and earlier for the distinction and affluence of his clients. The minister of the interior was Arborio di Breme, a Piedmontese marquis of ancient family. His style proving too gentle, he was succeeded in 1809 by the tough-minded Luigi Vaccari. The original minister of war was General Domenico Pino, who proved more politician than soldier, and was replaced in 1806 by General François Auguste Caffarelli, a Frenchman whose family was of Italian origin and whom Napoleon detached from the Imperial Guard. Caffarelli served with distinction until 1811, when he was given a command in Spain.

Of the ministers, the most successful was Prina, who was also the most hated, for the populace blamed high taxes on the finance minister and Napoleon, not Eugène. Vaccari was also despised, especially by the Milanese, never fond of Modenese, who considered him a ruthless megalomaniac. His predecessors, Felici and Di Breme, had been popular, as were most of Eugène's key officials. Bovara, minister of cults, handled the touchy Italian clergy with skill. Luosi insinuated the *Code Napoléon* into Italian jurisprudence with firm finesse, and his courts gained a reputation for fair and speedy rulings. Scopoli, in public instruction, proved an amazing organizer, and even the ministers of police, Guicciardini,

Mosca, and Luini, managed to function without arousing the ire of the populace.[12] Melzi, who took a seat in the senate in 1807, but remained in the background, had the deep respect of the Milanese.

The kingdom's constitution was that of the republic, modified by constitutional statutes promulgated by Napoleon with the advice of a *consulta* of state comprising eight prominent citizens. The government was nominally headed by the king, that is, Napoleon, whose powers were delegated to his viceroy. Beneath him was the ministry, a legislative council (council of state) which drafted laws for presentation to the legislative corps (parliament). The parliament of seventy-five members was elected by universal manhood suffrage, but through a system of electors with high property qualifications. A college of auditors, composed of promising young civil servants, assisted the legislative council.

At the first session of parliament (June 7, 1805), Napoleon introduced Eugène as his viceroy, and delivered a discourse in Italian. "Rival in zeal my Council of State," he told the assembly, "and by concurrence of wills . . . support my [viceroy]." Unfor-

12. *Ministers 1805–1814*

Justice	Spannocchi	1805–(interim)
	Luosi, Giuseppe	1805–1814
Interior	Felici, Daniele	1805–1806
	Di Breme, Arborio, Marchese	1806–1809
	Vaccari, Luigi	1809–1814
War, Marine	Pino	1805–1806
	Caffarelli	1806–1811
	Fontanelli, Achille	1811–
	Veneri, Antonio	1811–
	Biragio, Ambrogio	1811–1814
Cults (Ecclesiastical Affairs)	Bovara	1805–1814
Finance	Prina, Giuseppe	1805–1814
Treasurer	Veneri, Antonio	1805–1814
Foreign Affairs	(At Paris) Marescalchi, Ferdinando	1805–1814
	(At Milan) Testi, Carlo	1805–1814
	Aldini, Antonio (Sec. of State)	1805–1814
Public Instruction	Moscati, Pietro	1805–
	Scopoli, Giovanni	1805–1814
Police	Guicciardini, Diego	1805–1809
	Mosca, Francesco	1809–1811
	Luini, Giacomo	1811–1814
Roads and Waterways	Paradisi, Giovanni	1805–1814

tunately the legislators showed an Italian propensity for talk and an untoward zeal for provincial interests. Even the patient Eugène became irritated with their lack of dispatch. They refused to limit themselves to their assigned function, which was to reject or accept the proposals of the legislative council (or *consulta* of state for constitutional changes). Eugène dismissed the parliament in July 1805, and never called it again. By constitutional statutes of December 20, 1807, and March 21, 1808 the *consulta* of state was expanded into a senate composed of law members, the grand officers of state, and two representatives of each department; all were appointed by the viceroy. The senate thereafter took the place of both the *consulta* and the parliament. Proposals were presented to it by the legislative council (council of state) presided over by Eugène or the president he appointed.

The government became thoroughly authoritarian. The viceroy ruled with the advice of groups appointed by himself and with the technical assistance of his "French Cabinet," which we have already named.[13] In the senate sat "sure" supporters of the regime, among them Melzi, Paradisi, the marquis di Breme, Guicciardi, Codronchi, and Cardinal Caprara, the patriarch of Venice. But Eugène was honest, industrious, efficient, and progressive and so were the men he chose to serve him. If the viceroy never really understood the Italians, and tended to trust his French advisers more, he gained almost unanimous respect among his people. (Nothing could have made them love him; his soul was not Latin.)

The *Code Napoléon* went into effect in Italy on January 1, 1806. During 1805 a six-man commission had translated it into Italian and Latin (for Illyria). It struck down what feudal rights the republic had not eliminated, including those of the Church. The principles of civil and legal equality were reinforced. The legality of civil marriage and divorce (under extreme circumstances) was confirmed. Division of estates among heirs became the established principle. Trials were made public, and the remaining judicial rights of the Church eliminated. The penal and criminal codes proved more difficult to write. Luosi, minister of justice; Abrial, the French jurist; and Romagnosi, the leading Italian

13. See p. 28.

criminalist, with many assistants, labored over them until September 1807. The compilation they produced differed greatly from the corresponding French codes. Napoleon had approved some modifications, for example, eliminating jury trial. But there was too much secrecy in proceedings and too many inequalities in punishment for his taste. In November 1810 he ordered the French codes instituted without change. The commercial code, which went into effect in 1808, was a compromise between the French code and customary Italian law in the various provinces.

After its territory was stabilized (1809) the kingdom's area was 35,000 square miles, its population almost 7,000,000. It was divided into twenty-four *dipartimenti*[14] under *prefetti*, districts under *vice-prefetti*, and cantons and communes. The Republic had established departments, but divided authority between departmental councils and prefects. Councils remained, but only to settle disputes not covered by law and to advise the prefects. "All that is good, all that is beautiful, is invariably the result of a simple and uniform system," Napoleon had told the Italian parliament. Superimposed on these were six military divisions for purposes of conscription and military control, eight maritime syndicates (on the Adriatic coast), and sixty-one dioceses of the Church. A court system on the French model was installed in 1806 with justices of the peace in the *cantoni*, civil and criminal tribunals in each department, courts of appeal at Milan, Venice, Bologna, Brescia, and Ancona, and a court of cassation at Milan. Appeals from the court of cassation could in unusual cases go to the legislative council.

The public administration was centralized, symmetric, and very demanding of its functionaries. But it promised sure advancement and status to those who qualified, and the young bourgeoisie, especially, swarmed to the service of the state. So did the aristocrats, although they tended to gravitate toward the courts, the army, and high ceremonial office. Next to the French, the Italian bureaucracy became the best in Europe. Its competence was reflected in such diverse areas as the amazing fiscal success of the kingdom and the excellence of its educational structure, both of which we shall

14. See Map 2, p. 44.

discuss shortly. And it extended its talents to the improvement of the services of health and police, and even to cultural affairs.

Spurred on by Napoleon, who demanded improved communications for military and economic reasons, Eugène carried through an ambitious public works program. Roads were improved, as were the watercourses of the Po and its tributaries. A corps of engineers was established. Over-all direction was given to an autonomous directory of waterways and roads (*acque e strade*), in effect a ministry, organized and directed by Giovanni Paradisi, a "Renaissance Italian," who was politician, poet, and mathematician, among other things. His plans formed part of what André Fugier calls Napoleon's "*politique* of routes."

By the institution of the Continental System in 1806–1807 Napoleon deprived Europe (insofar as he could control it) of British goods, including colonial products carried by British vessels. Also, among other things, British control of the sea greatly reduced France's normal trade with Mediterranean countries. Early in his career Napoleon had planned to make the Italian peninsula an economic colony, specializing in raw materials for French industry. After the institution of the Continental System, he envisioned it also as an avenue for goods from the Levant and Balkans.

His plans were not designed to give the peninsula economic unification (or any other kind—it was too dangerous).[15] His major routes ran from the Kingdom of Italy, from the Principality of Lucca,[16] and from Naples through territory annexed to France, and then into France. Rivers and highways through the peninsula were expected to carry goods which had formerly reached France by ship from Italian and Near Eastern ports, now denied by the British blockade. The cargoes of ships from the Adriatic went by barge up the Po to river ports in Piedmont (part of France), where they were transferred to wagons for shipment into the French interior. Cargoes arriving at Trieste could reach Venice safely via a new coastal road, or at times by water. Improved

15. Napoleon did lay some groundwork for Italian unification, as the textbooks say, but not by design, as we shall discuss later.
16. Lucca-Piombino, ruled by Princess Elisa Bonaparte Bacciocchi, who was also grand duchess of Tuscany, which was part of France.

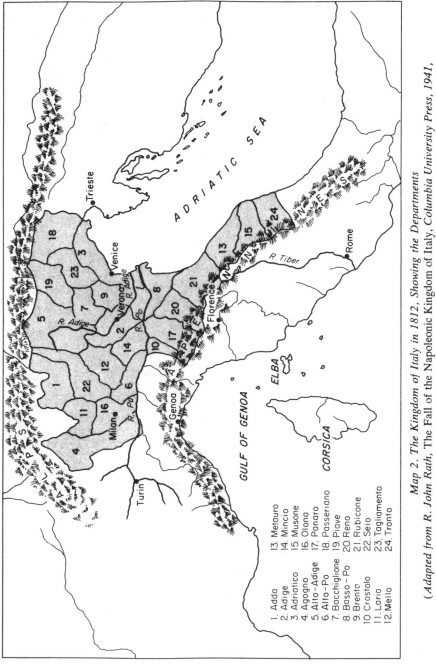

Map 2. *The Kingdom of Italy in 1812, Showing the Departments*

(*Adapted from R. John Rath,* The Fall of the Napoleonic Kingdom of Italy, *Columbia University Press, 1941, frontispiece*)

1. Adda
2. Adige
3. Adriatico
4. Agogno
5. Alto-Adige
6. Alto-Po
7. Bacchiglione
8. Basso-Po
9. Brenta
10. Crostolo
11. Lario
12. Mello
13. Metauro
14. Mincio
15. Musone
16. Olona
17. Panaro
18. Passeriano
19. Piave
20. Reno
21. Rubicone
22. Seio
23. Tagliamento
24. Tronto

highways connected Venice to Mantua and Milan, where traffic entered the passes of the Alps. To get control of the Simplon, Napoleon first made the Valais a republic and then annexed it to France. Under the direction of the French engineer Dausse, a major effort was made to improve the Mont Cenis Pass. Costs were shared by France and the Kingdom of Italy, and in spite of scandals involving contractors at Grenoble, Chambéry, and Turin, a spectacular new road was completed.

Goods from southern and central Italy, including Oriental cargoes reaching the port of Naples, were routed through annexed territory to France, bypassing the Kingdom of Italy. Though not fully complete until 1812, heavy traffic followed the new Corniche, which hugged the precipitous coastline along the French and Italian Rivieras, funneling goods from Parma, Piacenza, Lucca, Florence, Leghorn, and points south, to Genoa and Nice.

Eugène's directory of waterways and roads also left monuments to his regime. A number of arches of triumph were erected in Milan, the best known being that across the Porta Ticinese, designed by Cagnola. The *duomo* and the La Scala Opera House were given new façades. The royal villa at Monza was remodeled, and pavilions designed by Mirabellino erected on the grounds. Milan still bears the marks of the viceroy's city planners. In addition to its practical and decorative contributions the Directory left Italy a coterie of trained personnel. Their skills, endowed to the next generation, became a platform for greater progress in "High Italy" and the whole Italian peninsula.

FINANCES

"Uomo laboriosissimo, severo, incorruttibile," says Natali of Giuseppe Prina, Eugène's minister of finance. Not only industrious, severe, and incorruptible, but effective, he performed a feat matched in no other satellite kingdom. He kept the budget in balance, at least until the disastrous year of 1814. The kingdom incurred a small debt, but interest was always paid, and quotations on state paper were consistently high. In 1810, for example, when the notes of Joseph's Spanish government dropped to ten per cent of face value, Italy's were going at sixty-eight per cent.

Prina's basic levy was a capitation tax, set initially at 176 Milanese lire or 134 francs, and never increased. Following the example of the French government, he raised additional funds through indirect taxes. From the capitation were excluded children under fourteen, persons over sixty, fathers of twelve or more, and incapacitated persons. Tariffs favored France, but nevertheless brought in some income, and the state retained monopolies on salt and tobacco. Revenues were collected through nine directors general of finances, who supervised receivers of direct taxes and intendants who collected indirect taxes (one per department). Prina chose hard and honest men, and pounced ruthlessly on anyone suspected of fraud or venality. His glacial personality, meticulousness, and indifference to public opinion were assets in his profession. But they intensified the people's natural antipathy for the tax collector.

The tax system was not administered without difficulty. In the spring of 1809, decrees instituting new indirect taxes produced scattered uprisings among the peasants, who objected especially to a milling tax. But the violence was as much a product of the increased conscription for the Austrian war, the departure of the army, and Napoleon's quarrel with the Pope, as it was of the tax decrees. Nevertheless, one of the major grievances of the populace remained high taxes, no matter how fairly they were assessed.

Taxes were, in fact, slightly lower than in France. For this the equitable distribution of the fiscal burden and rigorous, impartial collection of revenues were largely responsible. But Prina's careful management of confiscated Church properties also served to reduce tax requirements. The republic had abolished some monastic orders and assumed title to their holdings; Eugène eliminated most of those remaining. The ministry of finance, as a result, assumed control of lands, buildings, furnishings, and other valuables worth over 500,000,000 lire. They were disposed of at public sales, so scheduled as to allow the government to benefit from rises in the market. Prina resisted the wholesale issue of certificates based on the properties, which in France (the *assignats*) and later Spain (Joseph's *cedulas*) became paper money, lost value, and hurt their governments' credit. Neither in Italy nor anywhere else did this property go to expand peasant holdings, as had been hoped. But at least Eugène's government profited from its sale.

The production of revenues of course depended on the king-dom's economic health, which could not but be affected by the Continental System and the "colonial" position Italy was compelled to assume. *Mercantilist* is the only suitable word for Napoleon's economic concepts. He was even a *bullionist:* "My object is [to export] French manufactures, and import foreign *specie*," he once said.

Republican Italy, however, had gone far in adjusting her economy to augment that of France, and Napoleon's further re-quirements caused relatively little discomfiture. Similarly, since the kingdom had few seaports, it was less shaken by the Continental System than other areas, for example, Naples, where even domestic trade had depended on coastal shipping. What losses Italy incurred in commerce were compensated by increased land and river traffic. The seaports, of course, atrophied. But over all the Italian economy boomed.

The initial effect of the Continental Decrees was to run up prices on sugar, indigo, tobacco, chocolate, cotton, saffron, and other colonial products, cripple the commerce of Venice and Trieste, and slow down commerce on the Po. But land shipments through Illyria and blockade-running kept the ports alive. And products of the kingdom and to some degree of French Italy and Naples increasingly came by land to the Po and were barged up-stream to French ports in Piedmont. Trade increased markedly in 1810, when a series of imperial decrees allowed dealing in captured British goods on payment of heavy tariffs (usually 40 per cent) and granted licenses for trading in colonial products. Throughout the period contraband-running was big business in the Alpine regions, especially Novara. And the British managed to get their goods into Italian ports. Transshipment through Vis, in the Adri-atic, which they occupied, caused the island's economy to boom; its population tripled between 1803 to 1811. The destruction of the warehouses of Vis by the Italian navy in 1810 proved only a temporary setback. Malta was a depot for British goods, and got rich by illegal trade with Italy, as did the ports of Albania and Morea. Corfu, under French occupation, carried much illicit traffic also.

Tariffs for the Kingdom of Italy, as elsewhere on the peninsula, were arranged to promote the sale of French manufactures and the export to France of raw materials. Initially the import duty on French manufactured goods was five per cent, and the export duties on Italian raw materials five or less. The tariff treaty of 1808 cut import duties to two-and-a-half per cent. That of 1810 prohibited Italy from importing any but French linen, vellon, gauze, cotton cloth, wool cloth and articles made therefrom, and allowed Italian raw silk to enter France without duty. Silk was the chief export of the kingdom. The value of shipments was 56,000,000 lire in 1809, 62,000,000 in 1811, and continued to climb.[17] The Tyrolean departments (annexed 1809) switched from tobacco to silk production to good advantage. Most trade was in raw silk, however.

The Italian "colony" supplied French manufacturers, whose products were returned to Italy and undersold those locally produced. Italian industry was crippled further by loss of markets to the French in the rest of the peninsula, and the tariffs against Italian manufactures of France's allies. Bavaria, for example, put a twenty per cent duty on Italian cloth in 1811. Considerable industry survived, however. Como and Milan continued to produce for German and Russian markets. Bologna and Modena sold their unique crepes and gauzes in the Levant. Salvation generally lay in producing fabrics which French factories could not make because of lack of experience, skilled workmen, secrets of processing, unfavorable climate, or such a simple thing as unsuitable local water supply. Changing the character of the Italian textile industry, which demanded the assembling of workers for training and supervision, accelerated the decline of the putting-out system in favor of factory operation. Bologna in 1812 had almost five hundred small factories, Modena four hundred. Together these two cities employed 25,000 weavers. Wool manufacturing persisted at Vicenza, Padua, Bergamo, Como, and Venice. Some of the cloth

17. The Milanese lira was valued at about 0.76 francs or about $0.15 U.S.

found a market in the Levant, but had Italian peasants not preferred the rough native cloth, these factories would not have survived the competition of those of Rouen, Amiens, Saint-Quentin,
Tarare, Roubaix, and Tourcoing. Hemp and linen production also
continued, although the French took a considerable part of the
Levant market.

Europe badly needed cotton, which the British were forbidden
to supply and which they prevented neutrals from carrying. Some
Egyptian and Turkish varieties came in by land routes, smuggling,
or blockade-running, but not enough. Italians began to grow
cotton, though the climate was more favorable, for example, in
Naples. Most of it was exported raw, although one manufacturing
center did appear near Vicenza which by 1814 employed 6,000
persons, mostly women. The Italian cotton cloth market was almost
monopolized, however, by the French. In 1809 their sales to Italy
totaled 43,000,000 lire, and by 1812 almost 90,000,000. French
cotton cloth undermined the domestic market for Italian silks.

Though exports of silk had greater value, the heaviest traffic
from Italy into France and northern Europe was in cereals. Wheat
was grown in the valleys of the Po and its tributaries and along the
Adriatic Coast. Rice predominated on the lower Po and Mincio.
Cattle and sheep were also exported in large numbers, as were
hides and wool. Herds declined somewhat, however, because of the
greater profits to be made in cereals. Though Modena continued to
be cattle country, Bologna put its pastures in rice. Sheep increased
in numbers in Romagna and the Varese, but declined elsewhere.
Modena and Mantua exported wine; eastern Venetia oranges and
lemons.

The balance of trade usually favored France. Had Italy not
had some markets in northern Europe and the Levant and carried
on contraband trade, the economy might have suffered more. As it
was, the kingdom enjoyed over-all prosperity throughout its life.
It was affected by the French depression of 1810–1811, but recovered rapidly. Revenues remained sufficient to enable Eugène to
sponsor public works, and welfare, charitable, educational, literary,
and artistic projects, but especially to finance the army, upon which
the survival of his regime depended.

THE ARMY

When Eugène became viceroy he inherited an army of 23,000 from the republic, and conscription was already in force, so that he escaped the stigma of introducing it. His problems were nevertheless great. He had to build a larger, more efficient army and establish a military tradition, which involved changing the attitudes of Italians radically. Generally they were willing to fight, and bravely, for personal, or at most, city interests. But they tended to view broader military service as something that should be done by mercenaries. In a word, military men had low status in Italy.

Napoleon felt that if the sons of the nobility and high bourgeoisie could be induced to regard the military as an honorable career, the feeling of the lower classes would soon change. "My object," he wrote Eugène ". . . is to effect a revolution in customs (*moeurs*)." The viceroy therefore gave personal attention to the recruitment of prospective officers and their schooling. Officers were trained for the artillery at Modena, for the infantry at Pavia and Bologna, and for the cavalry at Lodi. Cadets were mostly of the upper classes, predominantly nobles, but a few talented boys of the lower classes were also admitted. In addition to imparting the necessary military knowledge the schools strove to mold Milanese, Modenese, Bolognese, Venetians, and others into *Italians.* Only Tuscan Italian, foreign to all, was approved for speaking and writing. City-state loyalties were decried by instructors at every opportunity. The glories of Italian military accomplishments, however remote, were pictured. Loyalty and a sense of duty and gratitude to Napoleon were taught together with the principles of authoritarian liberalism. Religious discipline, as an adjunct to the military variety, was encouraged, but priests who dealt with cadets had to be certified Bonapartists.

Not all officers emerged ready to die for Napoleon, or even became pro-French, but most did become adamantly opposed to the return of the old regime. Many would be found in the ranks of Italian nationalist leadership later in the century. Royal guards were created in 1805 together with training units called guards of honor and royal *vélites* (light infantry). The guards of honor were recruited from the nobility, the *vélites* from the bourgeoisie, but in both cases parents bought places for their sons. According to the sentiment of the day, purchase of cadetship added prestige to the position, especially in Italy, as Napoleon well knew. Both guards of honor and *vélites* earned army commissions, but only the best remained in the royal guard. *Vélites* who remained generally served as sergeants. The guard developed a fierce *esprit de corps* which was well displayed in Russia, where a very high percentage of officers and noncommissioned officers died in battle.

The spirit of the guard carried over in some degree to the whole army. Eugène's personal leadership counted heavily also, as did the organizational ability of Generals Caffarelli and Biragio, ministers of war.[18] The Italian army was a model for others on the peninsula. Among the satellites, its units were rivaled only by those of Westphalia, where the Hessians, with a long military tradition, formed the core. Men of all provinces, serving in the same green uniform, under their own flag, developed a feeling of common citizenship. Generally, however, it did not extend to the other peoples of the peninsula. Concepts of general Italian unification were held only by a few exceptional men, mostly officers, even in 1814. The backbone of the army was its volunteers, of whom there were 44,000 over the years. Between 1805 and the end of the reign, 142,000 men were drafted—one of every three who reached twenty, and in the later years many of eighteen. Many deserted, usually prior to or just after being called, in some years one-quarter of those selected. Desertion on campaign was not heavy; although the figures taken by themselves seem shocking, the rate was only slightly greater than that in the French army. On the average less than 12,000 men a year were called up in the period 1805 through 1811; but for 1812 and 1813 the figures were 24,000 and 36,000 respectively. In French departments an average of three to four per cent (total) of the population was drafted between 1804 and 1814. In Italy during the same period the figure was just over two per cent. Nevertheless, conscription was much resented.

The Italian army grew from 23,000 in 1805 to 44,000 in 1808 and to 90,000 in 1813. It furnished almost half (18,000) of the "French" army which seized Naples in 1806 and most of the troops

18. Pino lasted less than a year. Fontanelli and Veneri were interim appointees.

which occupied the Papal States in 1808. It contributed 30,000 men to the French Army of Spain (of whom only 9,000 survived). Eugène led 27,000 on the Russian campaign (of whom 20,000 perished), and in 1813 sent 28,000 more to the Grande Armée in Germany. In addition to the regular forces there was a national guard of some 50,000 with units in the major cities. It proved loyal and useful in containing localized disturbances, for example the insurrections of 1809, which occurred in Eugène's absence.[19]

Wherever they served the Italians made a good record. They impressed Europe, and themselves. Sons of Italian merchants, bred to obsequiousness, became proud and forceful leaders. Men weaned on city-state parochialism gained a feeling of nationality, and a new pride in themselves. The Italian army was not only extremely useful to Napoleon, but of inestimable value in changing the outlook of north Italian society.

EDUCATION

One of the most remarkable achievements of Eugène's regime was the elevation of the ministry of public instruction to a position of real importance in the state. Established in 1802, the ministry had languished under the republic and accomplished little during Eugène's first two years. Its transformation began in 1807, when the rather lifeless Pietro Moscati relinquished its direction to Giovanni Scopoli. He developed even more effective control of institutions than did his opposite number in France. The Church's primary and secondary schools were subjected to government supervision. A system of *lycées* was established, and a college for young women in Milan, to which there was no parallel in France. For the universities at Pavia, Bologna, and Padua, his ministry appointed professors and endowed chairs for distinguished scholars and men of letters. (The poet Vincenzo Monti, for example, was nominally a professor at Pavia, although he seldom came near a classroom.) Where professorships were not possible, pensions supported the work of scientists and academicians much as research funds do today.

An institute had been established at Milan in 1802, but it had failed. Eugène's government revived and expanded it to include

19. See p. 46.

branches at Venice, Padua, Bologna, and Verona. Pensions of 1,200 francs were provided for members, and attendance at meetings insured by the threat of their cancelation. The institute promoted the work of a poet-priest Cesarotti and that of Giordani. The Hellenist Lamberti was a member of the institute and for a time inspector general of public instruction. "High Italy" had produced many scientists. Galileo had been professor of mathematics at Padua. In the eighteenth century Scopoli's father had gained a world-wide reputation as a naturalist at the University of Pavia. The government encouraged talented beginners with draft exemptions and scholarships, though often professional engineering or technological training took precedence over that in pure science. Scientists of reputation were honored and supported, for example the aging Alessandro Volta,[20] who was still experimenting in electricity, and the astronomer-priest Barnaba Oriani.

As noted above, one means by which provincialism was attacked was the establishment of a standard language. At Napoleon's suggestion, Eugène in 1809 and again in 1812 gave official approval to Tuscan, the dialect used by the first great writers of the Italian Renaissance. The viceroy approved the circulation of a dictionary produced by the Academy of Crusca at Florence under the sponsorship of Princess Elisa, grand duchess of Tuscany.[21] In the Kingdom of Italy, Vaccari, the minister of the interior, issued a vocabulary for his bureaucrats and a lexicon of proscribed terms. Interestingly enough, the latter held forth against Italianizations of French terms and has therefore often been described as anti-Napoleonic, which it was not.

To meet pressing needs schools of "roads and bridges" and veterinary medicine were founded. To improve farm methods and equipment and facilitate changes in land use required by Italy's "French colonial" position, an academy of agriculture was established. It summarized its findings and advice in a journal edited by Filippo Re of the University of Bologna. The regime also sponsored a conservatory of music, five academies of fine arts, and appointed a director general for the performing arts.

There was censorship from the beginning, but it was intensified

20. The electrical unit of force, the volt, is named after him.
21. Elisa Bonaparte Bacciocchi, Napoleon's sister.

after the insurrections of 1809.[22] In 1810 the system, which had undergone haphazard expansion, was regularized under two directors general, one installed in the royal library, the other in the government press. While the censors examined every scrap of printed matter, special police, selected by Lagarde, monitored performances at the theaters and opera. If however, one accepts the unstated Napoleonic premise that equality, opportunity (for the loyal), and government-directed "progress" are worth the loss of liberty, the educational system deserves unqualified praise, as does Eugène's whole government.

LITERATURE AND THE ARTS

Without question the Kingdom of Italy and Tuscany were the artistic-literary-intellectual centers of the Italian peninsula. The Kingdom of Italy boasted Vincenzo Monti and Ugo Foscolo, two of the most renowned poets of their day. In the early days both produced paeans to Napoleon, like Monti's "Il Beneficio." Both began to chafe under French domination, however, touted Italian culture as superior to any, and lent support to the proponents of Italian independence and unification. They were guarded in their attacks on Napoleon, however, not solely out of fear, but because his overthrow might bring back the old regime. Foscolo insisted on serving on Eugène's army in 1814.[23]

Many persons not native to the kingdom made reputations there. For example, the Neapolitan Vincenzo Cuoco edited the *Giornale Italiano* at Milan, and published a number of books. His *Platone in Italia* was a clear call for Italian unification, issued at a time when most intellectuals had a goal no higher than the liberalizing of the Napoleonic governments. Even in 1814 pan-Italian nationalists would be rare.

The Kingdom of Italy swarmed with artists. The sculptor Antonio Canova, born in Venetia, gained international fame. David, the French painter, once sent him a letter addressed simply "Canova, Europe." He produced busts of most of the members of the imperial family, and statues of some, of which the most famous

22. See p. 46.
23. Though after Napoleon's fall he favored Murat over Eugène since the former promised to unite Italy.

by far is that of Pauline. In white marble, the most voluptuous of the Bonaparte sisters reclines nude on an antique couch, wearing an expression of bored mockery. "Oh, the studio was quite warm," said Pauline. To Napoleon's outrage, Canova also produced a nude statue of him. The head was recognizable, but the herculean body, standing scepter in hand, was clearly not the emperor's. The thing shocked Napoleon, who had it hidden away in the Louvre. David, who could afford candid opinions, went about calling it "magnificent," but few people would discuss it with him. In 1815 the statue found an unlikely buyer, the duke of Wellington, who had it installed in his country house in England.[24]

On the surface Italy's entire artistic and literary effort seemed totally devoted to the support and glorification of the Napoleonic regime. But there was an undercurrent of resistance which came to the surface occasionally in the writing of men of stature, such as Foscolo and Monti. Lesser men resorted to allegorical verse and stories and works with ancient settings. Some produced classical plays denouncing tyranny—if the message were presented subtly enough to escape the police monitors. The majority, however, were willing captives of the government, either through sincere conviction or out of self-interest. Only in the secret societies did the voice of resistance speak loud and plain, and even there only in the last years of the empire.

THE CHURCH

In spite of Napoleon's conflict with the Pope, state-Church relations in the kingdom were generally smooth. The anticlerical policies of the Italian Republic had shaken the clergy violently. Eugène was inclined to abide more by the spirit of the Italian Concordat of 1803 than Melzi had been, and the simple fact that Italy had become a monarchy, which to most churchmen seemed a return to normal government, encouraged the hierarchy.

There were occasional conflicts over the investment of bishops (government-selected, Church-approved), and in times of crisis (as in 1809) there were generally enough recalcitrant clergy (mostly dispossessed monks) to stir up minor troubles. The abolition of monastic orders (completed by Eugène) and the seizure of

24. A replica resides in the state museum in Milan.

their properties were not accomplished without scattered violence. But the Italian monks rarely attempted to lead insurrections personally (as did the Spanish), and the peasants were not markedly devoted to them. Further, the government allowed them to enter the secular priesthood, to teach, or gave them pensions, so that the majority were not grossly discontented.

The minister of "Cults," Bovara, was judicious, diplomatic, worked closely with the hierarchy, and was generally respected. Cardinal Caprara participated as a senator in the decision-making of the government. The clergy generally supported the regime, and even produced a catechism for the schools declaring it God's will for all to support the emperor-king and his viceroy.

Eugène's policies, applied by a less skilled executive, might well have spawned widespread resistance in spite of the power he wielded. He took much of the Church's property, virtually eliminated its regular clergy, and robbed it of many of its functions in education. The *Code Napoléon* made possible a life cycle outside Church authority. Births were registered, marriages performed, and burials authorized by civil officials, so that those who wished (though few did) could ignore the sacraments. The Church was subordinated to the state, but Eugène used force sparingly, avoided embarrassing the clergy, placed them prominently in ceremonies, gave them office, and attended services publicly and regularly himself. While he ruled, an atmosphere of Church-state harmony generally prevailed.

Conclusion

The Kingdom of Italy was the most successful of the satellites. Eugène, if not popular, was widely respected. His administration was efficient and honest, his finances well managed, his army well drilled and effective. Italy had been well prepared for the viceroy, and he had some outstanding subordinates, but without his own sure, capable direction the government could not have been so effective.

Eugène devoted himself to Napoleon, but not slavishly. He served out of personal gratitude and by soldierly principle, which demanded that he put France before himself. He devoted himself.

to his people also, but without any thought of building a personal following, or using Italian nationalism to raise up a power against France, as would Murat. Natali, Lemmi, and other contemporary Italian historians are full of praise for the man and his government.

Conscription and heavy taxation bred discontent among the people. Many among the old ruling classes resented the social changes sponsored by the regime. Many clergy, if docile, wistfully remembered the Church's former eminence. Nationalism steadily gained strength among intellectual, political, and military leaders, though their objectives were various and vague. Economic dislocations left numbers of the middle class and workers disgruntled.

Nevertheless Eugène's government had massive popular support. Among the leaders he had assembled there was almost solid loyalty. Even among those who opposed him, few indeed yearned for the return of the old regime. In 1814, despite the fall of Napoleon, there was no revolution against Eugène's government. If he had not remained loyal to Napoleon to the end, or even thereafter if he had not been war-weary and disinclined to see his people suffer further, he might have become the independent king of Italy. We shall give evidence to support this assertion in a later chapter.

I have not heard that you have had a single one of the lazzaroni *shot. . . . If you don't make them fear you at the start, you will have trouble.*
—NAPOLEON TO JOSEPH

Death from starvation is ordinary here. . . . Surely something can be done about it. . . .
—JOSEPH TO NAPOLEON

chapter three

NAPLES UNDER JOSEPH BONAPARTE

Joseph Bonaparte

"*H*e must win glory! He must get himself wounded!" crowed Napoleon gleefully, referring to his brother Joseph.[1] The emperor wanted soldier-kings in his satellites; he had arranged for Joseph to win his crown by fighting his way into Naples. What could be more convenient! But his elder brother had never shown any inclination to win glory, nor did he in 1806. Concentrating on developing the royal presence, he left the war to his commanders—Masséna, Gouvion de Saint-Cyr, Reynier, and Lechi.

Though as a schoolboy Napoleon had advised his father that Joseph was better suited for the Church or the law than the army, as emperor he demanded that male Bonapartes in line of succession be soldiers. In 1804 he plummeted Joseph into the army as colonel of the Fourth Infantry, then at Boulogne. "Now, at least . . . epaulettes don't frighten him . . ." Napoleon told Miot. To justify Joseph's nomination to the senate, Napoleon recorded that he had been a battalion commander at Toulon (1793), had served as a staff officer in Italy (1796–1797), and had a wound. Actually

1. To Miot de Melito.

Joseph had no military experience.[2] At Napoleon's insistence Joseph had stayed with his regiment for three months, which until 1806 was all the time he had spent with the army. In Naples his military inexperience would not matter, but in Spain he would suffer greatly from it.

Though Joseph was not a military man, or even one possessing the hard qualities Napoleon admired in civil officials, he was a man of intelligence and marvelous magnetism. Men feared and respected Napoleon; they liked Joseph. Women yielded to Napoleon; they loved Joseph. Taller than Napoleon, darkly handsome, sympathetic, and soft-hearted, he loved society, philosophic conversation, literature, art, and the theater. A convinced liberal, he believed in progress through mass education and, far more than Napoleon, in individual freedom. Napoleon had gloried in the Revolution because it opened "careers to talent"; Joseph because it promised to fulfill the dreams of the *philosophes.* After the creation of the empire, Joseph's "Republican" manners incensed Napoleon. "I will call out [at court] 'good day, Prince Égalité!' and that word will kill you." While Napoleon was an "eighteenth century *cérébral*" (Lefebvre's description)—an organizer, believer in the efficacy of rational solutions—Joseph was a romantic. As late as 1799 he published a pastoral novel in the style of Rousseau.

Joseph (Giuseppe) was born in January 1768 at Corte, the ancient Moorish capital of Corsica, where his parents had joined Paoli to resist French occupation of the island.[3] He was the first child of Carlo and Letizia Ramolino Buonaparte to survive, and was inevitably coddled. After the rebels were defeated and most, including Carlo Buonaparte, pardoned, the family went home to Ajaccio, where in August 1769 Napoleon (Napoleone) was born. Received more casually, and less attractive, Napoleon learned to fight for attention, and early impressed his parents with his toughness and intelligence. Joseph, though probably equally bright, was never compelled to display anything but charm. Not surprisingly, when Carlo (classed as an "impecunious noble") found that Louis XVI would finance one son's education, he chose to send Napo-

2. He became so enamored of his bogus record, however, that he gave it in his memoirs.
3. Genoa ceded Corsica to France in 1768.

leon. The intendant of Corsica, however, agreed to pay Joseph's expenses, and both boys began their French schooling at the Collège d'Autun in 1778. While Napoleon, however, went on to Brienne and the École Militaire, Joseph remained at Autun to train for the priesthood. Bored, and excited by Napoleon's letters, Joseph announced in 1784 that he wanted a military career, but was returned to Corsica by his father, who died in 1785, leaving him head of the family. His mother, strong-willed and shrewd, could handle most matters herself, and when Jérôme (Girolamo, born 1784), the last of eight children, began to walk, she sent Joseph off to Pisa, where he earned a law degree (1788).

Fired with zeal by the French Revolution, Joseph in 1790 became a protégé of Paoli, who had been made governor of Corsica by the National Assembly, and rose rapidly in influence. But in 1793 Paoli, shocked by the execution of Louis XVI, accepted British aid and revolted against France. The Buonapartes were branded Jacobins (more because of the activity of Napoleon and Lucien than of Joseph) and fled. They arrived, penniless, at La Valette, near Toulon, where they were befriended by a Corsican member of the Convention, Saliceti. Through his influence Joseph became an army *commissaire* (supplier), and Napoleon commander of the artillery before Toulon (held by the British), where his performance gained him promotion from captain to general in three months.[4]

The family moved to Marseilles, where in 1794 Joseph married Julie Clary, daughter of a merchant-manufacturer. To some degree the match was promoted by the Terror: The Clarys were embarrassingly rich; the Buonapartes poor and suitably revolutionary.[5] Julie was not a great beauty (as the duchess d'Abrantès pointedly tells us), but in portraits with her children she seems quietly attractive—slender, with huge black eyes, soft hair, and a tiny, oval face. She bore Joseph two daughters (Zénaïde and Charlotte, in 1801 and 1802) and was always a faithful wife. But she shrank from public life, preferred to live in the country at Morte-

---

4. It is likely, however, that he would have remained in obscurity had not Saliceti insisted that he be recognized.

5. Napoleon played children's games with Julie's adolescent sister, Désirée, but the future Madame Bernadotte and queen of Sweden was barely old enough to flirt, and no romance developed.

fontaine, visited Joseph only once in Naples, and never went to Spain. Joseph cherished and respected Julie, though it is doubtful he ever loved her. In times of stress his letters to her always multiplied.

In 1795 Napoleon saved the Convention with his "whiff of grapeshot," and in 1796 he took command of the French Army of Italy. Before reaching his headquarters in Nice, he began signing his name "Bonaparte," a spelling his family soon adopted. Their fates were tied to his. He called Joseph to his army as a *commissaire,* and secured appointments for him as minister to Parma, then Rome. Corsica, reconquered, elected Joseph to the French Council of Five Hundred, which took him to Paris, where he remained while Napoleon campaigned in Egypt (1798–1799). According to Joseph, he sent the message which brought his brother back to France (in a hollowed-out cane carried by a Greek, one Bourbaki). If so, he did little thereafter to help Napoleon seize the government.

During the *coup d'état* of 18 Brumaire, Joseph seemed shocked by the unconstitutional proceedings, and immediately thereafter asked mercy for those who had opposed it. Among others his pleas saved Saliceti, Bernadotte, and Jourdan from deportation. Nevertheless, Napoleon as First Consul made him councilor of state and senator, and entrusted him with important diplomatic assignments. He was aware of Joseph's soft-headedness, however, and backed him with hard-minded professionals like Roederer, de Fleurieu, and La Forest. So seconded, Joseph negotiated the Concordat of 1801, and the peace with the British at Amiens (1802), where he became a fast friend of Cornwallis, another gentleman of rather foggy outlook. "Quel noble caractère . . . !" he wrote. If in the end Cornwallis was paid for his "nobility" by a treaty unfavorable to England, it was not Joseph's doing.

Made prince and grand elector of the empire in 1804, Joseph remained in Paris as chief of state during the 1805 campaign. Though he had declined the crown of Italy in 1805, he accepted that of Naples in 1806, because, as we know, Napoleon guaranteed his rights in the imperial succession, and was very persuasive. Miot took Joseph a summary of the emperor's arguments: "I recognize as relatives only those who serve me. . . . Tell him surely that [at] the least hesitation, he is lost entirely."

The Kingdom Established

THE CONQUEST OF NAPLES

As French armies moved toward Naples, the Bourbons made last futile attempts to save their throne. Cardinal Ruffo, as we have noted, pled with French diplomats in Rome. In late January the duke de San Teodoro met Joseph at Albano and on February 4 concluded an armistice with the French. Marie Caroline, compromised by her own diplomat, paraded with her children to the Church of Saint Anne of Chiaia, hoping to incite the lower classes (*lazzaroni*) against the French. Failing, she departed for Sicily on February 11.[6] The Bourbon army withdrew south into Calabria, and a regency, composed of Diego Naselli, prince of Aragon, the prince of Canosa, and the Councilor Cianciulli took over the government.

The regency and the Naples police superintendent, the duke d'Ascoli, outdid themselves to speed the entry of the French, fearing an assault on property by the *lazzaroni* before they arrived. The troops marched effortlessly to the capital, though the fortress of Gaeta had to be bypassed. Hesse-Philippsthal, her commander, refused to take orders from the regency or honor San Teodoro's armistice. Soldier to the core, he regarded the Neapolitans' behavior as shameful and traitorous, and with some justification. Cianciulli later became Joseph's minister of justice, and San Teodoro his grand master of ceremonies. Joseph's troops entered Naples in festive spirit on February 14, and Joseph himself on February 15, 1806. The city's senators welcomed him at the *Reclusorio*. Neither the ruling classes nor the common people showed any regret at the departure of the Bourbons.[7]

Oddly, the middle class and nobles had been the "republicans"

6. The queen declined to appeal to Naples' Patron Saint, San Gennaro, because he had performed a miracle for the Jacobins in 1799.

7. Not until March 30, 1806, however, did Napoleon decree Joseph king of "Naples and Sicily." He claimed both; the combination was generally called the Kingdom of the Two Sicilies.

of 1799. The *lazzaroni,* who had assisted the Bourbons' return, had been repaid with repression. Joseph passed under a hastily erected arch of triumph in the Largo San Dominico, and though the crowds were not enthusiastic, they were not unfriendly. On February 16 he attended Mass at the duomo di San Gennaro, celebrated by Cardinal Ruffo di Scilla. He presented the saint with a necklace of diamonds and received, ostensibly at least, the submission of the clergy. Napoleon, typically, was unmoved by Joseph's grand gestures. "I compliment you on your reconciliation with Saint January," he wrote sarcastically, "but . . . I hope you have [also] occupied the forts . . . [and] disarmed the city. . . ."

Bourbon armies remained to be beaten south of the capital. Masséna held one corps near Naples, and put Gaeta under siege. Reynier's French corps marched south along the west coast, while Lechi's Italians, who had entered by way of the Abruzzi, moved down the east coast. Lechi encountered little resistance, but Reynier had to fight. Bourbon regulars and some guerrillas under Roger de Damas gave battle near Morano, a center of guerrilla activity. The French scattered the enemy and swept into Morano, burning, pillaging, raping, killing indiscriminately.

After Morano the Bourbon armies were quickly evacuated to Sicily. They had counted on large-scale guerrilla support, for which a high command, under the marquis de Rodio, had been established. But the population had remained lethargic and generally neutral. Guerrilla bands were small and behaved more like bandits than soldiers, killing French stragglers if it did not inconvenience them, but mostly looting and robbing, often their own people. Rich merchants and monasteries in areas not yet secured by the French were prime targets. The irregulars did not slow the French march; Rodio was captured and shot on Masséna's order, though in uniform. (Joseph was outraged.) Without guerrilla support, the Bourbon forces had to withdraw. Reynier took Reggio, on the tip of the peninsula, on March 20. Civitella del Tronto, held by the valiant Irish officer Matthew Wade, was starved into submission on May 19. There remained Gaeta, under the flamboyant Hesse, whom we mentioned briefly earlier.

Louis, prince von Hesse-Philippsthal and von Hersfeld, count von Katzenelnbogen, Diez, and Ziegenhayn, was the son of William II, landgraf of Hesse-Philippsthal, whose estates would shortly be taken into the Kingdom of Westphalia. A noble soldier-of-fortune in the grand tradition, he had made a reputation in the Neapolitan army while his coquettish blonde wife shattered the poise of the court and provoked duels. Hesse was small, round, and almost comic in appearance, his face dominated by an over-sized hooked nose, beneath which drooped a cavalry moustache. But he was a superb leader of men, completely without fear, and in love with danger. Normally, he consumed incredible amounts of food and wine at all hours, but nevertheless was an incessant worker and a strict disciplinarian. His men feared him, but also gave him affection, because even his tongue-lashings were delivered in hearty good humor, and he shared their hardships. At Gaeta, Hesse gave the key to his wine cellar to the bishop, who brought him one bottle a day. He slept with the forward batteries, and stood shouting curses from the ramparts during French bombardments.

The supplies carried by the British navy to Gaeta were inadequate, but the fortress held stubbornly. Irate, Masséna arrived in June to direct the assault in person, deployed 10,000 troops and 107 guns. General Vallongue constructed elaborate siege-works, and Joseph came up in early July to give the signal for a renewed attack. The defenders were disease-ridden, and short on food and water. The pounding of French guns, reinforced by gunboats in the bay, took a steadily increasing toll. Still they fought, until on July 10 Hesse was felled by flying masonry, and carried off to Sicily by an English ship. Morale collapsed, and the garrison surrendered on July 18.

In the summer of 1806 French attention was held by Gaeta, and the few guerrilla bands still active, such as that of the colorful Fra Diavolo, who maintained liaison with Hesse. (He once went through the siege lines himself on a pass granted by a gullible French general.) They were taken off-balance when the British suddenly landed on the Gulf of Santa Eufemia.

MAIDA: COLUMN VS LINE

Sir Sidney Smith's British fleet landed the British expedition, 5,200 strong, on July 1, 1806. The fleet might have resupplied

and/or reinforced Gaeta. Instead, it became occupied in supporting a very small invasion, and allowed Gaeta to fall. Why? The
British knew that the people had grievances against the middle-
class merchants of the towns, whom the French had armed (the
civic guard), while they disarmed the peasants; that the French
had committed some atrocities (as at Morano); that many clergy
were disaffected, especially in the mountain areas, and might incite their parishioners against the "Godless" French; that the
Calabrian mountaineers, shaped by centuries of brutalizing poverty, were natural guerrillas, prone to violence and banditry, who
if given a profitable cause and a chance of success might still be
turned against the French and their affluent Neapolitan collabora-
tors. They calculated that a small, disciplined force might win victories over Reynier's corps, now in scattered occupation posts. If
so, the people might be encouraged to join a national uprising. If
the uprising occurred, Bourbon troops would return, but hopefully
under British restraint and guidance. If the people did not rise, the
British planned to withdraw after punishing the French to the
maximum. If nothing else, the French might be discouraged from
attempting an invasion of Sicily.[8]

General Sir John Stuart, the British commander, spent three
days assembling some 4,300 British, 650 Swiss, and 250 Corsicans
and Sicilians on the beach near the town of Santa Eufemia and
bringing his supplies, ammunition, and a few guns ashore. Reynier
reacted faster than Stuart had expected. Leaving garrisons at
Reggio, Scilla, and other points, he marched rapidly north, and
on the evening of July 3 deployed 6,200 men on the heights above
the village of Maida. During the day the reconnaissance parties of
the armies had made contact, and by dawn on July 4 both commanders had decided to fight. Both were overconfident; both
underestimated the enemy.

The French, above Maida, had an excellent position fronting
on the shallow Lamato River, their flanks screened by thick woods.
(See Maps 3 and 4, p. 66.) Initially the British moved south almost to the Lamato River, wheeled left in widely separated columns, and marched inland across marsh and scrub. His columns

8. Reynier had been ordered to prepare for one when Calabria was quieted,
and Napoleon had told Joseph to promise him a fief in Sicily.

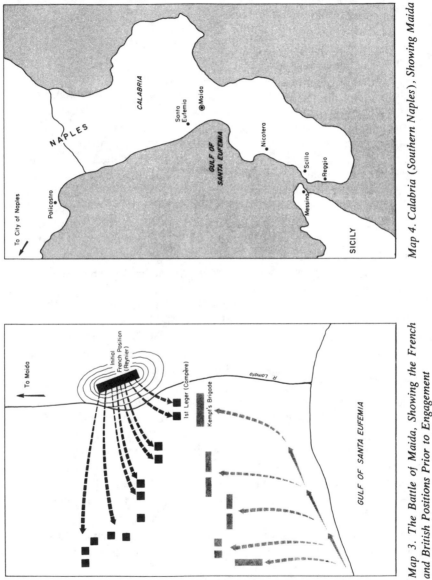

(66)

Map 3. The Battle of Maida, Showing the French and British Positions Prior to Engagement (Adapted from Sir Charles Oman, Studies in the Napoleonic Wars, Charles Scribner's Sons, 1930, pp. 47, 48)

Map 4. Calabria (Southern Naples), Showing Maida

echeloned to the left, Stuart planned for them to wheel right, make a front on the river, and attack the French on the other side. Until this maneuver was completed, however, the British flank was open. Noting this fact, and the separation of the British columns, Reynier ordered the attack. Off their heights and across the river came the French, wheeling left as the British wheeled right. The French left and British right flanks met first, and decided the battle.

Kempt's brigade, 1,000 British, 250 Corsican rangers and Sicilian sharpshooters, faced Compère's light brigade, 1,600 men. Kempt went into a defensive line, two or three men deep, with a front of 350 yards. The French attacked in two columns of 800 men each, each with a compact 60-man front. Down came the French columns like rams against the thin British line, trumpets blowing, men shouting: "Vive l'Empereur!" "En avant!" "A la baionnette!" This was a standard French tactic which had consistently broken European armies. Punching through the enemy's lines with speed and violence, they separated his forces, and finished him in detail. The charging columns were so terrifying that often the enemy infantry panicked before they made contact. The British, however, stood fast and waited for orders. At 150 yards their best marksmen almost decimated the front ranks of the columns; at 80 yards a second volley bit deeply into the ranks; at 20 yards a third broke the attack. The French fled, with Kempt's men in pursuit.

Reynier's left flank was turned, and although the battle went on until nightfall, the French never recovered. Reynier marched north, abandoning Calabria to the British. But though guerrilla activity did increase, the national uprising, which the British had hoped for, failed to materialize. Gaeta fell, and Sir John Stuart withdrew to Sicily after establishing Anglo-Sicilian garrisons at Reggio, Scilla, and other fortresses. Masséna rapidly reinforced Reynier, who marched south again to attack the fortresses. It was February 1808 before they were all recovered, but the British attack had not really shaken French control of Naples. What had it accomplished?

(1) The Battle of Maida confirmed for the British that the line was a better formation than the column—at least for themselves. The average British soldier was a stolid volunteer, well

disciplined, and trained in marksmanship. If they were "scum of the earth" who had enlisted for "drink," as Wellington once said, they stood like rocks in battle. The average French soldier was a young draftee whose marksmanship was abominable. He operated better in close formation, cheered on by his fellows, firing with them at a general target. Using the line against the column, Wellington would repeatedly beat the French in Spain. Usually, as had Kempt at Maida, he would stand on the defensive, but on ground he had chosen. He would take advantage of the impetuosity of the French commanders, who, like Reynier at Maida, could be counted on to attack. At Waterloo he would still be standing on the defensive, his men in lines and squares, allowing the French to dash themselves to pieces.

(2) The British determined that it would be better to leave Naples to the French and attack Napoleon elsewhere. The Neapolitans would not support "liberating" armies; though not altogether happy under French rule, they feared the Bourbons and distrusted anyone connected with them. Moreover, in the mass, they were people chronically suspicious of "causes" without immediate, concrete benefits attached. Similarly, the British show of strength determined Napoleon to abandon plans for invading Sicily for the time being.

(3) The expedition had made much trouble for the French. Their morale had been shaken. The garrisons at Reggio, Scilla, and a few smaller forts would keep the Army of Naples busy for months. The landing forced the French to stand alert for others. And the expedition's success had given limited new life to guerrilla activity. The wily Fra Diavolo was caught in November and executed, and others, such as the ferocious Baroness Laura Fava, fled to Sicily. But it would be years before the mountain areas were quiet, and some bands would still be operating in 1815.

JOSEPH AND NAPOLEON

The emperor chose Joseph, head of the Bonaparte clan, for the throne of Naples because in 1806 it was the most important territory of which he could dispose. It was not only an old, established kingdom, but the key to his Mediterranean policy. As was discussed earlier, he had hoped to deprive the British of bases'

through control of Spain, the north Italian coast, and Naples–
Sicily. The Neapolitan Bourbons ruined the scheme, and were
replaced with Joseph. But more went wrong. The French were
not even able to attempt an invasion of Sicily, more useful to the
British than continental Naples; and during the war with Prussia
Spain proved a more untrustworthy ally than ever.[9] Then in 1807
at Tilsit, Napoleon obtained Corfu, which, though the French
navy could barely resupply it, broke solid British domination of
the eastern Mediterranean. While efforts were made to improve
contacts with Turkey through Istria-Dalmatia (after 1809 part of
the Illyrian Provinces) and the Adriatic, Napoleon turned to the
task of seizing Spain and Portugal. Naples dropped in importance,
and before Joseph was fully settled there, Napoleon had developed
plans to move him to Spain.

Napoleon considered Naples a conquered country, and intended that she have no independence except that granted a fed-
erated state of the empire. Joseph was simultaneously king of
Naples and grand elector of the empire.[10] He was styled Joseph-
Napoleon (Giuseppe-Napoleone). The bees of the empire and
the eagle of the Legion of Honor appeared on the royal arms.
Six imperial duchies, and later two principalities,[11] were created
within the kingdom. The French army obeyed the king only as
a French general, and French military courts did justice in the
name of the emperor. By imperial fiat Frenchmen were authorized
to settle and hold property in Naples without loss of citizenship.
Napoleon envisioned an administration in which Frenchmen would
hold the key offices.

Though Napoleon's attitude was quite clear, Joseph showed
great independence and "nationalist" tendencies from the beginning. The emperor tolerated this behavior partly because Joseph
was the clan chief and a brother whose gentle qualities he respected, and partly because Neapolitan problems were minor
compared to those of the war of 1806–1807, and Spain. He displayed irritation: "I have the right to command a little where I

9. See pp. 16–7.
10. Imperial decree of March 30, 1806.
11. Talleyrand became prince of Benevento; Bernadotte, prince of Ponte-
Corvo.

have 40,000 men." But generally he let Joseph have his way. As a result the king developed habits which would work to his disadvantage in Spain.

In Naples Joseph refused to institute the *Code Napoléon,* approved a program for *gradually* eliminating feudal rights, with heavy compensation to the nobility, and declined to abolish all the monastic orders. He insisted on paying interest on the public debt. And most astonishing of all, he actually forced Napoleon to send money into the kingdom. "Let him provide . . . for my army; it is the only tax I levy on him," Napoleon told Miot. Joseph balked: French troops required French money. He was unimpressed by the equally simple argument offered by the emperor; no French army, no kingdom. Napoleon gave in, and by the time Joseph departed, the imperial treasury had sent 7,500,000 francs in specie to Naples. At the same time Joseph lowered taxes, which were never as high as those in France. "Naples," said Napoleon resignedly in September 1807, "deprives me of an army and costs me a lot of money." Joseph's Spanish kingdom would cost the emperor men, money, and much more.

Internal Affairs

GOVERNMENT AND ADMINISTRATION

Joseph was intelligent but lazy, sketched broad plans with ease but abhorred detail, wanted obedience but detested conflict. His conceptions were brilliant but he was a poor executive and a poorer commander, as would become glaringly apparent in Spain. In Naples his deficiencies were concealed because there a group of superb French bureaucrats organized his government for him, and because he never really had to function as a military executive.

In the early days he devoted four or five hours a day to administration (enough to astonish Neapolitans), made tours of the kingdom, and showed some interest in the military. In 1806 he visited Calabria and Apulia, was before Gaeta twice, and briefly commanded the reserve during the second conquest of Calabria. In 1807 he toured Apulia, the Abruzzi, and the Molise. In the blue uniform of his Royal Guard he occasionally rode sixty or seventy miles a day and seemed to some indefatigable, another Napoleon. He did have energy, when he chose to use it, and he displayed courage in, for example, touring Calabria. But the more perceptive noticed that he spent as much time viewing the excavations at Pompeii as examining the fortifications of Castellammare, and that his itinerary invariably included the villas where the hostesses were most beautiful.

Joseph's relations with his top military subordinates were not good. Masséna especially, a crusty old mercenary with the face of a debauched boxer, resented serving, even nominally, under a "civilian." The king was immensely relieved when he departed for the Grande Armée at the beginning of 1807. The volatile Swiss officer, Reynier, was almost as poor a subordinate as Masséna. It irritated the generals the more that Joseph had great popularity among the troops, which they felt he gained at their expense. Since they disciplined and commanded, he was free to concern himself with the soldiers' welfare, question them about their food and clothing, and visit their billets and hospitals.

The king was more at ease among his civil officials, men of cultivation as well as ability. Even the old Jacobin, Christophe Saliceti, sent by Napoleon to organize the police, now lived in aristocratic style and collected art works. Initially Joseph appointed ten ministers—more than necessary—to achieve a majority of natives. The top posts went to two Frenchmen and two Corsicans, whom the king announced would be replaced by Neapolitans in due course. He found, however, that his subjects readily accepted foreigners in high office, so long as Neapolitans shared honors with them. (They had long been ruled by outsiders; the Bourbons were not native, and had employed officials of all nationalities.) Joseph, therefore, felt free to cut the number of ministries to seven, and make appointments solely on the basis of ability.

When stabilized, the government included two Corsicans, Saliceti, minister of police and war, and Ferri-Pisani, minister secretary of state (coordinator and record-keeper); two Frenchmen, Pierre Louis Roederer, in finance, and André François Miot in interior; and three Neapolitans, the marquis di Gallo in foreign affairs, Michelangelo Cianciulli in justice, and the prince di

Pignatelli-Cerchiara in marine (navy).[12] Of the Neapolitan ministers, Cianciulli had the greatest responsibility. Pignatelli had a tiny navy, and though his authority extended to merchant shipping, ports, and seaways, he was not very busy. A grand seigneur of great tact, he also found time to supervise ecclesiastical affairs. Gallo's policies were dictated from Paris, though exceptional *savoir-faire* was required to keep both emperor and king content.

Joseph propitiated the Neapolitans by populating his council of state with them, and lavishing ceremonial offices on the high nobility. The prince di San Teodoro became grand master of ceremonies, Prince Stigliano, grand chamberlain, the duke di Cassano-Serra, grand master of the hunt, and two other princes first chamberlains. The queen, though absent, was provided with an immense suite, including the duchess di Cassano, the Princess Doria, and the marquise di Gallo. Nevertheless the chief figures in the government remained Roederer, Saliceti, and Miot. All were men trained in the French bureaucracy, but of "European," that is, imperial outlook.

12. *Ministers 1806–1808*

Finance	Christophe Saliceti	1806 (interim)
	Prince di Bisignano	1806 (Feb.–Nov.)
	Pierre Louis Roederer	1806–1808
War	André François Miot (de Melito)	1806 (interim)
	General Mathieu Dumas	1806 (Mar.–July)
	General Jacques Philippe d'Arcambal	1806 (interim)
	Christophe Saliceti	1806 July–1807 Apr.
Police	Christophe Saliceti	1806–1807 Apr.
War and Police	Christophe Saliceti	1807 Apr.–1808
(War and Police formally combined April 1807)		
Marine	Prince di Pignatelli-Cerchiara	1806–1808
Justice	Michelangelo Cianciulli	1806–1808
Interior	Miot de Melito	1806–1808
Foreign Affairs	Marquis di Gallo	1806–1808
Secretary of State	Ferri-Pisani (de Anastacio)	1806–1808
Ecclesiastical Affairs	Duke di Cassano-Serra	1806 (Feb.–Nov.)
(Ministry abolished November 1806)		
Royal Household	Duke di Campochiaro	1806–1807 Apr.
(Ministry abolished April 1807)		

Of those eliminated Bisignano took over the treasury of amortization, Dumas became Grand Master of the Palace, Cassano Grand Master of the Hunt, and Campochiaro minister to Austria.

Christophe Saliceti had befriended the Bonapartes during the Terror, but had opposed Napoleon's *coup d'état* of 1799, and had been saved from deportation by Joseph. He had since proved worthy of trust, though Napoleon preferred to use him outside of France. Some listed him later with the party of Italian unity, but no disloyalty to Napoleon was ever proved. Tall, thin, a somber figure with a sickly tint to his skin, always a man of mystery, he could have been cast on the stage as what he was—a policeman. Espionage, counterespionage, and domestic security always got his personal attention, whereas on military matters he usually took the advice of General Dumas, or later Marshal Jourdan.

Saliceti's organization included regular police, Neapolitan and French secret police, and a veritable army of spies and informers. (The trusted mistress of Colonel Hudson Lowe, who directed British espionage from Capri, was one of Saliceti's agents.)[13] The police were assisted, especially outside the capital by the *gendarmerie,* commanded by General Radet. They numbered about a thousand, and were assigned in foot or horse "brigades" to escort couriers and valuable shipments, or to rush to trouble spots. Many of them were old soldiers who preferred police duty to retirement. They were reinforced in the provinces by auxiliary gendarmes of units formed by the cities or individual nobles under the Old Regime. Kept in employment partly to prevent their becoming guerrillas, they were variously called—*armigeri, guardiani, torrieri, cavallari,* and the like.

Saliceti was accused of gross brutality, and probably used more force than Joseph would have condoned if the king had been fully informed. Yet Saliceti's ability to act ruthlessly on intelligence was invaluable. In the spring of 1807 his police suddenly seized several dozen notables and officers of the old court, hours before they had planned to stage a *coup d'état.* In June 1807 one of his traps closed on Agostino Mosca, sent by Marie Caroline, personally, to murder Joseph. The king could not have found a better policeman.

André François Miot organized an entirely new ministry, the interior, which was just gaining momentum when Joseph departed

13. The same officer, then General Sir Hudson Lowe, was later Napoleon's jailer at Saint Helena.

for Spain. Miot chose to follow him, which was perhaps just as well, because for all his brilliance, he was almost as softheaded as Joseph. Born at Versailles to a family of minor bureaucrats, he had entered the king's service, and had worked soberly under the various governments of the Revolution. Politically neutral, he had been in real danger only once, when accused of excessive moderation during the Terror. Initially employed by the war ministry, he had transferred to the diplomatic service, and under the Directory and Consulate had successfully completed a number of unusual assignments, such as reorganizing the government of Corsica after the reconquest of 1796. He had risen from lowly beginnings by hard work, but was nevertheless a man of almost effete sensitivity. "Savage," he wrote of Corsica, "people and mountains uniformly draped in brown." The *lazzaroni* of Naples brought a curl to his nostrils, though he pitied them in the mass. He retained enough republican sympathies to wince at Napoleon's arbitrary acts, but gloried in the title Joseph gave him—count of Melito. Thenceforth he was never anything but Miot de Melito, under which name he became one of the most famous memoirists of the period.

What Miot would have accomplished if he had remained in Naples is uncertain; his record is that of an inventive organizer-troubleshooter, never long in one place. One suspects that he found his niche in Spain, as Joseph's Chief of Household. But the ministry he left for his successor was prepared to do great things. Under its purview were general administration, agriculture, industry, public works, statistics, public welfare and charity, education, and the arts. Miot should be given great credit for creating the ministry of interior, which was of much use to Murat, and was retained by the Bourbons after 1815. During his stay, however, its activity was confined largely to administrative reorganization of the kingdom and the initiation of public works.

Pierre Louis Roederer headed the most valuable of the ministries, finance. Although it did not bring the budget into balance, it performed prodigies, considering the short length of Joseph's reign. Roederer, son of a lawyer of Metz, had been a Jacobin rabble-rouser in the early days of the Revolution, inciting the workers to rise against the bourgeoisie, "parasites who feed on the public body." But the Terror had sobered him; he had helped organize the *coup d'état* of Brumaire, and had supported Napoleon at every step. Humorless, precise, tireless, demanding, honest, Roederer was the perfect man for his post. His irascibility and caustic tongue generated a rumor that Napoleon had exiled him to Naples; actually Joseph had begged for months before the emperor consented to send him. We shall deal with his considerable accomplishments under another heading.

In secondary posts, Joseph had the services also of a number of talented Frenchmen. J. B. Cavaignac, an old Jacobin, was director general of the royal domains and a valued adviser. Louis Reynier, brother of the general, helped to regulate military subsistence and served as royal commissioner in Calabria.[14] Jacques-Philippe d'Arcambal held various posts, including, on an interim basis, minister of war. The Marquis François de Jaucourt, of ancient nobility, was useful in dealing with the grand seigneurs. "M. de Jaucourt is more a King [to them] than I," Joseph once remarked jokingly, watching his haughty first chamberlain go through his paces. Count Stanislas of Poland, son of the protector of Rousseau, was a man of many roles. He was grand equerry, and for a time commander of the royal guard; but as an intimate personal friend of the king, he had more influence than perhaps any minister except Miot.

The French divided into two general groups: the moderates, who were closer to the king, such as Roederer, Girardin, Miot, Dumas, and Jourdan; and the radicals, including Saliceti, Cavaignac, and César Berthier, brother of Napoleon's famous chief of staff. The moderates favored gradual reform and the merciful treatment of opponents; the radicals forced reform and the ruthless disposition of enemies. In police matters and the policy of the army in dealing with guerrillas, the radicals won out. In other matters, generally, the moderates held sway.

Joseph ruled by decree; he had no constitution or parliament. He was passionately committed to being a constitutional monarch ultimately, but placed quieting the country and administrative reorganization first, trying to draw the leaders to his side and deciding the basis for selecting a parliament in a country which had never had one. In 1808 he issued a constitution for Naples

14. Though he gained fame as a naturalist, archaeologist, and historian.

from Bayonne, shortly before assuming the crown of Spain. Since Murat had the task of enforcing it, we shall discuss it in the next chapter.

Beneath the ministry was a council of state of eighteen, divided into sections for legislation, finances, interior, and war and marine, each with a president. With their advice the king made decisions based upon which the ministers prepared decrees and regulations. Beneath the ministers were the intendants, one for each of the old provinces (fourteen), the boundaries of which remained unchanged. The provinces were divided into districts, governments, and communes.[15] Provincial and district councils advised the intendants and subintendants. Under normal circumstances, except in the Province of Naples, intendants had charge of civil and financial administration, police, the *gendarmerie,* and even the civic-provincial guards, the equivalent of the French national guard. The communes (municipalities) were governed by syndics (mayors) and city councils.

Elections of a sort were instituted in the provinces, where voters were persons who paid a minimum tax of twenty-four ducats[16] per year, plus professional people. In the larger towns the tax requirement was ninety-six ducats, and in rural areas master tradesmen and small businessmen qualified without reference to tax. In all communes the voters were few; they met once a year, selected a city council from among themselves, and nominated three candidates for mayor and a list for district and provincial councils. From the lists the king selected the mayors of the principal cities, and the councils; the intendants chose the mayors of smaller cities and towns. The lower classes had no vote; the privileged classes a limited one, though their nominations restricted the king's choices. Still, he chose and could remove at will any subordinate. The hierarchy was totally under the authority of the king and his ministers; the provincial and district councils were advisory only, as were the city councils. The system did nothing to disturb existing class divisions. Joseph hoped to effect a gradual social revolution by breaking up feudalism, redistributing land, and freeing industry and commerce from the control of vested inter-

15. There were altogether 42 districts, 495 governments, and 2,520 communes.
16. The ducat was worth 4.45 francs.

ests—which he expected to result in an enlargement of the classes holding wealth. At the same time the suffrage could be progressively widened as the schools produced more persons equipped to vote intelligently.

Authoritarian, centralized, the system should at least have been efficient. Unhappily it was not, largely because the personnel selected were the same, or of the same class, as those who had served the Bourbons. The classes in power chose officials who would keep them there, and perpetuate local business privileges, monopolistic arrangements, and legalized fraud. The officials, on the other hand, saw offices as *rewards,* not responsibilities, and felt they should be profitable—a traditional Neapolitan view. Though the central government even specified city taxes, the municipal councils were responsible for their allocation and collection and reviewed the accounts sent to the council of state. Here alone there was much room for favoritism and opportunity to conceal it.

The province and city of Naples had a unique organization. The syndic served directly under the intendant of the province, who was advised by both provincial and city councils. The latter, called the *senato,* had thirty members all named by the king without benefit of formal nominations. The city's prefect of police, Maghella, served directly under the minister of police, whereas in the other provinces the minister worked through the intendants.

Administratively, much remained to be done, but the way had been prepared for Murat, a much less bright but much more forceful executive than Joseph.

JUDICIAL AND LEGAL REFORM

Joseph had a worthy and forceful Neapolitan minister of justice, Cianciulli. But the legal profession, as firmly entrenched as that in eighteenth-century France, fought judicial and legal reforms doggedly, though with suave, disarming courtesy. As a result progress was slow, and compromises were many. More than a year passed before a decree was issued *proposing* (not establishing) new courts.[17] A court of cassation, in Naples, capped the structure, which included four courts of appeal, provincial courts (civil and criminal), and justices of the peace, plus special

17. April 30, 1807.

tribunals for commerce and maritime prizes. A committee was formed to advise the king on the institution of the courts. In May 1808 Joseph decreed that the system would go into effect on November 1, 1808, after his departure. Murat was saddled with organizing it. Joseph had operated during his entire reign with the Bourbon court system, minus feudal courts, which he did abolish.

Reform of the law also went slowly. At the moment of his departure (May 1808), Joseph promulgated three sections of a new penal code, and in June 1808, from Bayonne, he decreed that the *Code Napoléon* would go into effect in 1809. Problems of its introduction were left for Murat to solve, and, especially with the *Code Napoléon,* they were considerable. Joseph had been unwilling to offend Neapolitan traditionalists who were shocked at the prospect of civil marriage and divorce and at the equal division of inheritances.

THE CHURCH

Defying Napoleon's instructions, Joseph preserved the Franciscans, though he did abolish major monastic establishments. The Jesuit Order[18] went in 1806, along with thirty-three monasteries of minor orders; the Benedictines in 1807. In 1808 he suppressed all convents, of which there were thirty-eight in the city of Naples alone. The government assumed possession of property in all cases, of which the total value reached 30,000,000 ducats. Profit, however, was not the only motive. Clergy were so numerous that, although the Church had an income of 10,000,000 ducats a year (the Orders 5,000,000), most were shockingly poor. One adult male in ten belonged to the clergy; of these two-thirds were monks. They burdened the economy, and were not performing the charitable and educational services which had justified their predecessors' existence. Monastics were given the choice of either entering the secular clergy or accepting a pension. The government took over the direction of homes for orphans and the aged, hospitals, and some schools.

The Pope never recognized Joseph, but the clergy was instructed to cooperate with his government. Except that some

18. The Bourbons had restored the Jesuits' property in 1805, though the Order had been suppressed by the Pope in 1773, and was not restored until 1814.

monks participated in the Calabrian insurrection of 1806 and that there were some disturbances attending the confiscation of monastic property, there was religious peace during the reign.

FINANCES

Roederer's fiscal reorganization was far-reaching. He eliminated all Naples' banks but one, San Giacomo (Saint James), and equipped it to perform the same functions as the Bank of France.[19] To administer revenues and disbursements, he appointed separate directors-general for direct taxes, indirect taxes, and the royal domains; treasurers-general for receipts and payments; and paymasters for the army, navy, and civil employees. Treasuries of interest and amortization were established to manage the national debt, and another administration for the national properties (confiscated and certain royal holdings). Bureaus were created to keep accounts of each major tax or category of taxes, tariffs, and other incomes so that the government could easily estimate the productivity of each. In these offices a number of promising young Frenchmen and Neapolitans were given executive experience, among them Antoine Roederer, son of the minister. Each province had a director general and receiver general under whose authority receivers (*percettore*) operated in each district and collectors (*esattore*) in each commune. In towns and villages the collectors were appointed by the municipal councils, and in cities by the king. Beneath the *esattore* were a swarm of collectors specializing in the various direct and indirect taxes, necessary because Neapolitans paid nothing not demanded by a government official. Roederer required officials to swear not to use (customary) strong-arm methods, however, but to refer recalcitrants to the police.

Bringing the collection of indirect taxes under government control constituted a major problem. It involved eliminating tax farmers, who had bought their offices from the Bourbons, some with feudal titles attached, and the holders of *arrendamenti,* who were entitled to collect certain taxes in perpetuity and keep the proceeds. Sold at times when the crown was desperate for money, the *arrendamenti* were abolished first (June 1806) and their

19. Murat renamed it the Bank of the Two Sicilies.

owners compensated with bonds valued at 48,000,000 ducats. The government was obligated to pay 2,400,000 annually in interest, but gained 6,000,000 in revenues. The problem of the tax farmers was more difficult. Joseph abolished feudalism in August 1806, but tax farmers (and others with economic rights) continued to exercise their prerogatives until special tribunals determined the value of their offices. Though Roederer undertook to pay compensation for feudal offices, and buy up the others, the process was very slow. Gradually, however, a corps of salaried officials began to replace the old collectors of indirect taxes.

Revenues from indirect taxes could only be estimated, but for direct taxes allocations were given the provinces. These were proposed by the minister of finance and approved by the council of state, reallocated to the districts by provincial councils, and to communes by district councils. In the communes the municipal councils, supervised by commissioners of the district subintendant, determined individual and corporate levies. There were many abuses, especially at the local level, most involving the acceptance of false declarations of assets.

Roederer's principal direct tax was a single land and industrial tax which replaced twenty-three taxes of the Old Regime. All land was assessed, even that not under cultivation, according to its productivity. Land newly put to use was taxed as uncultivated land for the first five years to encourage expanded production. Business profits, and interest on all investments, including state paper, were taxed, but the wages of those without income-producing property were not. The tax increased revenues, and eased the burden on the lowest classes, but ruined many small proprietors. Schedules had to be revised by Agar, Murat's minister of finance, but the tax remained basic to his system, and after 1815 to that of the Bourbons. The finance minister was predisposed to eliminate all indirect taxes, internal tariffs, and government monopolies, but he found it impossible to forgo the revenues they produced. Taxes on food and on the sale, resale, and transfer of goods remained, though schedules were simplified. Duties of exit, at Naples and most other cities, were eliminated. But duties of entry remained, though with drastic reductions on items such as cattle and grain (an antiriot measure, to hold down food prices for the poor). Stamp taxes, in great variety, were retained. Experiments were made with free trade in salt and tobacco, traditionally state monopolies. Roederer found, however, that if salt were not forced on the people, and a tax taken, they would buy tax-free contraband salt from Sicily. When tobacco production and trade were released from control, revenues similarly dropped, and prices rose. The government felt forced to recover both monopolies. Respecting tobacco, a French firm under government license established a factory in Naples, and the old royal factory at Lecce was left in production. All tobacco (grown or imported) was bought by these establishments at fixed prices. A public lottery remaining from the Old Regime was left in operation, since it was both popular and profitable.

The existence of national properties eased fiscal problems. The bulk of them comprised royal domains (from which Joseph withheld only certain palaces and hunting preserves) valued at about 200,000,000 ducats, and including former Church holdings confiscated by or donated to the Bourbons, royal forests such as that of Sila, and estates which had reverted to the crown, such as Sora. To the domains were added Church properties seized by Joseph's government valued at about 30,000,000 ducats.

The properties were not disposed of wholesale. Many were retained, and their incomes applied to the support of charity, education, and the financing of public works. Some were made collateral for forced loans. Properties were sold for cash to cover current expenses, or to reduce the public debt, which, at Joseph's accession, stood at just over 100,000,000 ducats.

Cash purchasers paid one-quarter in specie (later one-fifth) immediately, one-half of the remainder the first year, and the rest over a period of two, three, or five years. For the government's creditors two plans were offered. They could reregister their claims on the great ledger of the state, and receive interest at five per cent, or take payment in national properties.

For debt payment, certificates were issued against the properties, good for their purchase, but not legal tender otherwise. Inevitably some did circulate as paper money, and their value dropped, but there was never runaway inflation such as that with the assignats of the French Revolution. Issues were kept in line with the real value of the property they represented, and those paid into the treasury were accounted for and burned.

By April 30, 1808, the debt had been reduced to slightly over 50,000,000 ducats, at which time quotations on debt certificates averaged sixty per cent of face value, a healthy figure for the time. The sale of national properties did not serve to increase the number of small-property owners, as Joseph and Roederer had hoped. Otherwise the program, broadly speaking, had been successful. Despite Roederer's careful organization, however, the administration of the properties had not been flawless. Enough venal officials had been discovered to cast doubt on accounts. Many properties had been sold too cheaply, often deliberately, and the titles were subject to question. In remote areas, much movable property had been stolen. Much work remained for Murat's minister.

Joseph rejected certain easy ways of improving his finances. He might have abolished feudal rights and the *arrendamenti* without compensation, and suspended interest payments for a year or so. He declined, however, to offend the propertied classes, which gave him their support in return for his moderation. Thus while the government liquidated half of the debt, and paid interest on the rest, it was always short of cash for ordinary expenses.

At the time of Joseph's departure, the ministries were due almost 2,000,000 ducats budgeted for 1806 and 1807, and 2,101,-552 ducats for the first half of 1808. The pay of civil employees was about 1,820,000 ducats in arrears. The pay of French troops was six months in arrears, though Napoleon had sent money to pay them, and Joseph's treasury owed the army, in addition, 23,400,000 francs (5,320,000 ducats) for food and supplies, which he had agreed to furnish. And the deficit for 1808 promised to be between 5,000,000 and 8,000,000 on a budget of only 15,000,000.

Roederer's performance should not be judged by these figures, however. His deficit had been smaller every year, despite the disruption of the economy by war and the Continental System. Without interest payments and the cost of Joseph's progressive projects, his budget would have balanced. He had laid the basis for a solid, orderly system of finances. Banks had been consolidated, administration of collection and disbursement modernized. Direct taxation had undergone major reform and indirect taxation had been regularized. Murat would complain loudly about the deficit, discrepancies in the national properties accounts (he took an inordinate interest in locating stolen church bells), and the shortage of cash. But he owed much to Roederer.

Joseph's government undertook to solve a multitude of chronic problems affecting the economy. Among these were feudalism and grand proprietorship, the servitude of peasants and artisans, internal tariffs, poor communications, an almost total lack of industry, primitive agriculture, a wild diversity of weights and measures, a perpetual scarcity of hard money, usury, persistent lawlessness—especially in Calabria—disease (malaria was most prevalent), general ignorance, widespread laziness (for which the nobles set the example), an excessive number of holidays and feasts, a superabundance of monasteries and palaces, and the small size of the middle class. The Bourbons had made some reforms, but, for the purpose of increasing revenues, not (necessarily) improving general economic health.

Joseph "abolished" feudalism in August 1806, but the nobles kept their domains as absolute proprietors and were guaranteed indemnity for tax offices and rights to rents and payments in kind, which they retained until tribunals decided the value thereof. Personal, jurisdictional, and prohibitive rights (the latter forbidding peasants to grow certain crops, improve their buildings, and the like) were abolished without indemnity. Watercourses were freed, and the mills utilizing them, but they were usually placed under municipal regulation, so that the peasants still paid for their use. Rights to the common lands, pastures, and forests remained in force until the commons could be divided among the users, a complicated process on which royal commissioners labored well into the reign of Murat. As lands were apportioned, a municipal tax replaced the old feudal dues. Again the peasants got freedom, but little or no immediate relief.

An easy-payment plan was established to allow peasant renters on certain national properties to buy their land. In addition certain previously uncultivated areas (e.g., the *Tavogliere* of Apulia) were offered at low rent, applicable for the first five years to the purchase price with the payment of five per cent interest. Joseph also encouraged the sale of noble lands by outlawing entail and perpetual trust, but the holders were only allowed, not required, to break up their holdings. Some new land was made available by draining swamps and marshes.

The land laws were enlightened, but did limited immediate good. Most peasants had difficulty paying their rent, much less scraping up an additional five per cent to secure titles. The British blockade tightened after 1806, and wool and grain prices dropped. Roads had to be built to carry goods previously sent by sea (including a large percentage of internal traffic). Meanwhile even goods badly needed in northern Europe rotted in warehouses. In addition, 1807 and 1808 were not good growing years. The government allowed temporary free export of wool and delayed payments on rents, but these were only temporary measures. Urgent revenue requirements prohibited substantial reductions in either internal or national tariffs. Much more was done in the areas of land reform and tariffs, however, than by any previous government.

With the cooperation of the French army, the communications problem was attacked. The navigability of the royal lakes Patria and Lucrino was improved, and the ancient canal of Corfinium at Sulmona restored. Routes to Rome via Terracina and Ceprano were improved. In Calabria, a number of new roads appeared, the principal ones connecting Lagonegro with Reggio and Cassano. Naples was connected to Brindisi via Benevento. In the Molise, which had been hit hard by an earthquake of 1805, roads and bridges were repaired. A new bridge was built over the Garigliano on the highway to Rome, and another over the Noce near Lagonegro. Port facilities were improved at Brindisi, Taranto, Gaeta, and Baia.

The scarcity of hard money, usury, banditry, and disease remained problems. Though the influx of coin to pay the French army increased specie in circulation, the real difficulty was an unfavorable balance of trade, difficult to improve because most trade was with France. Moneylending was placed under regulation, but illicit operations were kept alive by the ignorant and desperate. The army, police, and gendarmes worked constantly to stifle banditry, but since the "Robin Hoods" of Calabria were protected by their villagers, progress was slow. Disease continued to take a heavy toll. Miot's ministry endeavored to train more medical personnel and introduce the latest techniques and medicines, but French army doctors could give him only limited assistance because of the high incidence of sickness among the troops.

Agriculture adjusted to the needs of the empire. Napoleon, who saw Naples as a sort of tropical colony, hoped it would produce products denied by the Continental System and British blockade. Joseph, and Murat after him, opposed colonial status, and aimed instead to develop a balanced economy. But the demand for cotton and sugar, especially, promised large profits, and their production was encouraged. Cotton farms appeared near Castellammare, Torre dell'Annunziata, Salerno, and Otranto, which by 1809 could furnish three-sevenths of French needs. Less successfully, sugar beets, and even sugar cane, were grown. Raw silk and grain were also exported, though transportation difficulties kept prices down. Olive oil, the chief product of the Adriatic provinces, required ships to move large quantities, and could hardly be exported at all.

French experts tried to help improve peasant farming methods, but with scant success. Grain remained of poor quality, full of waste, dirt, weeds, mold; cotton was often taken before maturity. Animals, usually kept in the open and given no food supplements, were few and small. Grapes, habitually cut too late, made sour wine. Natural disasters, poor weather, the Continental System, military requisitions, and, during 1806, the disorders of war all tended to depress agriculture. Efforts of Joseph's government did help, however. And, whereas France had formerly sold colonial products to Naples, now she bought. Naples had products to sell— if they could be gotten to markets.

Industry expanded little. The new tobacco factory at the capital (already mentioned) was the major enterprise established during the reign. Capital was scarce; Neapolitan investors preferred government securities, land, or commerce to risky new manufacturing schemes. Foreign capital avoided Naples, where past experiences had been unhappy because of high taxes and tariffs, government interference, and the difficulty of finding educated and industrious workers. Manufacturers of low-quality wool, cotton, and silk cloth continued to produce for the domestic market. A few small plants made gloves, hats, soaps, and perfumes, some of which were exportable. The Bourbon manufactory which had fashioned items of shell and coral was given a new director, but its operations were drastically reduced by a shortage of raw material, most of which had come from the shores of Sicily, Corsica, and North Africa, now largely inaccessible. The royal porcelain plant continued to function, but without expansion. Iron was mined at Stilo, the Mongiana, and other locations in Calabria. Production was increased, and the foundries of the army and navy supplied, though most ore was exported raw or as pig. Marbles and some sulfur were also extracted. Progress was made, but great advances depended on improved transportation, which was slow in developing.

Contraband operations, a sort of national sport in Naples, contributed greatly to the nation's economic health. British goods reached Neapolitan markets in quantity, and there was considerable sale to British shippers and Middle Eastern markets. Ties between merchants in Naples and Sicily remained strong. Joseph issued decrees to enforce the Continental System, but could not change the venal habits of Neapolitan customs officials overnight.

Joseph's government worked for a freer economy, increased landholding, more varied production, and more industry, and not without some success. His programs were such, however, that more than two years were required to produce real results.

ARMY AND NAVY

Napoleon believed the Kingdom of Italy could produce an effective national army, but not Naples, whose population he considered irrevocably corrupt, prone to listlessness broken by spells of passionate violence, and chronically anti-French. "One cry . . . expel the [French] barbarians, and you will lose your whole army." He envisioned instead a sort of Neapolitan legion, with French, Italian, Swiss, and German officers and sergeants. Joseph insisted on organizing a national army, however, and regarded the French in Naples as a training corps for the Neapolitans. Napoleon allowed his brother to have his way, though what evolved was more "legion" than army.

A surplus of Neapolitan officers was available. To recommend which he should recommission, Joseph appointed General Parisi and Colonel Amato, late of the Bourbon army, and General Caracciolo, recently of the Italian army. To the Neapolitan officers selected were added a number of generals detached from the French army—Dumas, Maurice Mathieu, Dedon, d'Arcambal, Salligny, and Marshal Jourdan. The French and Neapolitan armies, both commanded by Joseph, were served by a single staff, headed initially by César Berthier (brother of Napoleon's incomparable chief of staff, but far from his peer), and later by Maximilien Lamarque. Dedon and D'Arcambal were chiefs of artillery and ordnance, respectively; General Parisi was chief of engineers, but was paired with the French General Campredon, who was something more than his adviser. Marshal Jourdan became commandant of Naples and counselor of the minister of war.

The Royal Guard was formed first, under Colonels-General Salligny and Maurice Mathieu. Napoleon dispatched a hundred former *garde-du-corps* of Louis XVI to serve as a nucleus, and its strength was quickly brought to 3,000 by enlisting soldiers from French, Italian, and foreign units in Naples. Regiments of grenadiers, infantry, cavalry, and mounted infantry were formed, plus companies of sailors and veterans. Status in the guard was also granted a company of dragoons of the civic guard of Naples, the only Neapolitans enrolled. The cavalry, under General Stroltz, wore the uniform of the Imperial Guard. For the rest a yellow-trimmed blue uniform was designed, with red and gold epaulets.

The army was fleshed out with Corsican and African regiments, and two "foreign" regiments—mostly Germans and Swiss—all transferred from the French army. The "Africans" had enlisted in the French West Indies, or in rare cases in Egypt; some had been captured by the British and repatriated after the Peace of Amiens. The effective strength was about 11,000 at the time of Joseph's departure. Of the total only some 2,000 were Neapolitans, concentrated mostly in one light infantry regiment. Four battalions of Neapolitan infantry were with the French army in Catalonia, however, and another regiment was in formation.

Joseph instituted conscription in March 1807—one man per year per one thousand population. The requirement was light; the Bourbons had taken eight men per thousand in 1805. Further, married men, sole children, brothers of soldiers, and professionals were exempted from the draft. The communes could designate draftees or hire replacements. Still the draft was extremely unpopular. The Neapolitans saw no glory in soldiering, and deserted at the slightest opportunity. In August 1807 recruits scheduled to parade on the emperor's official birthday were prudently locked in a fortress until march time. Of 4,365 men drafted in 1807 only 2,800 were in service at the year's end. Recruits were normally escorted by French or foreign detachments to Mantua or Verona (in the Kingdom of Italy) for training; in Naples desertion was too easy. Once trained, most went immediately to Spain, or other foreign service.

Joseph took most of his guard with him to Spain. Many of his Neapolitan troops were already there. Murat, though left the foreign troops in Neapolitan service, had to make a new beginning. But Joseph had given the army a basic staff organization and instituted conscription. He had also put into operation two military schools. The Bourbon Royal Military Academy, transferred to Annunziatella, and renamed the Military Polytechnic School, had been equipped to train engineers as well as line officers and to operate a topographic depot. An artillery school had been established at Capua. Further, some success had been achieved in getting the sons of the aristocracy into the schools. If most were sent merely to be educated or ingratiate their parents with the king, they could not but develop new viewpoints. Murat would depend heavily on the aristocratic graduates in developing a more spirited army.

The French Army of Naples had its difficulties. Joseph sought to abolish "requisition," by which the army took food, forage, equipment, horses and wagons, and even laborers and couriers, from the population. But, as his government could not supply the army, he charged General Féraud with regulating requisitions. The general did his best, but the army commanders were impatient with red tape, and their confiscations and impressments were the major cause of friction between troops and civilians. The peasants especially feared courier service; if bandits caught them with French messages, they were usually tortured, sometimes killed. The medical service struggled continually to care for exceptional numbers of disease victims. In September 1806 about 9,000 men, almost a quarter of the army, were hospitalized, only a fraction of them with wounds. Military doctors were too few, and civilian practitioners already overburdened. In 1806, 3,896 men died; in 1807, 4,277, mostly of fever.

Joseph's control of the French army was never very good. During the campaign of 1806 Masséna brooked little interference. Thereafter the army was scattered over the country, which tended to encourage independence in the French generals, especially Reynier, besieging the southern fortresses. The king was not a strong enough personality to get his way, nor did he spend enough time with the army to know its problems intimately, which put him at a disadvantage. Even without adequate central direction, however, the army went far toward restoring order in the rural areas and assisted in building roads and bridges.

The navy began with an excess of officers and little else. The Bourbon navy had sailed to Sicily, leaving behind one corvette and one frigate, both damaged. Reorganization was assisted by the French naval Captains Jacob and Lostanges, and the French Consul-General Blanc, but no other French personnel were imported. Pignatelli-Cerchiara, minister of marine, installed a reasonably efficient Neapolitan bureaucracy and officer corps, but concentrated on projects of commercial value. When Joseph departed the two Bourbon warships were still not fitted out for battle. His fleet consisted of about fifty gunboats mounting one cannon each, which served as a coast guard and on occasion as auxiliary artillery for land forces. Some building of ships had been begun, but there was a great shortage of material. Leather, hemp, and even wood had to be imported. The forests of Calabria contained suitable trees, but facilities for transporting heavy and cumbersome timbers and masts to ports were usually not available, and skilled timbermen scarce. As with the army, Murat had to begin anew in building a navy.

LITERATURE, SCIENCE, AND THE ARTS

Joseph maintained censorship, but a mild and liberal variety compared to that of the Bourbons, who had suppressed most French literature, even the *Code Napoléon*. Saliceti enforced it easily, since press and theater were largely concentrated in the capital. Miot had a plan for founding a press in each province, but it was abortive for lack of funds.

The government smiled on the intelligentsia. It included in its ranks three present or future members of the French Institute, and a number of persons who, like Joseph himself, interested themselves in literature and the arts. The king collected paintings, sculpture, ancient *objets d'art,* and books; he was constantly at the theater. Miot was very much of the same mind. Saliceti was a connoisseur of art, Louis Reynier an archaeologist and historian. The Neapolitan nobility had a strong sensitivity to art and music, though in general they read very little. Some took a more than casual interest in science, General Gabriele Pepe, for example, who made a study of the earthquake of 1805.

Literature and art under Joseph, as under the Bourbons, was dominated by non-Neapolitans. The leading painters were J. B. Wicar and Simon Denis, both Frenchmen. Wicar's "Concordat" had attracted Joseph, who bought it and brought the painter to Naples. His portraits of the King are probably the best ever done. Denis specialized in landscapes, some of which decorated Joseph's home near Bordentown, New Jersey, during his exile in the United States. The outstanding Neapolitan painter was Giuseppe Cammarano, who produced mostly frescoes for the royal palace. The leading practitioners of the plastic arts were also foreigners, with the exception of Raffaelle Morghen, born a Neapolitan but of Tuscan parentage.

Joseph offered local artists the examples of eminent working painters and sculptors, granted pensions, and sent promising students to Rome, Florence, and Venice for training. He established a museum to house paintings and sculpture from the confiscated monasteries, and added items from the royal collections at Capodimonte and Caserta, and objects discovered at Pompeii and Baia. Churches were encouraged to exchange their rare paintings for

NAPLES UNDER JOSEPH BONAPARTE

copies so that the originals could be safeguarded in the museum.

In literature the most renowned figure was the Milanese poet, Vincenzo Monti. He spent several months at Naples, was often at Joseph's soirees, and departed with a pension and gifts from the king. The court turned out *en gala* for the premier of his *Pythagoreans,* with music by the Neapolitan Paisiello. The outstanding native poet was Gabriele Rossetti, later famous as a leader of the *Carbonari.*[20] More than any living writer, however, Joseph revered Tasso, whose style and compassion for the innocent he felt had influenced his own writing. He ordered the road to Sorrento, Tasso's birthplace, improved, decreed his home a shrine and depository for his manuscripts and works, and built a monument before it.[21] In prose the great name was Vincenzo Cuoco, who had made his reputation in Milan. His history of the Neapolitan revolution of 1799 was republished, together with the final volume of his *Platone in Italia.* The liberal government also had printed some works previously banned, such as that of Mario Pagano on penal reform.

Joseph in 1806 established an Academy of History and Antiquity, which in 1808 became part of the Royal Academy, which also had branches for belles-lettres and fine arts. In addition he designated as "royal" the Society for the Encouragement of Natural and Economic Science, founded in 1806 by Augusto Ricci.

The university at Salerno had been famous for medicine since the thirteenth century, and still produced competent graduates. Joseph appointed the rector of the university, Cotugno, physician to the queen (who was absent until the last weeks of the reign), though interestingly enough his own surgeon was Paroisse, a Frenchman. Neapolitan doctors benefited by contact with French colleagues such as Paroisse, Mangin, and Chavassieu d'Audebert. The French in turn gained great respect for Neapolitans such as Miglietta, whom Joseph made director of vaccinations, and Amantea, an outstanding surgeon. Scientists other than medical men were few. We should mention, however, the names of the geologist-

20. Rossetti fled to London after the revolution of 1820, and his two sons and daughter made reputations as English artists and writers. Dante Gabriel Rossetti (1828–1882) is remembered as a founder of the Pre-Raphaelite school of painting.
21. Tasso's home has since been engulfed by the sea.

priest Savaresi, who demonstrated that Sicily and Calabria had once been connected, and Cagnazzi and Tupputi, who made reputations as agronomists.

Miot's ministry took possession of the ruins at Pompeii in the king's name, continued excavation, and banned exportation of artifacts and artworks from the diggings. Many valuable objects were nevertheless smuggled out of the country, but, except for the precedent set by Joseph and Miot, Pompeii would not be the attraction it is today. They safeguarded also the Temple of Serapis, unearthed at Pozzuoli, the Roman baths at Baia, and other ruins.

It was in music that the Neapolitans excelled. Miot supervised the consolidation of the two great conservatories, Santa Maria di Loreto and Pietà dei Turchini. On the faculty were two of the outstanding musicians of the day, Finaroli and Paisiello. Zingarelli, another outstanding Neapolitan composer, was made a member of the Royal Academy, but preferred to live in Rome. The major theaters of Naples alternately offered comedy, drama, and musical productions, including opera. A minor one featured dialect comedies. Joseph smiled on them all, and invited the more prominent actors and actresses to his intimate gatherings, especially at Capodimonte and Caserta.

The press, though under Saliceti's supervision, enjoyed greater freedom than ever before. The *Monitore Napoletano,* which had appeared briefly as a republican journal in 1799, was revived. Published twice a week, it was the official newspaper, but had to compete with others, most prominently the *Corriere,* to which General Colletta, later a leader of the Italian unification movement, and Cuoco contributed. For the French the *Moniteur* and *Journal de Paris* were imported. In these they had to be content with blandly optimistic versions of events in the empire, official statements, and often no news of Naples. Joseph's censors allowed too many accounts of violence to be sent, Napoleon ruled, and for long periods allowed nothing about Naples to reach print.

EDUCATION

The ancient university at Salerno was put under the charge of the ministry of the interior. Miot regularized its administration, but could do little to improve its faculty without offending Neapolitan sensibilities. At least immediately, little could be done either to modernize instruction, which was virtually all oral. An effort was made to encourage the preparation and use of texts, and to expand the library, but these were long-term projects. Miot did increase the student body through the liberal granting of scholarships and half-scholarships. Aid was also given to talented prospects for the Academy of Arts and Design, directed by J. B. Wicar, or the Conservatory of Music. In the latter (and in general) Joseph forbade the time-honored practice of castrating young boys to preserve their soprano voices. A great public clamor resulted, led by churchmen whose choirs were threatened, but Joseph stood his ground and approved heavy penalties for violation of his decree.

Joseph and Miot envisioned a public-school system. Each commune was ordered to establish a public primary school at its own expense. The central government undertook to found a college (secondary school) in each province, and two in Naples. Each province was also to have a school for girls. About 1,500 primary schools were organized (out of 2,520 planned), and colleges were established in Naples and three of the provinces (that is, five of fifteen planned). A model girls' school was created, but foundered for lack of interest; tradition too strongly opposed even secondary education for women.

Joseph's enlightenment was unquestioned. His efforts to aid the arts, literature, the sciences, and education were probably the maximum possible considering the situation and the funds available to him. If not all his schemes bore fruit, they set valuable precedents.

PUBLIC, COURT, AND SOCIETY

"From the duke of Ascoli . . . to the last Neapolitan, Fra Diavolo included, I have them all." So wrote Joseph to Napoleon on May 15, 1806. The violence of the ensuing summer proved that Joseph was much too optimistic. As would be the case in Spain, he was much too impressed by outward gestures and much too influenced by those near him. The ease with which he had entered the capital, the pleasant faces of the Neapolitan leaders which surrounded him, the ability of people made devious by oppression and poverty to cover their true feelings caused him to overestimate his popularity.

To the people at large, unfortunately, Joseph was the king of the propertied classes. Joseph fully intended to reward talent, but he most easily saw it in the friends and relatives of his courtiers. The people generally remembered the confiscations, the closing of convents, requisitions, the destruction of old customs, and conscription, rather than the opening of lands, improvement of communications, the abolition of feudalism, and improvement of education. Joseph's programs were long-term affairs; any immediate effects were offset by the impositions required to keep the government solvent. The nobles and bourgeoisie (more closely connected than elsewhere in Europe) stood by the government, which safeguarded their property even if it took away some of their privileges. The capital and the towns were the centers of the king's power. Civic guards kept the *lazzaroni* in awe, while the government saw they were fed. The rural areas were apathetic or hostile. If Joseph loved the peasantry, they saw too little concrete evidence of it.

Republicans exiled in 1799 returned with Joseph. They might have made problems, except that most had lost their fervor, and were willing to accept authoritarian liberalism as a practical compromise between republicanism and ancient monarchy. In Joseph's time the movement for Italian unification was in its infancy—the dream of a few intellectuals. The secret societies, such as the *Carbonari,* were very weak. The Masonic Society seemed completely innocuous, included many members of the government and military, and was patronized by the king. A desire for independence from all foreign powers existed in the kingdom, but Neapolitans generally opposed having their kingdom united with other Italian states.

During Joseph's reign the social life of the capital was brighter than it had been for many decades. The king set the example with lavish receptions and balls, hunting parties at Capodimonte and Caserta, and celebrations at the openings of operas and plays. His intimate soirees brought together the nobility, middle class, intelligentsia, and luminaries of the theater. He had an eye for beautiful women, and they were always present, even at the chase. His affairs were numerous, but short-lived except for that with the duchess d'Atri, daughter of the Prince Colonna di Stigliano. Upon his departure he created something of a scandal by leaving her

property worth 500,000 ducats. The life of the capital was en-
livened by the visits of brilliant and witty women from France,
among these the countess de Caraman (the former Madame Tallien), Madame de Staël, and Madame de Genlis.

On the surface at least, Joseph's reign was brilliant and successful. Though the peasants suffered, the middle class and nobility
made huge profits. Losses in trade were fairly well compensated by
higher returns from smuggling and army contracts. The king was
affable, soft-hearted, free-spending; his capital gave every impression of taking him to its heart. He in turn loved Naples and left it
an even more beautiful place than he found it. The Corso Napoleone, opened August 14, 1807, ran from the royal palace in
Naples to Capodimonte, and connected with the highway to Rome,
sweeping en route over the Sanita gorge, never before bridged, and
through a tunnel in solid rock. The Foro Napoleone was begun by
Joseph, and would be finished by Murat. The royal palace was
renovated and enlarged, the walks and gardens of the Loggetta a
Mare constructed, the Strada di Chiaia straightened and widened.
More than seventeen hundred oil lamps with parabolic reflectors
were installed along Naples' streets, making them safer and more
navigable at night, as well as more charming.

Exit Joseph

In December 1807 Napoleon called Joseph to Venice and
discussed with him his plans for Spain. According to Miot, Joseph
agreed to accept the Spanish crown, but this seems doubtful since
Louis, and probably Lucien also, later had it offered to them. In
March 1808, however, Napoleon began to press Joseph to come to
Spain, arguing that it was a greater and richer kingdom, and that
a Bonaparte king would be accepted without serious armed opposition. When Joseph hesitated, Napoleon dispatched Queen Julie
from Mortefontaine to Naples. She appeared in early April, and
immediately a pall fell over Joseph's sparkling court. As Napoleon
doubtless expected, her stultifying presence added an argument for
Joseph's departure, which he shortly announced. She was sent also,
however, to reassure the Neapolitans, who might assume the king's
withdrawal to mean that Naples would be annexed to France or

the Kingdom of Italy. Either prospect was unpopular, and might occasion violence. The public was told only that Joseph would visit Napoleon, and nothing more specific until after Murat had been designated to replace him.

The king left Naples on May 23 and on June 7 was in Bayonne, where Napoleon forthwith proclaimed him king of Spain. He did not abdicate the throne of Naples, however, until July 8. For a month therefore he was king both of Naples and of Spain, and took advantage of the fact to commit Joachim Murat to a new constitution, the *Code Napoléon* (as of 1809), and to honor a multitude of appointments, grants, and awards. Murat would enter Naples full of complaints. Joseph, he would say, had taken credit for reforms and gained popularity with favors, leaving him with problems and an empty treasury. This was, of course, an unfair appraisal. Joseph had created general and financial administrations; reformed finances and economic policy; made beginnings in improving communications; erected public works and planned more; taken steps toward judicial, legal, social, and political reform; involved the government in education, science, and the arts; created the nucleus of an army, and gone far toward quieting the countryside. Though the colorful Gascon cavalryman would appeal more to the Neapolitans, Joseph (and/or Roederer, Saliceti, and Miot) had done the basic work of organizing the kingdom.

chapter four

NAPLES UNDER JOACHIM MURAT

The Gascon

DOS DE MAYO

On the morning of May 2, 1808, horsemen of the French Imperial Guard escorted an empty carriage bearing the arms of the Bourbons of Spain to the steps of the royal palace in Madrid. It was to carry the last of the Spanish royal children, Don Francisco, to France. The king and queen of Spain, the prince royal, and other members of the family had already been dispatched. But now Madrid had waked from its stupor. Mobs followed the guardsmen out of the streets leading into the plaza, dragged their officer from his horse, and beat him as he fled up the steps of the palace. His men spurred their chargers and galloped away. The mob turned on the carriage and smashed it to bits. In the Puerta del Sol, the hub of Madrid, and in every open square, other mobs formed.

Marshal Murat, French commander, was unruffled; Madrid needed a lesson. To give it, a full division of the Imperial Guard—infantry, artillery, cavalry—and 40,000 other troops stood ready or moved according to prearranged plan. From all quarters troops converged on the Puerta del Sol, driving the people before them. Into the great central square galloped the Mameluke cavalry of the guard, scimitars slashing mercilessly. A few blocks away, before the royal palace, cannon belched grapeshot point-blank into the crowd. The people fled as best they could, leaving mangled corpses, blood and parts of bodies, and dying and wounded on the cobblestones. During the evening and the next morning, a tribunal under General Grouchy sent hundreds more before firing squads. Murat boasted to Napoleon that the Moslem Mamelukes had taken 'a hundred heads. This was literally true. Fired on from houses, they had entered, decapitated men, women, and children, and tossed their heads into the streets.[1]

Madrid quieted, Don Francisco was dispatched to Bayonne. The Bourbons were gone, and Murat was confident he would soon be king of Spain. The country was quieted. As the "Lieutenant of the Emperor in Spain," he had served his master well, as he had at Marengo, Jena, and Eylau. Surely he deserved a crown, even if his wife were not Caroline Bonaparte, who was incessantly demanding of her emperor brother that he get one.

At the moment when Murat was penning his self-satisfied reports on Madrid's Dos de Mayo, a courier was hurrying toward Madrid with a letter from Napoleon, telling Murat to choose between the crowns of Portugal and Naples.[2] Murat was disappointed, but his response was couched in terms of outrageous flattery of Napoleon and disparagement of himself. How could he serve without his emperor's personal direction? Napoleon had always been there for him "to adore" and "admire." Could he perform the "sacred duties" of kingship unaided? "I believe myself incapable." But he would take Naples. There was something of the oriental in Murat's personality. Surely there was nothing of which he believed himself incapable.

For the moment Murat was to remain in Madrid and prepare the way for Joseph Bonaparte. At Bayonne, Charles IV appointed Murat his "Lieutenant," then abdicated. Acting in the name of both the deposed king and Napoleon, the marshal arranged for a national assembly (*junta*) to meet with Napoleon at Bayonne, and induced the supreme council (provisional government) at Madrid to request that Joseph Bonaparte be made king. But Murat still did not abandon the hope of becoming king of Spain himself. He pressed Napoleon's ambassador, the count de la Forest, to emphasize in his reports that Spain needed a soldier-king, and that he,

1. The Spanish bitterly hated the Mamelukes, whom Napoleon recruited from the Egyptian warrior caste, which replenished itself by rearing Christian boy-slaves as Moslems. The guard never had over 150 members because they were so barbaric and difficult to discipline.

2. Napoleon found reason to ignore that he had promised a kingdom in Portugal to Godoy, who was no longer of any use to him.

Murat, was eminently qualified, whereas, by implication, Joseph was not. La Forest, who had seconded Joseph in diplomatic negotiations, agreed with Murat, and (cautiously) tried to plead his case. Their efforts, however, only brought down the wrath of Napoleon on them both. The die was cast.

Murat, his pride hurt, became impatient to leave. In early June he became conveniently "ill," suffering, he wrote Napoleon, from some unidentifiable malady brought on by the climate. Permission came the evening of June 28 for him to repair to Bayonne, and he departed at dawn the next day. Joseph could have Spain and be damned.

JOACHIM MURAT

Murat, as it was impossible to ignore, was a Gascon. His insolent carriage, his every gesture, his thick accent, his lapses into the patois of his native mountains when he was excited, all fairly shouted the fact. Born March 25, 1767, he was the son of Pierre Murat-Jordy, an innkeeper and sometime farmer of Bastide-Fortunière, and of Jeanne Loubières, a peasant girl of the region— hard, industrious, religious. As Murat's father was happily unambitious, his mother was the pillar of the family. Though perhaps somewhat less sophisticated, she had a great deal in common with Napoleon's mother, Letizia. Later she was apprehensive and embarrassed at Murat's meteoric rise to prominence, as if he might have sold his soul to the devil, and covered her pride with folksy adages. "When you can't see the jackass for his load, he is overloaded!" she flung at her splendid marshal.

When Murat was a boy, his mother dreamed of making him a priest, and her confessor, perhaps in self-defense, got him a scholarship at the College of Saint-Michel in Cahors, from which he went to the Lazarist seminary at Toulouse. When he arrived at the seminary he was eighteen, swarthy and handsome, with curly black hair, blue eyes, and flashing white teeth. At five-feet-eleven he was a giant among his contemporaries. The girls of Toulouse began to occupy his time, as did the serious occupations of drinking and gambling, and he was progressively less interested in his studies.

Then on a bright day in 1786 a regiment of the king's cavalry passed through Toulouse—*chasseurs des* Ardennes, resplendent in white-trimmed green uniforms—horses prancing, sabers rattling. At the sight of them Murat abandoned all thought of a Church career. He followed the regiment and enlisted. Within three years he had risen to the rank of *maréchal des logis* (master sergeant). But though the Gascon proved he could lead men easily, he was undisciplined himself, and was cashiered from the regiment in 1789.

For a while the best he could do was work in a grocery, but with the onset of the Revolution, new opportunities opened. In 1790 he was in Paris with the *fédérés* from the *département* of Lot; in 1791 a *chasseur* again; in 1792 out of service and a Jacobin, then lieutenant in the new republican army; in 1793 captain of hussars, then major. Imprisoned after the fall of Robespierre (as was Napoleon), he was soon cleared of suspicion and returned to service.

On the night of October 4–5, 1795, General Bonaparte prepared to defend the Convention; he needed forty guns from the artillery park at Sablons, on the outskirts of Paris; they had to be seized before the mobs thought of using them. Cavalry must go— under a commander who would not be stopped. Napoleon's eye fell on the Gascon Major Murat, whom he had never seen before. Bring the guns! Murat was off, three hundred horsemen lashing their mounts to keep up—through the narrow cobblestoned streets of Paris, crowds breaking in panic before them, through the suburbs —into the park at the charge, past defenders stunned and cringing. In the dark hours of morning the guns were wheeled into the gardens of the Tuileries. On the next day they belched grapeshot, nails, and lengths of chain into the oncoming Paris mobs, which fled the bloody and corpse-strewn streets. The Convention was saved. Bonaparte was again a hero, and Murat's future was irrevocably linked with his.

Murat, promoted to brigadier general, served under Napoleon during the first Italian Campaign (1796–1797). Hardly cool in battle, he seemed instead a man possessed. The sight of the enemy drove him to frenzy and blinded him to any danger. On the Egyptian campaign he led the charge which smashed the Turkish landing at Aboukir, and left the sea frothing with blood. He personally captured the Turkish commander. Promoted to general of division, he returned to France with Napoleon, supported the *coup d'état* of 18 Brumaire, and afterward took command of the Consular Guard, forerunner of the Imperial Guard.

In January 1800 he married Caroline Bonaparte, whose influence would carry him to positions beyond his ability, and to disaster. She was not quite eighteen, and had been possessed of a childish passion for Murat since she had first seen him, three years before, at Mombello. For her, at least, the marriage was one of love. But she very shortly became disdainful of her husband, who for all his spectacular appearance and courage, was a man of shallow intellect, offset by simple principles and loyalties. Caroline, on the other hand, rivaled Napoleon in intelligence, and in later years in ambition and ruthlessness. She was responsible for Murat's becoming a king, which took him beyond his depth. Though an incomparable cavalryman, he was not otherwise qualified even for high military command, for he understood little of strategy, tactics, logistics, and staff work. His one rule of battle was to form cavalry and charge. He was in no way qualified to administer a kingdom. Caroline might have ruled for Murat. But he was too proud to give her power openly, and she responded by exerting what influence she could through intrigue. The result was mistrust and rivalry between the two. Belying Caroline's cunning, hard-minded character, her face had a childlike cast, even in middle age. She did not have the seductive endowments of Pauline; her head was too large, her neck too short, and her bust and hips a little more than adequate. But she had vitality, regular, handsome features, a radiant smile, and the wit and guile to make herself more than beautiful. She was a charmer, an intriguer, a persuader, an amoral political animal whose every relationship, even love affairs, had practical objectives. She would both elevate Murat and drive him to his death.

The year of his marriage (1800), Murat distinguished himself on the second Italian Campaign. He remained in northern Italy to command French forces, produced delegates for the *consulta* of Lyons (1801), which made Napoleon president of the Italian Republic, supervised the conversion of Tuscany into the Kingdom of

Etruria (1801–1802).[3] With the creation of the empire, Murat became a marshal, grand admiral, grand eagle of the Legion of Honor, and, because Caroline insisted that the emperor's sisters and their husbands rank with his brothers, prince of the empire.

New honors did not diminish his courage or dash, however. In 1805 he was again a hero at Ulm and Austerlitz. While he campaigned, Caroline, in Paris, worked to acquire a new title for him. She became the mistress of Talleyrand, the foreign minister, and cultivated Maret, who would later succeed him. Her friends suggested suitable territories to Napoleon, and Murat's performance merited reward. In 1806 he was made grand duke of Berg,[4] and a prince of the newly formed Confederation of the Rhine. Caroline wanted the throne of Holland also, but Napoleon lost his temper, threatened to exile her to Berg, and gave Holland to Louis. Undismayed, she turned her sights on Poland as soon as the war of 1806–1807 began.

Murat took the cue. He appeared at Tilsit in a Polish uniform, modified to suit his own garish taste. Napoleon gazed at him in disbelief, told him he looked like a circus performer, and sent him to change. The Polish territories ceded at Tilsit became the Grand Duchy of Warsaw, under the king of Saxony. Murat and Caroline, after five months of negotiations, settled for an enlarged Grand Duchy of Berg.[5]

During the war Caroline had been winning friends and influencing people. She had become the mistress of Junot, governor of Paris, and was on intimate terms with Fouché, minister of police. (A clever woman who consorted with clever men, she kept knowl-

3. Tuscany, an Austrian tributary, was put at Napoleon's disposal by the Treaty of Lunéville (1801). He converted it into a Spanish secundogeniture (Etruria) in return for the cession of Louisiana and Parma-Piacenza (on the death of the old duke) to France. Both Etruria and Parma-Piacenza were annexed to France in 1808; the latter, however, had been under French administration since 1801. Tuscany subsequently became a grand duchy under Elisa Bonaparte Bacciocchi, already (from 1805) princess of Lucca and Piombino.

4. Actually he first became (March 1806) duke of Berg and Cleves, ceded respectively by Bavaria and Prussia, then with the creation of the Confederation of the Rhine (July 1806) grand duke, with the Duchy of Nassau and the Principality of Dillenberg added to his territories. He also acquired the postal monopoly of north Germany, held by the princes of Thurn und Taxis since 1615.

5. To which were added the Principality of Münster, the Counties of Tecklenberg and Lingen, and Mark (taken from Prussia). Murat ceded Wesel (a key Rhine fortress) to France.

edge of her numerous affairs from Murat until 1811—otherwise the imperial cabinet might have been decimated. Even in 1811, as we shall see, Caroline managed to confuse the evidence, and gained safety by turning the emperor against her husband.) She had no intention of allowing herself to be buried in Germany, trapped in the boorish society of Düsseldorf. At the Élysée Palace, her Paris residence since 1805, she continued to intrigue to become a queen. In 1808 she wanted Spain, but settled for Naples—for the time being. Napoleon could never satisfy her.

Gioacchino Napoleone

MURAT TO THE THRONE

When Murat arrived at Bayonne on July 3, 1808, Caroline had been there for a week, busily negotiating with the emperor. Still ostensibly very ill, Murat retired to the country house of Lauga, which had been taken by Caroline. On July 10, after a brief interview with the emperor, he left for Barèges to take the waters. While the grand duke soaked himself and reminisced with his old friends Ney and Lannes, also there for a cure, Caroline bargained hotly with Napoleon at Bayonne. On July 15 their foreign ministers signed the Treaty of Bayonne, by which Murat, as of August 1, 1808, would cease to be grand duke of Berg and become Joachim Napoléon (Gioacchino Napoleone) of the Two Sicilies.[6] The crown was to descend to his male heirs, but not surprisingly Queen Caroline was to succeed before her children in the event her husband died first. Murat remained "French," however—imperial prince and grand admiral. And his obligations to the empire were more specific than Joseph's had been. He was committed to govern under the Constitution of June 1808 (proclaimed by Joseph, approved by Napoleon). He agreed to pay French troops in Naples, and in case of war to furnish the emperor 18,000 infantry, 3,000 cavalry, and 25 cannon, plus a fleet of six vessels of the line, six frigates, and six brigs or corvettes. He was bound specifically to enforce the Continental System. He left not only his titles and property in Germany, but also all he and Caroline owned in France, including the Élysée Palace and the Château of Neuilly,

6. Naples and Sicily. Both were claimed.

with their paintings, works of art, and furniture. Caroline had her kingdom, but she had acquired it from a bargainer as tough as herself.

Thoroughly cured at the baths, Murat arrived in Paris on August 4 burgeoning with demands and questions for the emperor which he was compelled to reduce to writing. No, said Napoleon, to his request that Neapolitan troops be returned from Spain. Yes, pass through Rome, but don't see the Pope; he doesn't recognize you as king. No, don't prepare to invade Sicily as yet. Capri and Ponza? No reply. No, don't give naval construction priority over the army. Yes, you can have an Albanian regiment—if you can afford it. No, don't call the parliament, wait for a better time. No, Yes, No. Even Napoleon, a glutton for detail, became weary of Murat's questions. "It would give me considerable pleasure if you would leave for Naples as rapidly as possible," he wrote on August 18. It was time Murat went. Naples had been without a king in residence since May 23. Queen Julie had left early in July. The *lazzaroni* were surely becoming restless.

Reluctantly, the new king left Paris on August 22. A week later a delegation of Neapolitans joined his party at Turin—the archbishop of Naples, the princes di Torella and di Belvedere, several dukes and councilors of state. Escorted by those who could bear the strain, he galloped across Italy amid cries from the villagers, "Viva Napoleone il grande!" and "Viva il gran Gioacchino!" to Rimini and south to Tolentino (both to be scenes of triumph and tragedy for him in 1815), then across the peninsula again to Rome, for a spectacular entry, a brief stop at the Farnese Palace (Neapolitan crown property) and south to his kingdom. On September 5 French and Neapolitan military detachments welcomed him at Portella. In seven days he had traveled six hundred miles—Napoleonic! More energy was to be displayed. On September 6 Grand Admiral Murat entered Gaeta by sea—at five A.M. Splendid in naval uniform, he rode into port in a gaily decorated felucca, surrounded by armed barques, amid a cacophony of earsplitting martial music, artillery salvos, and ringing bells. At the docks he was welcomed by a very sleepy archbishop, a crowd of officers and civilians, and the garrison of Gaeta. The same day he pressed on to Naples.

Marshal Pérignon, commandant of the city, what remained of Joseph's royal guard, the municipal corps, and the ministers met him at the gates. The king was dressed modestly for this first appearance in his capital. By Napoleon's order he wore a simple campaign uniform, though above his hat floated one of the white plumes which were his badge. Huge crowds welcomed him, drawn by the reputation—military and erotic—of the first cavalryman of Europe. From balconies along the Via Foria and Toledo, legions of women waved as he passed to the Church of Santo Spirito for a *Te Deum* celebrating his entry. At nightfall he was ensconced in the royal palace, one of the most magnificent in Europe. Across the Bay of Naples Mount Vesuvius sent smoke and sparks skyward from an eruption which had begun on August 1—the day of Murat's accession. An evil omen, some said. In 1815 the superstitious would remember.

On succeeding days Murat appeared more spectacularly clothed, to the delight of the *lazzaroni,* who followed in crowds. Talleyrand had called Murat a *Carnaval* of Glory; Madame Staël, "the Chief Bedouin." Whatever he was, the Neapolitans loved his gaudy uniforms, white plumes, yellow boots, glittering decorations, and the way his carefully curled hair hung about his shoulders. He was a king after their own hearts.

Murat's children shortly arrived. Achille, the eldest boy, was seven, already tall and handsome, and showing signs of a temperament very like his father's; Lucien, five, somewhat overweight, more delicate and somewhat withdrawn; Letizia, six, pretty and lively, Murat's favorite; and the youngest, Louise, four, plain and quiet. A few days later Queen Caroline appeared, accompanied by the Baroness Exelmans, Madame Jourdan, and other ladies-in-waiting. Murat and the children met her at the gates, and all rode to the palace through cheering crowds. Caroline declined to attend a scheduled *Te Deum*—the churchmen would have to await her royal pleasure.

CONQUEST OF CAPRI

A military victory would lend luster to the soldier-king's accession. Where? Capri? Napoleon had not forbidden him to take it. A British outpost, the isle lay within sight of the capital, a center for espionage and contraband operations. But it seemed all but impregnable—a bastion of rock, well garrisoned, well supplied, guarded (intermittently) by the British navy. But Murat decided to take it, and succeeded, perhaps largely because the British commander, Hudson Lowe, felt all too secure. Capri lay in the sea like a ragged, half-submerged dumbbell, three miles long, half as wide. On the low center part were two small beaches, one on the north, one on the south. Elsewhere sheer rock cliffs met the sea. Atop the rock were five forts, manned by about 1,000 Corsican rangers and Maltese sharpshooters.

General Lamarque, who led Murat's expedition, planned well. On October 4 he struck suddenly, simultaneously, at the high, "impassable," ends of the island, which were the least well defended. Using ladders and ropes, his 2,000 men scaled the cliffs and gained the high ground. Once ashore he had Lowe outnumbered two to one, and his troops, virtually all French, were hand-picked, whereas Lowe's Corsicans and Maltese, though individually brave men, were ill-disciplined and confused by language differences. Lowe retreated into the town of Capri, in the low center of the island. The French consolidated the high ground, seized the northern beach, landed guns, and put the town under seige. A storm made life miserable for the attackers, but probably insured victory. A fleet under Admiral Macfarlane sailed from Sicily to relieve Capri with three regiments of infantry, but had to turn back. Lowe's supplies ran out, and on October 18, 1808, he surrendered. Lamarque, fearful that a British fleet might arrive momentarily, quickly made terms under which Lowe and his men were freed on the condition that they would not fight against the French for a year.

Murat ordered a *Te Deum* sung, paraded the conquering heroes, and presented their regiments with new flags "stitched by the Queen," and declared an amnesty for political prisoners. There were banquets and illuminations. Meanwhile Murat reported his victory to the emperor personally. The response stunned him. Since "my troops" were used, wrote Napoleon, the report should have gone to the minister of war, not the emperor. Lamarque had made dishonorable terms, and let the British escape. Murat must learn to await orders. Envy? Proper sense of discipline? Distrust of Murat's motives? Who can say?

Puzzled and embittered, Murat became more determined than ever to build an army of his own. He increased the conscription quota to two per thousand population, which produced 10,000 draftees a year. He recruited shamelessly in French, foreign, and Italian regiments, and even in Corsica and the Kingdom of Italy. By mid-1809 he had a standing army of 20,000; a year later 40,000. Meanwhile the provincial guard was expanded to provide a reserve of civilian soldiers.

THE CONSPIRACY OF 1808

If Murat alone could have dealt with Napoleon, his sense of loyalty and gratitude might have kept their relationship healthy. But there was always Caroline, who pushed him into intrigues, whetted his ambition, cultivated his distrust of the emperor, and in turn led him to behave so as to beget distrust. When Murat, on occasion, turned on her, she would run to Paris and take Napoleon's side against him. Her ambition was without limits, her intrigues continual, her loyalties zero.

Only three months after Murat's accession, Caroline involved him in an intrigue which very nearly cost him his crown. Joseph was driven from Madrid, the Grande Armée marched from Germany to his relief, and, in November 1808, Napoleon personally took command. Caroline, Fouché, and Talleyrand developed a sudden concern that the emperor might be killed in Spain. Should not those in influence, ignoring legalities, agree on a successor to whom Frenchmen would rally? And why not Murat? Talleyrand and Fouché agreed. Why not? He was a well-loved military hero, politically naïve, easy to control. It was arranged that if Napoleon died Murat would speed to Paris on signal. But the emperor survived, recaptured Madrid, put a small British army under Sir John Moore to flight, and inevitably learned of the plan.[7] In January 1809 he turned the army over to Joseph and hurried to Paris.

Fortunately for Murat, Austria was threatening war, and Napoleon suspected Talleyrand of intriguing also with Metternich, then Austrian ambassador in Paris. While the grand chamberlain was expendable, Fouché could not be removed without disorganiz-

7. Eugène intercepted a message from Talleyrand to Murat.

ing the police, and Murat, if alienated, might endanger Italy's
defense against Austria. It was Talleyrand whom the emperor dis-
graced: ". . . You have . . . betrayed everybody . . . You would
sell your own father . . . !" Talleyrand's riposte is famous: "What
a shame that such a great man should be so badly brought up!"

THE EVENTS OF 1809; THE AUSTRIAN MARRIAGE

Murat was not called to the Grand Armée in 1809, but perhaps he would not have been in any case. He stood ready to assist
Eugène against the assault of the Austrian Archduke John. After
the imprisonment of Pius VII, he sent Neapolitan troops to occupy
Rome (in the emperor's name). And there was always the danger
of British invasion, which justified his remaining in Naples.

On June 11, 1809, Sir John Stuart landed with 7,000 troops
on the island of Ischia, and 250 ships stood off the Bay of Naples,
ready to take them to the mainland. Murat excitedly called in
regiments from the provinces, the forts opposite Sicily, and Rome.
Caroline, with Napoleonic style, donned a semimilitary costume
and rode about the capital reassuring the people. But at the news
of Wagram, the British departed. Stuart's threat, however, had
displaced Murat's troops; as a result guerrilla activity in Calabria
reached its greatest intensity since 1806. French and Neapolitan
troops returning to the south had serious work to do.

Control of Calabria and the fortresses had not been lost, however, and in November Murat felt free to visit Rome. In the blue
and white of his guard, Turkish saber slapping his saddle, a black
Spanish cape billowing behind him, he and his charger one magnificent, prancing animal, he reviewed his troops. At the Borghese
Palace he entertained lavishly, but apprehension sent him back to
Naples within a few days.

He was refused any papal territory, and since Wagram the
emperor's letters had assumed a menacing tone. Nothing pleased
him, from the application of the *Code Napoléon* to the enforcement of the Continental System. He demanded payment of Murat's
debts to France and the Legion of Honor. The king feared Napoleon was building a case to justify retribution for the intrigue of
1808. When without explanation he and Caroline were sum-

moned to Paris, their fears mounted, but in early December they presented themselves to the emperor.

The found themselves cordially received—as members of the family council called to assent to the emperor's divorce and re-marriage. Their alarm grew. What would it mean? The Arch-duchess Marie Louise of Austria was the granddaughter of Marie Caroline of the Two Sicilies. Would the young bride soften Napoleon's attitude toward his old enemy? Napoleon's prospective son would be styled king of Rome, and he, or a second son, would eventually become king of Italy. Would Naples survive as a separate kingdom? They could not but oppose the new marriage—but in vain. Sensing the emperor's growing displeasure, Caroline gave in and undertook to repair their relations with him.

Murat, depressed and irritated, hurried back to Naples. Pub-licly he was unruffled; privately he railed against Napoleon's tyranny. He was full of plans for an invasion of Sicily—now or never. Surely after the marriage Napoleon would at least conserve the island for Marie Caroline. But before he could act, Caroline had persuaded Napoleon to invite him back to Paris. "Avec plus de joie" he replied. On March 22, 1810, Murat and Caroline were both present when Marie Louise arrived at Compiègne.

Caroline had played chess with Napoleon, arranged entertain-ment, radiated sympathy, and had won the honor of meeting the future empress at the border. With disarming motherliness, she had tried to undermine the eighteen-year-old's composure. Napoleon, lied Caroline, didn't like dogs; Marie Louise's beloved *Loulou* must go. Her favorite lady-in-waiting was sent away. Her accent, dress, and make-up were criticized—gently, helpfully. But Caroline could not erase a healthy, glowing charm which nervousness made even more appealing. Napoleon saw Marie Louise and took possession "sans souci d'etiquette." The queen of Naples smiled as if she had arranged it. Murat, however, kept muttering objections to the Austrian marriage. "Monsieur le maréchal Murat, I'll have your head cut off!" Napoleon snapped. But after the ceremonies in Paris he gave the king permission to assume an offensive posture opposite Sicily (though not to attack). Murat returned happily to his kingdom, leaving Caroline to pursue her machinations in

Paris.[8] The king's optimism was unwarranted, but before carrying the narrative further, we should deal briefly with his domestic endeavors.

Internal Affairs

GOVERNMENT AND ADMINISTRATION

On his initial entry (September 1808) Murat found the executive power in the hands of Saliceti and Cianciulli. Marshal Jourdan, appointed to share their authority, had elected to join Joseph in Spain, as had Ferri-Pisani and a crowd of lesser figures. Roederer also followed Joseph, but Napoleon recalled him immediately to administer the Grand Duchy of Berg. Vacancies were filled on an interim basis; only in the course of 1809 was the ministry stabilized. Saliceti remained minister of police until his death (possibly by poison) in late 1809. His post was given to Daure, a Frenchman, who was already minister of war and navy. Vulgar, barrel-shaped, and balding, Daure, ex-bureaucrat and army supplier, was efficient but venal and an intriguer. He was seconded by Naples' prefect of police, Antonio Maghella, a Genoan who would draw Murat into the Italian unification movement. Roederer's finance went to Count Agar de Mosbourg, a Frenchman who had served Murat in Berg; Miot's interior to Giuseppe Zurlo, a jurist and former Bourbon director of finances. Francesco Ricciardi became minister of justice; his predecessor, Cianciulli, president of the council of state. Prince Pignatelli-Cerchiara, Joseph's minister of marine, became minister secretary of state. The marquis di Gallo in foreign affairs, alone among Joseph's ministers, retained his original office. The key men in the ministry were Daure, Agar, Zurlo, and Ricciardi—two Frenchmen, two Neapolitans.[9] Initially Gallo, as under Joseph, sang harmony to

8. Not all were altogether political. She blasted a romance between the duchess d'Abrantès and Metternich by sending their letters to the duchess' husband, General Junot, who charged about threatening to shoot his wife. She thereby gained the gratitude of one former lover (Junot) and wreaked revenge on another (Metternich), though she hoped to use the latter's influence, and depended on Junot to keep her secret.

9. Interim ministers included General Reynier (war, navy), Zurlo (justice), Capecelano (interior), Pignatelli-Cerchiara (finance).

French diplomatic themes. His ambassadors and ministers, appointed to suit Napoleon in the first place, stayed at their posts (Monteleone in Paris, Mondragone in Saint Petersburg). Late in the reign, however, Murat would pursue an independent, by some definitions treasonable, policy, and his foreign ministers would assume new importance.

Though in some degree Joseph had become a Neapolitan nationalist, there had appeared during his reign no real party of independence. The shock of military invasion, the disturbances of 1806 and 1807, and the reorganization of the nation had occupied all talents. Under Murat, however, a party did form, which, moreover, rapidly became pan-Italian rather than merely Neapolitan. It should be noted here that the more important leaders occupied high positions in the government and army. Among these were the ministers Ricciardi and Zurlo, the philosopher-journalist-historian Cuoco, who was a councilor of state, the police prefect of Naples, Antonio Maghella, later minister of police, generals Colletta and Carascosa, and many others. In time, though their Italian sentiments found limited response among the masses, they captured the king. Opposing the group was the "French Party," headed by Queen Caroline, though for the sake of personal power, not out of loyalty to Napoleon. It included the minister of police, Daure, and Murat's aide La Vauguyon, successively the queen's lovers; the French ambassadors, d'Aubusson La Feuillade, then Durant de Mareuil; Colonel Sellier, head of the "counter-police," most of the French, and many conservative Neapolitans. We shall have much to say later of the clash of the parties.

From Joseph, Murat inherited a constitution, plans for a reformed judiciary, and a commitment to institute the *Code Napoléon*. The constitution provided for a one-house legislature apportioned equally among nobles, clergy, the intelligentsia (*dotti*), landed proprietors, and businessmen. All were to be appointed by the king; the clergy and nobles directly for life; the *dotti* for life from lists prepared by the university, academy, and high courts; proprietors and businessmen for one session from lists submitted by electoral colleges, which in turn were appointed by the king from among the highest taxpayers. The parliament was to meet at least every three years to approve the budget and changes in the "essential" law. Murat got no closer to applying the constitution than selecting electoral colleges. He instead continued to promise a new and more liberal document, which, however, he never issued, though he did style himself king "by the Grace of God and the Constitution." He installed a new system of courts, according to Joseph's plan, but issued a modified *Code Napoléon,* which, among other things, said nothing of divorce. The emperor read the arguments of Ricciardi for bending the *Code* to Neapolitan custom, but was unimpressed. He ordered the complete, unchanged *Code* made the law of the land as of January 1, 1810, and it was. Neapolitan judges, following an ageless, inbred pattern of resistance, sang its praises and ignored its more unpalatable provisions.

The governmental and administrative organization established by Miot, Saliceti, and Roederer was little altered. Murat must be credited, however, with considerable success in fighting venality and inefficiency. We shall deal with finances and the economy under another heading.

Joseph's program of public works was continued. If funds were short, however, the army took precedence. Murat paid great attention to the beautification of Naples and the improvement of roads in the immediate area, such as those to Posilipo and Capodichino. Buildings were demolished to enable the capital's main thoroughfares to be straightened, to clear a square opposite the royal palace (called first the Foro Napoleone, later the Foro Murat), and make way for a new avenue from the Gate of Capua to the Via Toledo. The city was liberally sprinkled with monuments, the most spectacular a copy of the arch of Constantine, covered with bas-reliefs in marble and bronze: Parthenope[10] presents the peoples of Naples to Murat; girls in provincial costumes surround Caroline; happy *lazzaroni* cheer Murat; Caroline and Murat are shown flanked by French and Italian generals. As Murat came to be celebrated as an early leader of Italian unification, Naples cherishes souvenirs of him today.

Banditry, especially in Calabria, was a severe problem, decades, even centuries, old. Poor soil, violent spasms of weather,

10. The siren who cast herself into the sea for love of Ulysses, and was cast ashore on the Bay of Naples. Naples (*neapolis,* new city) was built by Greek refugees on the site of the ancient city of Parthenope.

earthquakes, and disease had kept the people poor and the death rate high. The survivors of the hard life were callous to suffering and death. Their mentality showed in their cruelty toward animals, the gory character of the religious images in their churches—and in the prevalence of robber bands. The ranks of the outlaws had been swelled in 1806 and 1809 by genuine guerrillas, some of whom chose to remain, either because they could not renounce the benefits of the predatory life or because they had convinced themselves they still had a patriotic cause. Recruits came also from Sicily—mostly criminals released on the mainland. In 1809, 33,000 bandits (or guerrillas) were arrested out of a population of only 5,000,000.

The civic and provincial guard (mostly middle-class townsmen), police, and gendarmes proved ineffective against the outlaws. The French and Neapolitan armies had the general duty to assist, and were effective, but not always available. Murat renounced halfway measures and gave General Manhès orders to annihilate the bands. He was assigned picked regiments and given authority to order support by any other units necessary. Manhès, a French cavalryman, proved both ruthless and shrewd. Instead of galloping after the elusive mountaineers, he cut them off from their sources of supply. Villages were blockaded at night, with even cattle, sheep, and goats within the walls. The penalty for leaving a village after curfew was death, remorselessly imposed, even on mothers and children carrying food to their sons and brothers. Bandits who surrendered, however, were amnestied. By the bitter winter of 1810–1811 the system was fully in effect, and most of the bands collapsed. Proud chieftains persisted, however, like Parafante. On a black horse, cloaked in black, red feathers fluttering above his cap, he operated with two hundred men from the royal forest of Sila. No risk seemed too great for him, but he still could not feed his men, and his numbers fell to five. Still defiant, he was finally betrayed, ambushed, and shot. Other leaders were unfortunate enough to be captured, and were sent before firing squads, among them Capobianco, called (with flimsy justification) "the first martyr of the *Carbonari*." Calabria was not completely quieted, but travel became safer than at any time before our century. Murat rewarded Manhes by making him count and lieutenant general. Neapolitans gave him hate; whatever benefits he brought them, he was a foreigner and a "policeman."

THE COURT AND SOCIETY

The social life of Naples under Murat and Caroline made that of the preceding reign seem boorish; the capital would never see the like again. The vain, handsome, gregarious Gascon peacock and his still beautiful and lively queen loved display, costume balls, and lavish feasts. Yet in matters of protocol and etiquette Murat demanded of his court the formalities of the Old Regime, howbeit with certain parvenu touches. And no official, civil or military, was without a uniform. The chamberlains were in red; the prefect of the palace in purple; the equerry in blue. Knee breeches, silk stockings, shoes with buckles, and, as a concession to the *sabreur*-king, swords, were *de rigueur* at all hours. Joseph's court had been relaxed, informal, almost democratic, Murat testily demanded more deference. "How many kings do we have here?" he barked when asked how many places should be set at table. Only on special occasions, accompanied by rigid ceremony, did guests share his board; even *en famille* young noble pages stood in pairs behind the king, queen, and royal children.

Neapolitan grand officers generally kept their positions. The dukes di San Teodoro and di Cassano-Serra, and the Prince Colonna di Stigliano were confirmed respectively as grand master of ceremonies, master of hunt, and chamberlain. Cardinal Firao remained almoner. The French grand officers had mostly followed Joseph, and were replaced with favorites of Murat, for instance, Generals Lanusse and Exelmans, who had been with him in Madrid and who became respectively grand marshal of the palace and grand equerry.

The king arose attended by a horde of courtiers, each with some small duty in the *lever*. After breakfast his valet curled his hair, and more courtiers saw him into his morning costume, usually that of a French prince—white with gold trim. In the afternoon he wore the uniform of a regiment of his guard, usually of the lancers or the *garde-du-corps*. For solemn occasions and on gala days he wore purple velvet costumes of different cuts. For public appearances he fancied black capes and tall Polish-style caps or theatrical toques, always with immense egret plumes.

What plumes were to Murat diamonds were to Caroline. Tiaras, necklaces, pins, and bracelets set off the gowns of Chez Leroy, whose representatives rushed the latest creations from Paris. She was attended regularly by a dozen young ladies of the poorer nobility—a female *garde-du-corps* in yellow and white. At court functions and in public she was surrounded by the highest noble-women—the duchess di Cassano, the marquise di Gallo, and others—and the wives and daughters of French officials. She spent much of her day in her chambers "on the sky," as she put it— one-hundred-sixteen steps above the ground floor of the enormous royal palace. (She angrily renounced installing an elevator for her-self. It would have made her seem old.)

Morning visitors—ministers, generals, anyone—were invari-ably ushered into Caroline's bedchamber, where a world of white satin was broken only by the flowered bedclothes of Her Majesty, and her "English" hats, on which birds perched, flowers sprouted, and plumes waved, as she sat propped up in bed. Members of the government took her seriously. She was willful, persistent, and well informed (among other ways by her own spy net). Her in-fluence was so great that Murat had to be continually alert, and sometimes in outrage exiled her to Caserta or Capodimonte. Still, she was thoroughly female. Once she ousted a group of ministers in favor of the representative of Chez Leroy, just in from Paris. The queen was a creature of intrigue and power, jewelry and dresses, ruthlessness and feminine charm. "The head of Cromwell on a pretty woman," said Talleyrand.

Balls at the Theater San Carlo were social events of the season, especially the masked balls. The king and queen enjoyed costuming themselves, though at Caroline's insistence neither ever wore masks. Caroline and Murat entertained frequently and lavishly. Nobles, officials, and military officers followed the example of the monarchs—some happily, like Prince Pignatelli, who spent 50,000 francs on a single ball—some grudgingly, like Marshal Pérignon, commandant of Naples, at whose affairs there was little wine and sometimes no food. Premiers at the theaters and opera were occasions, though Murat was apt to doze. His real passion was hunting—pheasant at Caserta, ducks at Lake Agnano, deer on the Volturno. The pace was exhausting, but wine flowed and feasts were lavish. And a veritable pageant surrounded the king, who took as his hunting costume the uniform of his heroes—the Gascon musketeers of Francis I. Never was he happier or a better host than in the country.

While Caroline liked and cultivated the nobility, Murat distrusted and felt ill at ease with them. Despite the elegance of his retinue, he remained, emotionally, something of a crowned Jacobin, and enjoyed mingling with his people. Occasionally he went walking incognito, to the delight of the *lazzaroni,* who never failed to recognize him, but happily played his game with him, dropping outrageous flatteries of "the king" as they talked.

The king and queen were well liked; their personal conflicts were known only to the inner circle of the court. The classes upholding their power were, as with Joseph, the propertied ones. But they managed to gain more popular support than their predecessor, though their zeal for social uplift was less than his, perhaps largely because Murat's temperament and theatrical style appealed to Neapolitans. But emotional attachment, though reinforced with some concrete benefits, would not impel the masses to great sacrifice for them in 1815.

FINANCES AND THE ECONOMY

Roederer had predicted the 1808 deficit would be about 1,500,000 ducats. This proved optimistic, but Agar, by adjusting Roederer's land tax and easing national tariffs, almost balanced the budget in 1809, amassed a surplus of over a million ducats in 1810, and of two million in 1811. Exceptional military expenses during 1812–1815 produced deficits, but the fiscal system instituted by Roederer proved basically sound.

The system alone, however, was not responsible for the solvency of the government. Murat was more casual about enforcing the Continental System than Joseph had been. As trade increased, revenues climbed. At the same time the debt was reduced, and consequently yearly interest payments, partly by taking advantage of inflation. By late 1809 certificates against the national properties were issued sufficient to cover the whole national debt (though creditors could still choose to enter their claims on the state ledger). The paper, in part circulating as money, had already dropped to fifty percent of face value. While paying the debt at *face* value in paper, the government auctioned property at its *real* value, reappraising as inflation increased, gaining by the depreciation of its own notes. In 1810, when the debt had been whittled to about 20,000,000 ducats[11] (from 50,000,000), Agar's operation was terminated. The new debt was entered on the ledger, prices on properties were reduced, and the value of paper, which had fallen to twenty percent, began to climb.

After 1810 imperial licenses became available for trading, in effect, with the enemy, under heavy tariffs. Grain and oil especially, stockpiled in the kingdom, awaiting land shipment to France and northern Europe, now began to leave the ports for Middle Eastern and other markets (directly or indirectly). Neapolitan merchants took full advantage of new opportunities for illegal as well as legal profits, with the indulgence of the government. Traffic with Malta, always considerable, increased, and that to Sicily and Albania as well. Naples' economic health and the fiscal situation of the government improved.

Zurlo, minister of the interior, completed the eradication of feudalism according to the plan devised by Miot and Joseph. A royal commission, assisted by subordinate tribunals set compensation for property rights, and distributed common lands among their users. In the course of 1809–1810 some 8,000 decisions were approved by Dragonetti, chief magistrate of the commission, or his assistants, Borrelli and Winspeare. Thereafter their chief concern was preventing the former lords from exercising personal rights, for example, of jurisdiction, to which they were no longer entitled.

Generally there was prosperity in Naples during Murat's reign.

11. Ducat = 4.45 francs; lire = 1 franc = .22 ducats. Many secondary works confuse the Neapolitan financial picture by failing to convert. Roederer's report to Napoleon (1808) is often read to indicate a yearly revenue of 61,000,000 francs and expenditures of 15,393,912. The latter figure is ducats, however, so that there was a deficit. (Espitalier, *Napoleon and King Murat*, p. 53, uses the two figures to show that Murat began with a surplus in his treasury. Johnston, *Napoleonic Empire in Southern Italy*, I, pp. 214–215, gives figures in lire which should be read ducats; otherwise the government was operating cheaply indeed. Rambaud, *Naples sous Joseph Bonaparte*, pp. 364–365 and footnotes, gives the best picture of the situation in 1808.)

This factor, combined with his personal appeal and nationalist attitude, probably would have insured King Gioacchino unqualified popularity but for the draft, special taxes (after 1811), and the death of Neapolitans in battle (mostly in Spain; few joined the Russian campaign). Not only were the fortunes of propertied classes increasing, but the condition of the lower classes was improving as well. The reforms initiated by Joseph had begun to show effects, and were accentuated by a gradual brightening of economic conditions. Neapolitans were far from unhappy. Had only their opinions been in question, Murat might have maintained his throne indefinitely after the fall of Napoleon.

Napoleon and Murat

ON TO SICILY!

Murat returned to Naples in April 1810 with Napoleon's seeming approval of an invasion of Sicily, which quieted his fears that the emperor might enter negotiations with the Neapolitan Bourbons. His kingdom might still be in jeopardy if Marie Louise gave Napoleon an heir, but this was not an immediate problem, and the successful conquest of Sicily would strengthen his hand for future contests with his master. On advance orders Murat's army, almost 40,000 French and Neapolitans, had begun concentrating near Reggio, which had forced the Anglo-Sicilian forces to take up positions around Messina, across the strait. During the first week in May a British fleet sailed into the Bay of Naples, sank one of Murat's two warships, raked the deck of the other, killing most of its officers, and blew several gunboats to splinters. No landing at Naples seemed probable, however, as the allies could not risk moving troops from Messina. Murat on May 16 departed in high spirits for Reggio. His guard carried parade uniforms in their knapsacks, prepared to march in triumph through the Sicilian capital. En route south he provided spectacle and rhetoric for Cosenza, Nicastro, Monteleone, and Scilla. Palermo would be his in June, he told cheering crowds. Every village and town received him with arches of triumph, music, applause, and the tolling of church bells.

In Sicily a conflict raged between Marie Caroline and the British, whom she considered had undermined her power. "If it must be the foreign yoke, Sicilians prefer Murat to England. . . ." Furious over the failure of Sir John Stuart to invade Naples in 1809, she had accused the British of cowardice and treachery, and had begun forming her own fleet under the prince di Moliterno. Fearful that her ships would attack theirs, the British ambassador, Lord Amherst, and Admiral Martin forced her to scatter them. Meanwhile, they lent their support to the party of the prince di Belmonte, who controlled the Sicilian parliament, formed against the wishes of the queen. Unsupported by her ineffectual husband, opposed by her son, Prince Leopold, discouraged, and ill (she would die in 1814), Marie Caroline remained withal a dangerous adversary.

In the course of 1810 she sent two agents to Napoleon, D'Amitia, a Sicilian officer, and Donop, a French officer released from prison for the purpose. Both landed in Illyria, and were sent on to Paris by Marmont, the governor. What the queen proposed is uncertain, but Napoleon hinted to O'Meara at Saint Helena that she had plans to surprise and annihilate the British garrison on Sicily. At any rate her tentatives failed. Napoleon did not believe she would fulfill her promises even if she could. She also approached Murat, through Captain Cassetti of the Sicilian navy, who appeared several times in Naples, but again the negotiations were ruined by mutual distrust and Murat's inability to offer a suitable domain in return for her services (as Napoleon might have done). She gained nothing, and the British learned enough of her machinations to make them even more suspicious and watchful. Still, Murat had reason to feel that Anglo-Sicilian dissensions would facilitate his invasion.

Murat's army at Reggio comprised three corps under Partouneaux, Lamarque, and Cavaignac, all French, as was his chief of staff, General Grenier, named by the emperor. Under arms were 18,000 French, 17,000 Neapolitan regulars, and 5,000 Royal Guards. By mid-June all was in readiness except that Murat lacked warships to guard his transports. He was compelled to wait for winds which would drive the enemy fleet out of the Strait of Messina. At Reggio his troops were stationed to strike at the coast south of the city of Messina. Port facilities to the north enabled the British to guard the coast under almost any conditions. But a strong south wind might divest the southern coast of protection.

Even if favorable winds blew, however, Murat had no clear order from Napoleon to launch his assault. All summer he waited for one, killing time with inspections and reviews, drawing British ships into minor engagements with his gunboats, which attempted to bring them within range of shore guns, staging rehearsals to keep the British off-balance. Enemy naval guns bombarded his headquarters atop the hill of Piale at will—once blew some of his Neapolitan generals out of their tent. On the emperor's fete day (August 15) he staged a review in full view of British positions across the strait; fortunately for him they were too gentlemanly to fire. Caroline, still in Paris, was with her brother almost every day, and reported his puzzling performance to her husband. At first (before Murat was ready), he asked her repeatedly for news. "Have we taken Sicily?" Then he became steadily more cautious, mulled over the risks, Murat's impetuosity, and the strength of the British. Finally a letter from Clarke, minister of war, arrived: Patience. The emperor was forming another force at Toulon. Probably two simultaneous invasions would be attempted. Murat was incensed. The army from Toulon would get the glory! His role would be secondary! Sicily would be French, not Neapolitan. He had no specific orders *not* to launch his invasion, and he determined to do so at the first opportunity.

On September 17 winds drove the British fleet into port; Murat, exultant, ordered his army across the strait. Cavaignac, with a Neapolitan corps of 3,500, responded immediately, and landed successfully at Scaletta. But no other troops followed. Grenier, all deference to the king, refused to comply with his orders, protesting that he could not commit French troops without imperial authority. On September 18 Cavaignac withdrew, leaving 1,000 dead and prisoners behind.

Murat was convinced he had been betrayed—that Grenier had orders to undermine his expedition. Probably he was right; almost surely his men could have reached Sicily, and the forces opposing them numbered less than 6,000. On September 29 Murat took down the royal standard and returned to Naples by ship. So humiliated was he that he preferred to risk capture at sea rather than face his people on the route back to the capital. The invasion was canceled, he told his troops. "You have proved that enemy flotillas cannot [stop us] . . . Sicily will be conquered when *one* seriously wants her conquered." When *Napoleon* wants her conquered, he meant, as his bitter tone conveyed.

MURAT'S THRONE IN JEOPARDY

Perhaps Napoleon expected Murat to abdicate. During the summer of 1810 Napoleon had already forced Louis, king of Holland, from his throne, reduced Joseph's power in Spain so drastically that he threatened to withdraw, and humiliated Jérôme in Westphalia with calculated insults and unwarranted accusations. The emperor may well have intended to dissolve the satellite kingdoms in favor of a centralized imperial system. If, with this in mind, he willfully destroyed Murat's chances to win new glory and more territory, he surely did not authorize the threatened invasion solely for that purpose. With Murat poised to strike, the British had to forgo transferring troops from Sicily to Spain, where the French, for the moment, were winning. It also held the British fleet at Messina, which enabled the French to resupply Corfu. Perhaps Napoleon had intended Murat only to threaten invasion, as the conquest of Sicily might have created more problems than advantages, considering the magnitude of British sea power. Surely Napoleon had not meant for Murat to withdraw so abruptly. Neapolitan policy, he wrote angrily to the king, was part of imperial policy. The invasion should have been called off only by imperial order.

If nothing else, Napoleon thought Murat needed disciplining —before and after the abortive expedition. He was not apologetic about Murat's loss of face. The king had brought it on himself by launching his invasion without orders. To further impress Murat with his subordinate position, the emperor, in the course of 1810, rebuked him repeatedly for failure to enforce the Continental System, demanded the immediate payment of 5,000,000 francs which Naples owed France and money Murat personally owed the imperial treasury or the Legion of Honor, and ordered him to begin building three new warships. In addition Napoleon withdrew his ambassador from Naples and did not replace him, forcing the king to deal with a chargé d'affaires. He also expelled Murat's ambassador, Monteleone, from Paris, though he did accept a replacement, the duke di Campochiaro.

Murat was convinced that Marie Louise had persuaded Napoleon to abandon the conquest of Sicily. His fear returned that the emperor would make a settlement with his empress' grandmother. Napoleon's insults and demands Murat saw as evidence that he was doomed. Surely, he felt, even if the Bourbons were not allowed to return, his throne would not long survive the birth of an imperial heir. Perhaps he was right.

At any rate Murat's reaction was to become more intensely nationalist. Since, from his viewpoint, Napoleon scorned his loyalty, he determined to build a following in Naples. He associated himself, secretly, with the Freemasons, and probably also with the less influential but growing *Carbonari,* both favoring Neapolitan independence and gaining followers for the unification and freedom of all Italy. His most trusted associates became Zurlo, minister of the interior, and Maghella, prefect of police, both pan-Italian nationalists. Foolishly, Murat also openly flouted the emperor. He allowed the *Monitore* to adopt a guarded anti-French tone, and left off republishing all imperial decrees. In 1810 he had the Imperial Eagle removed from flagstaffs, and in February 1811 replaced the French tricolor with a new Neapolitan flag.

The emperor retaliated. He detained in Paris the ambassadors Murat dispatched to Saint Petersburg and Vienna. He proliferated his spy system in Naples, and warned Murat about associating with the nationalists. He continued to press the king to pay his debts, and excoriated him for his every real or suspected breach of the Continental System. A decree from Murat forbidding the exportation of cotton seed yielded the accusation that he was deliberately wrecking the imperial economy.

But Napoleon's difficulties with Russia prompted him (at least temporarily) to vacate conflicts with the satellite kings. In November 1810 the Baron Durant de Mareuil was appointed French ambassador to Naples. The tone of the emperor's letters softened, and Murat's representatives in Paris were no longer snubbed. The king, who truly wanted no conflict with Napoleon, whom he worshiped, grew optimistic. Caroline, who returned to Naples in the fall, did not share her husband's feeling. Invited to be godmother of the king of Rome (born March 1811), she declined to leave Naples, pleading ill health. Murat, however, went to Paris, where he was received warmly by the emperor.

In Murat's absence, the queen built her own political strength. She had become the mistress of Daure, minister of war, marine, and police. Middle-aged, stocky, shrewd, and energetic, but with the manners of a peasant, Daure was no Don Juan. But next to Murat, he was the most powerful man in the kingdom, and a natural leader of the "French party," into which Caroline also quickly drew Durant, Napoleon's new ambassador. The queen, at this stage, felt her best chance for retaining her crown was to display loyalty to Napoleon. She intended to expose the plots of the nationalists, and if necessary to implicate her husband. Daure's police labored to secure the evidence she needed. The nationalists, however, were also at work. Maghella, prefect of police, had his own spy net in operation, and was ready, when Murat returned, to feed his apprehensions, which were many.

In Paris the emperor had greeted Murat fondly, taken him hunting, radiated friendship. But it was obvious that he needed him to command the thousands of cavalry already forming for the war with Russia. After the war, what? Napoleon now had a son—the king of Rome. The Kingdom of Italy was to be his (unless a second son appeared); the empire eventually also. Even the cradle designed for him seemed to portend the doom of the satellite kingdoms. The sides displayed mythological figures representing the two capitals of the empire—Paris and Rome. In conversation the emperor had shown respect for Murat as a soldier, a thinly veiled contempt for him as a king. On his return Murat began to see every Frenchman as a potential enemy, and the French generals as men situated to seize his kingdom on order.

In June 1811 the king dismissed Marshal Pérignon, commandant of Naples, and replaced him with General Carascosa, a Neapolitan. The same month he decreed that all foreigners holding civil or military office must take Neapolitan citizenship or depart.

Napoleon's reply was prompt and devastating. All Frenchmen, he decreed on July 6, were also citizens of Naples. ". . . the Prince who governs [Naples] is French and a Grand Dignitary of the

Empire, and he has been placed and maintained on that throne only through the efforts of our people. . . ." Inescapably, the decree expressed a broader concept of the empire than had ever been put forward before. It gave Frenchmen an imperial citizenship, a special status akin to that of Roman citizens of the ancient empire. It adds weight to the thesis that Napoleon hoped eventually to create a centralized "Roman Empire," sans satellite kingdoms. Another decree followed making it a felony for Frenchmen to assume another nationality.[12] Simultaneously, all French troops were removed from Murat's command, and placed under Grenier, who was ordered to "protect" the kingdom.

Murat was checkmated. He became ill, left bed to stalk about, brandishing a brace of pistols and threatening to blow out his brains, and finally retired to Capodimonte for a rest. He emerged repentant, and at the same time guilt-ridden. He had defied the man to whom he owed everything. He was bested, humiliated, and yet as much ashamed as angry. He would never make a satisfactory traitor, even in later years when he had Napoleon at a disadvantage. Whatever he did, even when he set his troops against the French, he had to convince himself that *really,* somehow, he had the interests of France and his emperor at heart. "Your Majesty dishonors his brother-in-law, his lieutenant," he wrote ". . . I defy all my enemies to cite one deed contrary to your system . . . until the last supper, I shall be what I have always been, your most loyal friend."

Maghella, however, had another card to play. If Murat must of necessity submit to the emperor, he could nevertheless shatter the "French party." At the end of July he delivered to the king a packet of love letters between Queen Caroline and Daure, and other correspondence which gave the impression that Daure, Lanusse, the grand equerry, recently made marshal of the palace, Durant, the French ambassador, and others were conspiring with Caroline to eliminate Murat and give her full powers. Murat again seized his pistols, threatening to shoot the queen, Daure, and per-

12. It also forbade Frenchmen to accept titles or offices from foreign princes. It was understood in Naples that the satellite kings were not "foreign," but since the earlier decree had been directed at Murat, this was ambiguous elsewhere. In Spain Joseph was faced with the possibility that Miot, Ferri-Pisani, and others would resign and return to France. There were weeks of uncertainty before explanations arrived.

haps himself also. After an hour of theatrics, he galloped off to Capodimonte, then returned to Naples and ordered Caroline into "exile" at Capodimonte. Daure fled without passport to France. Maghella was appointed minister of police; Tugny took the portfolios of war and marine. The nationalists had scored a triumph. But, as usual, Caroline was not without resources.

Baudus, her boys' tutor, persuaded Murat to see her. Tearful, soft, feminine, coifed and dressed demurely for her part, she protested her innocence. The letters were not hers at all, she said. How could she take a pig like Daure for her lover? Most of the letters were not in her handwriting but in that of a secretary, she pointed out. Could he not see that the signatures were forged? Murat emerged less certain of the truth, but kept her at Capodimonte.

The queen, however, had not left herself at her husband's mercy. On the day Maghella had exposed her, while Murat still stormed about trying to make up his mind, she had sent copies of the letters in question to Napoleon by a friend, Captain Kesner, who had been granted leave in Paris. He also carried a letter from Caroline which accused Maghella of manufacturing evidence to alienate Murat from his emperor. Durant reinforced the queen's case: The "Italian party" was gaining control of the king; Murat had never publicly acknowledged the emperor's suzerainty over Naples.

The king protested his loyalty to Napoleon: "Sire I am so unhappy, oh oui! so unhappy, give me your love. . . . I will always be the first grenadier of the Emperor." He made friendly gestures toward Grenier, and reinstated Marshal Pérignon as commandant of Naples. But Napoleon's attitude had been fixed by Caroline and Durant. Again he moved to discipline the king. La Vauguyon, Murat's aide-de-camp, was expelled from Paris, his agent Aymé arrested and confined to Vincennes. The latter's papers provided new evidence connecting Murat with the Talleyrand-Fouché (-Caroline) plot of 1808, which was reinvestigated, together with charges, long suppressed, that Murat had made off with some of the Spanish crown jewels—both simply to embarrass Murat. Campochiaro, the Neapolitan ambassador, was sent packing. Again, Murat was defeated. Daily expecting to be dethroned, he swallowed his pride and sent Caroline to Paris to plead his case.

He gambled that Napoleon had enough affection for her to save their throne, but distrusted her too much to displace him in her favor.

In October 1811 Caroline was in Paris, and within a few weeks installed in the Tuileries and in daily contact with her brother. She ingratiated herself with Marie Louise, saw evidence of genius in the jabbering of the infant king of Rome, appeared smiling and diamond-laden at all the social functions. Murat, she told Napoleon, was weak, and had fallen under the spell of strong-willed Italian nationalists. He was repentant; the emperor must trust *her* to see that his loyalty remained constant. It would be well if Maghella were recalled to France (he was a native of Genoa, thus a French citizen). She would advise Murat to dismiss Zurlo, who was also dangerous, and give over the fortress of Gaeta to Grenier.

Napoleon, whose cavalry, now grouping in Germany, needed a commander, allowed himself to be won over. Murat, similarly, gradually, as his pride would allow him, did all that Caroline suggested. In early 1812 Grenier occupied Gaeta; Zurlo was dismissed, together with many minor officials suspected of "Italian" sympathies. Murat began to plead with Napoleon to give him a command so that he could prove his loyalty. He sent a new ambassador, the duke di Carignano, to Paris; he was accepted, a good sign. Finally, in March, the king ruefully submitted to the recall of Maghella.

In April Murat's orders arrived—the cavalry of the Grande Armeé was his. In Paris he agreed that Caroline would be regent in his absence. He was excited by the adventure before him, and by the vague possibility that a more secure throne might be granted him in Poland. But he deeply distrusted Caroline, and was not at all sure that Napoleonic victories would not bring his kingdom closer to dissolution. Nevertheless, in the early months of the Russian campaign, he would be the Murat of old, the first horseman of Europe, happily battling the Cossacks and basking in the praise of his emperor.

. . . never cease to be French.
—NAPOLEON TO LOUIS, JUNE 5, 1806

. . . I have changed my nationality. . . . I shall always remain Dutch.
—LOUIS TO DUTCH OFFICIALS, JUNE 23, 1806

chapter five
THE KINGDOM OF HOLLAND

Louis and Holland: Background

LOUIS BONAPARTE

*H*apless is the word for Louis Bonaparte. When he finally gave up trying to govern Holland, he could not even flee gracefully. Walking from his palace to his carriage, he fell into a ditch, crawled out, and was driven, wet, muddy, and sputtering toward exile. At such junctures in his royal career, one does not know whether to cry for him or laugh at him. Yet he was not a feckless clown. He was an intelligent, earnest, and kindhearted man, who in just four years managed to win the affection of his people. But he had also outraged Napoleon beyond remedy.

After the fall of the grand empire Louis wrote:

One would be in error to look for the principal difficulties of the Emperor Napoleon outside of the system called continental; it is that idea, mathematically valid, but impossible to execute perfectly; it is the extreme immorality of the blockade and all that went with it, which caused the . . . downfall of France.

As an explanation of the fall of the empire, the statement is ridiculously oversimple. It only places blame for the miseries of Holland, the like of which, Louis assumes, *must* have ruined the empire. And inadvertently, it reveals why he did not long retain his throne. His attitude is Dutch, not imperial. He calls the Continental System "immoral." Could a man capable of such a judg-

(127)

ment ever effectively serve Napoleon? To the emperor state policies were never either moral or immoral, merely practical or impractical, rational or irrational.

Louis was not quite twenty-eight when he became king of Holland in 1806, but he looked and behaved like a middle-aged man. He was overweight, flabby, nervous, and possessed of a waspish temper. Because his spine was slightly deformed, he walked with his body inclined to the right. At intervals rheumatism crippled his legs. A partial paralysis of his right hand forced him to write with his pen tied to his fingers. He was continually consulting new doctors and visiting mineral baths. No doctor every positively identified the source of Louis's maladies; possibly diagnosis would have been difficult even if he had lived in our time. All or at least part of his trouble was mental, and, to Louis's outrage, an occasional physician said so. Others opined that he had congenital tuberculosis or venereal disease or had sustained injuries affecting the marrow of his spine. Louis dated the decline of his health from age fifteen (1793), when he had been thrown by a horse at Nice. (Sergeant Junot, later general, duke d'Abrantès, had playfully slapped the horse on the rump, causing it to bolt.) After that, his coordination seemed to deteriorate, and his accidents multiplied. He became a hypochondriac, a semi-invalid, and developed a persecution complex which his experience in Holland deepened. If Louis's ills were not imaginary, perhaps the injuries did cause them, for he lived to be almost sixty-eight, and never showed signs of the sort of mental decline likely to accompany congenital disease. At any rate, in 1806 he was already a sufferer. "Phychisch was hij evenzeer een wrak . . ." says Van Houtte's history.

Louis was not unattractive, however. He had a good, pleasant face. When he felt up to meeting the public he was affable and smiling. He was generous, sympathetic, and compassionate, which won him love of his people (and accusations of weakness from Napoleon). No king ever had better intentions than he, or loved his people more, or became a more willing captive of them. Dutch ministers made decisions for him; Dutch administrators applied his policies to suit their individual interpretations; Dutch writers put words into his mouth. This was partly because he became one of them, and partly because he lacked the physical strength to be a full-time executive.

Born September 2, 1778, Louis was the third brother of Napoleon, and nine years his junior. He was fourteen when the Bonapartes fled Corsica, barely fifteen when Napoleon won fame at Toulon. Napoleon tutored Louis for examinations at the artillery school at Châlons-sur-Marne (though he never took them), got him a commission before he was sixteen, and let him have a look at static war on the Italian frontier (1794) and command artillery in garrison at Saint-Tropez. When in 1795 Napoleon became commander of the Army of the Interior, he called Louis to staff duty in Paris. "I am quite content with Louis," Napoleon wrote Joseph, ". . . he takes after me: passion, spirit, health, talent, exact reliability, good will, he combines everything." In 1796 Louis, seventeen, accompanied Napoleon on the first Italian Campaign. With Colonel (later Marshal) Lannes, he was the first to cross the Po. At Pavia he stormed the gates at the head of a company of grenadiers. From Mantua he was dispatched with a report to the Directory in Paris, where he turned eighteen and was promoted to captain. In November 1796 he was back in Italy for the battle of Arcola, the turning point of the campaign.

Peace came in 1797 and, for Louis, first love. On a visit to his sister Caroline at Madame Campan's school, the young captain was felled by the bright-eyed hero worship of the slight, impish Émilie de Beauharnais, Joséphine's niece. Louis proposed; Émilie accepted. Impossible! said Napoleon. The girl's mother had left her husband for another man. In matters involving his family's reputation, General Bonaparte could be a real prude. He whisked Louis off to Egypt (1798) as his aide-de-camp, and arranged a marriage for Émilie with General Lavalette, characterized by the acid-tongued Laure Junot as a boorish little man with a face like a roasting pig. Louis never recovered from this blow. Much later he would make himself and Émilie, thinly disguised, the central figures in a novel of tragic romance.

In February 1799 Napoleon could safely return Louis to Paris, and sent him on his way with a clutch of captured flags. The voyage, on a decrepit gunboat, was a nightmarish roller coaster ride broken by flights into friendly ports to avoid capture. Pursued by English warships in the Strait of Messina, Louis threw the flags overboard, and arrived in France weak and sick. The "new Louis" had begun to emerge. Ill all summer, he was unable to meet Napoleon when he landed at Fréjus in August.

Once Napoleon was First Consul, he made Louis colonel of Fifth Dragoons, with the mission of capturing and trying royalist rebels in Normandy. Louis did not have the stomach for the work, tried to halt executions, was overruled, left matters to his subordinates, then retired to Paris in disgust. Part of his regiment accompanied Napoleon on the second Italian Campaign, but Louis remained in Paris, where he fought another sort of battle.

Joséphine had assisted cheerfully in disposing of Émilie, because she had planned for years to marry her daughter Hortense to Louis. She would thereby provide a future for Hortense and additional security for herself, since the Bonapartes had never warmed to her, and were likely to abandon her if Napoleon were killed—an ever-present possibility. In the early years of their marriage, Joséphine usually got her way with Napoleon, despite her chronic unfaithfulness. Louis was doomed to a marriage which he later described as full or "horrors," and as having tinged his life with "une sorte de tristesse profonde." But he battled against the inevitable as long as he could.

Hortense had no lack of suitors. She was descended on her father's side from old nobility, had the highest possible connections in the new order, and was sure to have a large dowry. Moreover, she was pretty, intelligent, and vivacious. She had her mother's stunning figure and the blue eyes, blond hair, and finely chiseled features of the Beauharnais. Madame Campan had schooled her in music, literature, and the social graces. She had learned the conversational arts and not a little coquetry in her mother's salon. She was radiantly healthy, a tireless dancer, a skilled horsewoman, the star of plays and operas performed for the family circle. Most men would have found it easy to love her—but not Louis. He preferred to brood over the lost Émilie and nurse himself.

For two years Louis stayed as far away from Hortense as his health and Napoleon would allow. Playing on his brother's dwindling hope that he would develop into a soldier, he got permission to visit Berlin for Prussian army maneuvers (which he missed), Saint Petersburg (which he never reached), and Spain (for the comic opera *War of the Oranges* against the Portuguese [1801], which ended as he arrived, allowing him to retire to the baths at Barèges). But on his return to Paris, he found his fate decided. On January 4, 1802, he and Hortense were wed.

The connubial state held no charm for Louis, however. "During the years 1802, 1803, and 1804 [I] . . . was continually with [my] . . . regiment or at the mineral baths," he wrote later. Even when under the same roof, Louis and Hortense usually occupied separate apartments. (And Louis often protected himself further by having any connecting doors nailed shut.) They lived together as man and wife only for short periods in 1802, 1804, and 1807—a total of about three months. Louis in 1816 wrote Hortense an insulting letter in which he questioned that their children—one born after each period of cohabitation—were really his, especially the third, who was destined to become Napoleon III.[1] But there is no solid basis for doubting that they were. Considering Louis's treatment of Hortense, and the prevailing casual attitude of the upper classes toward marriage vows, Hortense was incredibly faithful. Her one real affair, with Count Charles de Flahaut, did not begin until 1807, and had solidified by 1810 (when she separated from Louis) into a second marriage in all but name. Czar Alexander paid her court in 1814, and helped her secure a generous property settlement from the allies. Perhaps he became her lover; if so the affair was short-lived.

While First Consul, Napoleon declined to advance Louis beyond the rank of colonel. His illnesses, the progressive softening of his personality, his affinity for intellectual circles all appalled the elder brother. "He has the air of an imbecile." Nevertheless, with the advent of the empire, Louis was promoted to general of a division and made prince and grand constable. In 1805 the emperor gave him command of the reserve of the army at Boulogne. True to form, Louis established his headquarters at a

1. The children were Napoleon Charles (1802–1807), Napoleon Louis (1804–1831), and Louis Napoleon (1808–1873).

convenient distance from the baths at Saint-Amand. When the army marched for Austria, the grand constable first took command of forces at Paris, then the Army of the North, formed to oppose a possible English invasion of the lowlands. At his headquarters at Nijmwegen, he made his first acquaintance with Holland.

THE KINGDOM OF HOLLAND

In early 1806 Napoleon determined to convert the Batavian Republic into a monarchy, though he would have preferred to annex it to France, as he considered its rivers "natural arteries" of the empire. He was trying to keep Prussia neutral, however, and was engaged in unofficial peace talks with England. The creation of a Kingdom of Holland would not greatly alarm either, while extending the boundaries of France might goad Prussia into war and destroy England's momentary will to peace. At the same time his control of the Lowlands would be improved by the installation of a docile king. (Louis seemed the ideal candidate.)

The Dutch, a nation of traders with little use for heroics, had for a decade bought a modicum of freedom from an aggressive France. The cost of their relative independence through 1804 they estimated at 500,000,000 francs. The value of the ships of war, transport vessels, matériel, and men they had contributed for Napoleon's descent on England had yet to be calculated. But they declined to dwell on the emperor's ingratitude for their material aid and the loyal service of Admiral Verhuel's naval units against the English. Instead they tried to bargain.

In April Schimmelpenninck's Great Committee[2] sent a deputation to Paris: Brantzen, ambassador to France, Admiral Verhuel, Gogel, minister of Finance, Van Styrum, a member of the legislature, and Willem Six, councilor of state. The emperor refused to see them, but allôwed Verhuel to present their proposition. "Holland" would accept a king, the admiral said, if Napoleon would guarantee her independence, government by natives, territorial integrity, traditional laws and liberties, religious freedom, the use of the Dutch language, the withdrawal of French troops, the inviolability of the national debt, a more favorable commercial

2. See p. 12.

treaty, a reduction of obligations to France, and agreement to a plebiscite on the change in government.

Napoleon refused to bargain—the republic must accept a monarchal constitution or face annexation to France. The treaty and constitution he offered, however, showed that he had taken cognizance of Dutch demands. No plebiscite, withdrawal of French troops, or reduction of obligations was promised, but all other guarantees requested were given. On May 24, 1806, representatives of the legislature and council of state signed the proffered treaty. Schimmelpenninck, who considered the change of government illegal without public sanction, went into retirement. Louis was accepted as king under the treaty, but during April and May he had shuttled nervously between Paris and Saint-Leu, his country estate, declaring that the Dutch people must approve his accession. But on June 5, when Napoleon summoned him to the Tuileries to be proclaimed king, he went. Between an interview with the Turkish ambassador and other business, the emperor heard a Dutch delegation request Louis as king, assented, and flung out advice from the throne: ". . . Holland owes her existence to France . . . protect her laws and liberties, but never cease to be French." He then escorted Louis into an adjoining salon where he was announced as the king of Holland. Such was his "coronation."

Why did Louis accept the crown? His *Documents et réflexions* show that Napoleon and Talleyrand had convinced him that only a monarchy could save the Dutch state. In no other way, save annexation to France, could her government be centralized and made efficient, liberal principles applied, and her defenses properly organized. Louis accepted the crown, therefore, in humility and with an attitude of service. Pathetically enough, he seems to have believed that the Dutch delegation truly wanted him as king. This conviction worked to his personal advantage, for it allowed him to approach his subjects, in all honesty, as friend and benefactor, and the Dutch remember him as such to this day. Of course the delegation *did* want him, and Dutch leaders would support him loyally—as an alternative to having their country annexed to France.

Never one to be rushed, Louis spent ten days preparing for the journey to The Hague and conferring with the Dutch delegation. On June 15, accompanied by Hortense and his sons, he finally left Saint-Leu for Holland. Crossing the border, he ceremoniously changed his French cockade for a Dutch one and, pausing only to greet local delegations, hurried on to the country palace of Huis-'Ten-Bosch, near The Hague. Along the route he had noted ". . . too many troops, too many arches of triumph, and among the people more curiosity than interest." For his entry into The Hague (June 23) he assembled an all-Dutch escort. His greetings to the legislature,[3] council of state, representatives of the provinces, religious bodies, and the universities were full of Dutch sentiment. "Your principles are mine . . ." ". . . You have the right to a Dutch King." ". . . From this day begins the true independence of the United Provinces."

Louis's selection of officials confirmed his determination to be Dutch. He reappointed three ministers of the old government: I. J. A. Gogel, Van der Goes, and Admiral Verhuel, respectively ministers of finance, foreign affairs, and marine. J. H. Appilius, secretary of the council of state, was also retained. His new appointees were Dutch patriots, although slightly more liberal than the ones previously mentioned. Roëll became minister secretary of state, Mollerus, Van Hof, and Van der Hem accepted the portfolios of interior, justice and police, and colonies. At Napoleon's insistence, Louis appointed a French minister of war, General Bonhomme, but shortly replaced him with a native, General Hogendorp. Virtually all of the members of the old council of state were confirmed in office, and Louis made strenuous efforts to induce Schimmelpenninck to accept the permanent presidency of the legislature, but he declined.[4] During the crisis of 1809–1810 Louis would complain that he was treated not as a king, but as "the replacement of Schimmelpenninck." In some respects Napoleon intended him to be just that—but more docile and

3. The exact nature of the legislature will be discussed below.
4. An honor allowed by the constitution, thus Napoleon's idea, not Louis's.

efficient. Unhappily for him, he became all too much like his predecessor.

As we shall note in detail below, Louis was faced immediately and continually with financial problems. At the time of his accession the treasury was almost empty and the deficit for the year already 44,000,000 florins.[5] The king turned to Napoleon: Could he repay 4,000,000 florins lent some years earlier to France? Should he not pay French troops in Holland? The loan had expired, replied the emperor, and he would not pay French troops, as they were protecting Holland. The new commercial treaty the emperor had promised? In due time . . . "You write me every day to sing of misery," wrote Napoleon. Find your own solutions; France cannot save you. Why not stop paying interest on the national debt? It alone amounted to 18,000,000 florins a year. No, said Louis, it would be like declaring his government bankrupt and would destroy public confidence. Schimmelpenninck's argument had been the same. Throughout his reign Louis would refuse to touch the interest on the debt. He also refused to institute conscription, which, he argued, was totally contrary to Dutch custom. He thereby committed himself to maintain an army of volunteers, or really, since Dutchmen seldom enlisted, of costly foreign mercenaries. Before he had been in Holland two months, he proposed to Napoleon that he cut expenses by reducing the size of his army and navy and closing a number of forts. Napoleon, outraged, threatened to make peace by giving the Dutch colonies to the English, and demanded that Louis expand the Dutch army to 30,000 and build more warships. How? wrote Louis. Interest must be paid on the debt; dikes must be repaired yearly or the country will be swamped. French troops must be paid. Greater military expenditures will "disorganize all my institutions." Napoleon was unimpressed: "It is notorious that the Dutch have all the money in Europe." There may be another war. If the Dutch want to be independent they will have to defend themselves.

Initially Louis was received politely, if without much enthusiasm. After a decade of upheaval and governmental turnovers,

5. Florin = 2.17 francs.

the population was inclined to be cynical, though docile. A mild hope for greater stability was as much as most citizens could muster. Most writers and poets celebrated his arrival perfunctorily, but in time they, like the masses, could sing his praises with sincerity. It was obvious that he was a good man, painfully intent on becoming Dutch. Willem Bilderdijk, the nation's most famous poet, undertook to teach the king Dutch; Louis showed his respect by sending the royal carriage to bring him to the palace. The great merchant and banking families easily accepted Louis. His fiscal policies were to their liking, and he gave them more protection from Napoleon than they had expected. There were a few recalcitrants, such as S. I. Wiselius and J. H. Van Swinden. Both refused any honors, and the former always referred to the king as "Heer Lodewijk Buonaparte." Generally, however, Louis encountered no open domestic opposition. A short-lived mutiny on three ships at Texel was the total of military resistance to his entry.

Try as he might, however, Louis would never completely understand the Dutch. Their stubborn provincialism exasperated him, as did their individualism. Congenitally *frondeuse,* he called them, i.e., if not exactly rebellious, antiauthoritarian. Louis, like many of his generation, was at once an authoritarian-liberal, a constitutionalist, and a believer in popular government. Unlike Napoleon, however, Louis had never quite made up his mind to support enlightened authority. He faithfully submitted all but emergency measures to his legislature, which met at least twice a year, but he never ceased to be shocked when his proposals were discussed, altered, and sometimes rejected. More disturbing to him was the behavior of his administrative subordinates, who applied a "rule of conscience" to his orders instead of carrying them out to the letter. "It is unity of movement which is the principal advantage of monarchy," he lectured. But he was too frequently ill or absent to follow up on all his instructions. Centralizing the police proved almost impossible. The Protestants Van Hof and Van Maanen were in turn entrusted with the ministry of justice and police; then in 1809 a Catholic, Hugenpoth, whom Louis hoped would have a better sense of discipline. All proved incurably Dutch.

The king never felt he had enough information on which to act. "A government is a pilot . . ." he began a pedantic plea for more thorough reporting by the whole administration. The ministers did not reform, not only because centralized administration was foreign to them, but because they wanted to keep some information from the king. His heart was with them, they knew, but he was too honest to lie to Napoleon, particularly about violations of the Continental System. After November 1806 smuggling became essential to even minimal prosperity. Louis wanted happy subjects and revenues; his ministers did their best to give him both without burdening his conscience. They liked him, but kept the government in their own hands.

Louis and Napoleon: The Early Years

The ardors of accession exhausted Louis. He spent August and September 1806 at baths in the Rhineland. Prussia meanwhile launched her armies toward states of the *Rheinbund;* Napoleon moved to counter them, leaving the Army of the North, which he ordered Louis to command, to guard the lower Rhine. The king responded with reasonable alacrity. By October 15 he had established headquarters at Wesel and disposed his 20,000 troops (half Dutch, half French). On October 14, however, the battles of Jena and Auerstädt had been fought and the major Prussian armies shattered. Louis was ordered to cooperate with Marshal Mortier (a corps commander) in reducing Prussian fortresses in western Germany and occupying the territories of Prussia's German allies, notably the elector of Hesse-Cassel. Louis dutifully occupied Münster, Paderborn, and Osnabrück, sent a Dutch division (General Daendels) to seize East Frisia, and laid siege to Hameln and Nienburg.

Before he could reduce the fortresses, however, Mortier asked aid in occupying Hesse-Cassel. Louis withdrew part of his forces from the siege lines and marched south, sending ahead to the elector a guarantee of his personal protection. (The king was embarrassed with his mission; he had recently received Hesse's ambassador with professions of friendship.) But on his arrival, he found that Mortier had already occupied Cassel and that the elector had fled. Testily, he forbade his troops to enter the city, only to discover that most of the troops with him had been added to the marshal's corps. His pride deeply hurt, he left Cassel to Mortier, and returned to the sieges of Hameln and Nienburg. En route, Dupont-Chaumont, Napoleon's ambassador to Holland, rode with Louis in the royal coach, prattling endlessly about imperial policy. Among other things, he opined that Holland would soon be annexed to France and, in the manner of a disinterested observer, that the emperor had never intended the kingdom to be permanent. Louis was tired and distraught over what he considered a humiliation by Mortier. Dupont's remarks threw him into violent depression. At Nienburg and Hameln he ordered his troops to blockade, not take, the fortresses. He complained that Napoleon was treating him like a French general, not a king; the Dutch army was a fiction—his troops were mixed with French—the top Dutch general was only a division commander. In mid-November he sent the emperor word that he was ill, and returned with his guard to The Hague. French generals completed the task assigned Louis in western Germany.

Napoleon made no attempt to return the king to his command, but ordered him to concentrate on raising 25,000 troops in addition to the 10,000 with the Grande Armée. This demand arrived simultaneously with news that the Continental System, sure to devastate the Dutch economy, had been established. The Berlin Decree (November 21, 1806) not only closed European ports to all ships from Britain and her colonies, or which had touched either or paid British tariffs, but forbade any commerce in British goods. The king wrote plaintively to Napoleon that he appreciated that the system was designed to ruin British trade, and drive them to make peace. But what of Holland? Her budget was almost twice her income. Trade was her life; revenues were sure to decrease.

Napoleon could not say bluntly "Holland be damned," but it was clear that he intended if necessary to sacrifice the Dutch economy for, hopefully, the good of the empire. He answered Louis's questions with orders. "Don't talk to me anymore of misery." You must have an army. Raise one. Leave your debts unpaid if necessary. The British are sure to attempt an invasion of Holland in the spring (of 1807), and if they succeed will exact a 200,000,000-florin contribution, he wrote, pulling a figure from the air as if revealing knowledge of dark enemy intent. Would your people rather defend themselves or face *that?*

Louis did his best to enlarge his army, but Napoleon called Dutch units into Germany almost as quickly as they were formed. By March 1807, 20,000 Dutch troops (actually mostly German mercenaries) were with the Grande Armée, though largely on rear-area duty. In the same month there was an invasion scare, but fortunately for Louis no enemy appeared. If there had been a landing he would have faced it with 3,000 guardsmen and 3,000–4,000 recruits from depots in Frisia and Helder.

Louis complained to Napoleon that, despite his efforts, Holland's defenses remained unmanned. The emperor shot back that it was Louis's fault. "You govern badly." Why had he not instituted conscription, as recommended? Amsterdam alone could furnish 20,000 men. Why had he not organized a national guard?

As we have noted in examining Napoleon's relations with Murat, his method of teaching obedience involved hammering away at a subordinate's mistakes and showering down irrational abuse on him until abject submission seemed the only way to salvation. It is a time-honored military technique, intended to teach men to respond to orders promptly without questioning their reasonableness, in short, to instill discipline. Napoleon applied it to military and civil officers alike, and to his satellite rulers. The more they complained, the more he abused them. The cannier ones questioned him as little as possible.

In Louis's case, the emperor seized on three measures promulgated by king and legislature in early 1807. They created marshals in the Dutch army, established two orders of knighthood, and recognized noble titles of the old regime. Marshals in an army no bigger than a French corps? scoffed Napoleon. Did Louis really think a French general would obey a Dutch marshal? (He well knew the problem would never arise.) Why did Holland need two orders when the Legion of Honor sufficed for France? How dare he elevate nobles of the old regime! Had he lost respect for the principles of the Revolution? What of equality, "careers open to talent," and rank proportionate to public service?

Louis appointed his marshals, protesting that they would command only Dutch troops, and conceded a point by retaining only one decoration, the Royal Order of Holland. He defended his recognition of old nobles on the basis that he was only following the emperor's example, allowing loyal subjects to use their titles socially, as they did in France; he would give new titles as a reward for service. Napoleon chose to let the Royal Order stand, but scorned to wear it himself. The matters of marshals and titles continued to provide fuel for his wrath (when needed) until the last days of the kingdom.

In the spring of 1807, while Napoleon fought the Russians, Louis continued to expand his army, toured the provinces, attended fleet maneuvers at Helder, and presented the legislature with an ambitious program of reforms and public works, which we shall discuss later. Before his people, he tried to radiate optimism; in the high circles of the government, he could not but show a growing despair. By mid-April the operation of the Continental System had severely dislocated the Dutch economy. Citing a mounting deficit, Louis suggested to Napoleon that Holland could be saved and the empire best served by making the kingdom a vast free port—the proposal advanced earlier by Schimmelpenninck.

Napoleon was appalled. Had Louis gone mad? Had he forgotten he was French? He must show strength and enforce imperial policy. "A prince called *good* in the first year will be mocked in the second." "You govern like a Capuchin!" Fatigued from travel and strain, continually berated by his brother, even on the treatment of Hortense ("One should not ask a wife of twenty to live as if in a cloister!"), Louis asked leave to spend the summer of 1807 at baths in the Pyrenees.

While he awaited the emperor's reply, the crown prince, Napoleon Charles, age four, fell ill and, despite the attention of a battery of French and Dutch physicians, died on May 5.[6] Napoleon, deeply saddened by the news, raised no objection to the departure of Louis and Hortense for Cauterets. There, under

---

6. Of a respiratory infection, described as "croup" by Louis in his *Documents*.

the impetus of their mutual grief, the king and queen again became man and wife after four years of alienation. As a result 1808 saw the birth of their third child, Louis Napoleon. The emperor, meanwhile, had undoubtedly begun to think of marrying again himself in the hope of producing an heir. The death of Napoleon Charles, designated to become the emperor's adoptive heir at age eighteen, cast doubt on the wisdom of staking the survival of the imperial line on Louis's second son. Further, Napoleon had become more certain of his own procreative powers, as we have noted.[7]

While Louis rested in the south of France, Napoleon defeated the Russians and made peace at Tilsit (July 1807). His attention then turned to the reorganization of Germany, the creation of Westphalia, the disciplining of Portugal and Spain, and, with a vengeance, to forcing the Dutch to respect the Continental System. French gendarmes arrested violators at Bergen op Zoom and Breda and carried them off to France. Louis was accused of allowing Dutch merchants to visit England (some had) and was told to discipline his officials or they would be replaced by Frenchmen. The French ambassador, Dupont-Chaumont, was recalled, leaving only a chargé d'affaires at The Hague. Louis feared for his crown, and was surprised when, as he passed through Paris in September 1807, the emperor received him cordially, and allowed him to return to his kingdom.

Napoleon apparently decided to temporize regarding Holland. Instead of destroying the kingdom, he annexed Flushing and its environs on the island of Walcheren—to bring major smuggling centers under direct control. In return he added East Frisia and Jevers to Holland.[8] In 1806 the emperor had rejected annexing Holland to France in the hope of keeping Prussia neutral and England peace-minded. At the end of 1807 Prussia (and Russia) were defeated, and all-out war, most prominently economic war, was in progress against England. There was no power-political reason to perpetuate the kingdom of Holland. His "Royal Prefect,"

7. See p. 37.
8. France also took the island of Loemel and part of that of Eertel and gave Holland the northern part of Gerstel. Louis, personally, became ruler of Kniphausen and Varel, in the Confederation of the Rhine (Treaty of November 1807).

had proved irritatingly independent. His presence hindered the effective operation of the Continental System. But Napoleon elected to maintain the *status quo* in Holland until he implemented his plans for Spain and Portugal, which he considered more urgent. Iberia would command his attention in 1808; the Austrian war would deter his solving the "Dutch problem" in 1809. All the while, however, he would become steadily more dissatisfied with Louis's performance. Immediately after peace was made in 1809 he would turn on the king mercilessly and systematically. Until that time Louis could dream of creating a kingdom for which history would praise him.

The Impact of the Continental System

FINANCES

"Pains, anguishes . . . continual and incredible," wrote Louis, wracked him as he worked, against his will, to enforce the Continental System. Because of it his government, in debt when he became king, settled ever deeper into bankruptcy—orderly, unadmitted, but real. Gains in revenues expected to result from tax reforms and a more efficient collection system instituted by Gogel were negated by a dwindling of usual tax resources as legal trade atrophied. The economy was kept alive by illicit trade, from which, however, the state got scant benefit unless profits were invested in its securities or converted into taxable property. The chart on p. 143 illustrates the gravity of Holland's fiscal sickness.

The real state of finances, however, was worse than is readily apparent from the figures. Amounts borrowed by the routine sale of state securities do not show in either the deficit or budget columns, nor do yields from extraordinary loans.[9] Money borrowed was invariably spent; the yearly additions to the national debt therefore represent a "second" deficit. The deficit figures, as they stand, seem to indicate an improvement, if slight, in the fiscal

9. In 1807 there was a forced loan of 40,000,000 florins; in 1808 an extraordinary loan of 30,000,000 (two-thirds forced, the rest virtually so); in 1809 a 6,000,000 special loan.

Financial Summary—Holland (1806–1809) *

	Budget	Income	Admitted Deficit	Added to National Debt	Interest on National Debt	National Debt a/o Year's End
1806	77,285,845**	50,693,272†	26,592,573	—	34,344,987	1,162,827,252
1807	78,140,368	about 55,000,000	23,140,368	89,112,590	42,263,367	1,251,939,842
1808	80,000,000	about 52,000,000	about 28,000,000	107,867,900	49,388,332	1,359,307,742
1809	70,000,000	about 52,000,000	18,000,000	estimated 116,000,000	55,128,332	1,475,807,742

* Derived from figures in Louis's *Documents et réflexions*. Amount of the national debt after 1806 had to be calculated from the interest paid at various rates. Totals of extraordinary loans only were given.

** Florins (florin = 2.17 francs).

† Figures included uncollected taxes. How much subsequently came in is uncertain.

picture. In reality they reflect only minor domestic economies. A more realistic picture could be presented by taking income as stated and lumping "Budget" and "Added to the National Debt" together as "Expenditures," thus:

	Income	Expenditures	Deficit
1807	55,000,000	167,252,958	112,252,958
1808	52,000,000	187,867,900	135,867,900
1809	52,000,000	186,000,000	134,000,000

Referring again to the first chart, one can see why Napoleon continually urged Louis to suspend or renounce payment of interest on the debt. In 1809 this expense exceeded the total national income. Included under "Interest" are 4,000,000 florins for 1807 and 7,000,000 for 1808 and 1809, representing funds retained in the treasury of amortizement for the payment of noninterest bearing forced loans. If we deduct these sums as not properly interest, or on the valid assumption that they were not really paid, interest still consumed the greater part of income:

	Income	Interest
1807	55,000,000	38,263,367
1808	52,000,000	42,388,332
1809	52,000,000	48,128,332

We may argue, as Louis did, that the state was living on loans, and therefore had to continue paying its interest faithfully. We must concede, however, that Napoleon was right in saying that there *was* money in Holland, and that it might have been secured through taxation rather than borrowing. Moreover, if one suppresses a sympathy for the Dutch and regards the whole empire as Napoleon did, that is, as a structure which would bring peace, efficient government, and progress to all of Europe—in the long run—then the empire becomes worthy of great sacrifice. Louis, from this viewpoint, was a poor executive. By his figures, the Dutch military budget for the army, navy, and French troops quartered in Holland averaged less than 35,000,000 florins a year. By introducing conscription he could have cut the cost. By suspending interest payments he could have saved enough to support a larger military establishment than Napoleon required. His domestic budget (less military expenses) amounted to only about 15,000,000 florins, including the vital *watterstadt* (department of dikes and waterways). His total budget, less interest, averaged around 50,000,000 florins. By his figures, he could have balanced the budget simply by suspending interest payments until the time of general peace. Of course his actual expenses, less interest, as we have seen, averaged nearer 130,000,000 florins. But if this fact had been faced and the resources supplying loans made to supply tax revenues, Holland could have better served the empire. It was because Louis lacked the will to make his people suffer for the long-term good of the empire—because he sympathized with them, could not bear the thought of being hated, and did not believe that (or understand how) Napoleon's system could bring eventual peace—that he was driven into abdication and replaced by a sterner executive, the Archchancellor Lebrun.

LOUIS AND THE CONTINENTAL SYSTEM

The Dutch had money, some accumulated in past decades, some earned in legitimate banking and commercial operations. But profits, as the reign progressed, came increasingly from smuggling, the financing of smuggling at high rates of interest, and dealing in contraband goods. Traffic in major ports declined drastically. (At Amsterdam the number of ships entering declined from 1,349 in 1806 to 310 in 1809.) But goods arrived nevertheless. Louis, in decree after decree, held for the enforcement of the Continental System. But at the same time he openly expressed his "extreme repugnance" for the "blockade," and declared that it "denationalized" Holland. Announcing the Berlin Decree to his ministers, he described Napoleon as so "blinded by passion" as to be able to "hurl himself off a cliff just to take his enemy with him." The measure was "gigantesque, impossible." When the general peace came, he promised, Holland would be a free port to the world. Officials charged with enforcing the *"blocus"* were responsible to Gogel, minister of finance, but dependent on the assistance of the police, army, and navy. All those involved responded more to the king's attitude than to his official pronouncements. They echoed his orders, but winked at violations and avoided bothering Louis's overdeveloped conscience by informing him of any except those of which they knew the French embassy or Napoleon's spies were already aware.

Louis's personal opposition involved delaying issuance of royal decrees to implement imperial decrees, taking advantage of any apparent legal loopholes, and giving as liberal an interpretation as possible to all regulations. These tactics thoroughly antagonized Napoleon, who always saw through them eventually. Both the Berlin and Milan Decrees[10] were a month old before Louis implemented them. The emperor sent angry reprimands. Louis's decree for enforcement of the Berlin Decree ignored East Frisia, which was not formally made part of Holland until November 1807, but was occupied by Dutch troops. That the king was on legally solid ground made Napoleon all the more furious. He allowed ships to enter ports with cargoes from "Java" (Batavia, the only important Dutch colony not seized by the British), knowing full well that Java was under blockade. Napoleon responded with orders for the seizure of specific contraband. After the Milan Decree, American and Swedish ships which could have been confiscated were simply told to leave Dutch ports. Even British ships which put into Holland's harbors to escape storms were allowed to sail off free until Napoleon personally and profanely told Louis to begin confiscating them. (French officials had begun seizing such vessels six months before.)

From the first, the emperor deemed Louis defeatist about enforcing the *blocus*. He was right. The task, proclaimed Louis, was like trying to "keep the skin from sweating." The emperor expected him to put under surveillance not only ports but every cove, beach, and sea dike. Impossible! But Paris brooked no excuses. "At the least contraband, at the smallest barque, [Napoleon] . . . cried scandal! treason!" Louis responded promptly to every

10. The Berlin Decree (November 1806) forbade trade in and ordered confiscation of all British goods found on the continent and barred from the continent British ships or any ships coming from or calling at British or British colonial ports. The Milan Decree (December 1807) "denationalized" and made subject to confiscation any vessel which had called at a British port, paid duty, or submitted to search according to British Orders in Council.

complaint or accusation from Paris—when pushed, he moved—
but never made innovations of his own. For example, during 1807
Napoleon repeatedly flung evidence at the king that Dutch fishing
vessels were picking up passengers, mail, and contraband in the
Channel. Each accusation brought half-measures, until finally in
January 1808 Louis ordered a Dutch officer to sail on every boat
and make a report on his return. Sufficient officers were not available, and those assigned too often shared the fishermen's sport
and profits, but the king was "covered"—he had given the appro-
priate order. More complaints on the same score brought more
orders, though often not in the spirit of the original ones. In July
1808 Louis instructed Gogel that if fishing boats returned with
passengers aboard—they were to be refused permission to land!
(In France the captain would have gone to prison and lost his
vessel.) The king responded in similar fashion to a multitude of
other problems.

Not surprisingly, Napoleon lost patience. In September 1808
he closed the entire continent to all colonial goods (even Dutch)
emanating from Holland. Only after Louis ordered all Dutch
ports closed until March 31, 1809, and promised to reorganize
his enforcement system completely was the imperial ban lifted.
When the ports reopened, a director general of tariffs, Van
Meeuwen, had been placed in charge of enforcing the blockade.
In May 1809 the king sent Gogel into retirement (with the odd justification that his sternness was damaging public morale) and made
Appilius minister of finance.[11]

Van Meeuwen's authority was undivided, and he was responsible only to the king. He was provided with regulations which
narrowed legal imports to thirty-two items, exports to fifty-two.
In all cases goods had to be proved of non-British origin and ships
identified as friendly, neutral, and guiltless of compliance with
British regulations. Even then they were allowed to enter only
specified ports. Goods coming overland had to be certified "sani-
tary" at the borders. In the latter case, however, French agents,
especially in the Hanseatic cities, had unofficial authorization to
allow certain badly needed English goods (cotton, wool, leather,

11. Verheyen replaced Appilius as secretary of the council of state.

oils, and the like) to enter. Dutch merchants made profits on transshipment, but Louis often found himself blamed for introducing the products onto the continent, a charge he bitterly refuted, with ample evidence—which Napoleon ignored.

It was too late for Louis to save himself. Once the Austrians were defeated at Wagram, Napoleon began systematically to build a justification for destroying the kingdom of Holland. The king had gradually moved, under constant pressure from his brother, to a harder, more determined position regarding upholding the Continental System. At the same time the emperor had been forced by shortages and economic distress in France to the decision that the blockade had to be loosened. (In 1810, after Louis's fall, licenses would be granted for trading in colonial products.) But this change of posture would not save Holland. Napoleon no longer trusted Louis to carry out imperial policy, whatever it became.

FINANCIAL AND ECONOMIC REFORMS

"Pitiful ideas . . . feeble sentiments . . . the small economies of an Amsterdam shopkeeper," wrote Napoleon of Louis's financial activity during 1806. He never changed his opinion. The king refused to touch interest payments on the debt, make major tax reforms, or strike down all the feudal strictures on the economy. To Napoleon's intense irritation, Louis seemed continually occupied with saving a few florins by trimming his civil service payroll or otherwise reducing his modest domestic budget (average about 13,000,000 florins), or devising some new scheme to fund the debt (each of which was then worked over earnestly by the legislature, but came to nothing, since no money was ever available for the purpose). The king announced in 1808 that the domestic budget was about 2,239,000 florins less than in 1807, and in 1809 that he had saved about 1,900,000 over 1808. Even if we ignore that borrowed money was not counted (for instance, 6,000,000 for dikes and waterways in 1809), the savings seem paltry when we note that interest payments rose over 7,000,000 in 1808 and almost 6,000,000 in 1809.

Tax reforms were proposed to the legislature by Gogel in

1806 and went into effect in 1807. The basic land tax (set at twenty-five percent of income from land, after cost) was made uniformly applicable to all owners. Great landholders, who had formerly evaded the levy, or shifted it to their renters, now had to pay. The burden of small landowners, whose margin of profit was less, was somewhat eased. Renters and sharecroppers paid no land tax, though their rents or shares were not controlled, so that eventually most shared their proprietors' burden indirectly. A "personal" tax, based on income from all sources (ten percent) fell on property owners and users, city and country alike. Businessmen in the cities were subject to a greater number of indirect levies; nevertheless the "reformed" system favored the merchants —the Netherlands' traditional oligarchy. The satisfaction of the ruling class with Louis was reflected in stock exchange quotations, which actually rose three and one-half points in 1806.

This reform had sufficient results to keep the states' revenues above 50,000,000 florins, but, as we know, produced nowhere near enough to balance the budget. Despite this fact no other significant tax increases, much less reforms, were made until early 1810, when taxes on real estate, dwellings, domestics, and farm animals were raised one-tenth, and a number of excise taxes (including those on gin, brandy, wine, and meat) were upped. These increases came, however, only after Napoleon threatened in unmistakable terms to annex Holland to France, and were inadequate to ease the government's fiscal distress. In 1808 the state had been forced to pay part of its salaries and pensions in bonds. In 1809 it met part of its obligations in "receipts," good for the taxes of 1810, which were in effect paper money.

Louis's attack on feudal privilege was halting and apologetic. In 1806 he allowed Gogel to cut milling rights (a feudal due) by one-half. But the tax schedule issued in 1810 raised them again by one-eighth. He appointed committees to suggest action against the guilds, but the members were city fathers and usually masters themselves. The guilds were mildly reformed, but far from destroyed, as Napoleon desired. Louis had reigned a year before hunting rights were eliminated. It was 1809 before communal property was ordered divided, and even then action was to be taken under a complicated law, devised by the legislature, which promised years of hearings and adjudication and compensation to former lords. It was November 1808 before a civil code, a watered-down version of the *Code Napoléon,* was even presented to the legislature, 1809 before it was instituted.

Louis, throughout, remained so fearful for his popularity that he shrank from instituting radical fiscal reforms or even the rigorous administration of the system in effect. He begged Gogel to consider the public morale and to remember that taxation was altogether but a matter of "arithmetic." He gave agonizingly apologetic justifications to the legislature for every financial measure. He seemed unaware that his one major reform (the land tax) was directed toward the landowners and peasants, not the persons who had the greatest wealth, the merchants and bankers who controlled the legislature and lent him money he could have taken by taxation. In 1809 Gogel began to speak of reforms and more rigorous collection as the alternative to bankruptcy or annexation by France. Louis dismissed the dour financier in favor of a more pleasant fellow, Appilius. The new minister was seconded by Robert Voule, director of the public treasury, a clever manipulator of records but as softheaded as the king.

Louis refused to face the fact that his survival as king depended on effective service to Napoleon, which meant pursuing ruthless short-term policies. He banked his hopes on the coming of peace and a resumption of trade or on some change of heart on Napoleon's part which would allow commercial activity to expand. At the same time he worked for a long-term readjustment of the economy to give a greater place to agriculture and industry and make Holland less dependent on trade. He tried to ease the tax burden on small farmers, put new areas into cultivation, and began projects for the desiccation of marshes and lakes, including the Lake of Haarlem. He forbade the mining of deep peat deposits, since the excavations left behind became lakes or marshes, whereas after shallow mining the land could still be cultivated. During his tours of the country, Louis made sure to visit the few industrial plants, admire their products, and compliment managers and workers. He pressed Amsterdam businessmen to invest in industry. His government sponsored industrial fairs and provided prizes of a thousand florins for outstanding products and new inventions and designs. In addition gold and silver medals in profusion were awarded producers, designers, and inventors. Louis's Institute of Sciences and Arts made special efforts to encourage practical science (technology). But the reign was short. Agriculture improved hardly at all; industry remained static. Scattered plants made cloth, clothing, hats, glassware; there were some iron foundries and tanneries; beer and gin were produced. But no new major industries appeared, and some of the old ones failed for lack of raw materials. Dutch industry, geared largely to local markets, did not benefit from the protection afforded by the Continental System. It could not compete even within a closed European system as did that of the Belgian provinces, already annexed to France. Both Louis's financial and economic reforms must be set down as failures, though the concept of introducing a better balance into the economy was forward-looking and intelligent.

Internal Affairs

GOVERNMENT AND ADMINISTRATION

The treaty of May 1806 guaranteed independence to Holland, but not to her king, whose arms were to be "the ancient arms of Holland, quartered with the Imperial Eagle of France, and surmounted by the Royal Crown." Louis remained prince and constable of the empire; he and his family were subject to the law of the imperial family. Holland's status as a puppet state was clear, her independence technical, even if Napoleon honored the treaty, which ultimately he did not. Holland was also to remain intact, in possession of her colonies,[12] and to have "most-favored-nation" status in trading with France. A new, favorable, commercial treaty was to be *"incessamment conclu,"* which translates as "immediately concluded," though in retrospect "incessantly concluded" seems to have been what Napoleon really meant—continually rewritten to

12. Though few remained. See below pp. 164–5.

suit the needs of the empire. Political, civil, and religious liberty was guaranteed Dutch citizens.

The constitution granted by Napoleon (June 1806) repeated all the guarantees of the treaty, and promised further that the public debt would be honored, and that Dutch would be the official language. It gave the king "exclusively and without restriction the entire exercise of the government," but entrusted lawmaking to a *corps legislatif.* The legislature was "normally" to meet twice a year, but clearly, if the king ruled conditions were abnormal, he could order as many sessions as he liked—or none at all. It was to comprise initially the nineteen "High Mightinesses" of the former legislature, plus nineteen new men chosen by the king from a list of nominees presented by them—thirty-eight members in all.[13] The term was five years, but each November beginning in 1807 the oldest seven members were to be replaced by new royal appointees (unless reappointed) selected from among the nominees of the younger members who retained their seats. Therefore, barring great hostility to the king among those making nominations, his power would grow yearly in the legislature.

The constitution called for four ministers—finance, foreign affairs, interior, and war-marine (combined). Two incumbent ministers, Gogel (finance) and Van der Goes (foreign affairs) were reappointed. Mollerus, experienced, learned, and fluent in French, was recommended to Louis (he says) by "public opinion," and received the portfolio of interior; General Bonhomme, at Napoleon's insistence, became minister of war. There remained, however, incumbent ministers willing to serve. Rather than give offense, the king reappointed the ministers of marine and colonies, Admiral Verhuel and Van der Hem. Then, because he had (vague) plans for a heavy program of public works and welfare under interior, and because Mollerus was a "spiritual" fellow, he created a ministry of justice and police for Van Hof. Finally Roëll, who had, like Mollerus, been recommended by "public opinion," and had quickly become the king's confidant and interpreter, was

---

13. Provinces were to have representatives roughly in proportion to their populations, as follows: Holland, 17; Gelderland, 4; Brabant, 4; West Frisia, 3; Zeeland, 2; Groningen, 2; Utrecht, 2; Drenthe, 1; Overijssel, 3. If the kingdom expanded, more members were to be added.

given the title minister secretary of state, i.e., coordinator and keeper of ministerial records. Thus Louis began with eight ministers instead of four.[14]

Gently, diplomatically, the king made changes. When Napoleon asked for Verhuel as Dutch ambassador to Paris, Louis gave Van der Hem both marine and colonies. In war, responding to blistering criticism from Napoleon, he relieved Hogendorp, then Janssens, but the former became minister to Austria and the latter secretary of the council of state. Mollerus proved an uninspired minister of the interior—so Louis created a new ministry of ecclesiastical affairs for him. Twent Van Raaphorst was given interior, but concentrated single-mindedly on his specialty, dikes and waterways—so he was made minister of *watterstadt*, and in-

14. *Ministers 1806–1810:*

Finance	Gogel	1806–1809
	Appilius	1809–1810
War	Bonhomme	1806
	Hogendorp	1806–1808
	Janssens	1808–1809
	Cambier (Provisional)	1809
	Krayenhoff	1809–1810
Marine	Verhuel	1806–1807
	Van der Hem	1807–1810
Interior	Gogel (Provisional)	1806
	Mollerus	1806–1808
	Van Leyden van Westbarendrecht	1808
	Twent Van Raaphorst	1808–1809
	Van der Capellan	1809–1810
Foreign Affairs	Van der Goes	1806–1808
	Roëll	1808–1810
	Mollerus (acting in Roëll's absence Nov. 1809–Jan. 1810)	
Justice and Police	Van Hof	1806–1807
	Cambier (interim)	1807–1808
	Van Maanen	1808–1809
	Hugenpoth	1809–1810
Colonies	Van der Hem	1806–1807
	(under Minister of Marine 1807 ff.)	
Ecclesiastical Affairs (created 1808)	Mollerus	1808–1810
Watterstadt (created 1809)	Twent Van Raaphorst	1809–1810
Minister Secretary of State (eliminated 1808)	Roëll	1806–1808

terior went to Van der Capellan. The aging Van der Goes retired in 1808; Roëll took over foreign affiairs; no new minister secretary was appointed. Van Hof, Cambier, and Van Maanen were successively shifted from justice and police to the council of state. "Minister," for Louis, was an indefinite term which in his *Documents* he applies freely to men whom he desires to give status, including former ministers retired to the council of state, the president of the heraldic college (which authenticated titles and arms), the chief justice of the tax court, and others. His references reveal that, for all his talk of centralized, efficient government, his concept of the administrative hierarchy was vague indeed.

Louis's reorganizing, soft and slow as it was, did gradually improve the direction of most ministries, however. Finance was an exception, as we have noted—Appilius did not approach Gogel in ability. But Twent in *watterstadt* and Van der Capellan in interior were exceptionally competent. Krayenhoff, Van der Hem, and Hugenpoth (war, marine, police) erred largely through patriotism. Mollerus was made to maintain a paternal surveillance over the churches, the disaffection of any of which, particularly the dominant Protestant congregations, could have given the Catholic king much trouble. Roëll, a patriot, but one who trimmed his sails easily to winds from Paris, was, under the circumstances, a good foreign minister. He was young and ruggedly handsome, graceful and at ease in the society of Amsterdam or Paris, and fluent in French. His charm and persuasiveness undoubtedly postponed the destruction of the kingdom.

The king had succeeded best, however, in reordering the ministries charged with domestic projects closest to his own heart (interior, *watterstadt*). The ministries in which Napoleon took greatest interest remained, from the imperial viewpoint, ineffective (finance) or uncooperative and inefficient (war, marine, police).

The evolution of the council of state was similar to that of the ministry. Louis's initial appointees were carryovers from Schimmelpenninck's council—Willem Six, Van de Kasteele, Vichers, Jan Goldberg, Devoss Van Steenwyck, Jacobson, and others—bankers, merchants, and part-time public servants. Mostly ex-ministers were added. The few others tended to be more sympathetic to the masses than the original appointees, but to vote with them on financial matters, under the assumption, apparently, that one could not help the poor by damaging credit or depriving the rich of investment capital by taxation. Robert Voule, the efficient but softhearted director general of the treasury, was typical.

Louis took his constitution very seriously, especially as to the role of the legislature. It met twice in 1806, three times in 1807, twice in 1808, three times in 1809, and was left in session during Louis's fateful trip to Paris, which we shall discuss shortly. As each meeting lasted two to four months, it was almost perpetually sitting. Napoleon expressed astonishment at this. "Does Your Majesty not govern with his Senate?" countered Louis. The king's health was affected by almost anything—family squabbles, war, travel, prolonged work, unpleasant social affairs, angry letters from the emperor, an inadvertent personal slight by a minister—but he bore up frighteningly under speechmaking. Reporting to the legislature was a task he would delegate to no one. At each session he held forth at length, driving to exhausted slumber some of the sour, harassed businessmen who sat before him. He reported on past legislation, proposed legislation, the work of committees and of the council of state, finances, the dikes, national health, war— anything and everything—mixing facts and figures supplied by his ministers with personal observations and elevated sentiments. He emerged exhilarated, his mind teeming with afterthoughts, which he wrote down and sent back to be read to the hapless parliamentarians. Except for implementing imperial decrees, Louis left anything that smacked of lawmaking to the legislature. In 1809, after a powder barge exploded, wrecking the center of Leyden, he issued regulations requiring munitions carriers to fly flags and move through cities without stopping. But when the legislature next met, he asked that his decrees be legalized. The lawmakers acted slowly, with much debate and committee work. Reform bills generally reflected compromises between the king's proposals and Dutch tradition. The less radical his proposals, the more quickly they were accepted. For example, his plan of administrative reorganization got quick approval since it involved only making the old provinces into departments (except Holland, which was divided into two).[15]

But two and a half years were required to pass a much-amended version of the *Code Napoléon*. A revised criminal code was not approved until March 1809 and not put into effect until February 1810. It was March 1809 before uniform weights and measures were established.[16] Louis angered Napoleon by recognizing old titles of nobility, but waited until March 1809 for a law allowing him to designate new "constitutional" nobles. The legislature spent most of every session struggling with financial problems. Since, however, it staunchly held interest on the debt inviolable, and refused to raise taxes on merchant-banking interests, no solution it proposed was very helpful. It did, however, approve with dispatch the loans which kept the government operating.

One thing can be said for Holland: Alone among the satellite kingdoms, it had an active legislature which participated in the government—possibly overparticipated. When the king was in his capital, it was almost invariably in session. It was very far from being a popular representative body, but was appointive and in some degree self-perpetuating. Still Louis was the only satellite ruler who allowed his parliamentary body its full constitutional role; this was one of the reasons for his downfall. Napoleon believed in legislatures, but not if they interfered with "progress."

From the beginning Louis disliked having his capital at The Hague. It was small and a center of nothing but government. A commercial country, Louis argued, required a commercial city for a capital; a constitutional nation, a center of population. Of course the Dutch had chosen The Hague originally because it had neither —so that no group of merchants would be favored and The Estates could deliberate without danger from city mobs. But the king was determined to move, and in October 1807, at the invitation of the city fathers, moved with his government to Utrecht, where he took up residence in the Grott Paushuizen, built in 1517 for Pope Adrian VI. Louis did not like the palace, which was drafty and

15. See p. 157.
16. The French metric system, but with Dutch names for units, for example, *kop* for *litre*.

uncomfortable, and still felt isolated. He began to bid for an invitation from Amsterdam, and it shortly came. In April 1808 he entered his new capital in the midst of a military parade, while thousands cheered. Finally he was satisfied. His ministers and legislators were not very happy—transferring their offices and staffs twice within six months disrupted their work and cost money —but they dutifully followed. The efficiency of the government meanwhile had reached low ebb for the reign.

By a law of March 1807 the provinces of Groningen, West Frisia, Overijssel, Gelderland, Utrecht, Zeeland, Brabant, and Drenthe became departments;[17] Holland was divided into two departments, Amstelland and Maasland. East Frisia was added in November 1807. (See Map 5, p. 158.) The departments of Holland were by far the most populous and richest, containing together over half the population (total 2,000,000) and paying three-fifths of the kingdom's taxes. Amsterdam, capital city of both the kingdom and the Department of Amstelland, was the largest city, with a population of 200,000.[18] Under the law, the king appointed a *landrost* to head the administration of each department.[19] The *landrost* in turn selected a council to advise him from a list of nominees drawn up by the leading citizens. Departments were divided into quarters, each under a *drost*. The municipal councils of cities of over 5,000 inhabitants selected a *burgemeester* (approved by the *landrost*) and councilors (*wethouders*) to assist him. No system was imposed for the selection of a muncipal council (*vroedschap*), which comprised "the notables of the city." Towns of under 5,000 retained their traditional governments, whatever they were. Thus some villages remained under seignorial rule, but, said Louis, all feudal rights could not be eliminated without "much preparation, management, and a long examination period."

17. Eight departments had existed under the Batavian Republic: the old provinces with Drenthe included in Overijssel. East Frisia was ceded to Holland in return for Flushing, which was annexed to France. See p. 141.

18. Utrecht and Leyden (34,000 and 28,000) were second and third largest.

19. The law specifically authorized Louis to appoint *landrosts* who were not natives of their departments (though they had to be Dutch). He was delighted with this "victory over provincialism" in the legislature, but decided to postpone using the power until the people were more receptive. He appointed a native *landrost* for each department.

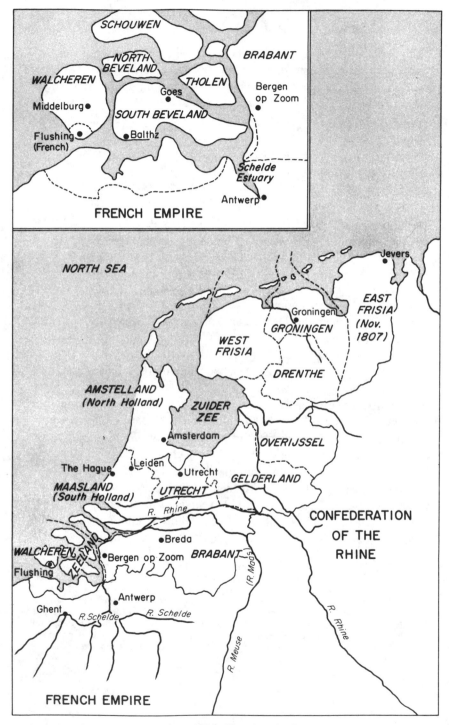

INSET:

SCHOUWEN

NORTH BEVELAND

BRABANT

WALCHEREN

THOLEN

Middelburg

Goes

Bergen op Zoom

Flushing (French)

SOUTH BEVELAND

•Balthz

Schelde Estuary

Antwerp

FRENCH EMPIRE

MAIN MAP:

NORTH SEA

Jevers

Groningen

EAST FRISIA (Nov. 1807)

WEST FRISIA

GRONINGEN

AMSTELLAND (North Holland)

DRENTHE

ZUIDER ZEE

Amsterdam

OVERIJSSEL

The Hague

Leiden

Utrecht

GELDERLAND

MAASLAND (South Holland)

UTRECHT

R. Rhine

CONFEDERATION OF THE RHINE

WALCHEREN

ZEELAND

•Breda

BRABANT

Flushing

•Bergen op Zoom

(R. Maas)

Ghent

•Antwerp

R. Schelde

R. Schelde

R. Rhine

R. Meuse

FRENCH EMPIRE

Map 5. Holland in 1809, Showing the Departments
Inset: Zeeland, Showing Walcheren

In November 1807 the king reported to the legislature that the system was fully installed. A certain symmetry and uniformity had been introduced into the administration at the higher levels. But as most Dutch towns housed fewer than 5,000 souls, traditional diversity characterized the governments closest to the people. Centralization was more apparent than real.

THE LAW AND THE COURTS

In 1806 Louis appointed the jurists Van Gennep, Scholten, and Loke to translate the *Code Napoléon* and adapt it for use in Holland. Almost two years later their code was finally presented to the legislature, after hearings, discussions with university experts and the heads of major religious bodies, parliamentary debates over parts of it (prompted by the king, who *had* to give status reports at intervals), and wrangling over the wording of the translation. It was passed in the spring of 1809, and became the law of the land. Napoleon was not pleased. Too much Dutch law had been incorporated; civil marriage and divorce were side-stepped; no provision was made for division of inherited property among heirs. But at least Holland had a uniform law and the key concepts— civil liberty and equality—were expressed. He let it stand.

Holland was much more in need of a uniform criminal and penal code, on which another royal committee was still at work.[20] Its proposals, presented to the legislature a month earlier than the civil code, had not passed, which alarmed Louis, for even he was appalled at the variety of laws in force. For example, adultery in some areas was punishable by death, in others by small fines. The king became more than usually insistent on action, and during 1809, amid torrents of rhetoric, the legislature settled the remaining points of difference and presented criminal and penal codes for his signature—but the codes to be effective in 1810. Before his departure, however, Louis saw the new laws being enforced.

The king's plea for a reformed judiciary, however, died in committee. Throughout his reign Holland retained the court system and most of the judges of the Batavian Republic. Louis tried to improve the administration of justice, however, by associating

20. Reuvens, Elout, and Musschenbrock.

himself closely with the high court, which heard final appeals. Under the constitution, granting "grace" (pardon, remission, or mitigation of sentence) was his prerogative, and he used it liberally. Moreover, he induced the legislature to pass a law requiring that the nine justices must vote unanimously to impose the death penalty, and then submit each case to him. "A mania of humanity," wrote Napoleon, and accused him of completely eliminating the death sentence. Not so, replied Louis, but almost no persons were executed whose cases reached the high court.

When Louis abdicated, codes of general procedure and commerce were still under study by committees.[21] Much remained to be done, but he had at least introduced civil and criminal codes, which, if not perfect, were in use throughout Holland. The Batavian Republic, before him, had in eleven years done virtually nothing but appoint committee after committee to study legal reform.

RELIGION

He tried to be, said Louis, a Catholic among Protestants and a Protestant among Catholics, by which he meant that he defended the rights of all religious minorities. He encouraged any sect under oppression to appeal to him directly and tried to give equal opportunities to all—for schooling and places in the government and military. There was little problem in guaranteeing the right granted in the constitution—of worship for all faiths within their own "temples"—so much had long been traditional. The king's problem was oppression by those in the religious majority, which varied with the locality. Where oppression amounted only to discrimination, he could do little but set a good example. But where it was more overt he could and did take quick action. In cases where Catholics, Jews, or minority Protestants were being forced to contribute to the Reformed Church (that of the majority in most areas) he ordered them exempted from levies. In rare cases where Catholic majorities existed (in some small villages), he forbade the exploitation of Protestants. He prohibited the widespread prac-

21. Under Farjon and Van Gennep, respectively.

tice of diverting city tax money to the dominant local church."
The Jews, whom he considered the most persecuted minority, got
special attention. He visited their communities on his tours, responded quickly to their complaints, and allocated civil and military offices to them.

Napoleon complained that Louis protected everyone better
than his own coreligionists, the Catholics. But Dutch Catholics
found little cause to complain, nor did any other group. The
king's stand on religion was generally approved, and his measures
effective. The minorities saw him as a protector; the Protestant
majority considered him fair and reasonable.

EDUCATION, PUBLIC HEALTH, AND PUBLIC WORKS

Louis dreamed of a centralized and improved educational system, but was compelled to defer any sweeping program to institute
one. In 1807 he appointed a director general of sciences and arts
who was also to supervise public instruction and the universities.
But the director, Hultman, a former secretary of state, had very
limited funds and insufficient personnel to inspect adequately,
much less reform, the schools. The universities at Leyden, Utrecht,
Groningen, Harderwijk, Franeker, and Amsterdam remained
largely independent, as was their desire. Improvements in other
schools were made on a hit-or-miss basis, generally as the result
of some suggestion, order, or gift of the king made during one of
his tours. Where he thought benefit could be derived, Louis sent
professional students to France—officers and prospective officers
of the army and navy, students of science and technology, medicine, and even veterinary medicine.

The duties of the director general of the sciences and arts
included overseeing museums; writing annual reports on the
status of the sciences, art, and education; and nominating artists,
scientists, and technologists for annual prizes. His primary responsibility was to administer the General Institute of Sciences
and Arts, which comprised four institutions: the Royal Society of

22. Voluntary contributions would not support parish churches, however. To
reduce their expenses Louis secured a law (1808) making clergy of all denominations state employees. But the legislature had made payment of salaries dependent
on funds being available, which they never were. The unfulfilled promise gave
congregations justification to continue, under various guises, to tap local revenues.

Sciences, the Royal Dutch Society, the Royal Society of History and Antiquity, and the Royal Society of Fine Arts. The Society of Sciences was heavily populated with naval officers, but included also men like the hydraulic engineers Jansz and Brunings, the physicist Van Swiden, and the astronomers Calkoen and Hennert. The Royal Dutch Society comprised Holland's literary elite, including Meerman, De Bosch, Bilderdijk, and Weyland. In the Society of History and Antiquity were enrolled such eminent scholars as Van Vyn, Valckenaer, and Wittembach; in the Society of Fine Arts, Thiebaut, Cobelt, and Van de Hart. Among those awarded prizes of the Academy of Fine Arts were the painters Alberti, Klein, and Teerling and the engraver Forssel.

At the king's urging the public library of Amsterdam was much enlarged. A number of monuments were erected, including one at Saardam to Peter the Great (a visitor loud in his praise of the Dutch and what they taught him) and one at Haarlem to Laurens Coster, according to some scholars the inventor of the printing press.[23]

Louis found public health matters in the hands of provincial councils whose efforts were coordinated only on a voluntary basis. There was pitifully little circulation of new medical information. Inordinately interested in medical matters because of his own precarious health, the king found this situation alarming, and in the early weeks of his reign laid plans to remedy it. Unfortunately he could not infect the legislature with a sense of urgency. It responded to his appeal for a centralized public health administration by placing the provincial councils under the surveillance of the minister of the interior. But this was some improvement. If the councils remained all but independent, there was at least a means for the uniform dissemination of medical information. And Louis, on his tours, never missed a hospital, orphanage, workhouse, or home for the aged. The royal indignation was easily aroused in these matters, and produced results, often because the king's attitude gave the local clergy the courage to fight for better conditions. For the population in general, Louis continually preached the value of smallpox vaccination, taking pains to test

23. Though Gutenberg is generally given the laurels.

the attitude of local clergy toward it, soliciting their help, and trying to win over those who feared inoculation was a sinful attempt
to thwart God's will. He campaigned also against antiquated customs which injured the health of mothers and children, and for
balanced diets and more medical attention for the young.

Louis's most grandiose plan was for a national medical college
to collect and disseminate medical knowledge. The college, he
hoped, would establish communication with physicians the world
over. It would take the initiative in organizing a Europe-wide, and
eventually world-wide, program to eliminate venereal disease,
tuberculosis, cholera, and other widespread maladies. His medical
college remained a dream, as did a really comprehensive public
health program, but his people remembered his deep concern for
their welfare.

A more dramatically evident menace than disease were the
floods, which annually broke dikes, inundated villages, destroyed
property, and took lives. Louis found the *watterstadt* merely supervised the activity of a national commission, which in turn coordinated the work of provincial governments. He gradually
induced the legislature to give more power to the director of
watterstadt (Twent Van Raaphorst) and in 1809 made him a
minister. Louis's public works program concerned primarily dikes,
waterways, and the draining of lakes and marshes to provide more
arable land. Twent was the key planner and administrator, though
credit must be given to previous governments for initiating some
of the projects he saw to completion, for example, the canal of
Katwijk begun in 1804 and finished in 1807.

During Louis's reign the dikes protecting Amsterdam were
raised, and many others improved. Communication between
Haarlem and Amsterdam was improved by new canals and locks.
A new canal was completed in South Holland, and two in Overijssel. Some 8,000 acres in the Amsterdam area were drained, and
smaller areas elsewhere. Louis had plans for recovering 50,000
acres by emptying the Lake of Haarlem, which was done in the
period 1840–1853.

It troubled the king greatly that winter after winter the floods
defeated the Dutch (in greater or lesser degeree) despite their
industry and valor. Considering a long-term solution, he was

much taken by a bold scheme advanced by the hydraulic engineers Brunings and Jansz (and earlier by Brunings's father). They proposed deliberately to open certain dikes on the Meuse and Waal, maintaining control of the rate of flow of the water, and to direct the flood overland to the sea. With suitable sluices and embankments, only selected areas, from which the population and vulnerable structures had been shifted, would be inundated. Nature could be defeated by surrendering to the waters in some areas, which would ease the pressure on the dikes elsewhere. Further, the controlled floods would leave behind alluvium, which would improve the fertility of the soil.

The scheme was shocking to the Dutch, accustomed to all-out war against the waters. Louis intended to implement it nevertheless, and had his government survived, would have. It is significant that he recognized and supported a plan which, when finally put into practice later in the century, greatly reduced the incidence of winter disasters in the areas involved.

Tribute must be paid to the Dutch experts who advised him, and the king's work and plans recognized as part of a continuing campaign against nature by Dutch engineers under all governments. Still, Louis's grasp of the problems involved and instinct for constructive solutions are impressive. In public works generally his work had long-range effects. For so short a reign, during a period of war and extreme economic stress, his concrete accomplishments were extraordinary.

COLONIES

Before Louis's accession the British captured Ceylon, Coromandel and Cochin (in India), the colony on the Cape of Good Hope, Surinam (Dutch Guiana), and Dutch establishments on the Guinea Coast. In 1807 they took Curaçao, in the West Indies. This left Dutch Java (Batavia), Amboina and Ternate in the Moluccas, one small island in the Celebes, and Borneo. Since the surveillance of the British navy over the East Indies was desultory, Louis was able to establish contact with his possessions. In 1807 he sent General Daendels to govern Java, the only really important one. Daendel's administration was so brutal that even Napoleon raised objections, but he defended the colony successfully against

the British, made it self-supporting, and delivered occasional cargoes of sugar, coffee, cocoa, and rubber to the homeland. The
British seized Amboina in 1810, but not until after Louis's abdication did they take Java (1811). The other colonies, ignored by
the British from choice and neglected of necessity by the Dutch,
remained in the primitive backwash of world affairs until 1814,
when the Dutch reestablished connection.

ARMY AND NAVY

"Prodigious" was the word Louis used over and over to
describe his efforts to produce the military establishment Napoleon
required. But he never did, and from his brother's viewpoint was
only "prodigious" in the volumes of complaints he wrote. Asked
for 40,000 troops in 1806, he mustered only 20,000, of whom
10,000 participated in the Prussian Campaign. In mid-1807 he
protested that he was supporting 50,000 troops, but actually had
about 30,000. This number remained constant in 1808. In 1809
Napoleon asked that he bring his army to 35,000. Louis raised
31,000, of whom only 20,000 were maneuverable.

Louis rejected conscription; the closest he got was requiring
male orphans to enter the army at age eighteen for enlistments
varying with the length of time the state had supported them.[24]
While he filled his regiments largely with foreign mercenaries, he
tried to encourage Dutchmen to volunteer by increasing pay and
bonuses, encouraging the promotion of competent enlisted men
into the officer ranks, advertising rapid advancement of talented
men, and staging parades and reviews and presenting medals to
bring the army to public notice. Foreign regiments, for instance,
those of Saxe-Gotha and Waldeck, had their names changed.

For all his efforts the Dutch army retained the pattern it had
assumed under the republic. Dutch officers usually chose to serve
in the engineers or artillery, which got most of the Dutch enlisted
men. Germans predominated in the cavalry and infantry. The
Royal Guard maintained the pattern in the ranks, although the
officers were, with few exceptions, Dutch or French. A royal mili-

24. There was rioting in Amsterdam when the first orphans were assembled
(1809), which distressed Louis greatly. He went to great pains to inform the
public that the policy was a substitute for conscription and that the orphans
would have better opportunities in the army than elsewhere.

tary school, established at The Hague, enrolled some cadets from the leading families, but most preferred the navy, which had more prestige. Louis kept hoping, however, to build an army which the Dutch could accept as representing them, not merely fighting for their pay. He was ready to accept small beginnings. ". . . The Army is composed almost entirely of foreigners," he wrote the minister of war in 1807, "[but] we must try to *treat* them as nationals." The only distinctly native troops at the king's call were those of the "Burgher Guard" (national guard). Organized under local auspices by the republic, untrained, variously equipped, armed, and uniformed, they were of little real value. Louis's efforts to reorganize them were thwarted by the legislature, which never gave him a clear-cut mandate to do so.

The Dutch had never maintained a large standing army. Since their decline as a colonial power, they had allowed their navy to shrink also, but had not destroyed its officer corps, *élan,* or tradition as a national, nonmercenary service. At Louis's accession the Dutch had a fine, efficient little fleet of fourteen armed vessels stationed at Den Helder, Amsterdam, Rotterdam, and Texel. Six frigates and a number of lighter ships were under construction. While there was a dearth of effective army commanders, the Dutch had a number of admirals of high merit including Verhuel, De Winter, Hartzinck, Kikkert, Bloys Van Treslong, and Lemmers. In view of Napoleon's demand for troops, however, the king asked that the navy be reduced to save money for expanding the army. The emperor refused, but Louis deemphasized the navy anyway, as is evident from his use of Verhuel as ambassador to Paris and Bloys Van Treslong as an aide-de-camp. He also curtailed building ships of the line in favor of gunboats, a signal that the navy was being converted gradually to a coast guard, with the primary mission of enforcing the continental blockade. Only one frigate was completed during his reign. The navy did harass the British during the invasion of Walcheren (1809), but could do little more.

The troops Louis supplied Napoleon served well. Dutch regiments in Spain (3,000 men total) were cited in imperial bulletins of 1808 and 1809. In 1809 (as we shall see in the next chapter) Gratien's division captured Stralsund, held by the Prussian renegade-hero Von Schill, who was killed in the fighting. Dutch artillery units, dispersed in the Grande Armée, proved themselves against the Austrians in 1809, and the Russians in 1812.

Louis's army, however, was always much below the strength Napoleon specified. Therefore when he supplied troops for imperial service, Holland was left almost defenseless. In 1809 the requirement was 35,000; Louis claimed to have this number, and actually had 31,000 on the rolls, counting 12,000 in Germany and 3,000 in Spain. But, when the British invaded Walcheren, Louis could only produce 3,000 royal guards and 6,000 other troops, of whom some 2,000 were untrained recruits or in hospital. Napoleon had repeatedly said that Holland did not deserve independence if she could not defend herself. He chose to view the Walcheren affair as a test.

The Invasion of Walcheren

The British, under the command of Lord Chatham,[25] arrived in the estuary of the Schelde on July 29, 1809. Seventy-four warships, 56 transports, and over 500 other vessels carried 40,000 British troops, 6,000 horses, a mass of artillery, and tons of supplies. The expedition's original objectives had been two: to trap and destroy the French fleet in the Schelde, and to create a diversion to take pressure off Britain's Austrian allies. News of the Battle of Wagram, and the armistice signed by Austria, had reached England on July 25. But the expedition, after three months of preparation, had been at the point of sailing, Austria had not yet made peace, French ships could still be sunk, and a foothold in the lowlands would make possible trade with the Dutch, at least temporarily. Chatham had ordered the expedition launched.

News of the landing found Louis taking the waters at Aix-la-Chapelle, but he departed without delay, and on August 2 was in Amsterdam; on August 3 he left for Antwerp with his guard. Meanwhile the British had occupied Walcheren, except for Flushing, defended by the French General Monnet.[26] General Cham-

25. Sir John Pitt (1756–1835), eldest son of William Pitt (1708–1778), 1st earl of Chatham, brother of William Pitt "The Younger" (1759–1806), England's great prime minister.
26. Flushing and environs was French, and the rest of Walcheren Dutch. Antwerp was French. See Map 5, p. 158.

berlhac, commanding French forces in Belgium, had rushed available troops to Antwerp, and the French fleet had withdrawn to Antwerp also, after throwing a boom across the Schelde and deploying a line of ships behind it. At Antwerp Louis assumed command of all French and Dutch forces. He ordered his Dutch troops (7,000 present including 3,000 guards) to defend the Coast and to hold Fort Bathz (on South Beveland between Walcheren and the mainland) at all costs. General Bruce, however, spiked the guns of Bathz, and abandoned South Beveland to the British, who also occupied the neighboring islands of North Beveland and Schouwen.

Louis was rapidly reinforced. A regular French infantry division moved up to the south bank of the Schelde, and four French national guard divisions arrived at Antwerp. A Dutch division was put on the march from Germany. The king, radiating optimism, ordered a huge celebration for Napoleon's fête day, August 15. In the midst of it news arrived that Monnet had surrendered Flushing, where the population had become uncontrollable under incessant bombardment by British naval guns, artillery, mortars, and rockets which had wrecked blocks of buildings and set raging fires. The king began a reconsideration of his dispositions, but to no avail. On August 16 Marshal Bernadotte arrived with orders to assume command. Disgruntled, Louis departed for Amsterdam with his guard.

French forces continued to grow. By September 1 Bernadotte had 30,000 troops at Antwerp, Bergen op Zoom, and along the south bank of the Schelde. The British, meanwhile, were falling like flies to "Walcheren fever." Every sizable structure on the island was filled with men delirious from high temperatures, dazed by bone-deep aches and spasms, their bodies puffed, their skin pale and covered with red spots. The medical men tried various remedies, but really could do little but try to make the sick comfortable and give brandy to those still unaffected, which doubtless improved their morale, but did little to ward off the disease. A month after the landing 8,000 men were in the hospital, and the numbers climbed by 500 a week. Lord Chatham, who was as fearful of his health as Louis, had spent most of the campaign in the abbey at Middelburg. Much of his time had been devoted to receiving highly placed sight-seers from London. One had brought him a turtle, so that his chef could prepare his lordship's favorite soup—a small gesture which caught the attention of wags in London and Paris, who characterized Chatham as doing nothing but reading reports and eating turtle soup, which, in fact, was not far wrong.

In view of the rapid French build-up and the collapse of his own forces—one-quarter sick, the rest demoralized—Chatham gave up hope of taking Antwerp. On September 14 he departed for London leaving General Eyre Coote with 16,000 men and orders to hold Walcheren. The fever began to abate, but victims still fell in sizable numbers. Coote pulled all his forces back onto Walcheren in October. On December 24, on orders from London, he withdrew to England.

On the allied side the expedition had accomplished little except that it had allowed tons of British goods to be sold in Zeeland. Its cost had been 17,000 casualties (4,000 dead, 13,000 others, mostly from disease) and 1,000,000 pounds sterling. It had caused Napoleon little worry. The French had experienced "Walcheren fever" earlier, and he predicted that it would stop the British. If not, with the Austrians beaten, overwhelming forces could shortly be sent against the expedition.

For Louis, however, as Napoleon interpreted events, it was a disaster of the first magnitude. The Dutch had not been able to defend themselves; the king had produced too few troops, and those present had performed badly. (Even Louis was outraged at Bruce's surrender of Bathz, and ordered him destituted.) Walcheren was the beginning of the end for the Kingdom of Holland. It provided Napoleon with a convenient new charge of incompetence to add to the old ones he hurled at Louis.

Louis Driven to Abdication

Since late 1806 Louis had felt insecure, and with justification. Napoleon pounced on his every deficiency, maintaining a "live" case against him. But as we have indicated, Napoleon, until 1809, was too fully occupied elsewhere to undertake a reorganization of the Netherlands. Still, he gave unmistakable indications that he intended to do so eventually.

In March 1808 he offered Louis the crown of Spain. Holland, said the emperor, was unlikely to escape ruin in the "turbulent state of the world." The climate of Spain would be better for Louis anyway, he argued. And why not exchange a bankrupt kingdom of two million people for a "generous nation" of eleven million? "Reply categorically:" wrote Napoleon, "If I make you King of Spain will you agree? . . . [say only] . . . yes . . . [or] . . . no . . ." Louis was incapable of a categorical answer, but in a few hundred words he said no. "I am not the governor of a province. Kings can only be promoted to heaven; they are all equal. How can I ask another people to swear fidelity to me when I have not remained true to the oath I swore . . . [to the Dutch]!" Napoleon did not press the matter. He had given his brother an "out," and all but told him Holland was doomed; if Louis chose to consider the offer insulting he would not argue with him.[27]

A year later (March 1809), after a campaign in Spain, during preparations to counter an imminent Austrian attack, Napoleon suddenly announced that the Grand Duchy of Berg would go to the prince royal of Holland, Napoleon Louis. Louis received the news with mixed feelings. Publicly he interpreted it as a gesture of good will toward himself and his kingdom. Privately he feared Napoleon had granted his son Berg as advance compensation for Holland, which he would never inherit.

His fears were justified. Immediately after Wagram (July 5–6, 1809), the emperor began a concerted campaign to discredit Louis and the Dutch. French newspapers made a scandal of contraband traffic between Oldenburg and Holland, though French and Dutch customs officials guarded opposite sides of the border. Louis complained. Napoleon shot back, ". . . it is France which has cause to complain. . . . Holland is an avenue for all English intercourse with the Continent. . . . M. de Starhemberg, sent by Austria, passed through Holland on his way to London. . . . Holland is an English province." Then, abruptly, dropping his imperial role, he signed, "Your affectionate brother, Napoleon." Louis was

27. Joseph had been offered the crown before Louis. Napoleon returned to Joseph and induced him to take it.

all the more pained. He could never keep their official and family relationships so neatly separated.

Through the summer and fall the abuse continued. At Amsterdam Napoleon's ambassador, the haughty former *émigré* La Rochefoucauld, called on the king's ministers for reports and behaved as if he were preparing to assume control of the kingdom. For a year Louis had been demanding that the ambassador be recalled. Napoleon refused. "I do not have an Englishman in my service [to send as replacement]." After the Walcheren invasion the emperor concentrated on Holland's defenselessness. "That power is bound by treaties to have 40,000 troops, plus a squadron, plus a flotilla . . . everything has been destroyed by false economies." Louis was not surprised when in November he was ordered to Paris.

The king tried to avoid going, but Admiral Verhuel hurried from Paris to tell him that the emperor wanted family approval for his divorce from Joséphine. Holland was in jeopardy, but Louis, if anyone, might save her by using his position in the family council. Louis, with Verhuel, Roëll, and other advisers, traveled to Paris at the end of November. Louis gave his consent for the divorce, but hurt his bargaining position by pressing for a legal separation from Hortense, which the family council refused.[28]

Meanwhile the British withdrew from Walcheren, but French troops remained in Brabant and Zeeland. Napoleon's pronouncements on Holland were unspecific but alarming—she was "astride the arteries of the Empire" [the Rhine, Meuse, and Schelde], and unable to enforce the Continental System or defend herself. Louis, considering flight to Amsterdam, moved from the Trianon to his country estate, Saint-Leu, but found imperial police behind every bush. He sent off coded orders by Count Charles Bylant that Dutch troops were to oppose French occupation of any more cities. In response the French were denied entry into Bergen op Zoom and Breda. "Go to see the King of Holland," wrote Napoleon to Clarke, his minister of war, "and inform him if he does not remedy the affront to my troops, I will march on Amsterdam,

28. Napoleon granted the two separate establishments, however. Though Hortense accompanied Louis to Holland in the spring of 1810, she left almost immediately. They never again lived together.

and declare the reunion of Holland to France." Louis ordered the cities to yield; but Napoleon was determined to show the Dutch that the king's orders in such matters could not be obeyed with impunity. He forced Louis to dismiss Mollerus, acting foreign minister, and Krayenhoff, minister of war. At the end of January a French "Army of Brabant" was created, under Marshal Oudinot, whose troops secured Breda and Bergen op Zoom and began to inch northward. In a feeble gesture of appeasement, the Dutch legislature raised taxes and repealed the laws regulating the nobility and creating marshals to which Napoleon had so long objected.

Louis, now desperate, offered Napoleon Brabant and Zeeland for the Grand Duchy of Berg plus certain of the Hanse cities. Champagny, the French foreign minister, responded: In the interest of France Louis must be prepared to obey the emperor. The same day Champagny wrote Roëll that Louis was to be recalled for failure in his duties as a Frenchman and in enforcing the Continental System. Louis's sense of doom was relieved only by Napoleon's sudden decision to approach Britain with the offer to preserve Holland if she would make peace. (The Walcheren fiasco had brought a new British ministry into power; it might treat.) The emperor could hardly sue for peace directly, but Louis jumped at the chance to make the necessary tentatives. In February he sent Labouchère (head of Hope and Company) to London where he exchanged notes with Wellesley, the foreign secretary, but accomplished nothing. The British were willing to negotiate only if Napoleon first softened the regulations of the Continental System.

Again, all seemed lost; Louis, by his own account, fell "dangerously ill." He recovered quickly when Napoleon, without warning or explanation, offered to compromise. Louis accepted. By a treaty signed March 16, 1810, he ceded Zeeland, Brabant, and Gelderland south of the Waal to France, and agreed to allow French troops and customs officials to enforce the Continental System on the Dutch coast and rivers. In return he got only the assurance that he would not have to renounce the interest on his debt or enforce conscription.

In view of subsequent events, it is astonishing that Napoleon made a treaty at all. Perhaps because of his approaching marriage he felt the time inopportune to dethrone Louis. Conceivably, he was moved by pity for Louis, whom he loved as a brother. Possibly, he felt Louis's traumatic months in Paris had rendered him totally submissive, so that he would be satisfied merely to wear his crown while French officials gradually assumed control of Holland. (If so, Louis was worth keeping, for he had the love of his people.) Perhaps he hoped only to tranquilize the Dutch and facilitate gradual, peaceful occupation of the country. At any rate the document was signed, in apparent good faith, by both French and Dutch representatives.

After the emperor's marriage, Louis took his leave, gratified that at their last meeting (April 5) Napoleon had accepted and worn the Royal Order of Holland, which he had previously scorned. In May the king left Amsterdam to greet Napoleon and Marie Louise during their tour of Belgium. The brothers would not meet again. French newspapers had already resumed their attack on Louis and Holland. Napoleon wrote Louis suggesting that in Holland's interest he must become "more French," or the Dutch themselves would evict him. Baffled, despondent, the king went before his legislature and offered to abdicate if it would benefit Holland. The members unanimously opposed the suggestion.

Louis's presence was Holland's only guarantee of even nominal independence. But the vestiges of his authority and prestige were dwindling daily. On May 23 the coachman of the French ambassador, La Rochefoucauld, was pulled from his box and mauled. La Rochefoucauld, who probably staged the incident, demanded his passports and left for France. He was not replaced. On June 1 French tariff officers demanded to enter Amsterdam. By treaty they were to regulate commerce on the coasts and rivers. Whether Amsterdam, which stood on both, was under their authority, was a matter of interpretation. Louis forbade them to enter, whereupon Oudinot moved troops to the outskirts of the capital, and on June 29 demanded free entry.

Louis sent Valckenaer to Paris to discuss the problem with Napoleon. He then announced his intention to defend Amsterdam to the death, and called on his top army and navy commanders, General Dumonceau and Admiral de Winter, for advice. Both opined that the capital was indefensible. Astonished, Louis summoned all his ministers. In his opinion, he told them, a fight had to be made for Amsterdam if negotiations failed; there was no other honorable course. Their hearts were with him, but all agreed that what he proposed was foolhardy.

Louis, deeply shocked, chose to interpret this opinion as a vote of no confidence. On July 1, 1810, at Haarlem, he proclaimed his abdication in favor of his eldest son. ". . . convinced . . . that I am an obstacle to the return of good feelings between my brother and the country. . . . I will never forget such a good and virtuous people; my last thought, my last wish will be for your welfare." During the night of July 1–2 he drove away toward the German border. At the end of the month it became known that he had reached Töplitz, in Bohemia, where the Austrian emperor had given him asylum.

Napoleon did not respect the terms of Louis's abdication. On July 9 Holland was incorporated into France by imperial decree, and the Archchancellor Lebrun shortly arrived to organize the former kingdom into French departments. Louis penned a protest to the crowned heads of Europe, declaring the annexation of Holland unconstitutional, contrary to the treaties between the kingdom and France, and a violation of the rights of his son, Napoleon Louis. His legalistic arguments perforce fell on deaf ears, though some, surely, were touched that a Bonaparte could be so naïve as to offer them. In 1810 Napoleon was the fount of Europe's law. Holland was no more, and at the time her division into imperial departments seemed to portend a like fate for the other satellite kingdoms.

Conclusion

Louis had been "captured" by the Dutch. From his and his people's point of view, this was good; from Napoleon's, disastrous. Louis had not governed Holland in the interest of the empire; Napoleon had felt fully justified in forcing his abdication. The ex-king, however, could never admit that he had not served both Holland *and* the empire. He even thought he had enforced the Continental System as well as anyone could. This alone shows how Dutch his attitudes had become, and that he was always more the intellectual than the executive. He *had* issued the proper decrees and instructions, but had given limited attention to having them enforced.

Louis had, however, "captured" the Dutch as surely as they had captured him. When he abdicated, his subjects immediately recalled that in 1809 he had spent weeks in villages devastated or threatened by breaks in the great Waal dike, truly risking his life to help victims and direct repair operations. If the engineers were unsure his direction and presence did not hinder operations, the people were impressed and pleased to see him there. In the same year he had rushed into an epidemic area, visiting hospitals; giving advice; exhorting doctors, ministers, and priests to greater efforts; visiting the sick; and, to the alarm of his staff, sitting through the night at the bedsides of the dying. His dictum that finances were not all "arithmetic" had endeared him to the peasants. His painstaking review of cases before the high court, his reluctance to exact the death penalty, his opposition to injustice and discrimination in any form had won general approval.

The informed few appreciated Louis's administrative and legal reforms, public works projects, and encouragement of education, the arts, and sciences. The people remembered the man. Sometimes they found his behavior wildly funny—as when he campaigned to convince mothers of the superiority of breast feeding over bottle feeding of babies, or when he ordered twenty-four identical foot warmers for the council of state. But they liked and trusted him. "Goed en deugdzaam volk" he called them. Good and virtuous they thought him too.

Dutch historians today reveal a sympathy for Louis which they are not at pains to defend, since tradition supports their attitude. They lament his fragile health and melancholy, but praise his humanity, respect for Dutch traditions and the constitution, his liberalism, constructive reforms, and, not least, his patriotism and the courage he displayed in resisting Napoleon's will. They credit Louis with fidelity to the motto he gave the Royal Order of Holland: "Doe wel en zie niet om."

I do not know whether I am King, Prince, or subject!

—JÉRÔME BONAPARTE IN 1812

chapter six

THE KINGDOM OF WESTPHALIA

Jérôme and Westphalia: Background

KÖNIG JÉRÔME NAPOLÉON

O n July 2, 1808, King Jérôme Napoléon addressed the parliament[1] of Westphalia at its first meeting. Behind him, emblazoned on silken drapes, a stern Imperial Eagle united under its wings (and claws) another eagle, two lions, and a horse, representing Prussia, Brunswick, Hanover, and Hesse-Cassel, states to which the delegates had formerly owed allegiance. Delegates, councilors of state, and ministers, in newly designed uniforms of office, occupied the floor. The elite of the kingdom jammed the galleries. Behind the tribune sat the queen and her ladies, admiring eyes fixed on Jérôme, slender and handsome in white silk. "We shall work in concert," said the boyish figure of twenty-three to the formidably mature and dignified assemblage before him, "I as King and Father, you as obedient and loyal subjects."

Jérôme's speech, however, had made a generally good impression. The meeting of the parliament, he had said, was an earnest avowal that he intended to observe the constitution. Unity among the peoples of the kingdom was essential; his government would promote their welfare, and insure liberty and opportunity for all. He intended ultimately to assemble a government of natives; careers would be open to talent. He had praised the warlike qualities (beyond dispute in Hesse, certainly) of his peoples' ancestors, pledged that when a Westphalian army was formed, French troops would depart, and pointedly remarked that so proud

1. *Ständeversammlung.*

(176)

a people would understand that conscription was "a grand development."

The new king's performance had been precisely what Cassel had expected after observing him for seven months. He had arrived thunderously, on horseback, surrounded by his guard cavalry, and strode into the hall, aides-de-camp in trail, a purple cloak flying from his shoulders, white plumes waving above a black toque set at a rakish angle. He looked the fairy-tale prince, a man of whom stories of romantic exploits, already circulating, could easily be believed. But he had made a sober speech. He was young, blazingly undisciplined, but no fool, rather a man to be reckoned with—self-assured, intelligent, informed, and forceful. Tales of his marathon amusements at Wilhelmshöhe (Napoleonshöhe), "the Hessian Versailles," of the "royal guard" of pretty young women who flocked with him to the theater and opera had reached Paris. Napoleon fired off scorching reprimands and volumes of advice. But he knew that his brother had ability and courage. "*Mon ami*," he wrote, "I love you, but you are so furiously young." The average Westphalian's reaction was much the same. Jérôme's antics amused more than offended them. Somehow his ability to slip effortlessly from the role of playboy to that of king, administrator, soldier—to be convincing in both—made him even more impressive. They were not displeased with him.

THE PRODIGAL BROTHER

When Jérôme was born in November 1784, Napoleon was already at the École Militaire in Paris; he was nine when his brother became a hero at Toulon. If as boy and man he behaved as if born to the purple, it was because he barely remembered the time when the Bonapartes were poor and unknown. Napoleon, fifteen years older than Jérôme, was more father than brother to him, and as indulgent as a grandfather. At thirteen (1797) Jérôme played staff-officer at Mombello after the first Italian Campaign, and then went off to school at Juilly. When Napoleon returned from Egypt in October 1799, Jérôme was on vacation, and celebrated by not going back to school at all. Instead he lived with Joséphine, an experience which, says Masson, spread over his whole life a sort of "*odeur de femme*." He quickly learned to be

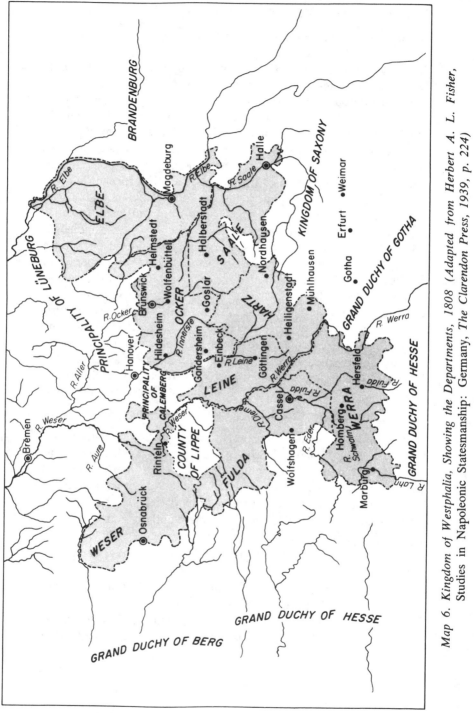

Map 6. *Kingdom of Westphalia, Showing the Departments, 1808 (Adapted from Herbert A. L. Fisher, Studies in Napoleonic Statesmanship: Germany, The Clarendon Press, 1939, p. 224)*

at ease among the beautiful and worldly women of Joséphine's circle, how to win their friendship—or more—arts he would practice with astonishing success in later years.

In 1800 Napoleon placed Jérôme in the Navy, where in the next three years he saw action in the West Indies with the fleets of Admirals Latouche-Tréville and Villeneuve. Combat excited him —but there was too little of it. Ashore, in Santo Domingo, Martinique, Brest, or Paris, he led his young cronies in an unrelenting pursuit of pleasure, exhausting his pay, private allowances, and loans from his brothers (especially the softhearted Joseph), or colonial officials dazzled by the Bonaparte name. In 1802 he was made a lieutenant and given command of the *Epervier,* whose captain had fallen ill (not surprisingly, since Jérôme and his playmates were the ship's officers). After wintering (1802–1803) in Fort-de-France (Martinique) with occasional sorties in search of English merchantmen, Jérôme was ordered to sail his ship to France.

Lieutenant Bonaparte had decided, however, to visit the United States. At Guadeloupe he turned the *Epervier* over to another officer.[2] Accompanied by his friends Meyronnet, Reubell (the wastrel son of the former director), Le Camus, a physician, and a number of servants, he boarded an American pilot boat bound for Portsmouth, Virginia. Late in July he appeared at the French embassy in Washington, where he demanded a house and funds. Afraid to do otherwise, Pichon, head of the legation, gave what he asked, and wrote frantically for instructions from Napoleon. Before a positive order came to withhold funds, however, his visitor had relieved him of thirty thousand dollars.

Jérôme had meanwhile entered Baltimore society and fallen hopelessly in love with Elizabeth Patterson, daughter of a prosperous merchant and shipowner. Nymphlike, black-haired, brown-eyed, with exquisitely modeled features, Elizabeth had a regiment of admirers. But the dashing brother of the world's most famous man was too much for her to resist. On Christmas Eve, 1803, they were married in a Catholic ceremony performed by Archbishop John Carroll of Baltimore.[3]

2. The ship was captured en route to France by the British.
3. Brother of Carroll of Carrollton, signer of the Declaration of Independence.

Jérôme was ordered to return to France and Pichon refused him more money, but he stayed on. Meanwhile in May 1804 the senate had proclaimed Napoleon emperor. In August Talleyrand informed Jérôme that his marriage was invalid—if he wished to remain a member of the imperial family, he must return and make peace with his brother. Convinced that Betsy's beauty would shatter the family's resistance, Jérôme sailed with her for France in October, but their ship was turned back. In the spring of 1805 they again embarked, and reached Lisbon in April, only to find that "Mademoiselle Patterson" could not be permitted to land. Jérôme went on alone to Turin (Napoleon was touring Italy), but the emperor refused to see him until he agreed to renounce his wife. If he did not he would have no title, his debts would not be paid, and he might face a court martial for desertion from the navy. Jérôme agonized for ten days, but seeing no alternative to submission but beginning a new life abroad (if he could escape), dependent on the charity of his father-in-law, he agreed to an annulment of his marriage. Betsy meanwhile had been denied permission to land at Amsterdam, and had finally landed in England. In July 1805, at Camberwell, in the suburbs of London, she gave birth to Jérôme's son, christened Jerome Napoleon Bonaparte. Napoleon offered her a pension if she would cease using the Bonaparte name, but she refused. All her life she fought for her son's recognition and inheritance, with qualified success under the Second Empire.

In May 1805 Pope Pius VII refused Napoleon's request for a bull annulling Jérôme's marriage. The Pontiff considered the marriage legal, and was disinclined to listen to contrary arguments after his brusque treatment at Paris during the Emperor's coronation. He was aware, moreover, that a new coalition was forming against France, and declined to make any gesture which might make him appear to support Napoleon, whose success he now feared would mean even greater erosion of the Church's power. He never granted an annulment, though he did remain silent when the archbishop of Paris approved one in December 1806.

Jérôme was returned to duty with the navy. During the Summer of 1805, in command of five vessels, he sailed to Algiers, and by threat of force (and payment of 150,000 francs) obtained the release of French and Italians held prisoner by the dey. The French press made him a hero. In the fall he again sailed for the Antilles, captain of a ship in the fleet of Admiral Willaumez. He was soon up to his old tricks. In the summer of 1806 his ship, the *Véteran,* disappeared from the fleet. Willaumez combed the seas for it for weeks, only to find it at Fort-de-France, Jérôme's favorite port.

Shortly thereafter, without orders, Jérôme sailed for France via Newfoundland and the Azores. En route he blundered into a British merchant convoy, captured eleven ships, and made port safely. His arrival in Paris (August 1806) suited Napoleon's plans. Jérôme was acclaimed a hero (deservedly so this time, if his indiscipline is ignored). He was finally made a French prince, and promoted to rear admiral.

During the 1806–1807 campaign he commanded a corps of Bavarians and Württembergers, made a creditable record (mostly reducing fortified places in Silesia), and emerged a major general. After Tilsit Napoleon apprised Jérôme that he would become king of Westphalia; and in August his designation was announced to the French *corps législatif.*

In August also Jérôme acquired a new wife, Catherine of Württemberg.[4] Napoleon, in 1805, had made her father a king; he in turn had promised his daughter would marry a member of the imperial family. The emperor was delighted with Catherine. She was attractive, poised and regal, sturdy (Napoleon wanted his brothers to have healthy male children), of spotless reputation— and she spoke French like a native. Jérôme pronounced her not bad, but not pretty either. Before the honeymoon was over he was ignoring his bride and chasing after Stéphanie de Beauharnais, Joséphine's sparkling cousin, herself recently married to the duke of Baden. Catherine, who to all appearances had fallen in love with Jérôme at first sight, seemed not to notice. At least publicly, she would ignore her "Fifri's" philandering as long as she lived. She became a model queen, wife, and mother, and stood by Jérôme even after Napoleon's fall.

WESTPHALIA

Westphalia, recognized by the powers at Tilsit (July 1807), comprised territory seized from German princes who had dared to oppose Napoleon during 1806–1807. The former Electorate of

4. Katharina Sophie Dorothea, princess von Württemberg (1783–1835).

Hesse-Cassel and the Duchy of Brunswick formed the nucleus. Prussian territory west of the Elbe, and southern Hanover (of which the king of England was duke) had been added, plus other minor states. Some fragments of border territory had been contributed by Saxony (Napoleon's ally) but with ample compensation provided elsewhere.[5] The kingdom, with its capital at Cassel, lay in the upper Weser valley, and stretched northeast to the Elbe and southwest to the borders of the Grand Duchies of Berg and Hesse.[6] With an area of 17,000 square miles, adequate resources, and a population of 2,000,000 noted for its industriousness and warlike qualities, it was expected to be the anchor state for the Confederation of the Rhine. Its eastern outpost was the fortress of Magdeburg, guarding the Elbe frontier against Prussia.

The territories of Westphalia had since 1806 been under the control of French generals, the nucleus of the kingdom under Lagrange, military governor of Hesse-Cassel, the rest comprising all or part of five other military governments.[7] In August 1807, while Jérôme was acquiring a bride, Napoleon dispatched a "regency" of three French bureaucrats to establish a central Westphalian government at Cassel. Joseph Jérôme Siméon was to organize the courts and prepare for the introduction of the *Code Napoléon;* Jacques Claude Beugnot and Jean Baptiste Jollivet to establish general and financial administrations.

The regency found Westphalians cooperative. The peasants, unaccustomed to questioning their rulers' right to govern, had gen-

5. Westphalia's territories in detail were: Brunswick (Braunschweig); Hesse-Cassel, with Rinteln and Schaumburg, but without lower Katzenelnbogen and Hanau; those parts of the Prussian Altmark and Magdeburg province situated on the west bank of the Elbe, the province of Halle, the land of Hildesheim, and the city of Goslar, the land of Halberstadt, the county of Hohenstein, the province of Quedlinburg, the county of Mansfeld, the Prussian county of Stolberg-Wernigerode, the Eichsfeld with Treffurt, the cities of Mühlhausen and Nordhausen, the Bishoprics of Paderborn, Minden, and Ravensberg; the Hanoverian provinces of Göttingen and Grubenhagen with Hohenstein and Elbingerode, the Harzdistrikte, the Bishopric of Osnabrück; the "organic land" of Corveh and the County of Rietberg-Kaunitz.

6. The Grand Duchy of Hesse (Hesse-Darmstadt), not included in Westphalia, and Hesse-Cassel (included) had been separate states since 1567.

7. Those of Generals Loison, Gobert, Bisson, Thiébault, and Clarke. Each (and Lagrange) had been paired with a civilian intendant. The six intendants reported to Daru, intendant-general, whose superior was the receiver-general of the Grande Armée. The military governors reported to the minister of war.

erally accepted the fact of conquest, though there was some unrest in the Prussian territories, especially Magdeburg.[8] One might have expected them to be excited over the imminent abolition of feudalism and serfdom, heralded by the military governors, but few understood what was involved. For many of the intelligentsia, of course, such promises had appeal, as did the prospect of constitutional government. The nobles preferred a monarchy in which they would have some influence in seeing their homelands annexed to France—the only apparent alternative. The business community hoped to profit by operation within a larger state and from the French connection. Over all, Westphalians were peaceful and cautiously optimistic.

As the regency departed Paris a Westphalian delegation had arrived to assist in framing a constitution for the kingdom. It was a mixed bag of clerics, nobles, burghers, former officials, and professors, including the historian Christophe Wilhelm Koch and the legalist Georg Robert.[9] At the insistence of Napoleon, Johannes von Müller, the "Swiss Tacitus," joined the group. A year before, the historian, then in the service of Prussia, had met the emperor at Berlin and overnight had changed from francophobe to francophile. The group was received by the emperor, met with Jérôme, the French foreign minister, Champagny, and Cambacérès, the archchancellor, and began deliberations. It produced few constitutional proposals, however. The members proved principally concerned with avoiding having to support French troops, the establishment of imperial fiefs in Westphalia, and the imposition of the *Code Napoléon*.

The emperor grew impatient. In a maneuver reminiscent of that he had used at the *consulta* of Lyons (1802), he arranged for

8. There had been a serious revolt in Hesse-Cassel in December 1806, involving former Hessian soldiers and some peasants. The French intended to recall Hessian regiments (assumed to be mercenary) and put them in imperial service. They found that there was loyalty among them to their former prince. Even so, the rebellion might not have started if the soldiers had been aware they were going into honorable military service rather than to prison or to the galleys, or if their officers, already in prison or on parole, had been recalled with them.

9. The most influential members were: The Abbot Henke (Brunswick), graf (count) von Alvensleben (Altmark), von Hagen (Halberstadt), von Pestel (Corveh), Prof.-Dr. G. F. K. Robert (Hesse), count von Merveldt (Hildesheim), count von Schulenburg-Emden (Magdeburg), count von Kesselstadt (Paderborn).

the delegation to appoint a committee of five to produce a draft constitution. The committee then had a constitution virtually dictated to it which in turn the delegation accepted.

The constitution, issued at Fontainebleau on November 15, 1807, reserved half the alodial lands of the former princes for distribution as imperial fiefs, and required that Westphalia have and army of 25,000 and support 12,500 French troops. The king's subjects[10] were guaranteed equality before the law and religious liberty; serfdom and feudal rights were abolished; noble titles were affirmed, but were to command no special rights, privileges, or offices. Taxes were to fall equally on all classes in all parts of the kingdom. Provision was made for a ministry, council of state, and a parliament of one hundred (seventy landowners, fifteen merchants and manufacturers, fifteen savants and distinguished citizens), of whom one-third would be replaced every three years. But only the king could convoke the parliament; he could name its president, and prorogue, adjourn, or dismiss it; and it could consider only bills he proposed. For local government a departmental structure was specified, with officials at all levels appointed by the king. Departmental electoral colleges were to elect members of parliament, present nominees for departmental executive and judicial offices—but the king named the electors. Effective January 1, 1808, the *Code Napoléon* was to be the civil law. The judiciary was to be "independent" but was appointed by the king, who could review his appointants every five years. Conscription was to be a "fundamental law" of the kingdom. The constitution was terse but quite comprehensive. Little room was left for innovation by Jérôme and his ministers.

Initially, at least, Napoleon hoped to create a model state for the edification of the other *Rheinbund* states—a liberal, progressive, constitutional monarchy that would demonstrate the value of "French principles," as well as creating a productive and militarily useful satellite. The location for the first venture in French government beyond the Rhine was deeply German. The lands of Westphalia (". . . der Name war zwar absurd . . ." says Kleinschmidt) had been a battlefield of the Carolingian wars, of the

10. A word avoided in the constitutions of Italy and Holland. The usages of the empire became more traditional by the year.

Reformation, and of the Thirty Years' War. It was also a center of German learning, with no less than five universities—Göttingen, Marburg, Halle, Rinteln, and Helmstedt. German tradition was deep-rooted in the people; pride of accomplishment, in addition, stirred the intellectuals. So much the better, thought Napoleon. What better place to demonstrate the benefits of "the Revolution"? He urged Jérôme to be a constitutional monarch. "What people would want to return to . . . arbitrary . . . government after they have tasted the benefits of a sage and liberal administration?"

Organization of the Kingdom

GOVERNMENT AND ADMINISTRATION

Jérôme and Catherine reached Cassel on December 7, 1807. The same day the new king decreed the regency dissolved and appointed his own ministry, initially all French—the regents and Lagrange, with Cousin de Marinville added as secretary of the cabinet. Within a few months, however, Jérôme had removed all but Siméon. To his intense irritation, Jollivet remained in Cassel as a sort of imperial watchdog, but outside the government; Beugnot and Lagrange departed; Marinville became the king's first chamberlain. The replacements were well chosen, except where Jérôme was overly influenced by friendship. As was noted by Karl Friedrich von Reinhard, Napoleon's ambassador, Jérôme's intuitive powers were remarkable. He judged men quickly and usually rightly; his grasp of problems was often better than that of subordinates who had labored over them. Two Westphalians were installed in ministries with major roles in domestic affairs— Ludwig Viktor Hans von Bülow in finance and Gustav Anton von Wolffradt in interior. Siméon retained the portfolio of justice with the enthusiastic approval not only of the king, but of his West-phalian colleagues. The spare, assiduous Siméon had won the German's respect and also the special affection they seem to develop for professorial types. Brilliant and practical, he was still at heart a scholar. Appointed interim minister of war for a few months in 1810, he startled an aide with the question: "Do you know the Roman Law?" Siméon's ministry was staffed in large part by Germans. He had assembled the best native legalists to translate and interpret the *Code Napoléon,* and given assurance that the courts, when reorganized, would be staffed by Germans. In time Westphalians accepted him almost as their own. Bülow and Wolffradt, as we shall note below, did outstanding work, as did Wolffradt's subordinate, Johannes von Müller, director of public instruction.

Less wisely, Jérôme made ministers of two of his cronies— General Joseph Morio (war) and Pierre Alexandre Le Camus (secretary of the cabinet). Morio was a graduate of the École Polytechnique and had served honorably in combat. But Napoleon considered him an erratic dandy ("You a general? In my army you would not even be a corporal!"), and seems to have been right. Before the year 1808 was out Jérôme relegated him to command of the *gardes-du-corps*[11] and gave the portfolio of war to General Jean Baptiste Eblé. (Napoleon insisted that a Frenchman hold the post.) Le Camus, a Creole who had shared Jérôme's adventures in the West Indies and United States, remained in the government. But instead of performing as coordinator among the ministries, the *Staatssekretär*'s normal task, he devoted himself to foreign affairs, for which there was no ministry, and no real need for one (so that he did little harm).

After 1808 the ministry remained remarkably stable.[12] Bülow

11. In 1809 Morio commanded the Westphalian division sent to Spain. Late the same year he was évacuated, ill with fever. He returned to Cassel, where he served as grand equerry until 1811, when he was assassinated by a French blacksmith whom he had dismissed.

12. *Ministers 1807–1813:*

Justice	Siméon	1807–1813
Interior	Siméon	1807–1808
	Von Wolffradt	1808–1813
Finance	Beugnot and Jollivet	1807–1808
	Von Bülow	1808–1811
	Malchus	1811–1813
War	Lagrange	1807
	Morio	1807–1808
	Eblé	1808–1810
	D'Albignac	1810
	Siméon (Interim)	1810
	Salha	1810–1813
Staatssekretär (*Secretary of the Cabinet*)	De Marinville	1807–1808
	Le Camus	1808–1813

was brought down in 1811 by accusation of treasonous connections with Prussian nationalists, apparently generated by a subordinate, Karl August Malchus, who became his successor. Nothing was ever proved against Bülow; he retired honorably and evidently remained loyal to Jérôme to the end. But because he was a relative of Prussian Minister Hardenberg, he was kept under police surveillance. There were three war ministers after Eblé, but General Valentin Salha was his permanent successor; the terms of the two span almost the whole reign.[13]

More powerful than most ministers was Le Gras de Bercagny, director general of police. His counterespionage organization was widespread, and hardly a scrap of mail entered or left the kingdom without being examined by his censors. His German was weak, however, and his native officials signally lacking in subtlety. All documents got the most literal interpretation, which often meant much of their meaning was lost, or they were misunderstood. A feeling that he saw all "through a glass, darkly," whipped up his suspicion of Germans, especially Bülow and Wolffradt, to paranoid proportions. His spies infiltrated every ministry, the ministers' homes, and even the king's household. He was encouraged by Jollivet, "Ambassador of the [Imperial] Family." In 1809 some of the operatives blundered, and the proportions of Bercagny's activities came to light. Jérôme gave direction of the police to General Jean François Bongars, chief of the gendarmerie; Bercagny became prefect of police of Cassel, later Magdeburg. The king demanded that Napoleon recall Jollivet. "I myself surprised one of my ushers going through the papers in my desk . . . he told me, throwing himself at my feet, that . . . he was paid by Jollivet, who told him it was by order of the Emperor! Your Majesty's name is being used . . . ! the scandal . . . is more than your brother's dignity can suffer!" Napoleon did not reply; Jollivet was too valuable an informer to dismiss. His continued presence, like Bercagny's, served to breed distrust between French and Germans.

13. Jérôme granted titles to most of his ministers. Salha became count (graf) von Hoene, Le Camus count von Fürstenstein, Malchus count von Marienrode; Bülow and Wolffradt also became counts. Siméon, who had been since 1804 an imperial councilor of state, and was made a count of the empire, had more prestige than any of them.

Essential to the government's operation was the council of state, which Jérôme formed four days after reaching Cassel. Its functions were to advise the king, and propose and formulate laws. Despite Jérôme's professions of egalitarianism, he appointed largely nobles, partly because they were still accepted leaders of the masses, whose support he needed, partly because few others were qualified. Of the original members only two were of lesser rank than *freiherr* (baron)—Professor Leist of the law faculty of Göttingen and Karl August Malchus, whom we have already mentioned. Malchus had ingratiated himself with the French by betraying the location of certain treasuries within Prussian territory, including those of monastic orders.

Wolffradt organized the Westphalian departments quickly and effectively. The prefects and subprefects he recommended to Jérôme proved efficient, strong, and loyal. The electoral colleges, formed in 1808 as required by the constitution, endorsed the key men already in office. Despite the suspicions of Bercagny, and the envy of Le Camus, Jérôme gave him steady support, a tribute to the king's good judgment. Initially there were eight departments run on geographical lines, as the names Elbe, Harz, Saale, and the like indicate.[14] The prefects were all German and mostly nobles, some with the highest connections, like the count von Hardenburg, in Fulda. Göttingen and Marburg, to the joy of their merchants if not their scholars, became departmental capitals as well as university towns. Police prefects were often French, but after 1809 were subordinated to the departmental prefects. The local police were reinforced by Bongar's Royal Gendarmes, in companies of fifty men per department. A mixture of French and Germans, all were required to be bilingual.

To match the new administrative organization, a new system of courts was installed by Siméon early in 1808. Judicial com-

14. Department	Capital	Population	Prefect
1. Elbe	Magdeburg	253,210	Graf von der Schulenburg-Emden
2. Fulda	Cassel	239,502	Graf von Hardenberg
3. Harz	Heiligenstadt	210,989	Borcke
4. Leine	Göttingen	145,537	Freiherr von Hoevel
5. Ocker	Braunschweig	267,878	Friedrich Christian Ludwig Henneberg
6. Saale	Halberstadt	206,222	Wm. Christian Goszler
7. Werra	Marburg	254,000	Reiman
8. Weser	Osnabrück	334,965	Von Pestel

petency centered in a court of appeals (*Appellationsgericht*) at Cassel, and in descending degree, was held by criminal tribunals (one per department), civil courts (one per district), justices of the peace (*Friedensrichter*) in the cantons, and police courts in the municipalities. Later a *Petitionskommission* was established to advise the king on giving "grace," and a special court of appeals for commercial cases was established. The judiciary was German throughout, and of unexampled quality. Siméon, with the assistance of Wolffradt and Professor J. C. Leist of Göttingen, chose men not only learned and experienced, but amenable to enforcing French-style codes. Leist supervised the translation of the *Code Napoléon,* which was printed in September 1808, though the courts had begun enforcing it at their inception. In 1809 revised codes of civil and criminal procedure were issued, and by mid-1810 penal and commercial codes had rounded out the basic law. All vestiges of feudal law, together with seignorial and church courts, disappeared in the first months of 1808. Though completion of the codes required time, Westphalian law was completely revolutionized in practice by the end of the year.

Pending the election of a parliament, Jérôme, on January 1, 1808 assembled two hundred and seventy-five notables of the estates of the former provinces at Cassel, laid out his general program, and asked their support. He emphasized unity, his intention to observe the constitution, and the wisdom of German states returning to the "sane *politique*" of the early eighteenth century, that is, a policy of alliance with France. "It is necessary," he told the delegates "that Westphalia finally have citizens . . ." All men would be equal before the law and eligible for office. The nobles were unruffled; they had already noted the rank of Jérôme's councilors and prefects. The representatives of the Third Estate were encouraged. Napoleon warned Jérôme to be more reserved in the future; the princes of the *Rheinbund* must not take him for a Jacobin. But these princes too were more interested in the king's behavior than his words. They held rightly that he, like Napoleon, was a liberal, but no democrat. The *Westphälische Moniteur,* established by the regents prior to Jérôme's arrival, gave wide publicity to the king's remarks, and helped to generate wide interest in the first meeting of the parliament.

The *Ständeversammlung* met twice in 1808, each time to vote taxes and little else. Under the direction of Von Wolffradt, president, the delegates proved amenable to all the king's proposals. By 1810, however, when the third session was called (The Austrian War prevented a meeting in 1809), Westphalians had found their voices. With count von der Schulenburg-Wolfsburg in the chair, the representatives challenged Von Bülow's tax program, and made drastic modifications before passing it. Jérôme was disgruntled at their performance, though surely his repeated pronouncements on the importance of parliament had encouraged independence among the delegates. After 1810 Jérôme chose ·to meet Napoleon's ever-increasing demands without reference to parliament. The fate of Louis, who had been too faithful to his constitution, was fresh in his mind.

The king's abandonment of parliamentary government caused little stir. The intelligentsia kept cynically silent; the masses had never understood its possible benefits; the nobles tended to accept its failure as inevitable. Some of the electors had never taken their responsibilities seriously. In Leine, the name of a notoriously stupid peasant had been placed on the list of nominees for seats authorized for intellectuals. Another department sent two illiterates to the parliament who were later found to have voted "no" to every proposal. If, they explained, the bill were good, it would pass anyway; if not, they would have voted right. Still, save that of Holland, Westphalia's parliament had played a larger role than that of any other satellite kingdom. And nineteenth-century developments would demonstrate that Jérôme had taught some Germans "bad habits."

A diplomatic corps was gradually assembled under Le Camus, the *Staatssekretär*. The count von Wintzingerode went to Paris; Balthazar Siméon, the son of the minister, to Berlin—for Westphalia second in importance only to the imperial court. It was essential that Cassel be abreast of developments in Prussia, just across the border, the state of former allegiance of Jérôme's most recalcitrant subjects, potential seat of subversive activity, and potentially a dangerous enemy. It also behooved Westphalia's ambassador to cultivate as cordial relations as possible. Siméon both collected information and radiated good will. His successor,

Freiherr Hugo von Linden, a touchy diplomatic ferret, concentrated on the former, kept Jérôme's fear of Prussia at an unnecessarily high pitch, and ruined what chances existed for amity. Prussia's official attitudes were perforce dictated by Napoleon's policies and moves. But a more capable ambassador, personally, and by his influence on Jérôme, might have eased Prussian resentment of the very existence of Westphalia. Westphalia ultimately had diplomatic representatives in Saxony, Holland, Russia, Denmark, Austria, Bavaria, Württemburg, and the minor German capitals. In Germany they were useful in handling problems such as those concerning the *Rheinbund*. Elsewhere they served largely to keep Jérôme informed.

The ranking foreign diplomat in Cassel, Napoleon's ambassador, Karl Friedrich von Reinhard, deserves special notice. He was one of a special breed of imperial bureaucrats, non-French by birth and schooling, "European" in outlook. A Württemberger educated at Tübingen, he had become impressed with the dynamism of Revolutionary France, migrated, and served in the French foreign ministry under the republic, consulate, and empire. Convinced that France would produce a "New Europe," he was unswerving in his loyalty to her emperor. Napoleon longed to produce this sort of man, but had never warmed to Reinhard, partly because of his glacial personality, partly out of suspicion that he might still be a republican. Reinhard had been dispatched to obscure posts—in Switzerland, Hamburg, and Moldavia. Cassel was his first good assignment since 1799, but he was far from embittered; Napoleon could not have chosen a better man. Proud of German cultural achievements, a friend of Goethe and Müller, at home among the *Gebildeten* of his homeland, he was unashamedly German. And yet he was certain that his people were politically backward, and that Westphalia could both teach them and serve the empire. He was a superb diplomat and an earnest and meticulous reporter; Napoleon never lacked information. At the same time he gave Jérôme sound advice, encouraged him to employ Westphalians in his government and opposed the police methods of Bercagny. Because the king was wise enough to hear Reinhard's recommendations, and in part to accept them, his government had much strength built on the self-interest of Westphalians in its survival.

Jérôme took his kingly duties seriously, but Jollivet accurately reported, "His Majesty [has] . . . ardent passions and an irresistible penchant for prodigality." "A Roman circus," said Goethe of his marathon entertainments. "France has not asked that the court of Cassel rival . . . the Imperial Court," wrote Napoleon. In the Orangerie of Cassel and the Wilhelmshöhe, the "Hessian Versailles," Jérôme had theaters for play of which he took maximum advantage. The Orangerie, erected between 1692 and 1728, was a massive baroque structure liberally sprinkled inside and out with statues of mythological figures in erotic poses. Wilhelmshöhe (renamed Napoleonshöhe), had been built a century before by the Landgraf Karl as a country residence and showplace. It boasted a sumptuous palace, a pyramid topped by a gigantic statue of Hercules, cascades dropping three hundred feet, and immense gardens and parks. It was the country chateau which the king favored and which, says Alfred Rambaud, Germans came to view as a *"babylone napoléonienne."* At his masked balls hundreds of guests played at identifying the king, who gleefully changed costume, wig, and make-up a half-dozen times. Between balls there were spectacles, musicales, and rounds of feasting, drinking, and dancing that went on for days.

The public easily accepted the most bizarre tales about Jérôme, such as that he sustained his awesome vitality by bathing in Rhine wine. And occasionally his performances topped anything that could be invented, as when he and a bevy of beautiful ladies, all dressed as miners, gaily toured the mines of the Harz. The king's chamberlain, Cousin de Marinville, became notorious for recruiting pretty young women to enliven the court. Not that his task was difficult. Parisian and German actresses and daughters of the nobility and bourgeoisie trouped happily to the palaces. "Careers" were open to beauty and charm; marriages could be made to young men of promise or older ones of fortune; influence could be gained outside marriage; an occasional lucky one might take the king's fancy. If nothing else there was gaiety, escape.

With the old social structure threatened and a new one yet undefined, escape was enough for many.

Jérôme's loves were many. The queen, a model of propriety, went her own way, giving no sign of objection. Few women held the king's interest for long, however, and fewer still had any real influence over him. In the first year the countess von Waldburg-Truchsess, described by Reinhard as *"jolie et intrigante,"* had his confidence. But as both grand mistress of the queen's household and the king's favorite, she was all too vulnerable. A scandal broke and she was exiled to the provinces. Afterward Jérôme's name was linked with that of madame de Pappenheim, whose husband Jérôme made a count, and others. Eventually, however, the Countess Ernestine von Löwenstein-Wertheim-Freudenberg became "Mistress in Title." Beautiful and worldly, she was a woman of intelligence, refinement, passion, and understanding, a combination the king found in no other. Her hold on him was such that she could tolerate his passing affairs with others. Madame d'Escalonne, a German beauty of seventeen, married to a courtier for convenience, accompanied Jérôme to Poland in 1812, but returned abruptly, alone. The king was followed back to Cassel by a Polish favorite, who, like Escalonne, proved no match for the Countess Ernestine.

The king's court, women, and amusements perforce attracted more attention than his constructive labors. But his people viewed him more fairly than could German historians in the next century. Francophobe and nationalist, they would exaggerate his vices and ignore his virtues and accomplishments. His people found much to admire in him, as their loyalty during the crisis of 1809 would demonstrate.

THE ARMY

His constitution required Jérôme to raise a Westphalian army of 25,000 (20,000 infantry, 3,500 cavalry, and 1,500 artillery), and to support 12,500 French, already present when he arrived. In all sincerity, the king expressed the conviction that they would go as soon as Westphalian troops could replace them, which encouraged financial support for his army, the acceptance of conscription, and voluntary enlistment. On all scores enthusiasm waned as the years passed, the "general peace" seemed even further away, and the French, though usually concentrated on Magdeburg, remained.

Napoleon dispatched three hundred bilingual French veterans to Cassel to serve as a nucleus for the royal guard, which was organized first. To these he told Jérôme to add nine hundred young Westphalians *de famille,* good bourgeois or sons of farmers, whose parents could help pay their expenses. The guard, as in the other kingdoms, was to be an instrument of social revolution. Napoleon emphasized that the recruits were to be young, "even eighteen," and without previous service, at least under the old princes. Jérôme was to select them carefully, even if two years were required to bring the guard to full strength. With special status, training, pay, and privileges, its members were expected to develop an *élan* and loyalty to the dynasty which would carry over to the rest of the army as guardsmen matured, were promoted, and assumed leadership of other units. The king was to consider ennobling the higher officers, who would initially be mostly French.

Jérôme violated his instructions. By the end of 1808 he had 2,100 men in the guard, rather than 1,200. He had not only light cavalry, grenadiers, infantry, and military police, which the emperor had authorized, but also *gardes-du-corps,* which he had not. But Napoleon, with a war in Spain and one with Austria in the offing, raised no objection. The guard, though hastily formed and greatly dependent on German officers for leadership, seemed solid and dependable. It would prove itself in 1809.

The Westphalian army numbered 14,000 at the end of Jérôme's first year. In addition to the guard there were 8,000 infantry, skirmishers (*Jäger-carabiniers*), ten companies of artillery, military police (*gendarmes*), and regiments of light and heavy cavalry (*chevauxlégers* and *Kürassiers*).[15] All 14,000 were trained, armed, equipped, and maneuverable. Another 4,000 were in training, and 7,000 conscripts arrived in depots in February 1809. In slightly

15. The German designations were a phonetic rendering of the French, except for the *Jäger* ("hunter"), and *Jäger-carabiniers,* which were the equivalent of the French *tirailleurs,* used to lead and screen an advance of infantry in column.

over a year, therefore, and in time for the Austrian War, Jérôme had 25,000 troops, as required.

Westphalia continued to produce troops, and superb ones, to meet Napoleon's demands. Considering her financial difficulties (to be discussed shortly) the record is remarkable. Here is a summary:

	Location	Number	Total
1809	Germany	16,000	
	Spain	9,500	25,500
1810	Germany	28,000	
	Spain	2,500	30,500
1811	Germany	25,000	
	Spain	2,000	27,000
1812	Germany proper	12,000	
	Spain	1,000	
	Baltic Fortresses	4,000	38,000
	Russia	17,000	
	Russia (replacements)	5,000	
1813	Germany	27,000	
	Spain	200	27,200

The figures are more impressive when we consider that to maintain the required strengths about 70,000 men were drafted and some 30,000 volunteered between January 1808 and October 1813. In 1809 the army lost only some 2,000 in Germany (killed, severely wounded, or missing), but in Spain the toll was disastrous. Of the 9,500 dispatched to the peninsula, 2,500 remained at the end of the year. Over 5,000 had been killed or died of fever, 2,000 evacuated wounded or ill, mostly with fever. General Morio, who commanded the Westphalian division in Catalonia, was himself evacuated with fever.[16] Jérôme asked that all Westphalians be returned from Spain. Napoleon refused, but cognizant of the effect of such severe losses on public morale, asked for no more complete units, only replacements. By 1813 he had allowed all units to withdraw but one, the First Westphalian Light Cavalry Regiment. Meanwhile, however, the kingdom had lost another 2,000 men on the peninsula; the unit remaining had 200 of its

16. Only 1,500 remained of Morio's division of 8,000. Artillery and cavalry units elsewhere in Spain fared better.

authorized 600 men. These fought on with the French in eastern Spain after Joseph had withdrawn to France. In 1812 only some 1,500 of the 22,000 men sent to Russia returned; some 2,000 more were isolated in Baltic fortresses. The units returned from Spain yielded only 200 veterans. Nevertheless Jérôme produced an army of 27,000 for the 1813 campaign.

Westphalians served with distinction everywhere. Thirteen earned the Legion of Honor in Spain; ninety-three in Russia. Commanders like General Adam Ludwig Ochs (who replaced Morio in Spain) and General Count Hans von Hammerstein were among the finest in Napoleon's service. Both fought in Spain, Germany, and Russia; both won the Legion of Honor. No satellite troops served Napoleon better in war, nor remained loyal longer. No kingdom produced as many troops per capita as did Westphalia. The kingdom moreover supported French troops—12,500 in 1808 and 1809, 18,500 during part of 1810 and in 1811, 24,000 in the first half of 1812, and at least 30,000 during ten months of 1813. The key fortress of Magdeburg was provisioned to withstand siege in 1809 and in 1813 stocked to sustain 30,000 men for three months. The army, throughout, had a desertion problem, but the rate was little worse than in France. In the latter years the population grew restive, and isolated places were rebellious, under the pressure of taxes, levies, conscription, and news of heavy casualties. But Westphalia contributed to Napoleon's military strength far out of proportion to her size.

Why? Westphalians had a military tradition; her native leaders had deeply ingrained penchants for order and discipline, and they feared Napoleon. But within the army Jérôme's policies and personal leadership ability counted heavily. The king took his soldiering seriously. He emphasized the *German* character of his army. The majority of the officers and noncommissioned officers were German, though Napoleon insisted that the minister of war and most of the division commanders be French.[17] Except in the guard, commands were given in German, and uniforms, though gaudy enough to suit the king's taste, showed the mark of German tailors. Jérôme moved easily among his men and obviously cared

17. Roughly one-quarter of the officers were French or Polish. Except in the guard and gendarmes non-German NCO's were rare.

about their welfare. His was the first German army where officers were forbidden to strike men. Movement from noncommissioned officer to officer rank was made easy. Pay was higher than in any German army, and regular. The army promoted patriotism and weakened provincial attitudes, softened class distinctions, and encouraged religious toleration. Hessians, Prussians, Hanoverians, Saxons, and other Germans marched together in the same uniform. Officers came from all classes, though nobles were in the majority. Catholics, Calvinists, Lutherans, and, for the first time in any German army, Jews served together in the officer corps. The ranks were a similar amalgam. All of this proved to the advantage of the army. There was rank, pay, and glory enough for the old leadership elements; those of the lower classes who gained position were loyal to the system which gave them the opportunity.[18]

The medals of the Royal Order of the Crown of Westphalia were awarded infrequently and worn with pride. Napoleon accepted and wore the highest decoration, that of grand commander, not once, ceremonially, as he did with those proffered by Louis, Joseph, and Murat, but frequently. The sons of the most prominent families populated the *"Pagenkorps,"* of the royal military schools at Cassel and Brunswick. These centers inherited the facilities, faculties, and traditions of the schools of the elector of Hesse and the duke of Brunswick. It was not difficult to bring the curriculum in line with French doctrine on strategy, tactics, weapon employment, staff methods, drill, and leadership, and not too startling that the institutions produced good line officers (cavalry, infantry). What was surprising was that engineer and artillery officers second to none in the imperial armies were graduated from the entirely new branches added to the military school at Cassel.

Jérôme was a good judge of men. Few whom he gave command disappointed him; still fewer betrayed him. (Dörnberg, the outstanding exception, we shall identify shortly.) When with his army, the king set a good example. He was alert and active, made decisions quickly, and gave positive, clear orders; his subordinates

18. Jérôme employed most of the officers of the former princes, and had an excess of generals. But he considered it good policy, and worth the cost, to keep their loyalty by giving them status in the new regime.

were never in doubt as to his wishes. He was sometimes wrong, but always abreast of the situation, unafraid to accept responsibility, and ready to accept a better course. He eagerly exposed himself to danger, even in practice. Once, on maneuvers, a soldier fell into a swollen river. Jérôme leaped into a rowboat and went after him, was swept downstream and saved himself (and the soldier) by seizing a bridge piling and holding on. The events of 1809 allowed him to demonstrate forcefully both his physical and moral courage. He was a very good soldier, a natural leader, and an instinctive master of tactics. His alleged failure in Russia has no basis in fact, as we shall show in a later chapter.

The Crisis of 1809

During 1808 French reverses drew to Spain the bulk of the Grande Armée and Napoleon himself. In northern Europe his enemies raised their heads. Austria, her army reformed and expanded by the Archduke Charles, had 400,000 men, including her *Landwehr*.[19] Count Stadion, the foreign minister, and Metternich, ambassador at Paris, urged on by the treacherous Talleyrand, openly joined the "war party," which included the archdukes; Maria Ludovica d'Este, the new empress;[20] and Baron Hormayr, historian and proponent of Austrian and pan-German nationalism. In Vienna and Prague, the elite of European exiles blared encouragement—madame de Staël, August and Friedrich von Schlegel, Pozzo di Borgo, baron vom Stein. War spirit, whipped up by French-style propaganda, songs, poems, and plays, swept the populations of Austria, Hungary, and Bohemia. Prussian, and to a lesser degree other German intellectuals and patriots, discouraged by the caution of their rulers, reluctantly looked to Austria for leadership. Their people, however, reflected little of their enthusiasm. The Emperor Francis, despite his failure to find allies, other than the British, plumped for war.

In February 1809 the Tyrolean mountaineers of Andreas Hofer revolted against the king of Bavaria (by grace of Napoleon their

19. Composed of old soldiers and volunteers, with a high command of regular officers, a sort of national guard.
20. Third wife of Francis I.

ruler since 1805). True to the promises of Hormayr and the Arch-
duke John, Austrian troops supported the rebels. The Archduke
Charles, however, delayed marching into Germany. Meanwhile,
Napoleon, in January, had returned from Spain and in three
months rebuilt the Grande Armée by reinforcing the 90,000-man
Army of the Rhine and calling up the troops of his satellites and
Rheinbund allies.[21] In March Charles proclaimed a war of German
liberation; on April 9 he invaded Bavaria, but by that time the
French emperor was marching across south Germany at the head
of over 200,000 men. In Italy Eugène's army, reinforced with
French divisions, stood ready to meet the Austrians under the
Archduke John. In the face of Napoleon's rapid recovery Prussia
remained neutral; Czar Alexander prudently stood by the Erfurt
Agreement of 1808, hoping to gain at Austria's expense.

On May 12 Napoleon was in Vienna. The campaign seemed
almost over when on May 20 the French established a bridgehead
on the north bank of the Danube. But on May 21–22, at Aspern-
Essling, the Archduke Charles struck. Napoleon's advance divisions were forced back onto the Island of Löbau. Not until the
end of June did he attempt another crossing, which led on July 5–6
to the victory of Wagram. Meanwhile his enemies exulted. The
British decided to attack Holland; the Pope (in effect) excom-
municated him; Frederick William of Prussia inclined toward
joining Austria (but procrastinated until events decided him otherwise), and German recalcitrants struck at Westphalia.

In April 1809 Jérôme had been placed in command of the
tenth corps (reserve) of the Grande Armée. It comprised the
Westphalian army (15,500 with about 8,500 fully maneuverable),[22] 14,000 French garrisoned at Hanover, Hamburg, Bremen
(10,000 maneuverable), 3,000 at Stralsund, Küstrin, and Stettin
(unusable except in dire emergency), a Dutch division (7,000)
and some 2,300 Mecklenburgers.[23] Other French units (totaling
about 18,000 men) were prepared to reinforce him if necessary,
principally from Hanau and Mainz. Reubell was Jérôme's chief

21. An amazing feat, since he had left 300,000 men in Spain under Joseph's
command.
22. Another 9,500 were in Spain, as noted, p. 195.
23. The Magdeburg garrison, though most of it had marched with Napoleon,
was under another command, the "Corps of Observation of the Elbe."

of staff; his top generals, D'Albignac, Du Coudras, and, when he finally arrived, the Dutch General Gratien. His corps was hardly a cohesive unit; even the Westphalians were scattered for provisioning. Time would be required to assemble troops either to defend Westphalia or take part in the campaign.

Those most interested in attacking Westphalia were her former princes. The duke of Brunswick-Oels had joined the Austrians in Bohemia with a "Black Legion of Vengeance." The former elector of Hesse-Cassel was there also with a few troops. Prussia constituted the greatest potential threat, was alive with anti-French agitation, and succored the leadership of pan-German nationalism, with which such eminences as Scharnhorst, Blücher, and Gneisenau were (rightly) suspected of being involved. Despite all pressures, however, Frederick William declined to risk another debacle such as that of 1806. Without his support, as it turned out, no one was able to seriously endanger Westphalia. The kingdom became a battleground, all the same, and Prussian subjects were among the invaders. One made legend, but the first was hardly made of the stuff of heroes.

Friedrich Wilhelm von Katte, a former lieutenant of Prussian infantry, responded to the Archduke Charles's appeal to the Germans before the Austrian commander had himself begun the war. On the night of April 2–3, 1809, he appeared with a few companions at Stendal (north of Magdeburg), intimidated the local officials, announced that the "war of liberation" had begun, collected some money, and induced a few innocents to follow him. On the approach of troops from Magdeburg, however, he fled, ultimately to Bohemia. There were those who might have joined the young romantic, but he had not bothered to coordinate with any of the dissident organizations. His king declared him a traitor, but he had already escaped.

Really serious trouble was brewing, however, inside Westphalia, a conspiracy led by a colonel of the guard and royal chamberlain, baron von Dörnberg.[24] A Hessian, Dörnberg had served in the Prussian army. In 1806 he had been among the last to surrender, and retired to his estates only after failing to persuade the elector of Hesse to fight on. Offered service by Jérôme, he had

24. Wilhelm Kaspar Ferdinand, Freiherr von Dörnberg (1768–1831).

accepted, and played a major role in organizing the guard. All the while, however, the mustachioed, dashing colonel had been plotting rebellion.

Dörnberg's group had headquarters at the convent of Homberg, which housed only noble ladies, among them Marianne vom Stein, sister of the famous Prussian minister. The conspirators included former officers, nobles, and a middle class group led by one Sigismund Martin. Directly and through the high-born nuns, the leaders were in contact with Chazot, in Berlin, Vom Stein, and other nationalists as well as the elector of Hesse-Cassel and the duke of Brunswick.[25] All supported the return of the elector and other deposed princes; otherwise, they disagreed. Dörnberg's immediate followers were vaguely pan-German; Martin's were Hessian patriots, but wanted the elector to accept a constitution; others were merely traditionalists. They were fully united on one proposition: The French had to be expelled. Dörnberg pinned his hopes on an army revolt; Martin on an uprising of the masses. They tried to produce a combination of the two.

On April 22 the conspirators began their operation. At Homberg Martin, attired in a colonel's uniform tailored for the occasion, organized a crowd of peasants (armed mostly with pitchforks, axes, and farm implements), ex-soldiers, and foresters. At other neighboring villages similar groups formed. They expected to march on Cassel the following morning on signal from Dörnberg. The colonel, in Cassel, planned to induce all or part of the guard to defect, capture Jérôme, and hold him in the palace until his "army" arrived and took the city. He also counted on help from the Prussian Major Ferdinand von Schill (of whom we shall say more shortly).

The uprising had been scheduled and canceled twice, while its leaders perfected their plans and waited for the optimum moment to strike. Nevertheless, amateurism marked the whole operation. In the countryside armed peasants moved about in broad daylight, and Cassel was alerted. Dörnberg, afraid he had been betrayed, rode off hell-for-leather for Homberg. Arriving at dusk, he found

25. The duke (*Herzog*) von Braunschweig-Oels, heir to the Duchy of Brunswick (Braunschweig), fourth son of Karl Wilhelm Ferdinand, whose military career had begun in the Seven Years' War, and been ended by a mortal wound at Auerstädt in 1806.

a detachment of Westphalian troops under Colonel Marshall, whom he summoned to join the revolt. Marshall, nonplused, simply led his men away. Martin, earlier in the day, had tried to win over two squadrons of *Kürassiers,* but most of them had departed also.

Dörnberg decided to attack Cassel anyway. The next morning (April 23) he led the insurgents away from Homberg, flying a flag on which the ladies of the convent had embroidered "VICTORY OR DEATH IN THE CAUSE OF THE NATION."[26] Groups from other villages joined him along the way. Most local officials prudently stood aside; one mayor who emerged sounding warnings was thrown into a cesspool. Dörnberg soon had 5,000 men behind him.

The preceding day Jérôme had sent toward the trouble area two screening forces, each of less than three hundred men, under Reubell and D'Albignac. This left him 1,500 guardsmen in Cassel. He called for French troops from Mainz and Gratien's Dutch division, but knew it would be days before any help arrived. Some of the king's advisers suggested he withdraw to a safer place; he coolly refused, but did send Catherine off to Strasbourg. After a sleepless night he faced his troops and called the German officers forward. Choose, he told them—go freely and join the enemy or take a new oath to your king. To a man his officers swore loyalty.[27]

Meanwhile, five miles from Cassel, Reubell confronted Dörnberg. The French general had some two hundred infantry, twenty-five cavalry, and two cannon, but almost all were Westphalians. Dörnberg had five thousand men, but mostly without firearms. Both hesitated, assessing their chances. The rebels taunted the troops and called on them to desert. Seeing quickly that delay might be fatal, Reubell opened fire with his cannon. The rebels fired back, and the Westphalian troops, once engaged, attacked viciously. Dörnberg's "army" scattered to the winds. The first real

26. SIEG ODER TOD IM KAMPFE FÜR DAS VATERLAND.
27. There was risk involved, but Jérôme was making an intelligent gamble. Obvious suspects had already been arrested, and he knew that most others with strong rebel sympathies had fled. His gesture was calculated to win the respect of men who set high value on courage, and force them into making a clear choice. Napoleon could not have sized up the situation better.

crisis was past; Jérôme's courage and leadership ability had been proven. His troops would not waver thereafter until the last days of the empire, and surprisingly few of them then.[28]

Before the dust cleared, however, Westphalia was beset with invaders—the freebooters of Major Ferdinand von Schill. A seemingly nonchalant, likable, but extremely cunning soldier, Schill had made his reputation in 1806. Captured at Magdeburg by the French, he had escaped, though wounded, with two men. Within weeks he was leading a thousand partisans, and had become the terror of the French in north Germany. His captives included Marshal Victor, taken enroute to Stettin. After Tilsit "Battalion Schill," now a Prussian army unit, marched first in the escort of Frederick William when he reentered Berlin. Schill disdained spit-and-polish, but maintained rigid discipline. His punishments, such as making men dress as women and walk behind the battalion, were more feared than the cane, which he forbade his officers to use.

Probably with the blessing of General Blücher (though officially he had to deny it), Schill marched from Berlin on April 28, ostensibly to exercise his troops, who were unaware of their destination. En route to the border he announced to his men that they were the vanguard of a Prussian army in the "war of liberation." Before the day was out he had orders to return to Berlin, but he ignored them, and moved south into Saxony, then went through Anhalt into Westphalia. Schill's troops were in a holiday mood, their commander exultantly announcing in every village that Blücher was on his heels with 13,000 men. He appropriated the city treasury at Halle, returned to Anhalt, where he recruited and seized cannon, then crossed the Elbe again into Westphalia. Meanwhile he learned that Frederick William had declared him an outlaw, that Dörnberg had fled, and that forces dispatched by Jérôme were closing in on him, Gratien's division from the west,

28. Dörnberg was hidden by sympathetic peasants and escaped in disguise to Bohemia. Martin was arrested and condemned to death, but Jérôme pardoned him and later made him a royal notary. Most of the handful of officers and men who had defected were captured, but few were executed. The convent at Homberg was closed, and Marianne vom Stein and a few others imprisoned briefly. Over all Jérôme was merciful, which, since he was firmly in control, was accepted as a gesture of benevolence rather than weakness.

D'Albignac, much reinforced, from the north. It was evident, moreover, that the best he could expect from the Westphalian people was neutrality. No man to court suicide, he struck at a weak Westphalian-French detachment at Todendorf, broke out of what would soon have been an encirclement, and began a forced march for Swedish Pomerania. On May 24 he stormed into Stralsund, catching its French defenders (200 artillerymen), in the process of unpacking equipment, captured them, took control of the city, and made contact with British ships lying offshore. He was informed that George III would make him a colonel, and the royal navy evacuate him and his troops.

Schill now had 6,000 men, however, recruited partly in the Prussian and Brunswickian provinces of Westphalia, but mostly in Mecklenburg and Pomerania. He decided to defend Stralsund, assuming that the French would react slowly, giving him time to organize the fortress. This time Schill guessed wrongly. As soon as Jérôme had intelligence of the path of Schill's force, he had ordered Gratien and d'Albignac into pursuit, reenforcing the Dutch with 1,500 Danish troops. Gratien reached Stralsund first, and on May 31 attacked alone. Schill's men, concentrating pell-mell to repulse the assault, left one gate totally unguarded. The Dutch found it and poured through. In the ensuing melee Schill was killed, his makeshift army overwhelmed, and all but three hundred of his men killed or captured.

Schill's heroic death made his place in the German nationalist pantheon unshakable. (Even today German school children know his name.) Napoleon, who knew that the major had won a victory of the spirit, wreaked venegeance on his followers. All were treated as stateless renegades, many executed, hundreds condemned to the galleys in France.

Hardly had Schill been dealt with when Saxony was invaded by the duke of Brunswick-Oels with his "Black Legion of Vengeance," 2,000 strong, supported by some 7,500 Austrians and 500 men under the elector of Hesse. On June 11 Brunswick took Dresden, on June 19 Leipzig. At Napoleon's order Jérôme and D'Albignac marched with 11,000 men to reinforce the Saxons of Thielmann (2,000) who had retreated toward the Westphalian border. (Most of Saxony's troops were with the Grande Armée.)

Gratien followed rapidly. By June 21 the king had assembled 20,000 men at Weissenfels, on the Saale. On June 24 he smashed Brunswick's advance guard, on June 26 captured Leipzig, and on June 31 Dresden, but allowed the Austrian Kienmayer to recapture Leipzig without a fight. The enemy began to consolidate for a new effort; Jérôme maneuvered and tried to contact Junot, marching with a small corps to his aid.

Before any serious action could occur, however, news arrived of Wagram (July 5–6) and the Austrian armistice with Napoleon. Kienmayer withdrew to Bohemia, and Jérôme, with some justice, concluded that the war was over. More trouble in his kingdom seemed unlikely. There had been an uprising in late June, led by a rickety Don Quixote, retired Colonel Emmerich, and his Sancho, an equally ancient professor, but they had found no support and had been ingloriously arrested by the police.

The war was not over for the duke of Brunswick, however, who made a move so militarily illogical that Jérôme can hardly be condemned for not anticipating it. Gambling on an English landing in the north of Germany and/or an uprising among his former subjects, he marched for Brunswick with his legion and some of Hesse's men.[29] Cassel was alerted; at Halberstadt, General Meyronnet threw 3,000 Westphalian troops in Brunswick's path, but the duke's black-clad veterans cut through, capturing Meyronnet and killing 600 of his men. On July 31 Brunswick was in his hereditary capital, where his people greeted him warmly, but showed no signs of fighting spirit. Jérôme's corps, meanwhile, had left Saxony and was drawing closer by the hour. Taking the initiative, the duke on August 1 sought out the king's advance guard, under Reubell, and scattered it, but aware that D'Albignac, Gratien, and Thielmann were close behind, he beat a retreat. Sending a decoy force in the direction of Bremen, Brunswick made for Elsfleth, at the mouth of the Weser, where ships of Admiral Stuart's British fleet took him and his men aboard. A little later, the rest of the Black Legion was picked up at Bremen. In London the duke became the hero of the hour.[30]

29. Hesse went into exile in Bohemia.
30. He was pensioned by George III and remained in England until 1813, when he returned to Prussian service. He was killed at Quatre-Bras (1815) during the Waterloo campaign.

Napoleon raged over the Black Legion's escape, and insisted that Reubell be destituted for allowing the occupation of Brunswick.[31] He condemned Jérôme for not winning decisive victories in Saxony: "You make war like a satrap!" But in fact the king had done well. The rear of the Grande Armée had been adequately protected. Further, he had kept the loyalty of most of his people, and shown himself capable of firm, energetic leadership. Surely fear of Napoleon influenced Jérôme's officials and people, but he deserves credit for having established a government and army which held together in time of crisis. During the entire hectic spring and summer fewer than a hundred officers and men defected. All the prefects and subprefects remained loyal, and all but a few municipal officials. In Germany, especially, leadership meant everything; the defection of any sizable number of Jérôme's military and civil officers could have meant disaster. He had chosen them well.[32]

Westphalia's financial problems had multiplied. The population was not insensitive to the loss of men in battle, some 2,000 in Germany, 6,000 in Spain. But peace was in the offing, the challenges Westphalians had met in 1809 had given them an enhanced sense of nationality, and their king seemed better identified with them, or at least established beyond hope of remedy. Jérôme accepted his brother's criticism as disciplinary; he had come to expect little praise. He knew he had done well, and expected to have Hanover[33] added to his kingdom as a reward.

In November 1809, Jérôme traveled to Paris for the family council which preceded Napoleon's divorce from Joséphine. It was confirmed that he would receive Hanover, which made him even more amenable to his brother's divorce, which he favored anyway despite his affection for the empress. The proposed second marriage, which would make the Habsburg emperor Napoleon's father-in-law, could not but improve Jérôme's standing in Ger-

31. Reubell emigrated to the United States.
32. It is to Jérôme's credit that he did not try to blame his Saxon "failures" on Junot. Napoleon's chief complaint was that Jérôme had not made contact with Junot, so that if the war had continued Kienmayer might have defeated each in turn. But whereas Junot had known Jérôme's location, the reverse had not been true, and Junot had equally failed to establish liaison with Jérôme.
33. The kingdom already possessed the southern fringe of Hanover, but the bulk of it had been under French military government since 1806.

many. Over all, the future seemed bright, despite Westphalia's serious financial problems, which the king hoped (vainly) the wealth of Hanover would alleviate.

Finances

Napoleon, says Rambaud, "financially ruined his own creation." He initially saddled Westphalia with a debt of 34,000,000 francs,[34] allocated 7,000,000 francs a year to himself from the royal domains, designated lands with incomes totaling 5,000,000 a year to be distributed as imperial fiefs, and claimed 26,000,000 owed the former princes by foreign courts.[35] The requirement to support 12,500 French troops added some 10,000,000 a year to Westphalia's expenses, and more after 1810, when requirements were increased.[36] These assessments were crippling for a kingdom with annual revenues averaging only 34,000,000 francs and which at the outset had domestic debt of 47,000,000 francs amassed by the former rulers.

What really "ruined" Westphalia, however, were the economic disadvantages under which she labored. The uncertainties of the time drove domestic capital into hiding. Considerable risk was involved even in investing in the "national properties" (those confiscated from the churches, Catholic and Protestant, and rebel nobles, plus some of the royal domains), which might revert to their former owners. Foreign capital, where available, went to the more promising industries and commercial houses of France, Switzerland, and Italy (or into illicit commerce). Dutch bankers refused to lend even to Jérôme's government. The kingdom did not control the mouths of the Elbe and Weser, its principal arteries. Foreign trade was hampered further by the Continental System, and domestic trade by a multitude of internal customs barriers, most of which were left intact until the "general peace" (which

34. The constitution required that French denominations of money be used. Accounts were kept in francs, though the currencies of the former states continued to circulate.

35. Spelled out in the Treaty of Berlin (April 22, 1808), negotiated by Daru for Napoleon and Jollivet (nominally) for Jérôme.

36. To 18,500 with the addition of Hanover, reduced again when Napoleon repossessed Hanover, but expanded in 1811–1812 in preparation for the Russian campaign, and in 1812–1813 to support operations in Germany.

never came), because they produced ready revenues and protected provincial industries which would have collapsed without
them. Westphalian agriculture prospered, but industry declined
slightly, and mining and commerce greatly. Revenues, therefore,
in spite of increased taxes, remained static; the budget never
balanced.

To meet its obligations the government sold the national
properties, including by 1813 virtually all of the royal domains,
resorted to forced loans, and in the last year of the kingdom confiscations of money and property. The national debt climbed
steadily. The chart below shows the course of Westphalian finances:[37]

Year	Domestic Budget	Revenue	Deficit	Domestic Debt Year's End
1808	42,000,000	34,000,000	8,000,000	47,000,000
1809	50,000,000	32,000,000	18,000,000	93,000,000
1810	45,000,000	35,000,000	10,000,000	113,000,000
1811	45,000,000	35,000,000	10,000,000	160,000,000
1812	56,000,000	32,000,000	24,000,000	189,000,000
1813	58,000,000	27,000,000	31,000,000	220,000,000

The "Domestic Budget" figures above include the cost of the
Westphalian army, but not of supporting French troops. Income
is only that from taxes and tariffs. During the reign some 100,-
000,000 francs, not shown, was required for pay and subsistence
of French troops; another 100,000,000 was expended to furnish
them horses, forage, matériel, and supplies. About 120,000,000
francs was obtained by the sale of the National Properties, including virtually all the royal domains. The rest came from forced loans
and confiscations. Only the loans (and the domestic deficits) are
reflected in the "Debt" figure. The only compensation the kingdom
got was cancellation, bit by bit, of the debt to France (34,000,000
francs).[38] In short Westphalia was not only deeply in debt when
the kingdom fell (October 1813), but bereft of public property,
and drained of everything of any use in war.

37. Figures in francs.
38. But first the debt had been whittled down in consideration of the
transfer of royal lands to Napoleon, the assumption of Hanoverian debts, and
other concessions.

Taxes had been revised the first year, making the basic land tax (*Grundsteuer*) applicable to all lands, even those of the crown. Feudal and corporate privileges were abolished for the hearth tax, movable-property tax, and indirect taxes. Most indirect levies, including salt and stamp taxes, remained about the same, though made uniform in all areas. National tariffs were standardized; internal tariffs, as noted above, changed little. Thereafter imposts rose yearly. In 1809, the hearth tax, which had begun at an average of four francs (on heads of families) was pushed to five and three-fifths francs; food, salt, and stamp taxes were increased, and licenses required for all businessmen, artisans, and peddlers. In 1810 and 1811 more varieties of indirect taxes were elevated, and fines for desertion and draft-dodging (on heads of families of offenders) raised. In 1812 a graduated personal tax became applicable to all males above sixteen, with exceptions for officers (captains and above), miners, those in arms industries and foundries, invalids, foreign students, and others. The land tax, begun at 5 percent, had reached 20 percent by 1812. In addition there were emergency taxes and confiscations, especially in 1812 and 1813. Special taxes were levied on Magdeburg province and other formerly Prussian areas, where French troops were normally concentrated, and where the population was the most recalcitrant. Moreover French commanders sometimes levied without the king's permission. In Magdeburg the burden on property holders was so great that some emigrated, abandoning their holdings.[39]

From a domestic viewpoint the reign had produced fiscal disaster. From the imperial viewpoint Westphalia had served outstandingly. Jérôme *met* every requirement established by Napoleon —to the very end. That he did this, and with a totally German financial administration—from the minister of finance to the lowest collector—is almost incredible. Even in 1813 he did not fail. Magdeburg was supplied with a war chest and stocked for 30,000 troops for three months, horses and material were supplied, and the Westphalian army was rebuilt. No area of the empire, even France herself, served the emperor better than Westphalia.

39. Three hundred empty houses were reported in 1810.

The Affair of Hanover

By a treaty of January 14, 1810, Hanover became part of Westphalia, making the latter larger than any state in the *Rheinbund,* save Saxony.[40] Revenues of 15,000,000 francs a year were expected. The duchy had a large reserve of manpower; it produced surpluses of grain and livestock, famous breeds of war horses, and had arms plants and foundries which could be fed by the iron and lead mines the kingdom already possessed. Westphalia's domestic trade benefited little, nor, on a legal basis, her foreign trade. The Hanse cities remained under imperial control, though the kingdom's boundaries did impinge on Bremen, Hamburg, and Lübeck, the first two on the North Sea estuaries of the Weser and Elbe, respectively, the latter with access to the North Sea. If the "general peace" ever came, of course, trade prospects were good.

But Napoleon never gave anything away. Jérôme agreed to support 18,500 instead of 12,500 French troops, and the 6,000 added were all cavalry, so that the total cost to Westphalia went from 10,000,000 francs a year to 20,000,000. Property yielding 5,000,000 francs a year was allocated for imperial fiefs. And Westphalia had to assume Hanover's foreign and domestic debts, together 180,000,000 francs. Considering these commitments, acquiring Hanover seemed of doubtful value, without much question unprofitable in the short run.

Even so, the emperor began to hedge on his bargain. He denied Jérôme full authority in Hanover until a detailed settlement could be completed establishing exact boundaries and designating imperial land and incomes specifically. Le Camus and count von Wintzingerode negotiated for over two months with French diplomats, and in March 1810 a lengthy "Act of Cession" was completed. But Napoleon, after more delays, refused to ratify it. The status of Hanover remained uncertain. Jérôme struggled to meet his treaty obligations, while imperial officials appropriated a good share of ordinary revenues and all of the income from the postal service, customs, and royal forests.

40. Her territory increased from 18,000 to 30,000 square miles, her population from 2,200,000 to almost 3,000,000.

Jérôme, nevertheless, sent a *Hohe Regierungskommission* into Hanover which served as an interim government until September 1810, by which time three new departments[41] were ready to operate, new courts had been organized, the *Code Napoléon* introduced, and provision made for representation of the new departments in the Westphalian parliament. Meanwhile the king's officials clashed almost daily with the officers and procurers of Marshal Davout, commanding the French Army of the North, and the minions of Barrois, director of imperial domains. In the absence of an Act of Cession, defining areas of authority, conflicts were settled by contests of will, by referring them to Paris, or by the earlier arrival of one or another set of officials. Tempers flared, tension between French and Westphalians led to fist fights, duels, and minor demonstrations. Davout seized what his troops needed at random. A taciturn, humorless, professional soldier, he executed Napoleon's orders with machinelike efficiency. Bald, heavy-shouldered, his face frozen in an expression of disdain, he displayed his contempt for the "playboy" king in an exaggerated courtesy combined with total disregard of his authority. Jérôme developed such an antipathy for the "Iron Marshal" that later, in Russia, it critically influenced his behavior.

Napoleon maintained a warm personal relationship with Jérôme and Catherine. They were at Compiègne when the emperor met his new bride, traveled to Paris for the wedding, and accompanied the imperial couple on their spring tour of the Lowlands. Officially, however, Napoleon seemed to favor Davout. When the pay of French troops fell into arrears, he ordered the marshal's headquarters moved into the city of Hanover to "facilitate" the collection of revenues. When Davout threatened to seize Magdeburg (city) if the fortress were not supplied, the emperor ignored Jérôme's protest. (The threat was not carried out, however.)

Since the fall of 1809 Napoleon had bombarded Jérôme with complaints about the violations of the Continental System. The tempo had increased after the "annexation" of Hanover, and become more violent after the abdication by Louis of the Dutch

41. Nord, Nieder-Elbe, and Aller with capitals at Stade, Lüneburg, and Hanover.

throne. Jérôme had exerted himself to enforce the system. His agents and gendarmes had cut deeply into the contraband traffic between the Hanse cities and Strasbourg, which for a time had followed the Weser to Münden (just north of Cassel), and gone overland to the Rhine.[42] In September 1809 a single raid had netted a hundred wagons of British goods. In 1810 he expanded his customs service, and ordered all his officials, police, and gendarmes to give French agents in Hanover their full cooperation. He gave evidence to Napoleon, at the same time, that French officials were probably more venal than his. Nevertheless, the French got orders to penetrate into Westphalia proper. Jérôme protested, but tried loyally to facilitate their work; still he was treated to abuse from Paris.

The king had begun to fear that he would share the fate of Louis. Davout had declared publicly that he meant to pinch Westphalians until they screamed for union with France. Napoleon consistently refused to ratify the "Act of Cession" for Hanover, which territory had only served to derange Westphalia's finances and shatter the morale of her officials. "I pray Your Majesty," Jérôme wrote Napoleon on October 30, 1810, ". . . positively to make known . . . his intentions . . . I am ready to . . . do his bidding . . . but if he leaves me [King] . . . he cannot deny me the means to maintain myself with honor . . ." Napoleon's reply was short and ominous. "It seems unnecessary to repeat that you have made agreements with me which ought to be kept, and they have not been kept." Throughout the fall he had emphasized that pay of French troops was late, and on October 20 had instructed Champagny to inform Jérôme that pay must be produced or Hanover would be repossessed.

His "case" against Jérôme thoroughly prepared, Napoleon, by a *senatus consultum* of December 13, 1810, annexed the northeastern half of Hanover to France, along with Osnabrück and most of Minden, both held since 1807.[43] Westphalia retained

42. Minden and Osnabrück also fed contraband to Strasbourg.
43. More specifically, Westphalia lost all territory north of an irregular line running roughly northeast from the confluence of the Rhine and Lippe (south of Wesel) to the North Sea east of Travemünde, leaving Münster, Minden, Nienburg, and Lauenburg on the French side. The same *senatus consultum* joined to France the Hanse cities, the Duchy of Oldenburg, part of the Grand Duchy of Berg, and other small territories.

half of Hanover and had 250,000 more people than in 1809. But the territories lost had produced above average revenues, so that the estimated yearly income of the kingdom dropped 2,000,-000 francs. In the final bargain,[44] the number of French troops to be supported was again made 12,500, some imperial domains were returned to Jérôme, and he was allowed to purchase others with Westphalian bonds (adding 14,500,000 to the national debt). Westphalia remained responsible for part of Hanover's domestic debt, however—about 40,000,000 francs—but in the course of negotiations her debt to France had been reduced to 10,000,000 francs, and would be eliminated in the next two years.

The settlement could have been worse. But the arbitrariness with which the emperor had redrawn boundaries made Jérôme's real status glaringly clear. He had, in effect, no rights not voidable by Napoleon. The *senatus consultum* of December 13 was issued without prior notice to the king or his ambassador. Champagny wrote Reinhard of the action on December 14, but not until December 17 did the emperor authorize Champagny to inform Jérôme, in general terms, of the disposition of territories. Both before and after the *senatus consultum* the efforts of Le Camus and Wintzingerode to negotiate terms were futile. Wrote Jérôme to Napoleon: "If it is part of your political design to annex Westphalia to the Empire, like Holland, I have but one desire, that is to know about it at once . . ." In the end the emperor granted the kingdom life, but on such terms as he chose, disregarding all previous commitments.[45]

What was the meaning of the affair of Hanover? The usual explanation is that Napoleon concluded, after ceding the territory to Jérôme, that the Continental System could only be enforced if France possessed the North Sea Coast, the Hanse cities, and their hinterland. He had temporized in treaties with both Louis and Jérôme; he broke both, forcing Louis to abdicate, making a new treaty with Jérôme. But it seems apparent that the emperor's

44. Treaty of May 10, 1811.
45. Westphalia was again reduced to eight departments: Elbe, Fulda, Harz, Leine, Ocker, Saale, Werra, and Aller. Aller comprised newly acquired Hanoverian territory and what remained of the old Weser department (i.e., part of the Bishopric of Minden); Leine was slightly expanded with new Hanoverian territory.

actions, up to the end of 1810, were directed toward forcing Jérôme to abdicate also. The measures taken to destroy the king's morale and authority were the same used in Holland. French customs officials invaded his kingdom, the French military defied his laws, French obligations were ignored while accusations of faithlessness and treason were showered on him. But for the decision of the czar to defy Napoleon, made positive when he renounced the Continental System on December 31, 1810, the Kingdom of Westphalia would probably have disappeared. As we have noted, all the kingdoms were in jeopardy in 1810; in 1811 Napoleon began to retrench for war on Russia. The creation of a "Roman Empire" of French departments to replace the satellite system was postponed. Westphalia, and the other kingdoms, were saved. But probably their lives would have been short if the emperor had won in Russia.

The Universities, Education, and Cultural Life

"Your universities are good for nothing: I'll burn them all; I want nothing but soldiers and ignoramuses," Jérôme flung at Müller in 1809, when student unrest was adding to his problems. Expressed in anger, this was far from the king's true attitude, as his director of instruction knew, but it added to Müller's sense of disillusionment over the progress of education in Westphalia. Convinced by Napoleon that French rule would bring enlightenment, peace, and the blessings of liberty and equality to Germany, he had happily entered Jérôme's service. But Westphalia had perforce become Sparta, not Athens. If the king did not mean to burn the universities he was bent on closing three of them. Müller's despair surely hastened his death, which occurred within weeks of Jérôme's outburst.

Initially Westphalia inherited five universities, Marburg and Rinteln from Hesse, Helmstedt from Brunswick, Halle from Prussia, and Göttingen (the "Georgia Augusta") from Hanover. Müller set out to make Göttingen, his alma mater, a *Kern Deutschlands*—center of new enlightenment—for which no German university seemed a better choice. Founded in 1734 by George II of England, it had quickly acquired a place in the top rank of European universities, with unexcelled faculties in law, classics, economics, politics, philosophy, theology, and science.[46] Halle had an excellent reputation, but had been too much a school for Prussian bureaucrats; Marburg was good; the other two of questionable quality, though all were old, and subjects of pride for their people.[47] While planning to concentrate on Göttingen, Müller considered it vitally important to preserve and improve all of the schools, for the sake of public support, if nothing else.

The king, the faculties, the students, the police, and local officials all seemed bent on frustrating the director of instruction. Jérôme, beset with budget problems, argued that two universities were more than enough for a small kingdom, though he did visit the institutions, praise their work, and offer prizes to their scholars. The faculties, especially Göttingen's, refused to recognize that France deserved to lead Germany intellectually, and perhaps rightly. As H. A. L. Fisher observed: "In Germany a new literature, a new philosophy, a new humanism, a new pedagogy had been the product of a generation. In France there was no divinity, no philosophy, no Greek, no political science. There was only Chateaubriand, Barante, and the *Moniteur*. In Germany there were all the kings of European scholarship and thought." The aging philologist, Gottlob Heyne, expressed the opinion of many. The king's prizes were attractive, he said, but he could not "rise to the French hyperbole." The students reacted violently to the government's bans on dueling, the wearing of caps of their ancient fraternities, the presence of police spies or censors. Though they usually gave Jérôme a polite reception, they flaunted regulations, clashed with police, joined pan-German clubs, and could be counted on to riot when times were troubled. Their activity helped such as Bercagny to convince the king that ever more severe surveillance of the universities was necessary, whereas initially he had listened to Reinhard and Müller, who favored a more liberal attitude. As a result many students migrated,

46. For which it is still famous. In the 1920's its faculty counted such eminent physicists as Max Born and James Franck, and Robert Oppenheimer, Edward Teller, and Enrico Fermi were students. Since World War II Göttingen has undergone a revival, and is again renowned for its physics faculty.

47. Halle dated from 1694, Marburg 1527, Helmstedt 1575, Rinteln 1624. The University of Berlin was founded in 1810 to replace Halle, which had been Prussia's major university.

especially to Heidelberg, and after 1810 to the University of Berlin (founded to replace Halle), along with some of their professors. Even friends of education sometimes alarmed Müller. The Leine department's prefect, Von Hoevel, proposed the introduction of technological and agricultural courses at Göttingen. The director opposed staunchly, fearing the university would turn into a "trade school," but in part lost the battle. "Wir will wider der Strom schwimmen?" he wrote disconsolately just before his death. Still, some of his innovations at Göttingen survived after 1815, to wit, the department of French literature, which grew apace in the nineteenth century.

Müller was replaced by Baron Justus Christoph Leist, professor of law at Göttingen, one of the translators of the *Code Napoléon*. Though a dedicated man, Leist was more of a realist than his predecessor, and his compromises probably kept the universities from disintegration. He acquiesced to the closing of Helmstedt and Rinteln (late 1809), but saved Marburg, as well as Göttingen and Halle. The suppressed institutions' endowments went to a state fund for subsidizing the others; their professors were transferred to the surviving universities or pensioned, if they did not choose to emigrate. Though unpopular, the action had advantages. Initially, the educational fund almost compensated for endowment monies lost because of property confiscations. The government was also enabled to adjust the incomes of the institutions according to need. For example, Marburg had two hundred students but more private income than Göttingen, with seven hundred; the latter got more from the educational fund. Unfortunately, the fund shrank as military requirements forced Jérôme to sell the national properties. Still, through 1812, at least, the surviving institutions never went begging.

The universities remained amazingly strong though conscription reduced their enrollments, and the government's restrictive policies prompted many students to go elsewhere. Among the luminaries at Göttingen was Karl Friedrich Gauss (after whom the unit of magnetic force is named), who was professor of astronomy and mathematics and director of an observatory built under Jérôme's sponsorship. (The observatory was appreciated, but not the king's other major contribution—a "natural history" collection, featuring a huge, moldy, elephant's foot brought by Napoleon from Egypt.) Until his death in 1812 Heyne was still active at Göttingen; prominent also were Johann Eichorn, Niklas Vogt, Johannes Falck, and Ludwig Wachler. Halle boasted the philologist Schütz, and the physicians Reil and Menkel. Marburg was not without eminent men, among them August Niemeyer, the great Calvinist theologian, whom Jérôme made chancellor and rector of the university.

Primary and secondary schools, some 3,100 in all, held their own; little more can be said. Schemes were hatched for reorganizing them, but never executed beyond placing all—public, private, and Church—under the director of education, and establishing two pilot institutions in Cassel. Through 1812, however, the 1,000,000 francs necessary to support the schools was always found, though largely by the prefects of departments.

Though hardly a *cérébral,* the king earnestly lent his support to the promotion of enlightenment and cultural elevation. The *Societät der Wissenschaften,* under his sponsorship, drew members from all the universities and the intelligentsia generally. The French were represented by Garnier, Jérôme's physician, Norvins de Monbreton, who later wrote anti-Napoleonic history, and others. Though Heyne snidely pronounced the membership "no Knights of the Round Table," the society did successfully bring together Westphalians, other Germans, and French with scientific and scholarly interests. Jérôme encouraged the young philologist Jakob Grimm, who was an auditor of the council of state and royal librarian.[48] Thanks to the influence of Reinhard, he financed the publication of Joachim Heinrich Campe's famous dictionary,[49] and new editions of the works of Goethe and Schiller. The atmosphere was hardly favorable, however, for new literary production. As Rambaud observed, "literature" had taken a practical turn, "toward the *Code Napoléon,* statistics, and the Constitution of the realm." The only regularly printed periodicals were *Der Westphälische Moniteur,* edited by Murhard, and a review dedi-

48. During Jérôme's reign he published *Über den Altdeutschen Meistergesang* (1811), and with brother Wilhelm the first volume of *Kinder- und Hausmärchen* (Grimm's Fairy Tales; 1812).
49. *Wörterbuch der Deutschen Sprache,* 5 volumes (1807–1811).

cated to clarifying the law codes and explaining decisions. Both were committed, naturally, to giving the regime favorable publicity.

Jérôme took much greater interest in art, the theater, and music. The superb art collection of the former elector was opened to students and the public. Prior to Jérôme's accession, Denon, the emperor's director of fine arts, had made selections from among its some fourteen hundred canvases, most of which had gone to the Louvre or Malmaison, Joséphine's residence.[50] Much remained, however, including many works of Dutch and Flemish masters—Rubens, Snyders, Van Dyck, Gerard Dow, and others —an astonishing treasure-trove for a small capital.

Cassel's theaters played to packed houses, which, on opening nights, invariably included the king when he was in his capital, and sometimes the queen. With groups of ladies he returned to see his favorites several times. The best companies of Paris and Vienna were brought to Cassel to supplement the efforts of German performers. As was the rule everywhere under the empire, "safe" classics were done most frequently in both French and German. Some of the German standards, however, became vehicles for subversive messages, and had to be banned. These included, embarrassingly, some of Schiller's for which the king had underwritten republication. Most new productions undertook to flatter the king or emperor. One celebrated Jérôme's rescue of Italian prisoners from Algiers. Posturing before the dey, the hero threatened to reduce the city by "blood and iron"—an interesting phrase for a francophile author to have chosen. Concerts and musicales were scheduled frequently for the public and royal circle. Jérôme tried vainly to induce Ludwig van Beethoven, who was at Vienna, to become musician to the court. The *Opéra* of Paris and lesser companies lent variety to the fare of Cassel's stages.

Over all the little Hessian city had never seen such brilliant seasons, such exotic performances, such diverse talents, such cosmopolitan audiences. Society during Jérôme's reign made anything before or after seem drab and provincial. In matters of edu-

50. Most of Joséphine's collection later went to the Hermitage in Saint Petersburg (Leningrad), where most of them still reside.

cation, literature, and the arts, the king's accomplishments were small, made possible largely by the presence of outstanding native talent, and built on foundations laid long before his appearance. But intellectual and cultural life was influenced by his passing— much more than was apparent when his kingdom collapsed.

Preparation for the Russian Campaign

The year 1811 began unpropitiously, with General Campans discharging his duty to "plant . . . [the] Imperial Eagles" at the boundaries of that part of Westphalia annexed to France, and Napoleon angrily taking offense at Jérôme's telling his former subjects to "love the Emperor as you have loved me." But the fear soon passed that all of the kingdom would be annexed. The emperor turned brotherly and amiable toward Jérôme, and, significantly, requested that 2,400 of his troops reinforce the garrison at Danzig. "These dispositions do not mean war . . ." he wrote. "Things are tranquil for the moment." But in fact preparations for the Russian Campaign had begun. Jérôme was invited to Paris for the christening of the king of Rome (June 2, 1811); he went early, returned late, and spent most of his time discussing means of expanding his military forces with the least possible alarm to his people and other German rulers. On his return the army and finances became his consuming interests—together with amusement, ever more violently pursued as the great adventure grew nearer.

The army grew; the French garrison increased much beyond 12,500. Conscription quotas increased, taxes climbed, sales of national properties accelerated. Construction of public buildings was halted to save money. Jérôme spent more and more time with his troops; his attitude toward nonmilitary problems became increasingly cavalier. He was not, however, insensitive to the growth of anti-French sentiment and the success of pan-German propaganda among his people. "The powerful cause of this dangerous movement," he wrote to Napoleon on December 5, 1811, "is not only . . . impatience with the yoke of the foreigner, but . . . in the total ruin of the classes, in the excess of impositions, contributions of war, maintenance of soldiers, passage of soldiers, and exactions of all sorts . . . the despair of the people, who have nothing more to lose because they have been completely robbed, is to be feared."

Apprehensions notwithstanding, Jérôme did what was necessary to build his own and provide for French forces. Napoleon continued to pretend that there would be no war, but in January 1812 he told Jérôme to prepare to march. The Westphalian army numbered over 30,000 (by summer 38,000) including 4,000 men at Danzig, 1,500 *Kürassiers* already with the emperor's cavalry reserve (shortly under Murat), and a few hundred troops still in Spain. Jérôme concentrated at Halle 17,000 designated the Eighth (Westphalian) Corps of the Grande Armée—two infantry divisions, a cavalry brigade, and artillery, all under Westphalian generals.[51]

In March the king went to Paris, where he was informed that he would command the right wing of the army, which at the opening of hostilities would "cover Warsaw." His force comprised 80,000 men in four corps—the Poles of Prince Poniatowski, Saxons under Reynier, cavalry of mixed nationalities under Latour-Maubourg, and his own Westphalians. The king was exultant. He was for the moment unconcerned with the fact that Napoleon was giving greater responsibility to Davout. Jérôme was to enter Poland in early April and establish headquarters near Warsaw. Meanwhile Davout had the major role in assembling the main body (left wing) of the army (250,000) on Thorn, and in addition, was issuing orders in the emperor's name to Jérôme's corps, among others. On Napoleon's arrival, he would revert to corps commander, but obviously be available for greater responsibility. Perhaps Napoleon planned from the beginning to give Davout the right wing; certainly he had the marshal in reserve for the purpose.

From early 1812 Jérôme's behavior reinforced rumors that he expected to leave Cassel and not return. At any rate he began rewarding his favorites lavishly, in disregard of his government's bankruptcy, as if he would not have another chance. In January alone he distributed 400,000 francs in largess, and gave away some of the better estates remaining from the royal domains, the largest, valued at 200,000 francs, to Siméon. Other gifts followed.

51. Ochs, Wellingerode, and Hammerstein. At Napoleon's insistence the French general Tharreau was later given one of the infantry divisions, however.

Cassel believed that Jérôme would become king of Poland; the courts of Europe thought it likely; Napoleon maintained a "positive" silence, neither confirming or denying the possibility. Jérôme denied the rumor, even in later correspondence with the queen. But his most durable mistress, the countess von Löwenstein, let it be known that she was preparing to travel to Warsaw as soon as Jérôme's elevation was announced. The resurrection of Poland, which had disappeared from the map in 1795, seemed more than probable. Surely the Poles of the Grande Armée believed that since Russia was now the enemy no obstacle remained to Napoleon's fulfilling his promise to restore their nation. No foreign troops had fought more valiantly for the emperor—in Italy, Germany, Austria, Spain, or Portugal. None were more trustworthy; Poles had guarded the emperor's person, escorted Neapolitan recruits bent on desertion, furnished cadre for satellite armies. Nevertheless, Poland would not be restored. But it is evident that until the Russian Campaign was underway Napoleon still toyed with the idea. It is equally obvious that if Jérôme were not intended as king, he had a political role to play in Poland, and was aware of the fact.

Jérôme delayed in Cassel only ten days after returning from Paris. Leaving the queen as regent, seconded by Siméon, president of the council of ministers, he departed on April 7, 1812, for Kalisz, in Poland, to assume command of his troops. Ahead of him traveled his latest love, the seventeen-year-old Madame Escalonne —with her mother. His performance in the next four months was destined to overshadow everything he had ever done, or would do, and establish him in history, undeservedly, as a prodigal deserving of mention only because he was Napoleon's brother. We shall leave discussion of his experiences in Poland and Russia for a later chapter. At this point, however, we can attempt a judgment on his success as king of Westphalia.

Conclusion

Jérôme was a playboy, but he was also a remarkably successful executive. Much credit must go to his subordinates, but after the first few months they were his appointees. He chose them well and directed them forcefully, without trying to do their work for them. He was "lazy" in the sense that most really good executives are, that is, he limited himself to making policy decisions, assigning tasks, and examining results.[52] Those beneath him had to "produce" or give way to men who could (excepting always old cronies, like Le Camus). The crisis of 1809 served to reveal his qualities as civil, military, and personal leader.

No satellite ruler save Eugène de Beauharnais made a better record of domestic accomplishment. Jérôme introduced the *Code Napoléon,* reformed the criminal, penal, and commercial codes, reorganized the courts, abolished feudal privilege and serfdom. He ruled with a parliament as long as he dared, and reformed the administrative and local government systems. He created, at some risk, what closely approximated a native government. Its solidness was proved in 1809, and it would weather more serious tests in 1812 and 1813. But for his obligations to Napoleon, his finances would have remained in good order, and by amassing a modest national debt he could have supported a Westphalian army of 25,000 with ease.

In terms of service to the empire, Jérôme's record is unexcelled. His troops had no peers among satellite contingents; his commanders gained the respect of their French comrades and the emperor. By liquidating the national properties and levying mercilessly on his people (however distasteful it was to him), he met all of Napoleon's demands. French troops were paid (if sometimes late); food, supplies, matériel, and horses were produced for them.

Despite what many took to be his incurable profligacy, there was no more competent man among the satellite rulers than Jérôme Bonaparte. None was a better governor, lawmaker, administrator, or soldier. None was more useful or loyal to Napoleon; none more successful in keeping the loyalty of his people. We shall try to demonstrate all this further in later chapters, and to show that his military record in 1812 was better than historians have generally supposed.

52. Karl von Clausewitz, in his famous *Vom Kriege,* opined that brilliant and lazy officers were the best commanders, brilliant and industrious ones usually fit only for staff duty, since they tended to get too involved in detail to make big decisions.

. . . that miserable Spanish affair turned opinion against me and rehabilitated England. It enabled them to continue the war. The markets of South America were opened to them; they put an army on the Peninsula . . . [which] became the agent of victory, the terrible node of all the intrigues that formed on the Continent . . . [the Spanish affair] is what killed me.
—NAPOLEON AT SAINT HELENA

chapter seven
SPAIN

The Spanish Fight Back

THE SPANISH REBELS

*A*t the end of June 1808, Napoleon, at Bayonne, saw little reason to doubt that Spain was his. Murat had viciously disciplined Madrid; the Bourbons had abdicated and gone quietly into exile in France; French troops were gradually occupying the country without marked interference from contingents of the small Bourbon army; a Madrid junta had requested that Joseph Bonaparte be made king; a national junta, at Bayonne, had echoed the request and accepted a liberal constitution. It was true that, of the ninety-one members of the Bayonne junta, seventy-one had been hand picked and only twenty elected. But there was present an impressive array of illustrious Spaniards: the prince de Castelfranco; the dukes del Parque, d'Infantado, and de Frias; Pedro de Cevallos, former first secretary of state; Don Gonzalo de O'Farrill, former minister of war; Don Sabastian Piñuela y Alonso, former minister of justice; Don José de Mazarredo y Salazar, general, admiral, and former ambassador to Paris; Count François de Cabarrus, former minister of finance. Churchmen had been uncooperative; of eight archbishops only two had appeared. But the renowned archbishop of Burgos, Manuel Cid Monroy, had come and moreover had agreed to officiate at Joseph's coronation, scheduled for July 7.

In Spain there were inescapable signs of growing popular opposition to French domination, but Napoleon paid little heed. The masses needed leadership, and generally, he felt, were conditioned to accept only that of the upper classes. Many of the traditional leaders had already accepted the change in government; the rest would submit, he was sure, when his troops completed occupying the peninsula. He had thought Spain pitifully weak when the Bourbons controlled a centralized government, and had a standing army. How could she resist when the only central authority was French, and Bourbon forces had scattered or surrendered?

Napoleon's assessment was rational, but he was wrong. Spain would fight, irrational though the attempt seemed. Beginning slowly, spreading rapidly after the *Dos de Mayo* of Madrid, a national spirit had infused the people. The spirit was anachronistic, even medieval, but very real—the nationalism of Crown and Church. Suddenly spoiling for blood was an overwhelmingly peasant population, ready to defend the Bourbons (whom they saw as descendants of the "Hero Kings" who had crusaded against the Moors), convinced, with their clergy, that Napoleon was the servant of the devil. Thorough provincials, they saw themselves not as Spaniards, but as Aragonese, Galicians, Catalans, Castilians. But they were willing to fight for Crown and Church against the invader. Most nobles and clergymen shared their peoples' feeling, and additionally feared the impact of French liberalism on their authority and property. To them Napoleon was a dangerous, unprincipled revolutionary. The middle class, though liberally inclined, was very small, not very vocal, and faced in the cities by a proletariat wracked by unemployment, hunger, and rising prices, all of which were blamed on France. (She had forced Spain into alliance, used and robbed her, provoked the British to blockade her ports.) The liberal intelligentsia, including a sizable representation of nobles and clergy, were mostly francophiles, and saw hope for progress under a Bonaparte king. But as the strength of the national movement became apparent, the majority elected (some after going to Bayonne) to be Spanish first and liberals afterward, lest they lose all influence with their people.

In May and June 1808 rebel juntas had seized the governments of all provinces not under French occupation. The count de Toreño had sailed to London to ask aid for the "war of independence." The people, eager for action, struck out blindly at first. In a country where suffering was widespread, even in the best times, and literacy rare, the masses took easily to violence when invited suddenly, even by many of their priests, to take revenge for all their ills on a single oppressor. Charges of treason were hurled at those who urged caution. In La Coruña, Seville, Badajoz, Ciudad Rodrigo, Jaén, and Málaga temporizing governors were killed by mobs.

Public enthusiasm resulted in more than disorder, however. Positive, uncompromising leaders got solid support; Bourbon officers found plenty of recruits. In a few weeks whole armies were built around a few loyal regiments of regulars. In Andalusia General Castaños raised 30,000, and drew to his side not only Spanish officers but outstanding foreign soldiers such as the Swiss General Redding, the French *emigré* marquis de Coupigny, and the Irish soldier of fortune General Felix Jones. Llamas raised an army in Valencia; Montijo and O'Neill in Murcia; Palafox in Aragon, Cuesta and Blake in Old Castile and Galicia. The armies would later prove pathetically fragile, but their sudden appearance threw the French badly off balance. They scored a few dramatic successes, and gave the Spanish rebels a taste of glory which sustained them in the lean years that followed.

BAILÉN

In June 1808 a French corps of 20,000 under General Dupont pushed south through the Sierra Morena into Andalusia. Peasant bands pursued the column, falling on stragglers, couriers, and small parties. French soldiers were stoned, blinded with pikes, crippled, then killed or left to perish in the withering sun, or castrated and allowed to bleed to death. At La Carolina a hospital was burned by irregulars, who waited outside to butcher those who escaped the flames. Captain Schumacher, a Swiss cavalryman of the Imperial Guard, found the charred and mutilated bodies of almost two hundred sick and wounded. His vivid memoirs reflect the outrage felt even by a hardened professional soldier. And "the Barbarians," he says, thought God approved their actions. General René, captured enroute to join Dupont, was lowered inch by inch, toes first, into a caldron of boiling water. The peasants were entertained by his screams for a whole afternoon before he died.

Dupont seized Córdoba; then, hearing rumors that rebel armies were forming to the south and alarmed because he had lost contact with Madrid, he retired to Andújar and took a defensive position on the north bank of the Guadalquivir. On July 11, General Castaños, with his newly formed Spanish army of 30,000, found him there. Though outnumbered, Dupont declined to withdraw. He had nothing but contempt for the Spanish, and he feared that if he retreated he would have to abandon the sick—some nine hundred —and trains, loaded with loot from Córdoba. He simply waited, and Castaños seized the initiative. By midnight on July 18, when Dupont, alarmed by Spanish movements, finally decided to withdraw, half the enemy army was behind him, at Bailén, blocking the road to Madrid. On the morning of July 19, Castaños crossed the river and followed the retreating French. By midmorning Dupont was surrounded. His trains, heavy with loot and packed with sick and wounded, made dashing tactics impossible. Further, his troops were sluggish from weeks of idleness, tired from a night march, and by the time the scorching summer sun had reached its peak, entirely without water. Instead of making a maximum effort, however, Dupont pushed small attack after small attack up the road toward Bailén, losing men and getting nowhere. In late afternoon, hard-pressed front and rear, his demoralized troops giving up on all sides, he surrendered.

Almost 18,000 French became prisoners of the Spanish. Napoleon could stand to lose the men, but the blow to French prestige was shattering. News from Valencia heightened the effect of Bailén on Spanish and European opinion. Marshal Moncey, with 20,000 men, had failed to take the capital and, menaced by a superior force under Cervellon, had retreated to Madrid.

Joseph: King and Commander

Meanwhile on July 7, at Bayonne, Joseph Bonaparte was crowned king of Spain and the Indies. Napoleon looked on, for once declining to make some dramatic gesture, while Spanish grandees, nobles, and bishops paid homage to his brother. On July 8, under escort by imperial and royal guardsmen, the king departed happily for Madrid. But as soon as he entered Spain, the optimism his Bayonne experience had engendered began to fade.

His people did not fawn, as had the nobles at Bayonne, or even cheer as he passed. In village after village no one appeared at all. The king looked out at deserted streets, shuttered windows, barred doors. His kingdom, hot, dusty, and silent, seemed to be populated by occasional stray animals, bony dogs dozing in the shade, distant shapes of people darting for cover like frightened deer. During his twelve-day trip to Madrid he wrote Napoleon every day, and on five days twice, his tone becoming increasingly plaintive. Did no one want him? Had all his supporters been at Bayonne? Replied Napoleon reassuringly, "You have a great number of partisans in Spain, but they are intimidated: they are all the better men." Joseph's alarm, however, grew apace. In the beginning his ministers of finance, justice, and ecclestiastical affairs had most frequently been invited to the royal coach; they were displaced by Gonzalo O'Farrill, minister of war. At least 100,000 troops would be needed to hold the kingdom, Joseph wrote the emperor. It boded evil for the future that he did not know there were *already* over 100,000 French in Spain; of their disposition he knew little, much less of enemy forces. Nevertheless, Joseph, en route, asked for and got command of French forces in Spain, relieving Savary, who had replaced Murat at Madrid.

The king got occasional cheers as he entered his capital on July 20, but mostly the populace stood silent. On some streets an unsubtle mockery was evident. Rags instead of bunting had been hung from windows and balconies in response to Savary's order that the city be festooned for Joseph's entry. The *Madrileños* did exhibit surprise, mingled with grudging respect, that the king entered their city at all. They were proud that Madrid was dangerous—doubtless more dangerous than Joseph realized. After July 23 when news of Bailén began to circulate in the streets the atmosphere became steadily more quiet and ominous, and some of the king's more timid followers, without explanation, disappeared from court. But Joseph knew nothing of the disaster until July 29, when a soldier who had escaped capture reached Madrid.

The king suddenly felt the weight of the military responsibility he had so casually demanded. Dupont was lost; Moncey, in Madrid, had been chased from Valencia. How strong were the rebel armies? Should he retreat or fight for Madrid? Joseph could have called up 80,000 troops (not counting Duhesme's corps in Catalonia), most of which were closer to Madrid than Castaños and Cervellon. At hand were Moncey's corps, the royal guard, some of the Imperial Guard, and other troops, together over 30,000. Napoleon, answering Joseph's letter of July 29, told him that he had more forces than he needed to subdue Spain, if they were "directed with proper precision." For commanders the king had Moncey and, a few days' ride away, Bessières, both senior marshals, the latter a Gascon habitually entrusted by his emperor with guard cavalry, and General Savary.

Joseph could have fought, but he could think only of retreat. As soon as news of Bailén came he began the evacuation of 3,000 sick and wounded from Madrid. Reporting to Napoleon on July 30 he wildly exaggerated the danger of his position and gave the false impression he had no Spanish followers left. By midday on July 31 he had abandoned Madrid and was marching north. Timidity had marked Joseph's first major decision as a commander. Without seeing a rebel soldier or hearing a shot fired in anger, he had ordered retreat.

By August 9, Joseph had established headquarters at Vitoria; by August 30, the entire French Army of Spain, save outposts and a corps in Catalonia, was north of the Ebro. The siege of Zaragoza, in progress since June 15, was lifted on August 15 because of the king's retreat. "War to the knife!" Palafox, the Spanish commander, had spit out when General Lefebvre[1] demanded his surrender. It was no vain boast. The whole city had fought—men, women, and children. Their dead lay in heaps, and every shelter housed wounded and sick. But the French had failed to reduce the city, and had left 2,000 dead behind. Palafox was a hero; the rebels took new heart.

In Paris General Dumas fell heir to Napoleon's wrath. Why had Joseph not halted at the Duero? To cross the Duero *and* the Ebro was evacuating Spain. "This coat must be washed in blood!" the emperor shouted, clutching Dumas's lapels. Turning away, he added, "I can see very well that I must return and set the machine in motion again."

There was more to the French humiliation. In Catalonia Duhesme's forces were able to hold only Barcelona and a few strong points on the route to France. In Portugal Junot, faced

1. Lefebvre-Desnouettes, not the marshal.

with a British landing, dashed impetuously to attack and was defeated at Vimiero by Sir Arthur Wellesley (later duke of Wellington). So demoralized were the French that Junot felt lucky when the British allowed him to surrender on condition that he and his army be returned by sea to France.

In the summer of 1808, then, the French met general defeat on the peninsula. In their defense one can say that Napoleon had underestimated both the spirit and virility of the Spanish nation and the capacity of the British to intervene on the continent. French commanders had not expected determined resistance. French troops were numerous, but in the bulk raw, one-third being from the levies of 1808 and 1809, both called up in advance. Still, French strength had been adequate to counter the organized enemy forces, which, despite the effect of irregulars on the invaders' morale, had scored the victories. French *leadership* had been found wanting.

In long-term effect, Joseph's failure was the most serious. A Bonaparte king had advanced to the capital, stayed a week, and fled with his army before an unseen enemy. Ludicrous! Though the decision to retreat might have been made by a more experienced general (neither Savary nor Moncey strongly contested it), *Joseph* had given the command. He was vulnerable in that he had no military reputation. His action could easily be attributed to gross ineptitude, stupidity, or simply a loss of nerve. Rebel propagandists took every advantage. From this time forward, while they painted Napoleon as agent of the devil, they made fun of Joseph. He became *"Pepe Botellas," "Protector de los Jugadores," "Pepe Coxo,"* "squint-eye"—a vice-ridden incompetent. The confidence of his Spanish followers was shaken; as he left Madrid some of the most influential deserted, including Pedro Cevallos and the dukes del Parque and d'Infantado. French generals thenceforth would be prone to regard him with condescension, an attitude encouraged by Napoleon's scornful condemnation of his brother's decision. After 1808 it was much more difficult for him to be king and commander.

Burdened by a sense of failure, wounded by the emperor's sarcasms, Joseph tried to abdicate. Neither honor, conscience, nor "the secret instinct which motivates all my actions" would allow him to keep his throne against the wishes of the people, he wrote

Napoleon. The conquerer of Spain would become an object of terror. "I am too old to repair all that evil." He begged to be allowed to return to Naples. Napoleon did not bother to reply. Instead he ordered Joseph to hold his army behind the Ebro and prepare to receive reinforcements.

THE MARQUISE DE MONTEHERMOSO

At Vitoria the king took up residence at the villa of the marquis de Montehermoso, whose much younger wife had set her heart on being the royal mistress. Perfection in Latin beauty, sharp-witted and accomplished, she soon got her man, though during the first weeks Joseph, unaware of her interest, disconcerted her by sharing his bed with an overblown chambermaid of eighteen. The marquise de Montehermoso remained mistress-in-title throughout the reign. Like a second wife, she tolerated Joseph's other affairs of the heart (which were numerous but short-lived), and extended her power over him by taking advantage of his little-boy guilt about them. Joseph depended on her, rushed back to her in time of trouble, and in many matters was dominated by her.

The marquise played her role proudly. She saw no immorality in her position, felt no shame. She attended mass and confession sedulously. In his memoirs the crusty General Bigarré speaks of her "spiritual" qualities. She managed the social life of the court with grace and skill; Joseph got her entire devotion. But as the king's mistress she demanded her due. Cavalry of the royal guard escorted her when she traveled; ministers felt her wrath and paid her court. She was a power, and yet men melted before her merely feminine charms. Says Grandmaison, with Gallic simplicity, "Elle charmait, car elle était charmante . . ." Jean Abel Hugo (brother of Victor Hugo), once a page in Joseph's palace, wrote so rapturously of her after twenty years that as a little boy he must have loved her from afar. In the first days at Vitoria she gave solace to a depressed Joseph who could make no move with his army until the emperor arrived.

The Emperor!

In October 1808, at Erfurt, Napoleon promised Czar Alexander to support Russian interests on the lower Danube, and received (in effect) the czar's pledge not to support France's potential enemies, Austria and Prussia. The danger to the empire in the north thus reduced, Napoleon turned his attention on Spain, where troops from France and Germany had already been directed. By the end of October Joseph found himself in command of 286,000 men. With them had come the elite of French commanders, whose names conjured up memories of already legendary Napoleonic victories: the lean and towering Marshal Ney, duke d'Elchingen; Marshal Lannes, duke de Marengo; the small, tough, remorseless Marshal Soult, hero of Austerlitz; Junot, duke d'Abrantès, spoiling to repair the reputation sullied in Portugal; Victor, Mortier, Lefebvre. . . . Marshal Jourdan was assigned as Joseph's chief of staff.

"The war must be terminated by a single *coup par manoeuvre* . . . My presence will be necessary," wrote Napoleon from Erfurt on October 13. On October 18 he was back at Saint-Cloud (Paris), his mind already running on the coming campaign. He wrote Joseph that he would be in Bayonne in a few days. Had a reconnaissance of the Ebro from Tudela to Frias been made? How were the roads to Logroño? What was the condition of the fort at Burgos? Was it manned? Could loyal Spaniards be found to analyze the terrain of Soria, Montana, and Santander? On October 19 (still from Paris) he complained that Jourdan's reports were inadequate. What was the exact situation? "Tell me about every skirmish—how many are killed and wounded, everything, to the last detail." On November 3, at three in the morning, he announced he had arrived in Bayonne. On November 4 he told Joseph he would see him the next day; but: "I intend to arrive incognito. Make sure that I do."

On the morning of November 6, 1808, the measured reports of a sixty-gun salute began to echo in the misty air over Vitoria. Napoleon had arrived the evening before, as planned. Now, in proper theatrical manner, his presence was announced to his troops, encamped for miles about. Cheers of excitement and relief went up. The emperor had arrived; the Army of Spain was now the Grande Armée. The rumor that "José" (Joseph) would command was false. Napoleon, in fact, gave Joseph no place in the army; when it marched, the king followed in its wake.

The emperor's plan was swiftly to convince the Spanish that

resistance was foolhardy by smashing rebel forces pitilessly under the weight of superior numbers. Napoleon was a professional soldier to whom war was no sport. The greater his advantage the better; the more crushing the victory the greater the effect. Earlier, on Napoleon's orders, propaganda letters, written by Joseph's Spanish advisers, had been sent to rebel political, religious, and military leaders. Their message was simple: "The time for illusions is past. . . ." The Grande Armée is in Spain. Make terms now or take the consequences. Napoleon also found time to instruct Spaniards personally. To a group of monks, members of whose order had led rebel bands, he shouted "*Messieurs les moines* if you are determined to meddle in military affairs, I promise you I will cut off your ears!" For others there were threats and insults. "I am here with the soldiers who conquered at Austerlitz, at Jena, at Eylau. Who can beat them? Without doubt not your miserable Spanish troops who do not know how to fight!"

THE REBELS

The rebels were indeed in a desperate situation. In September 1808 their leaders had formed a new central junta in Madrid and placed the government under the aging Count Floridablanca. The thirty-five members were agreed to fight for the restoration of Ferdinand VII, whom they crowned *in absentia*. On all else they had displayed alarmingly provincial attitudes. Spain, wrote the marquis de Lazan to Ferdinand, was "very confused."

Gradually the junta had managed to array 88,000 men opposite the French. The command, however, was divided. Deployed (except on the left) south of the Ebro, with huge gaps between them, stood six separate "armies" (of Galicia, Castile, León, Andalusia, Aragon, and Estremadura). Each commander was independent, pledged only to cooperate with the others. Moreover the bulk of the troops were green, untrained, poorly armed, and miserably supplied. Blake's Galicians, at Villarcayo on the left, were one hundred miles from Palafox's Aragonese and Castaños' Andalusians, on the right between Lodoso and Zaragoza. Concentrated, the rebels' chances against the French would have been poor; as they stood only a miracle could save them.

By November 10 the Grande Armée was fully in motion. Spanish forces resisted bravely but could not stand. The French main body, under Napoleon, shattered the defenses organized at Burgos by the valiant Belvedere and advanced almost without pause to the pass of the Somo Sierra, in the Guadarrama Range, beyond which lay the plateau of New Castile and Madrid. There on November 30 the Grande Armée, strung out in column along a narrow road cut into the cliffs above the raging Duratón River, found itself blocked by 9,000 Spanish with cannon emplaced at the head of the pass.

Napoleon spurred forward with his escort, the Polish light cavalry of the Imperial Guard, eighty-seven men, young noblemen all. Behind him was the world's finest army—infantry, artillery, a cavalry reserve of 50,000—but in this pass only the lead elements could engage the enemy. Days would be required for infantry to claw their way to the crest and flank the guns. Furious, the emperor ordered the Poles to charge the guns. Forward they galloped, Colonel Korjietulski in the lead, but the cannon bit into their ranks, and they took cover. "My Guard will not be stopped by peasants. . . ." shouted Napoleon. Again the Poles charged, full-tilt into the blazing muzzles of the guns and across the crest, driving the Spanish gunners before them. Its guns lost, San Juan's army disintegrated before the oncoming French. The charge of the Poles had won the day, but half of them lay dead, including Korjietulski, and hardly any were without wounds. The emperor assembled the survivors and with tears in his eyes announced the Legion of Honor for both living and dead.

Essentially unopposed, the army marched on to Madrid, from which the rebel junta had fled (to Aranjuez, Seville, and ultimately Cádiz). After minor disorganized resistance, the city submitted, and on December 4 Napoleon made his entry in a magnificent parade which most *Madrileños,* behind closed shutters, pretended to ignore.

JOSEPH RESTORED

The king, following the Grande Armée by stages, saw appalling scenes of pillage and destruction. Peasant villages were stripped, sometimes burned. At Burgos nuns had been driven from their cloister and some raped; the tombs of their predecessors had been torn open, robbed, and the corpses left strewn in the court-yard. "His people" came to him with petitions for protection which he was powerless to grant. Sickened by what he had seen, angered that French commanders ignored his wishes, overcome with hu-miliation and frustration, he stopped short of Madrid, at the Pardo hunting lodge. There he saw rebel cartoons depicting him as a bloated drunkard asleep among bottles, or staggering after women, a crucifix invariably under his feet.

Deeply depressed, he again tried to abdicate. But the emperor ignored the offer and proclaimed to the Spanish that they had a choice between Joseph and himself as king. As he had expected *Madrileños* flocked to sign an oath of loyalty to Joseph. Napoleon was pleased, but intended to strike at the Church and nobility before he stepped down. By imperial decree he abolished the In-quisition, ordered most convents and monasteries suppressed, pro-claimed the end of feudal rights and privileges, eliminated seignorial courts, and confiscated the property of all rebels. He expected the Spanish masses to be grateful, but they were not. Even in the case of the Inquisition the belief was still general that it protected Spain from subversives—Moors, Jews, heretics, masquerading as Chris-tians—at once enemies of the Church and Crown, though in recent years it had acted principally against liberals and liberal literature, mostly French.

As always, Napoleon was in search of funds. The treasury of the Inquisition netted 613,193 francs. Twenty millions' worth of wool was shipped from Burgos to France. At Santander Soult took possession of quinaquina valued at several millions. Certain of the more valuable rebel estates were declared imperial property. In Madrid, Savary made lists of "suspects," confiscated their prop-erty, and even held furniture sales in the streets.

To Madrid's relief, the emperor's stay was suddenly terminated after only two weeks. On December 19 word came that an English army of 30,000 had appeared in the north near Valladolid. Its commander, Sir John Moore, unaware that the Spanish armies had fled south, had marched from Portugal to reinforce them and blundered into the rear of the Grande Armée, ten times the size of his.[2] "It is a gift of Providence . . ." said Napoleon, barely able to believe the reports. He would meet the British—on land—with the odds all against them!

Hastily restoring Joseph to his throne, Napoleon pushed north with the Imperial Guard through the ice and snow of the Guadarrama. Moore meanwhile awoke to his dangerous position, however, and made for Coruña, where British naval units could evacuate his army. Marshal Soult, who had been maintaining contact with Moore, pursued. Napoleon, rapidly overtaking Soult, was stopped by couriers from Paris with news that Austria was preparing for war and that Tallyrand, Fouché, and his sister Caroline were intriguing to have Murat named his successor. He turned back to Valladolid and on January 16, 1809, departed for France, leaving behind orders restoring Joseph to command of the Army of Spain (that is, the Grande Armée, with only slight losses). ". . . If nothing prevents, I shall return toward the end of February," Napoleon wrote. But he would never return. On the day the emperor departed, Soult fought Moore at Coruña, but most of the British army escaped by sea, though its commander was killed. The British would return, and the conquest of Spain, which Napoleon had skillfully begun, would never be completed.

Joseph spent Christmas and New Year's at Aranjuez, at a villa formerly occupied by Goya's *amie délicieuse,* the duchess of Alba, then remained at the Pardo for some weeks. On January 22, 1809, he finally made an official entry into Madrid. As in the previous July it was a military spectacle, but he tried to give it a more Spanish flavor. The Royal Guards, displaying their startling new white and lavender uniforms, led the march. They were followed by Joseph's "Spanish" troops—a regiment of mixed foreigners, an Irish brigade, and two half-filled regiments of Spaniards, mostly ex-prisoners of war. Most of the marchers, however, were from Sébastiani's Fourth French Corps.

For the next few days Joseph concentrated on establishing a benevolent image. He visited institutions of charity and hospitals —military and civilian, French and Spanish. To the outrage of some of his aides, the king showed exaggerated concern for the

2. The Spanish government, first ill informed itself and later too proud to admit the extent of rebel defeats, had not kept the British representative with the junta properly informed.

enemy wounded—"his people." At prisoner-of-war compounds he freed those who agreed to enter his army. Generally they cheered lustily, drew their arms and equipment, and promptly disappeared. For years the pattern of enlistment and desertion would continue. "*El Capitán Vestuario,*" the rebels called Joseph, and with reason. Napoleon, at that time, and often later, angrily damned the king's recruiting policies. But Joseph held to the belief that he must show faith in "his people."

The war went on. French commanders contended with strong Spanish armies in Aragon and Catalonia, and elsewhere with fragments of armies and ever-multiplying bands of guerrillas. Soon a British army would again appear in Portugal. The south of Spain was unconquered; elsewhere the effective boundaries of Joseph's kingdom were in continual flux. No area was safe for the French. The king chose, however, to decline exercising active over-all command and to devote himself to organizing his court and government.

Internal Affairs

THE CONSTITUTION

Joseph took the constitution of Bayonne very seriously; he would not be a "legitimate" monarch, he reasoned, until it was in force. In 1809 he had it published and explained in the press as a contract between himself and the people. From the outset he strained to apply as much of it as possible. "Tell me," wrote Napoleon sarcastically, "if the Constitution prohibits the King of Spain from commanding 300,000 Frenchmen . . . if the Constitution says that in Saragossa [Zaragoza, enduring its second siege] one can jump over the houses one after another?"

The constitution called for a single-chamber Cortes comprising eighty members named by the king and ninety-two elected (indirectly) by universal manhood suffrage, though elected delegates had to meet stiff property requirements. A ministry, council of state, and (honorary) senate were to be appointed by the king. Titles of nobility were affirmed, but feudal rights (personal and property) were to be abolished and entail limited. Minimal civil rights (inviolability of homes, freedom from arrest without charge) were guaranteed, and jury trial if the Cortes approved. A uniform system of courts was to be installed. The Bourbon debt was guaranteed. Guilds were to be eliminated, as was the *mesta,* the sheepman's organization, long the scourge of farm property owners. Internal tariffs were to be struck down. "The Catholic, Apostolic, and Roman" Church was declared the sole and established church, though its courts were to be suppressed. All provisions of the constitution, however, had to be put into effect by royal decrees.

To his dismay Joseph could not in 1809, or ever, put the constitution in full effect. Initially, even respecting individual rights would have jeopardized public order. He supplied a decree detailing the terms on which feudalism would vanish, but could not prevent feudal practices from persisting in remote areas. He ordered plans produced for administrative and court reform, and for funding the Bourbon debt. But the only strict and positive compliance he could make to the constitution was to organize his ministry and council of state as it specified.

THE GOVERNMENT, ADMINISTRATION, AND COURTS

Of the ministers Joseph had appointed in 1808, five were present, two with the rebels, and one in retirement in a monastery. During 1809 he filled the vacancies, and thereafter no minister was removed except by death, though some changed positions.[3]

3. *Ministers 1808–1813*

Minister Secretary of State	Mariano Luis de Urquijo	1808–1813
Finance	François de Cabarrus (Died April 1810)	1808–1810
	Francisco Angulo	1810–1813
Interior	Gaspar Melchior de Jovellanos (Named 1808; ignored appointment and joined the rebels)	
	Don Manuel Romero	1809–
	Almenara (José Martinez Hervas)	1809–1813
Justice	Sebastian Piñuela y Alonso (Retired to monastery Nov. 1808)	1808–
	Don Manuel Romero (and Interior) (Died 1812)	1809–1812
	Almenara (and Interior)	1812–1813
Foreign Affairs	Pedro Cevallos (Deserted to rebels July 1808)	1808–
	Campo-Alange (Manuel José de Negrette)	1809–1811
	Santa Fé (Azanza)	1811–1813

The key figures were three: Count François de Cabarrus (finance), born a Frenchmen but a Spanish noble, financier, founder of Madrid's Bank of San Carlos, and former Bourbon minister, but more easily identified for Frenchmen as the father of the beautiful and shocking Madame Tallien; Don Gonzalo de O'Farrill (war), descendant of an Irish adventurer of an earlier era, sometime Bourbon minister, ambassador, and captain-general; and Don Manuel Romero, one-time prosecutor of the Council of Castile.

Joseph's ministers were all capable, some brilliant, but most were old. The most eminent, like Cabarrus and Romero, had served the progressive Charles III (1759–1788), and were chosen partly because they had national reputations. (Under Charles IV Romero had lost favor and Cabarrus had been imprisoned briefly by the Inquisition.) The average age of the ministers was sixty (an age few men reached in that era). Several were in poor health; three were destined to die of natural causes during the reign— Cabarrus in 1810, Romero and Mazarredo (minister of marine) in 1812. Most were reformers, but lacked the energy to create efficient machinery to execute policy. Cabarrus, for all his intelligence and financial acumen, was becoming feeble and often over-fortified himself with wine. (Once, while enthusiastically inspecting a distillery with Joseph, he fell and bruised himself badly.) Romero, who charted the king's domestic reforms with great skill, did not have the strength to direct his ministry properly. Francisco Angulo, who succeeded Cabarrus, was more energetic, but inherited organizational problems multiplied by his predecessor's neglect and the interference of the French military. As an executive, Joseph lacked force; so did his chief subordinates. From the beginning, lack of strong direction plagued the government.

In 1809 also a council of state was formed with working sec-

War	Gonzalo de O'Farrill	1808–1813
Police	Pablo de Arribas (de facto Minister)	1808–1813
Marine	José Mazarredo y Salazar (died 1812)	1808–1812
	O'Farrill (and War)	1812–1813
Indies	Azanza (Made duke of Santa Fé, 1810)	1808–1813
Ecclesiastical Affairs	Piñuela (and Justice) (Retired to monastery Nov. 1808)	1808

(After Piñuela's retirement under various ministries, usually interior) lions for justice and cults, interior and general police, finance, and war and marine. Among the progressive councilors were Juan Antonio Llorente, former vicar-general of Calahorra, a long-time foe of the Inquisition; the count de Montarco, a liberal whose career in government had been frustrated by Godoy; and Ferri-Pisani, count de Saint-Anastacio, a Corsican who had served Joseph in Naples. These were seated with reactionaries, such as General Thomas Morla, and members whose appointments were largely honorary (including a poet and a playwright), but over all the council was an impressive pool of talent. Unfortunately, it was a planning and advisory body, and could contribute little to fill the government's greatest need—positive leadership.

Beneath the central organs of ministry and council of state, government and civil administration depended on the system left by the Bourbons, headed by the intendants of the ancient provinces and/or that of military governors. During 1809 Joseph sent out commissioners who filled vacancies in the civil system left by men who had joined the rebels and replaced a few others. The king was anxious to be accepted as "Spanish," however, and confirmed in office almost all who professed *willingness* to take an oath to him, though often they avoided doing so, or took it with tongue in cheek. In 1810 he decreed the gradual abolition of provincial administrative areas in favor of thirty-two prefectures, each subdivided into subprefectures, cantons, and communes. The plan, drafted by Romero, would have provided an orderly hierarchy of officials—prefects, subprefects, and mayors—each advised by elected councils. Unhappily the disruptions of war prevented implementation of the scheme except in the Madrid area. Throughout the reign, in areas where civil administration was possible at all, the system remained that of the old regime. Inefficient under the Bourbons, it functioned even more poorly under Joseph. Jobs which had been created as rewards continued to be filled. At the lower levels, capable men were seldom very energetic, for the king's favors, like God's rain, seemed to fall on the "just and unjust" alike, whereas the people might mark an overzealous official for revenge by the rebels. Venality was common and, in various forms, supported by tradition. In remote areas, where guerrillas kept towns and villages under terror and sometimes held them for extended periods, officials did the king's bidding only when French troops were present, and Joseph's government, when functioning, was, admittedly or otherwise, military.

Military governors had authority, in varying degree, in every province. In areas not fully conquered, Napoleon gave French corps commanders (like General Suchet in Aragon) governing power; for dangerous provinces and those guarding the high road to France, he designated officers to be governors (for example, General Thiébault in Valladolid). The corps commanders were required only to keep Joseph informed and forward him surplus revenues (if any); governors like Thiébault were supposed to establish a civil bureaucracy, answerable immediately to Madrid, but were slow to relinquish their own power. In "safe" areas, principally New Castile, Joseph was allowed to assign governors, usually French officers attached to his service. They were supposed to concern themselves with police, security, communications, and providing for French troops and occasionally the king's Spanish troops. Invariably, however, they became involved, especially if forceful men, in civil matters, for instance, tax collection and the operation of the courts. In some places the development of the civil bureaucracy was unnecessarily discouraged. In others, the military governors were compelled to rule. In Guadalajara, for example, General Sigisbert Hugo spent years alternately chasing the guerrilla chief Empecinado into the hills and herding his reluctant Spanish clerks and judges back to their posts.

Except for special tribunals, most of them military, Joseph retained the complex and inefficient Bourbon court system. Romero produced plans for establishing justices of the peace at the local level, courts of first instance and appeals courts, and a court of cassation at Madrid. But it was not implemented in 1809, and never would be.

In sum, the king's civil servants were supervised by French officers, except in New Castile; there, part of them were so supervised, and the rest shared power with military men. With local alterations the Bourbon local government, administrative, and court systems persisted. From the beginning the government lacked uniformity and clear channels of authority. Even in New Castile, where both military and civilian officials were responsible without qualification to Joseph, his reluctance to define their areas of authority left issues to be settled by contests of will, usually won by the military. Unhappily, the government was least effective where the king's power was greatest. Had the war not continued, the government might have improved—though not surely.

At any rate Napoleon had no interest in excuses. At the end of 1809 he ruled that Joseph had failed as civil executive (among other things) and, as we shall see shortly, took drastic action.

FINANCES AND THE ECONOMY[4]

French troops in Spain, unlike those in the other satellite kingdoms, were paid by the imperial treasury, though after mid-1810 some military governors, notably Suchet, were able to support a small percentage of them from Spanish sources. By the end of 1809 the French Army of Spain had cost France over a billion reals in specie alone and, by the end of the reign, over three billion. The total outlay is difficult to estimate. It would include the cost of equipment, arms, ammunition, supplies, and services not secured by force in Spain. One might well add also the cost of furnishing replacements for the army; in five years there were 300,000 casualties, of whom some 150,000 to 200,000 were killed or required evacuation.

In addition to supporting French troops, Napoleon lent Joseph money—234,000,000 reals in 1808 and 1809—620,000,000

4. The chart below supports the discussion. Figures are in vellon reals (15.06 reals to the peso); 1 franc = 3.75 reals. The vellon peso did not have the value of the silver peso (piece of eight) of eight reals, which was minted only in the American colonies, and for which the U.S. silver dollar had been made exactly exchangeable.

Finances, 1808–1813

Total at the end of	Bourbon Debt	New Domestic Debt	Debt to France	Cost of French Army of Spain
1808	7,194,000,000	36,000,000	107,000,000	532,000,000
1809	(Paid beginning in 1809 in *cédulas hipotecarias* secured	80,000,000	234,000,000	1,064,000,000
1810	by national properties)	68,000,000	306,000,000	1,702,000,000
1811		142,000,000	409,000,000	2,444,000,000
1812		269,000,000	537,000,000	2,976,000,000
1813 (June)	1,000,000,000	327,000,000	620,000,000	3,242,000,000

reals by the end of the reign. In spite of these concessions, the government's debt climbed steadily—to 116,000,000 reals by the end of 1809—327,000,000 by the end of the reign. These figures seem modest, but were compiled by the minister of finance, acutely aware that Napoleon would scrutinize the records and determined to present as favorable a picture as possible. They represent the *admitted* debt, but even if they are precise they do not include the debt to France, which would bring the debt (as of June 1813) to 947,000,000 reals. They are no indication of the true state of the economy, for obligations totaling some 2,000,000,000 reals were settled in paper exchangeable for "national properties," that is, in effect, the crown had expended its capital to meet expenses not covered by income.

The "national properties," confiscated monastic and rebel holdings, were valued at 9,700,000,000 reals. According to a plan prepared by Cabarrus, Ferri-Pisani, and others, part were to be liquidated to pay the Bourbon debt (7,200,000,000 reals). The rest were to be reserved to produce income, house and support public schools, hospitals, and institutions of charity, and for other purposes.

Paying the Bourbon debt seemed desirable. Domestic creditors who accepted payment would be committed to the Bonapartist government. Payment should revive the government's domestic and foreign credit. There would be a redistribution of property, which would operate, Joseph hoped, to strengthen the middle class and increase the number of landowning peasants. Joseph signed decrees to implement the program in June 1809. Bourbon credit paper was to be replaced with "mortgage notes" (*cédulas hipotecarias*), which would be turned in for property, then burned.[5] Similar notes were to be given (if necessary) to meet new obligations. The system was simple and seemed workable. But it was poorly administered, and the king himself made ruinous modifications of the original scheme. Before the issuance of *cédulas* had fairly begun, he authorized new notes of "indemnity and recompense," also exchangeable for properties, which he distributed to

5. Bourbon *vales reales,* large denomination notes renewed yearly, were made directly exchangeable for property. Further, creditors had the alternative of registering their claims on the "great ledger" of the state for interest at four percent per annum.

his favorites. Other sorts of paper followed, always based on the dwindling properties. Worst of all, however, his government's poverty drove Joseph to sell properties for specie. Buyers with coin or bullion increasingly took precedence over those with paper. When buyers with hard money could no longer be found, properties were pledged as collateral for loans.

From the beginning the *cédulas* circulated as paper money, and their value became increasingly unrelated to the value of the properties they supposedly represented. Inflation began, in fact, before the first issues were off the presses. Notes received in November 1809 were worth only twenty-five percent of face value. With occasional slight rises (always at times when French armies scored triumphs) the worth of the notes spiraled steadily downward. The government gained short-run benefit by paying its debts in paper. Nominally it kept its deficits low and paid a large portion of the Bourbon debt. Actually it expended its capital and ruined its credit.

The poverty of Joseph's government stemmed basically from a general disruption of the economy by the war, but was increased by administrative bungling. And initially his revenues were decreased by his *laissez-faire* program, universally accepted as progressive by the liberals of the time, but damaging to an economy where risks were extreme and private capital unlikely to replace government capital. During 1809, urged on by Cabarrus, the king destroyed government monopolies on the manufacture and sale of playing cards, brandy, aromatic liqueurs, hard liquor, sealing wax, and tobacco. He closed the royal china and crystal plants, conveyed various government cloth works to private owners, abandoned the operation of royal gambling establishments, and began a gradual reduction of internal tariffs.

Perhaps as much as 100,000,000 reals a year in income were sacrificed by abandoning the monopolies and gambling houses. Losses from tariffs were immediately evident. The royal factories declined under private management, to no great loss since they had never been very profitable, but hundreds of workers were left jobless, adding a surly element to an already embittered and hungry proletariat. Almost immediately Joseph began restoring, even raising, internal tariffs (the rights of entry at Madrid climbed to twenty-eight percent ad valorum). By mid-1810 he had abandoned the whole *laissez-faire* program. In the interim, however, his losses had been severe.

Initially the king retained the Bourbon tax system, and he never made basic modifications. Still, if he had administered it properly, allowing for the fact that he did not control all of Spain, he should have netted 20,000,000 reals a month, which would have supported his government. His actual collections seldom exceeded 10,000,000.

By the end of 1809 Napoleon had many complaints against Joseph, but none more damaging or justified than that his financial administration had failed miserably.

THE ROYAL STYLE

In April 1809 Wellesley again landed a new British army at Lisbon. In Andalusia, Spanish armies gave evidence of new strength. Everywhere guerrilla activity was increasing. Joseph, however, bent on establishing a reputation as benevolent, progressive, and Spanish in spirit, let the French armies fend for themselves. He pressed plans for a public school system and discussed converting the *Prado* into a museum. He considered proposals for parks and fountains for Madrid, road improvements, bridges, and canals, some of which he ordered executed. To impress the Spanish with his appreciation of their culture, he commissioned busts of Lope de Vega, Pedro de Calderón, Guilhen de Castro, and Agustín Moreto.

The royal court, though less lively than that of Naples, was vital and colorful. The setting was the magnificent palace designed for Philip V, its walls lined with paintings by Europe's masters— Raphael, Michelangelo, Veronese, Velázquez, Murillo, Van Dyck —and, jarringly, a copy of David's *Napoleon Crossing the Alps,* hung there not by Joseph but by the hapless Charles IV. The throne room was dominated by Tiepolo's gigantic fresco depicting the peoples of the Spanish empire. Before it king and court observed the rigid forms of the old regime. Elsewhere the atmosphere was more relaxed. The fastidious Miot de Melito, chief of household, and the marquise de Montehermoso managed a leisurely sequence of ceremonies and social events, allowing time for the king to rclax at Casa del Campo, his favorite spot. In the evenings, French and Spanish courtiers mingled with the elite of Spanish literature, art, music, and the drama. The writers Meléndéz Valdés and Leandro Moratín, the actor Maiquez, the artists Maella and Ramos, the dramatist Manuel de Gorostiza joined Joseph's circle, as did the reigning beauties of the Madrid stage.

By summer 1809, the king had established a pleasant daily routine. In some five hours he performed, very well, he thought, the duties of civil executive. There was time for riding and hunting aside from his social schedule. The *raffinée* Countess Jaruco added excitement to his personal life. In Naples he had lived a similar life, leaving military matters to others, and had been popular and successful. Spain, however, was different. In July, the war suddenly compelled his attention; armies which he had seldom or never seen awaited his command.

The Peninsular War Continues

TALAVERA

In May 1809, two weeks after landing at Lisbon, Sir Arthur Wellesley surprised the single French corps (Soult) in Portugal and drove it into northern Spain. He then moved south and joined forces with the Spanish army of Cuesta. In July he marched east along the Tagus toward Madrid at the head of 60,000 British, Anglo-Portuguese,[6] and Spanish troops. Joseph, notified on July 22 of the enemy movement, responded with amazing alacrity, and produced a strategic plan of Napoleonic quality. (No one denied that Joseph could *plan,* even militarily; execution was another matter.)

The king ordered Marshal Soult to march south from Salamanca with 60,000 men (his own corps plus those of Marshals Ney and Mortier) to block Wellesley's line of retreat. Joseph, with 40,000 (the Guard, corps of Marshal Victor and General Sébastiani) went west along the Tagus to meet the enemy head-on. (See Map 7, p. 246.) As Napoleon would later point out, the strategy

---

6. Portuguese troops trained and in great part led by British officers and NCOs.

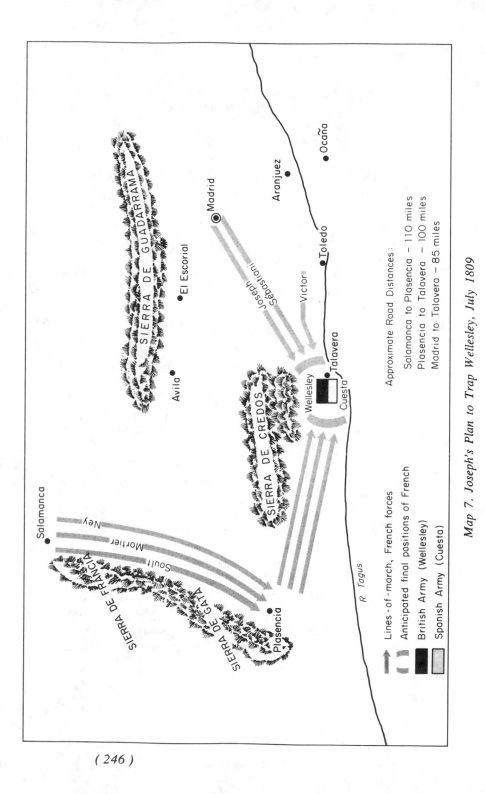

SIERRA DE GUADARRAMA

Avila

El Escorial

Madrid

Aranjuez

Ocaña

Toledo

Victor

Josephian

Sebastiani

SIERRA DE CREDOS

Talavera

Wellesley

Cuesta

Salamanca

Ney

Mortier

Soult

SIERRA DE FRANCIA

SIERRA DE GATA

Plasencia

R. Tagus

Lines-of-march, French forces

Anticipated final positions of French

British Army (Wellesley)

Spanish Army (Cuesta)

Approximate Road Distances :

Salamanca to Plasencia – 110 miles
Plasencia to Talavera – 100 miles
Madrid to Talavera – 85 miles

Map 7. Joseph's Plan to Trap Wellesley, July 1809

was dangerous in that it required bringing two French armies together in the face of the enemy. Still, if Joseph had adhered to his plan, it probably would have worked.

On July 26 Joseph's advance elements clashed with the allied army east of Talavera. Cuesta's Spanish broke, and had to be reorganized after nightfall behind the British and Anglo-Portuguese. By dawn the next day Wellesley had taken up a defensive position anchored on high ground north of Talavera. Joseph occupied the hills opposite; Soult had not been heard from, but the king could have waited, probably for days, for the marshal to appear in the allied rear. The British general, unable to depend on the Spanish (half his force) and their mulish relic of a commander, was unlikely to attack. If he did, Joseph was on defensible ground with an army which, if smaller than the enemy's, was well disciplined and almost solidly French. If Wellesley tried to retreat, he would have to lower his defenses; Joseph could attack him when he was most vulnerable.

But the king did not wait. Bullied by Marshal Victor, who did not want to share laurels with Soult, he ordered the attack. In doing so he played into the hands of Wellesley, probably the best defensive tactician alive, as he would prove again and again, for the last time (as duke of Wellington) at Waterloo. On July 27 the French attacked by day, then again by night, and each time, exhausted by their climb to the enemy positions and decimated by the accurate musket fire of the British, were beaten back. The night assault ended in utter confusion. In the darkness, stunned by noise and the flash of explosions, serenaded by the eerie howl of the bagpipes from the British squares, the men became disoriented, some even firing on each other. Nevertheless, on July 28, Joseph consented to another attack, which also failed. Wellesley, however, was pinned down, and Soult, though late, was on the march to close the trap around him.

Until July 29, Joseph's strategy was succeeding in spite of his tactical setbacks. On that day, however, he got word that a small Spanish army was threatening Madrid from the south. Horrified at the thought of losing his capital again (Napoleon's jibes of the previous year still rankled), he left half his force to watch Wellesley and marched off to cover Madrid.

With less than 20,000 men opposite him, Wellesley could risk a fighting retreat. He withdrew rapidly down the Tagus before Soult arrived to block him, and marched to safety in Portugal. Had Joseph stood fast, the allied army would almost surely have been destroyed. Instead, Wellesley was credited with a victory and rewarded with a new title—viscount of Wellington and Talavera.

Joseph, meanwhile, won a battle and saved Madrid, and since Wellesley had fled the country, he felt he was victor in the campaign. ". . . Sire, I have maneuvered with 40,000 men against 100,000 enemies and embarrassed them in the worst way," he reported proudly to Napoleon. In reply he received angry reprimands; the emperor saw only that Joseph had risked battle with only part of his army, failed to defeat Wellesley, and let him escape. Marshal Jourdan, the king's chief of staff, was made the official scapegoat and recalled to France. Joseph was stunned; most of his generals felt that he deserved *some* praise. In retrospect, however, Napoleon's assessment seems just.

Talavera was a stalemate, but the campaign was a British victory. If Wellesley had been trapped, the British effort on the peninsula might have ended in 1809. Instead he survived to construct the lines of Tôrres Vedras, around Lisbon, which he would hold against massive French assaults until he was ready to emerge, carry the war into Spain, and drive them from the peninsula. Napoleon's Austrian Campaign of 1809 gave the empire new life; the Talavera Campaign, since it was lost, revitalized the cancer on its body. The British remained on the peninsula. But for them, the French might have won the Spanish War; instead it grew in intensity and costliness, steadily draining the strength of the empire.

THE CONQUEST OF ANDALUSIA

For a time, however, the French seemed gradually to be gaining the upper hand. In January 1810 Joseph invaded the south of Spain (Andalusia). Wellington was seeing to his defenses in Portugal, and the major Spanish armies were pinned down in the east by the corps of Suchet and Augereau.[7] The king, therefore, was almost unopposed. Except for Cádiz, where the rebel government took refuge, the conquest was complete by mid-March.

The campaign was a personal triumph for Joseph. The Andalusians, who had spent centuries longer than other Spanish under Moorish rule, could fatalistically accept a ruler who displayed seemingly overwhelming power. They turned out en masse to welcome Joseph; their new nabob, in turn, was captivated. Crowds cheered, girls threw flowers in the king's path, splendid processions accompanied him through the streets of the cities, the *Te Deum* was sung in the cathedrals. Joseph was presented with Andalusian horses, magnificently harnessed, and fighting bulls, and, according to his aide-de-camp, Bigarré, some of the nobles put at the king's disposal "their wives, their daughters, and their homes."

Joseph quickly forgot that these same people had butchered Dupont's men. He rejected all evidence that cold power underlay his new popularity. No! Rebel propaganda had told the people that Joseph Bonaparte was ugly, one-eyed, stupid, a drunkard, and a wastrel who doted on sacrilege. Now that they had seen the "real Joseph" they knew better. In his letters to Napoleon he crowed with happiness: ". . . Your Majesty will be charmed by the progress we are making here . . . the triumph of our enemies was founded on the most absurd and black calumnies, which are now being dissipated . . ." Posterity might doubt it, wrote Bigarré, but Joseph was truly "the idol of the peoples of Andalusia and Granada," and gave interesting proof:

One of the most beautiful women . . . [of Málaga], belonging to one of the best families of the kingdom, delirious with enthusiasm for her new King, begged him, in writing, to do her the signal favor of visiting her in bed.

In the cathedral of Córdoba (the magnificent *Mesquita,* with its hundreds of jasper pillars, eternally more Moorish than Christian), Joseph was presented the French standards captured by the rebels at Bailén. Determined to treat this as a gesture of love

7. Suchet was invading Valencia; Augereau was attempting to quiet Catalonia, which Duhesme and Gouvion Saint-Cyr, in turn, had failed to do.

rather than of submission, the king leaped onto a chair and with choked emotion proclaimed his love for Spain and her people. In gratitude for his reception at Granada, he ordered the Opera of Madrid to perform there forthwith. It came escorted by Joseph's only complete Spanish regiment, whose uniforms, newly designed, outshone the costumes of the artists. Shortly most of the king's ministers were adding to the splendor of his entourage (while their work piled up in Madrid).

Touched by the appeals of seemingly repentant rebels (and by the weeping entreaties of the wives and children of many still fighting against him), Joseph ordered a "reconsideration" of the status of confiscated rebel properties. (The accounts of the national properties, already confused, were further complicated.) With incurable optimism he guaranteed the jobs of rebel bureaucrats who pledged loyalty to him, recommissioned Spanish officers who had earlier betrayed him (some twice), filled up his Spanish regiments with ex-rebels, even including some guerrillas. Most of his recruits—civil and military—remained loyal only as long as it was profitable.

Joseph a Figurehead: 1810–1812

THE MILITARY GOVERNMENTS

Unimpressed by Joseph's triumphal procession through Andalusia, exasperated by his persistent softheadedness, and generally unhappy with his performance, Napoleon decided to reduce his brother's authority. During 1809 the king had failed to establish an effective governmental-administrative system; he had bungled the Talavera campaign, and had given no direction to his commanders in northern Spain, where guerrilla activity was proliferating; his finances were in disarray. The emperor had other complaints as well. For example, Joseph had delayed for eight months before implementing the imperial decree disbanding the monastic orders. Even then he had allowed ex-monks to take refuge in the Escorial!

On February 8, 1810, Catalonia, Aragon, Navarre, and Biscay were removed from Joseph's control and placed under imperial military governments; in May the system was extended to Burgos and Valladolid-Palencia-Toro.[8] (See Map 8, p. 252.) The emperor's justification was succinct: ". . . I cannot stand the enormous cost of Spain . . . there is only one way out, that is to administer the provinces for the benefit of France." Specifically, Spain had cost the French treasury 300,000,000 francs in specie during 1808–1809, and was still devouring money at the rate of 13,500,000 francs a month. Joseph, in short, had failed to make Spain pay; the military would. (In part, the governors lived up to expectations, but Spain remained expensive.[9]) Not one for half-measures, Napoleon proceeded next to divide the Army of Spain into six separate armies, all directed from Paris. Joseph was given direct command of only one, the reserve Army of the Center, at Madrid. Marshal Soult, commanding the Army of the South, was given power which virtually made a military government of Andalusia.

Nominally, Joseph remained king of Spain, but he ruled only the "Center," that is, New Castile and the southern half of Old Castile.[10] Even there the French commanders were authorized to collect and use part of the revenues. He could have controlled the French military in the Center and Andalusia if he had been forceful enough, which he was not. In addition, Napoleon specified that Joseph could command *any army* with which he was *present,* but the king returned to Madrid and declined to budge. Thus without him the Army of Portugal, under the crusty old *condottiere,* Marshal Masséna, marched against Wellington, in Portugal; Marshal MacDonald's Army of Catalonia pursued the never-ending task of subduing the Catalans; Suchet's Army of Aragon

8. León and Zamora were added to the sixth government in July. Governors were as follows:

Catalonia	Augereau, shortly replaced by Macdonald
Aragon	Suchet
Navarre	Dufour, shortly replaced by Reille
Biscay	Thouvenot
Burgos	Dorsenne
Valladolid, etc.	Thiébault (replaced for a few months in 1810 by the younger Kellermann)

9. See chart p. 241, footnote 4.
10. Namely, Ávila and Segovia.

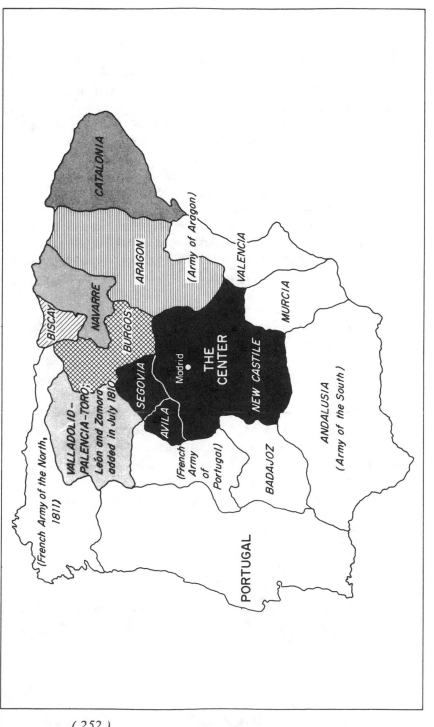

Map 8. *Spain in 1810, Showing Military Governments and Joseph's "Center"*

quieted that province and marched against Valencia; and the Army of the North battled guerrillas from Galicia to Navarre.

First news of this sweeping reorganization found Joseph at the peak of his Andalusian triumph, when, to all appearances, the Spanish were finally beginning to accept him as king. He returned to Madrid in May, shocked and humiliated. He had announced a new era in Spain; promised constitutional government and progress in a reborn, united kingdom. Suddenly he was powerless; Spain was parceled out to soldiers to be conquered and robbed. Was Napoleon envious of his personal success, as Miot de Melito suggested?

The emperor, unruffled by Joseph's initial protests, calmly announced that it might be necessary to annex northern Spain to France. Within weeks Joseph had two of his ministers in Paris to protest the unconstitutionality of Napoleon's acts. The constitution guaranteed Spain's integrity! The military governments came close to violating the provision. If part of the country were annexed, how could he face his people? It became obvious that Napoleon did not care. Spain must be conquered, must show a profit. All else could wait.

Probably Napoleon expected Joseph to abdicate; his policy in 1810 seemed directed toward eliminating the statellite kingdoms in favor of a "Roman Imperial" system, as we have indicated elsewhere. The king, however, merely asked to be recalled, and got no reply. It was desirable that Joseph flee Madrid (as Louis had Amsterdam), in which case Spain would revert to the emperor, and he could dispose of her "legally." Joseph did not oblige, though in great part he abdicated the functions of government remaining to him. In public he affected optimism; privately he was despondent. Much of his time was spent at Casa del Campo; he had, La Forest observed, "a veritable need of dissipation." Haunted by the feeling that abdication was the only honorable course, he could still not bear to cast away his kingship, the trappings of which he dearly loved. At the end of 1810, when he seemed at last to have mustered the courage to leave, Napoleon began to patch up relations with him. The menace of Russia had induced the emperor to change his plans. Joseph, along with the other satellite kings, save Louis, was to be rehabilitated.

THE CÁDIZ CORTES

With British help, the rebel junta held Cádiz against all French assaults, and in September 1810 assembled there a Cortes which assumed nominal leadership of rebel Spain. Piece by piece, the Cortes assembled what was later known Europe-wide as the "Constitution of 1812," a charter more liberal than the constitution of Bayonne.[11] Considering that the Spanish rebel armies were actually led by conservatives, and that the guerrillas and people generally were moved largely by the nationalism of Church and Crown, it is an astonishing document. The explanation is that the Cortes was packed with liberals who had assumed election from their home districts or had been selected by liberal underground groups in French-controlled areas.

As noted earlier, most liberals had cheered Napoleon's expulsion of the Bourbons but, after noting the bitterly anti-French sentiment of the people, had espoused the rebel cause, hoping to infiltrate its leadership. As Ramos-Oliveira put it: ". . . the most clear-sighted among the Spanish progressives led the revolution against Joseph Bonaparte, whose policy coincided in general with that of the intelligentsia." With the establishment of the Cádiz Cortes the liberals came into their own. The British, weary of dealing with the stiff-necked reactionaries of the former junta, gave the Cortes support and distributed its propaganda. The active rebel leaders, still mostly conservatives, bided their time, ignored disagreeable orders from Cádiz, and concentrated on winning the war, confident that when Ferdinand VII returned he would reject the constitution and its makers (which he did). Meanwhile the Spanish cause was credited in Britain and northern Europe with a liberal character, which it really lacked. The provisions of the Cádiz constitution were trumpeted abroad by Argüelles, Toreño, De la Huerta, and others.

Napoleon, noting the liberals' work, felt challenged; it took validity from his oft-repeated claim that he had intervened in Spain to reform her government and benefit her people. In late 1810 he

11. The Cádiz constitution: (1) declared the abstract sovereignty of the nation, (2) provided for hereditary parliamentary monarchy (Bourbon), (3) established a single-chamber Cortes to be elected by *universal manhood suffrage* and to meet annually, (4) established ministerial responsibility, (5) separated executive, legislative, and judicial powers, and (6) gave the king a three-year suspensive veto.

suggested that Joseph try to negotiate with Cádiz, and authorized him to accept the Cortes as his legislature if it would recognize him as king and adopt the constitution of Bayonne. He recommended, however, that Joseph wait until Wellington was expelled from Portugal, so that he could bargain from a position of strength.

The British, Napoleon recognized, were the greatest obstacle to French success on the peninsula. During 1810 Spanish armies had made difficult work for Suchet in Valencia, but were clearly losing. Wellington's defenses at Lisbon, however, had held against Masséna's assaults, and at year's end the marshal, unable to feed his troops in Portugal, had withdrawn to the Spanish border. Wellington had credit for victories against Joseph in 1809 and Masséna in 1810. The British enabled Cádiz to hold out, supplying troops and provisions and backing her defenses with fire from naval vessels. They were supplying Spanish armies still in the field. As long as Wellington threatened the French from Lisbon, rebel commanders would tolerate the Cádiz Cortes. If he were expelled the Cortes would be in jeopardy, even if the British continued to support the rebels; the delegates might well make a deal with Joseph. If they did, it might shorten the war. If not, then the war would probably be short anyway. Neither the French, the British, nor the Spanish themselves believed that the Spanish regular armies could defeat the French. The only real Spanish successes were being won in the war of attrition being waged by their guerrillas. Terrible as was the punishment they were inflicting on the French, however, they could hardly expect to expel the invaders if the Spanish armies were destroyed.

THE GUERRILLAS

In April 1809 the rebel junta, discouraged with the record of its regular forces, gave official sanction to guerrilla warfare against the French. Churchmen, though not the Church officially, encouraged the *partidas,* furnished them hideouts, and sometimes joined them. (The Spanish priests and monks were a fierce breed and never ceased to astonish Napoleon, who expected them to behave like Italian clergy.) A catechism circulated in Aragon read in part: "Are we at liberty to kill the French? . . . It is our duty to do so."

In Galicia and Asturias, bands were in action under Marquerito and Ballesteros. In León the leader was "Capucino," an un-frocked monk. In Navarre the roads were menaced by Mina, called "The Student," and, after his capture, by Espoz y Mina, his uncle, a less romantic but more vicious fighter. In Catalonia, Aragon, and Old Castile, Villacampa, a Spanish marquis, carried out raids from the mountains. El Empecinado (Don Juan Martín) dominated the highlands of Guadalajara and occasionally sent bands galloping into the outskirts of Madrid.

The numbers and ferocity of the *guerrilleros* increased as the war progressed. Some French observers tried to pass them off as former contraband runners and bandits. Doubtless some were, since guerrilla activity was often lucrative. French convoys were plundered; "tariffs" were levied on Spanish food destined for French-occupied cities, and even on goods coming from France. But for most bands the "take" was too small to have kept them fighting solely for profit. Most partisans surely had other motives, though there was little nobility, or even valor, among them. Bands of four or five thousand seldom attacked French units of over five hundred; even then they often fled if hotly opposed. Usually they struck from ambush, and if successful killed wantonly and indiscriminately. Prisoners were taken only for the pleasure of torturing them to death, or to be held for ransom. Some leaders, notably Villacampa, were civilized, humane, and honorable, but they could not always control their men. All bands included some men who killed for the love of it. Some small bands specialized in silent murder, at night, using the knife and garrote, with no object but terrorizing the enemy.

Admirable or not, the *guerrilleros* were an important part of the rebel forces, perhaps the most important part. Bigarré esti-mates, quite soberly, that they often killed a hundred Frenchmen a day during the latter years of Joseph's reign. (If so, they prob-ably accounted for half the French killed in Spain.) Miot says they caused many times more casualties than Spanish armies. Both probably exaggerate, but their statements show how deeply the irregulars were feared. They kept the French in a constant state of anxiety, perpetually alert against an unseen enemy. Thousands of troops were tied up on escort and guard duty. In mountain areas companies and sometimes battalions protected single mes-sengers. Battalions and regiments traveled with large convoys.

After 1811, the *guerrilleros* began to participate in orthodox military operations with British and Spanish armies, and some bands became uniformed troops. In 1812 Longa and others struck from the mountains at French forts on the north coast while simultaneously Sir Home Riggs Popham landed British marines to attack from the beach. These operations tied the French Army of the North in knots and contributed to Wellington's success farther south. In the earlier years, however, the guerrillas forwarded the rebel cause by destroying, capturing, killing—making the war expensive in money and blood. Assignment to Spain came to be viewed as a death sentence in all the armies of the empire.

JOSEPH TO PARIS

In December 1810 Joseph received letters from members of his family urging him to stay at Madrid "for the good of the [Bonaparte] dynasty." He well knew only Napoleon could have inspired them. Simultaneously the emperor's suggestion for eventual overtures to the Cádiz Cortes arrived, with the implied promise of the restoration of his powers. His anxieties were somewhat relieved, but his morale remained low. Too soft to exert the authority he still possessed, the king was at the mercy of the French military, even in the "Center." His government was poverty-stricken and a sham. "His people" grew daily more sullen and rebellious, a development he blamed on the brutality of French generals such as Dorsenne, the bull-necked hangman who governed Burgos and commanded the Imperial Guard in Spain. In the south Soult not only ignored Joseph, but spoke openly of his "Nation of Andalusia," as if he were a king. Guerrilla bands were everywhere. Only Suchet's Army of Aragon seemed to be winning victories. Joseph fully believed that Spain could be salvaged only if he were allowed to fulfill the promises he had made in Andalusia. As he saw it, Napoleon had ruined his prestige just when he was about to be accepted by the Spanish. If he could restore their faith in his good intentions, all would be well. To the astonishment of his courtiers, he even opined that Spain might accept him more quickly if French troops left the country. He feared that the emperor was being deceived about Spain by his ministers and ached to go to Paris and tell his brother "the truth."

In March 1811 an opportunity presented itself. Napoleon announced the birth of his son by Marie Louise, and expressed the hope that Joseph would be the child's godfather. It was not an invitation to Paris, but Joseph decided, nevertheless, to present himself for the christening of the "king of Rome." With difficulty the minister of finance produced funds for the journey, and Joseph traveled north, stopping at Spanish towns along the route to promise an early return and better days for the nation. In Paris he got a chilly reception; the Austrian emperor (*in absentia*), not he, became the king of Rome's godfather. But Joseph finally saw Napoleon privately, and came away with promises that his power would soon be restored, and that the imperial treasury would lend him money.[12]

To all appearances the emperor, as of old, could deny his elder brother nothing when the two were face to face. Actually Napoleon intended to "restore" Joseph only when he marched for Russia—if he decided positively on the war. The emperor reasoned that while he fought Russia he could not trust a marshal with Spain. They were all *condottieri,* as he himself had been, and might well betray him. Further, if he gave a marshal over-all command, he would be more powerful than Joseph, and the king would have to be removed, which would spread fear in the satellites of annexation to France, and damage their usefulness and that of their rulers. Authority in Spain could not safely be left divided, however, while Napoleon was in Russia—too far away to coordinate activities, difficult enough even from Paris. Joseph had his faults, but he was trustworthy. Surely the king could maintain a modicum of control over Spain—at least avoid a disaster—while the overwhelming force Napoleon planned to assemble speedily crushed the Russians. Joseph would be king and commander again—*when,* and for how long, the emperor would decide later.

RETURN TO REALITY

Joseph returned jubilantly to Madrid, expecting to hear momentarily that Napoleon had announced his "restoration." The money he had been promised began to arrive (in irregular installments), but the year slipped by, and his prerogatives were ex-

12. See chart p. 241, footnote 4.

panded not at all—he ruled the Center only. Meanwhile his debt mounted in spite of the emperor's loans, and the value of his paper sank steadily.

In an effort to maximize receipts from taxes due after the summer harvest, Joseph assigned ministers and councilors-of-state as local supervisors. Unfortunately the French military gave them little more respect than the regular officials, and denied them adequate troop support, without which nothing could be collected. Moreover, the guerrillas took extra pains to thwart their efforts. At Toledo, Almenara was menaced by *partidas* so continually that he fled precipitately to Madrid without finishing his task. Returns were less than in preceding years.

The Center produced bumper harvests during 1811, but grain convoys (taxes in kind and normal supplies) were frequently attacked en route to Madrid. Enough were captured to cause a drastic food shortage in the capital during the fall. Bread prices reached four times the 1810 level. Food riots were common, and starvation an everyday affair. To maintain order, troops had to be placed on constant alert to reinforce the Madrid police. Many of the king's bureaucrats were in dire straits, as were even members of the government. Joseph was almost reduced to tears when Admiral Mazarredo, minister of marine, member of the Golden Fleece, ex-minister of both Charles III and Charles IV, asked that his family be issued army rations. As 1812 began Joseph's usual level geniality had given way to moroseness punctuated by spells of exaggerated good humor and fits of temper. He talked frequently of abdication, but made no move to leave Madrid.

THE WAR

In 1811 General Louis Gabriel Suchet became the twenty-third marshal of the French empire, a rank he richly deserved. During the year he crushed the Spanish Army of Catalonia, advanced against those of Valencia and Murcia, and at year's end was besieging the city of Valencia, where the remnants of the latter two armies had been rallied by Don Joaquín Blake. He took the city in January 1812 and captured the rebels' most renowned commander, together with their largest remaining regular force.

On the western side of the peninsula, however, Wellington had won victories in 1811. His army had become the rallying point for the remaining maneuverable Spanish forces on the peninsula. Under his personal command were 30,000 British and 20,000 Anglo-Portuguese; operating under his orders was Beresford (later Hill) with an additional 11,000 British and 15,000 Anglo-Portuguese. The furtive Spanish armies of Estremadura and Galicia (5,000 and 12,000) gave him occasional support, as did various guerrilla bands, though the latter served him best by supplying information on French movements. In succeeding years his Spanish contingent would constantly grow larger and more cooperative.

In 1811 Napoleon ordered Masséna to attack Lisbon again, drawing reinforcements from the Army of the North if necessary, and directed Soult to support him with the Army of the South. Without an immediate superior, however, the marshals cooperated poorly. Soult made a half-hearted thrust at southern Portugal, but it was parried by Beresford. In the north Masséna was hit off-balance by Wellington's main army and driven back on Salamanca. He called for reinforcements from the 90,000-man Army of the North, whose commander, Marshal Bessières, responded personally—at the head of 1,200 cavalry of the Imperial Guard. "I come like a French cavalier, at the head of a small band of heroes!" announced the blond Gascon. Masséna marched for Portugal anyway, only to have his army shattered by Wellington just after he crossed the border; Napoleon recalled him. Marshal Marmont, who took over the Army of Portugal, did little better, however. At year's end his outpost was Ciudad Rodrigo, inside Spain, and most of his army was at Salamanca.

Joseph Commands Again

During the winter of 1811–1812 the harassed Joseph was forced to allow Marmont to seize provisions in the Center for the Army of Portugal. The king's mood was improved, however, by Suchet's announcement of the capture of Valencia (January 1812), whose revenues, he hoped, would repair his finances. But Napoleon also had need of money, and before Joseph could furnish a civil administration for the province, the emperor had sent officials to assist Suchet, who was appointed military governor of Valencia (as well as Aragon, which he had ruled since 1810).

Conditions worsened at Madrid. All civil employees had to be put on army rations. The price of bread spiraled upward; *Madrileños* were surly and desperate; at every dawn bodies of victims of starvation or violence were found in the streets. New bands of *guerrilleros* had appeared under ever-bolder chieftains like "El Medico" who in January 1812 stormed the gates of Madrid, killing a number of French soldiers. Illness removed Romero and Mazarredo from the cabinet. Every day there seemed to be new portents of doom for the jittery French—as when a mad dog attacked a guard before Bigarré's quarters.

Joseph determined to abdicate. In February and twice in March he asked to return to France, ". . . where I should have been for a year." But the time had arrived for his "restoration." Napoleon, as he left Paris on March 16 for the Russian campaign, had issued orders appointing the king commander of "all my armies in Spain" and placing all military governments under his control. He was again king in fact as well as name.

Before all else, Joseph was to give direction to the resurrected Army of Spain (all the armies), for which Marshal Jourdan had returned to organize a staff. It numbered 300,000, and, although it included some foreign troops, mostly Italians, essentially constituted the largest French army in Europe. (The Grande Armée of 1812 boasted 611,000, but only one-third were French.) During 1811–1812 Napoleon had withdrawn selected troops from Spain, including Imperial Guard regiments, redistributed the remaining veterans, and filled up units with draftees, some under age. But the amalgam was strong; Joseph had a first-rate army. Some famed commanders had also been recalled—Ney, Junot, Bessières, and Victor, among others—but most of them were difficult subordinates for anyone but the emperor. (Victor had served Joseph poorly at Talavera; Ney, Junot, and Bessières had been partly responsible for Masséna's failures against Wellington.) The commanders still present, save Soult, though hardly enthusiastic over following Joseph, could be expected to follow his orders.

The military situation did not seem dangerous. Only Wellington posed a threat to deployed French armies. At base his strength depended on the performance of a mere 40,000 British regulars (30,000 normally under his direct command). He had never massed more than 50,000 (British, Portuguese, and Spanish) against Masséna. Nothing irritated Napoleon more than having to assign major importance to such a small army. Yet he had; Marmont's Army of Portugal stood at 60,000, reinforceable from the north and center to 100,000. It seemed probable that Marmont could handle Wellington no matter what Joseph did. As it turned out, however, much depended on the king, as we shall see in the next chapter.

Conclusion

Spain cannot be rated as of 1812 on the same basis as the other satellite kingdoms, which had, in a sense, reached the prime of their existence when the Russian campaign began. She had not yet been conquered, and never would be. But we can make a judgment on Joseph's performance as king (civil executive), which was all but finished, leaving his military record for later examination.

On the face of it, as executive–administrator–lawgiver, Joseph planned well, meant well, but accomplished little. But conditions were abnormal during 1809, the only year (until 1812) he was even nominally in complete charge of French-controlled territory, and he spent considerable time on campaign. One might argue, as did his friend Miot de Melito in his memoirs, that Joseph would have done great things if Napoleon had not curtailed his authority. But it becomes doubtful when one considers that he never effectively governed the Center. There, in 1809 and thereafter, civil officials and military governors were *his* appointees, and *he* commanded the French army. No one in authority answered to anyone but him. War or not, if he could not efficiently organize the Center he was surely lacking in executive ability.

The king's control of his ministers was slack. The inbred inertia of his Spanish bureaucrats and the willfulness of his military subordinates were both encouraged by his inattention to duty and reluctance to make decisions. He tolerated, at all levels, too many experts at obstruction, marathon talking, and the devious scuttling of projects. His magnanimity toward his enemies won over few of them and alienated his friends. Perhaps he was too "good" a man to be an effective executive; perhaps he lacked the moral courage to rule. In any event his record was poor. His finances were mismanaged; his administration and courts remained inefficient, nonuniform, and burdened by useless officials; his progressive dreams largely failed of fulfillment. Though he doubtless would have had somewhat more success in peacetime, chances are that he would not have been an outstanding reformer or more than a mediocre governor.

It would be unjust, however, to deny Joseph credit for planting seeds of progress in Spain. Undoubtedly his attempts at constitutional, fiscal, legal, administrative, judicial, and educational reform left their mark. So much is attested to by Spanish historians, e.g., Altamira. Today's political map of Spain reflects his projected prefectural system, and the organization of Spanish courts owes much to his plan of 1812. The Prado museum is a monument to his inspiration, though few Spanish guidebooks confirm it, as are the restored Alhambra and palace of Charles V. Spaniards, and unfortunately Spanish language students the world over, are likely to remember Joseph only as *Pepe Botellas.* (Rebel propaganda left a mark too.) But *Madrileños* would have to be blind to ignore the parks and fountains he left behind. To them he is the *rey de las plazuelas* as well as *protector de los jugadores,* and like people everywhere, they do not bother themselves with contradictions.

But whether we blame Napoleon, Joseph, or the situation, Spain was the least successful satellite kingdom. Its cost far outweighed the contributions of the others. By the end of its life, in June 1813, it had cost the empire 300,000 casualties, almost 4,000,000,000 reals (over a billion francs) in specie, and untold amounts in matériel, armament, munitions, and supplies. If the Spanish adventure were not responsible for Napoleon's downfall, as he himself suggested more than once, it surely lessened the empire's chances of surviving the shock of defeats in Russia.

Are we not still the soldiers of Austerlitz? . . .
Marchons donc en avant. . . .
—NAPOLEON'S PROCLAMATION
TO THE GRANDE ARMÉE, JUNE 1812

chapter eight
THE EAGLES AT BAY: RUSSIA AND SPAIN

Russia

THE GRANDE ARMÉE OF 1812

T hough by 1812 Spain had bled the empire white, and extraordinary exactions made its people restive, the imperial military machine shone with un-exampled brilliance. In June the Grande Armée, 611,000 strong, stood behind the Niemen in East Prussia and the Bug in the Grand Duchy of Warsaw; supporting it were another 130,000 troops in depots and garrisons from Mainz on the Rhine to Königsberg on the Baltic. Ready to march were 200,000 French, 100,000 from Dutch, German, and Italian departments of France, 30,000 Austrians, 20,000 Prussians, 130,000 other Germans, 90,000 Poles and Lithuanians, 32,000 Italians and Illyrians, and 9,000 Swiss.

From the satellite kingdoms had come 17,000 Westphalians, 27,000 Italians, and the 5,000 man Neapolitan Royal Guard. (To bolster Murat's confidence in the permanence of his kingdom, Napoleon had withdrawn French troops from Naples; the king's army stayed at home to guard against a possible British invasion.) Joseph had contributed no troops; the few Spanish and Portuguese present (in French uniform) were volunteers, volunteer or im-pressed ex-prisoners of war, or survivors of units sent Napoleon by Charles IV before 1808.

The main body of the Grande Armée, the left (north) wing comprised 250,000 under Napoleon. In the center and somewhat to the rear, Eugène comanded 80,000, including his "Army of Italy."[1] On the right Jérôme commanded 80,000, of which his Westphalian army made up one corps.[2] On Jérôme's right was the Austrian army, under Schwarzenberg. On Napoleon's left were the corps of Macdonald and Yorck's Prussians. Murat, with the main army, commanded the Imperial Guard (47,000) and two corps of cavalry (40,000). Two Russian armies faced this immense array: 120,000 under Barclay de Tolly, opposite Napoleon, and 70,000 under Bagration, opposite Jérôme and Schwarzenberg. Other Russian armies, under Tormasov, Kutuzov, and Tchitchagov were for the moment not in play. Such was the picture at the beginning. We shall not attempt an account of the Russian campaign except as necessary to describe the part of the satellite rulers in it.

JÉRÔME IN POLAND

Jérôme had assumed command of the right wing on April 22, at Kalisz, established his headquarters in Warsaw (Praga) in May, and remained there when it moved to Pultusk in early June. He had gained notoriety for his intimate parties, populated preponderantly with Polish beauties, a number of whose names had been linked with his, especially that of the Princess Dominique Radziwill. Nevertheless, he had paid close attention to his military duties, and had also played a political role.

After Jérôme's arrival, Napoleon appointed an ambassador to Warsaw (the marquis de Pradt, archbishop of Malines) and allowed the revival of the Polish Confederation. These and other signs pointed to the end of the Grand Duchy of Warsaw[3] and the resurrection of the Kingdom of Poland, long expected as a reward from the emperor by the Poles, who had served him in every corner of Europe. By appointing Jérôme commander of the Right Wing (including the Polish army), Napoleon had brought to Poland European rumor-mongers' favorite for the throne. But he was not an avowed candidate; thus the emperor could test the

1. Eugène's army comprised the Fourth Corps (Italians augmented by two divisions of French), the Sixth Corps (Bavarians), and the Third Cavalry Corps.
2. Jérôme commanded the Eighth Corps (Westphalians), Fifth Corps (Poles), Seventh Corps (Saxons), and the Fourth Cavalry Corps.
3. Created in 1807 from Prussia's Polish provinces; expanded at Austria's expense in 1809.

Poles' attitudes toward his brother without risking embarrassment if they were adverse.

The Polish nobles quickly made their views known. (No other class was politically active.) Most feared the advent of a "revolutionary" Napoleonic government, and despite Jérôme's reputation as a profligate, they well knew he had forcefully implemented liberal policies in Westphalia. Virtually all, even the few liberals, preferred a native king, but they were badly divided on whom to support. Establishing a dynasty which would please even a majority seemed next to impossible. This discouraged Napoleon, already displeased with the small army the Duchy of Warsaw had produced. (The Poles' faith in his promises was wearing thin.) Moreover, he had to consider that his allies, Austria and Prussia, hoped to recover their Polish possessions, and that the czar might be more amenable to early negotiations (assuming quick initial French victories) if Poland's status remained unchanged. For these reasons Napoleon gave up the idea of creating a Polish kingdom; exactly *when* is uncertain, for his decision did not become apparent until after the campaign had begun.[4]

Jérôme meanwhile played out his role, probably assigned him in March during his visit to Paris. He almost consistently denied the prospect of a new throne, although he did promise the countess von Löwenstein (she said) that he would bring her to Warsaw when he had the crown. Napoleon, similarly, never confirmed that Jérôme was a genuine candidate. But it is striking that he failed to deny it either. Under the circumstances his silence assured that his brother would be so considered.

Jérôme did not leave Warsaw for his headquarters at Pultusk until June 17, after his troops had been in motion for some weeks. It has often been assumed, therefore, that he delayed as long as possible before dragging himself away from the pleasures of the Polish capital. Actually he had waited to see Prince Adam Czartoryski,[5] recently elected marshal of the Polish Confederation, who arrived in Warsaw on June 17. Apparently this interview

4. In July, at Vilna, he found the Lithuanians lukewarm to being included in a Polish kingdom, at least a French-sponsored one, and announced the creation of a Duchy of Lithuania, comprising territory which had belonged to Poland before the eighteenth-century partitions.
5. The "Old Prince," not his more famous son, who was in the Russian camp.

convinced him that he had no future in Poland. On June 19 he wrote Queen Catherine protesting that he would never be king of Poland in terms more positive than ever before. At any rate, through June 17, Jérôme had business in Warsaw. His performance on the Russian campaign will have to be judged by his actions thereafter.

JÉRÔME, COMMANDER

Napoleon's main army crossed the Niemen on June 24–25, and on June 26 captured Vilna. Earlier Napoleon had thought Bagration might attack Poland. Jérôme had been directed to place the bulk of his troops north of the Narew River, leaving Reynier and Schwarzenberg to screen Warsaw. If Bagration attacked, Jérôme could defend the river line until Eugène and/or units of the main army reinforced him. On June 22, however, Napoleon learned that Bagration was marching east, probably to join with Barclay de Tolly. He ordered Jérôme to advance (abreast of the main army) and seize Grodno. (See Map 9, p. 268.) The king was delayed by Reynier, who had conflicting orders from Napoleon and Jérôme, and who himself was held up by the slow progress of Schwarzenberg. Nevertheless on June 30 Jérôme captured Grodno, where he remained four days to reorganize and rest his troops. It was not an excessive delay. Torrential rains had made the roads almost impassable, lowered the soldiers' morale, and made operations generally difficult.

Meanwhile Napoleon had word that Bagration was moving northeast. He directed Marshal Davout, with a corps of 35,000, to march on Minsk, and ordered Jérôme to find and pursue the Russian. Surely Napoleon did *not* want the two to attempt to trap Bagration between them; it would have been too dangerous. If their coordination were not perfect he might have a chance to attack each separately, and if his superb Cossack scouts alerted him to their movements, he would surely have the chance. (He had almost two-to-one numerical odds on Davout, and even odds on Jérôme, since Reynier's corps lagged behind.) Probably the emperor expected them to fall into parallel lines of march and goad Bagration southeast (to delay or prevent his junction with

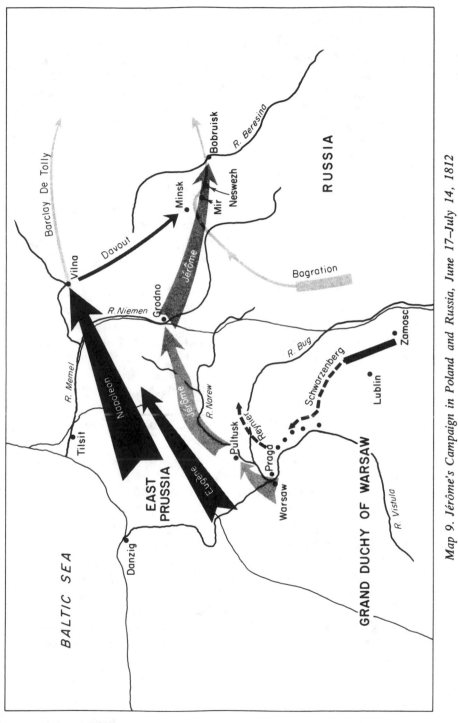

Map 9. *Jérôme's Campaign in Poland and Russia, June 17–July 14, 1812*

BALTIC SEA

Danzig

Tilsit

R. Memel

EAST
PRUSSIA

Napoleon

Eugène

Barclay De Tolly

Vilna

Davout

R. Niemen

Grodno

Jérôme

Jérôme

Minsk

Mir

Neswezh

Bobruisk

R. Beresina

RUSSIA

Bagration

R. Narew

R. Bug

Schwarzenberg

Zamosc

Lublin

Pultusk

Reynier

Praga

Warsaw

GRAND DUCHY OF WARSAW

R. Vistula

Barclay de Tolly), joining together before they pressed him too closely so as to outnumber him if he turned to fight.

As Davout approached Minsk, he mistook roving Cossack cavalry and a "lost column" under Docturov for Bagration's advance guard. He held up and reported to Napoleon that the Russian army was north of Minsk, and then that it was in Minsk. Belatedly discovering otherwise, he occupied the city and awaited orders, complaining that Jérôme had failed to appear. The king, meanwhile, was in hot pursuit of Bagration, who had veered off south. On July 10 his Polish cavalry flushed the Russian rear guard from Mir; he moved up to Neswezh and located Bagration's main body at Bobruisk. Apprised that Davout was in Minsk, Jérôme sent a courier on July 14 asking the marshal to join him and prepared to press on.

Within hours the same courier returned with a curt note from the marshal and Napoleon's orders placing Jérôme under Davout's command. The emperor had chosen to believe Davout's reports rather than Jérôme's and on July 6 had given the "Iron Marshal" command of the Right Wing. Though Jérôme had since heard from Napoleon or his chief of staff (Berthier) almost every day, he had not been told of the change in command.

With some justification, Jérôme stormed and raged. Not only had he been subordinated to Davout, but the maddeningly haughty bald eagle had been given the pleasure of telling him! The king had followed orders and, considering conditions, had fought a flawless campaign. His four-day delay at Grodno, condemned by Napoleon, had the same military justification—reorganization—as the emperor's two-week halt at Vilna. And of all the marshals, Davout! He and Jérôme had clashed continually when the marshal commanded French troops in Westphalia.

Jérôme felt sincerely that Napoleon had deliberately left him no honorable course but to resign his command. Even if he swallowed his pride and remained, how could he do anything but complicate the chain of command? Davout would have to maneuver all five corps; why should he route orders for four of them through an extra commander? He would be useless, Jérôme wrote Catherine, a "parade general"; he would have none of it. The king placed his army under Marchand, his chief of staff, who was to await Davout's orders. He sent a courier to Napoleon announcing his decision, waited two days for a reply which did not come, and then left the army. Some days later Napoleon legalized Jérôme's departure by sending him permission to retire to Westphalia, where he appeared on August 11.

Meanwhile Bagration passed the Beresina at Bobruisk on July 18–20 and by long detours eventually joined with Barclay de Tolly at Smolensk. His "escape" has generally been blamed on Jérôme, which is patently unjust. When the king departed, his Right Wing was all but united with Davout's corps and prepared to march under his chief of staff, who was fully cognizant of the situation. He left the army under the man whom Napoleon had designated, Davout. If Bagration marched away without having to fight, it was Davout's fault, not Jérôme's.

Napoleon's conduct is more easily understood if one considers that he probably intended Jérôme's appointment to be temporary in the first place. Davout had been kept informed in detail of the Right Wing's situation and strength from the beginning. Further, the emperor gave Davout command before he knew that Jérôme had "failed" or *if* he had failed. Probably Jérôme had been given the Right Wing (including the Polish army) only to facilitate his role as prospective king of Poland. Or perhaps Napoleon intended that he retain command if his army served only to defend Poland while the main army forced a decision elsewhere. In any case, he did not inform Jérôme, who took his command seriously; the king's violent reaction to his brusque reduction was natural. Doubtless it was not expected, however, by the emperor, who never saw his brother as more than tentative army commander. His reason for demoting Jérôme was tersely expressed by Maret, his foreign minister, in a letter to Reinhard, at Cassel: ". . . an army of 120,000 men needs a commander of great experience." Davout fitted the bill.

"*Jérôme destitué* . . . ," writes Georges Lefebvre in his account of the Russian campaign, and dismisses the king from further mention. Such has been the general view. But the king was not destituted; he could have marched on to Moscow with his troops. Napoleon was angered by Jérôme's precipitate departure from the army, and his own pride was wounded also, because he knew his high-handed action had deprived him of a very promising young commander. Even if Jérôme were not ready to manage an army, he, alone among the emperor's brothers, had true talent for military leadership. Not until Waterloo would Napoleon again trust Jérôme with troops in combat, but because he had been insubordinate and offended his brother, not because he had shown incompetence in Russia.

Westphalian troops (the Eighth Corps of the Grande Armée) went on to distinguish themselves in Russia. At Borodino they were in action under Marshal Ney in the center of the line. While Napoleon was in Moscow they helped keep open the Smolensk road, the army's main supply route. During much of the bloody retreat, the Westphalians led the way, supported at critical moments by Poniatowski's Poles and the Imperial Guard. Throughout, the record of Von Hammerstein's cavalry was unmatched in the army. At the end of the retreat General Ochs mustered the Eighth Corps at Kustrin (January 1813)—of 17,000 who had marched in June and 5,000 replacements, only 760 remained. Of the living and dead, eighty-one had been awarded the Legion of Honor. Around the hearths of Westphalian homes, the king's reputation would have been infinitely better if he had stayed with his men—even as a "parade soldier." For all his flightiness, one feels that Jérôme would have marched with them if he had foreseen the horrors they would face. Of courage he had more than most; at Waterloo he would fight on after Napoleon left the field.

MURAT AND EUGÈNE

Murat led the march of the main army, playing the part for which he seemed to have been born. In a uniform of his own design, wearing a tall Polish cap topped with a huge plume, astride a black charger with a leopard-skin saddle cloth, he could be mistaken for no one else. On the dusty plains beyond Vilna he galloped about before his cavalry, brandishing his gold cane and shouting insults at the Cossacks of the Russian rear guard. The Cossacks loved him, and gave him salutes instead of firing at him. Platoff, their commander, had ordered that the "King of Naples, with the great plume," was to be captured, if possible, but not killed. Hearing this from a Cossack prisoner Murat gave the man his own jewel-encrusted Order of the Two Sicilies and set him free. Ney was infuriated by the antics of "the Emperor's plumed cock," and on several occasions Murat and Davout almost drew swords on each other. But Napoleon, who knew that there was no better cavalry leader in the world than Murat, did not discourage his posturing. On a single day (August 11), near Krasny, Murat led forty cavalry charges against Barclay de Tolly's rear guard in an effort to make him stand and fight, but his retreat continued.

Before Smolensk the main elements of the Grande Armée came together to face Barclay de Tolly and Bagration, who had united, but the Russians withdrew. The city taken (August 17–19), Murat went into pursuit, perpetually mounting attacks against the Cossacks. Behind him the French column, hard pressed to keep up, became much elongated, to the disgust of Davout, who was trying to keep his troops tightly massed and preserve their strength. Napoleon, ever hoping to force the Russians to stand, sided with Murat. The king's morale was high—he was clearly enjoying himself. Alone among the marshals, he retained his optimism about the outcome of the campaign.

At Borodino (September 7) the Russians, now under Kutuzov, finally made a stand. Eugène commanded the left wing of the French army, which attacked the city itself and the "Great Redoubt." Murat's cavalry was committed both in the center and on the right, and sustained heavy losses. Eugène, stolid and professional, did his job. Murat, in the frenzy that often seized him in battle, charged continually to the places of greatest danger, and galloped back to Napoleon's hilltop command post to give him advice. At dusk he begged the emperor to give him the Old Guard to deliver the *coup de grâce,* but was ordered to charge again with his tired and bloodied cavalry. The Russians gave ground, but held. The guard's artillery was in action, meanwhile, under Sorbier, who had backed Eugène at his first triumph, the Battle of Raab. As night fell he had registered on the Russian's new line, and their artillery was answering. Another day of battle seemed imminent. During the night, however, the Russians began a precipitate retreat on Moscow.

Murat was up all night. He walked the battlefield, toured the hospitals dispensing wine to the wounded, and put his own surgeon to work performing amputations on French and Russians alike. At dawn he was off, leading his cavalry toward Mozhaysk. He was first into Moscow, where his cavalry flushed from buildings gaunt and bearded convicts, freed to create problems for the French, perhaps to set the fires which soon began to burn.

Once the emperor had installed himself in the Kremlin, Murat took over a defense line southwest of Moscow, opposite Kutuzov's outposts along the Nara River. There, for weeks, Murat's cavalry and the Cossacks observed a sort of armed truce. The king himself frequently rode the lines of the Cossacks, who invariably cheered for him, and he talked with their chiefs and Russian officers.

His head turned by the Cossacks' admiration, Murat was happy during the first days. He even boasted to friends that the fierce horsemen might join the French if he offered to lead them. To his disappointment he learned gradually that though the Cossacks saw him as a fellow spirit, they believed the French doomed. His outlook was muddled also by Russian officers' repeated profession that the czar had not wanted war, and would make peace if the French withdrew. And as the weeks passed Murat's troops were decimated by disease and made listless by lack of action and hunger. The king became daily more pessimistic and querulous; Caroline's letters deepened his mood. He almost expected her to be unfaithful, but was she also seizing permanent control of his government? Why didn't his ministers report to him more frequently? What was she doing?

Eugène's troops were in and north of Moscow; he was frequently with the emperor. Though he was becoming restive and apprehensive also, he had no worries about his government or his wife. For Augusta, especially, he tried to paint a cheerful picture. He was doing his best to keep up the emperor's spirits, he wrote, talking and playing "twenty-one" in the evenings. The Kremlin was not bad, but there was "more ice than tea," and no billiard tables. As late as October 1 he told her that Napoleon would soon bring the opera from Paris, and perhaps invite some artists from La Scala in Milan.

THE RETREAT

All the while the situation became worse for the French. They were hungry and freezing; the snows would soon come and slow or stop the trickle of supplies reaching Moscow. The czar had shown no inclination to negotiate, and his armies, now locally larger than

Napoleon's, were inching nearer the city. On October 17 the emperor ordered preparations to withdraw. The next day, before the French began to move, the Russians broke their unofficial truce with Murat and viciously attacked his positions in the southwest. For a time the king was surrounded and in danger of capture. With a small group of cavalry, however, he cut his way out, and managed to reform his lines. Napoleon marched from Moscow, joined Murat, and the great retreat began. The king and emperor were seldom apart during the agonizing days that followed.

Napoleon planned to avoid the devastated route the army had followed to Moscow, and instead to march south of it, where food and forage were more plentiful, via Kaluga and Elnya to Smolensk, where the army would go into winter quarters. Eugène, with his Italians, led the way toward Kaluga, and on October 23 occupied Maloyaroslavets and secured the single bridge across the Luzha River. The next day Kutuzov attacked, and a battle as savage as Borodino ensued. In ten hours the town changed hands seven times. Without assistance from an ailing Napoleon, Eugène won the day by committing his Royal Guard, which covered itself with glory, but was all but wiped out. Wrote Eugène sadly to his secretary, Darnay, "The Italians fell like flies; the Royal Guard has [left] no more than two hundred men."

Though Eugène won, it was clear Kutuzov was intent on denying use of the Kaluga route. Gathering his marshals at Gorodnia, Napoleon asked their advice on the next move. All but Murat were for taking the shortest road to Smolensk, that by which they had marched to Moscow. The Gascon bellowed that he would "cut a path" to Kaluga for the emperor, but the decision went against him, and the army took the barren route west. On November 4 the first snow fell; after November 6 the temperature was always below freezing. With ice underfoot, men and horses slipping and falling, wagons and artillery more difficult to drag along, the pace of the army slowed to ten or twelve miles a day, or less.

Napoleon, traveling mostly by carriage, was not himself. Listless and vague, he only occasionally broke his seeming stupor to appraise the situation and issue orders. Early in the campaign he had been nervous, short-tempered, and prone to snap decisions, like that regarding Jérôme; now he let the army drift. Exhausted and ill, he concentrated less on the ever more disorganized retreat than on how France and Europe would take the news, and what must be done to recapture his prestige and power.

Smolensk was untenable as winter quarters, and the retreat had to continue. The army straggled away—the Westphalian advance guard on November 12, other units during the next five days. On November 18 Ney finally marched with the rear guard, only to find that Kutuzov's main army had moved in to block him. "A Marshal of France does not surrender!" the towering red-head shouted at the Russian officer who offered him terms, and, as never since 1805, proved himself the Ney of legend. Disdaining the odds he attacked the Russians frontally, but could not break out. That night, leaving his fires burning, he marched north and managed to cross the Dnieper on the ice, leaving his wagons and artillery behind. The next day found him musket in hand, among his men, fighting off Platoff's Cossacks. But for Eugène, however, Ney probably would not have escaped, despite his heroism. Hearing of his plight, the viceroy turned back with some 4,000 men. Marching and countermarching, he apparently convinced the Russians that the whole army had returned. They withdrew, and he brought Ney back to the main body—but with less than 1,000 of the marshal's 6,000 men.

In the last days of November Napoleon suddenly came alive, and utilizing all the skill of his commanders and fading strength of his troops, defended and bridged the Beresina. He got the army across, and burned the bridges behind him. Murat and Eugène figured prominently, but the hero of the operation was General Eblé, formerly Jérôme's minister of war, who built the bridges, dismantling most of the buildings in Studenka for lumber. Some 10,000 French stragglers were left behind, and hundreds perished in the icy water. But the crossing of the Beresina was more victory than tragedy. Under a lesser commander the Grande Armée might have expired east of the river.

MURAT COMMANDS THE GRANDE ARMÉE

With the main body of the army west of the Beresina, Napoleon determined to return to Paris. There was little more he could do for the army; at his capital he could begin building a new one. Rumors that he had died in Russia needed to be spiked. Already General Malet had made an abortive attempt to overthrow his government. His communications had deteriorated; he was out of touch with domestic and international developments. If he delayed much longer he might lose control of France, or Europe might rise against him, or both.

On December 5, at Smorgoni, the emperor made Murat commander of the army and departed for France. The king, who for weeks had thought of nothing but returning to Naples, was far from happy. Secretly, he feared the empire was finished; if so, he wanted to salvage his kingdom. If the empire survived, he still wanted to be in Naples in case Napoleon turned on him, as he seemed to have before 1812. The emperor tried to reassure Murat against the latter possibility by returning property he had confiscated, promising more licenses for Neapolitans for "contraband" trade, and making Murat's son prince of Ponte Corvo.[6] Already he had withdrawn French troops from the kingdom, and returned his ambassador, Durant, to Naples. The king, however, remained uncertain of Napoleon's ultimate intentions, and was sick with worry that Caroline might betray him, the emperor, or them both. While Napoleon was present, Murat's personal loyalty to him overrode all other considerations; once the emperor was gone, the king's urge to fly to Naples grew apace.

Since Murat had shared the imperial coach during much of the journey from Moscow, Napoleon knew he was obsessed with returning to Naples. He was aware also that the king was no strategist and that as a tactician had the same solution to all problems— *attack*. The emperor gave him the army because (1) he did not want Murat to return to Naples, and (2) the king's specialty— leadership in person and by example—was the only kind to which the exhausted army would respond. If Murat returned to Naples he might defect—on his own or under Caroline's influence. Unless he were made commander, the proud Gascon would surely not stay with the army, since as one of the original marshals he ranked with any officer present, and as a king outranked them all. As to leadership, no man save the emperor could better inspire the men, and nothing was possible which required refined military skills. Complex maneuvers were out of the question; staff work had virtually stopped; there were not even horses left for messengers.

6. Formerly property of Bernadotte, since 1810 heir to the throne of Sweden.

In sum, it was safer to keep Murat with the army, and he could command it well—if he would.

On December 9 the army reached Vilna, where there were large stocks of food, supplies, clothing, ammunition, and arms. Murat had orders to hold the city, which he might have done for many months. But not he! Besieged? Probably cut off from all possible escape to Naples? "I will not be trapped in this *pot de chambre!*" Reflecting their commander's impatience the troops swept supply personnel aside and sacked the warehouses. After barely one day in Vilna, the army plodded on. On December 19 Murat's headquarters was at Königsberg, well inside East Prussia. Three weeks later he had withdrawn to Posen.

The king's temper was short, his orders confused, his mind constantly on Naples. Notes from Caroline urging that he stay with the army and trust the emperor drove him to frenzy. What was she up to? In letter after letter he begged Napoleon to let him return to his kingdom. He could better serve his emperor there, he said, and also recover his health, which (conveniently) he found to be breaking down. Actually he had lost faith in Napoleon, and could think only of saving his crown, a fact he artlessly revealed a dozen times a day. At Königsberg he had told Berthier, Ney, and Davout that no one would make peace with the emperor, because his word was no good. "[But] I can make peace with the English! Why not? I am the King of Naples just as the Emperor of Austria is the Emperor of Austria."

After reaching Posen Murat could stand the tension no longer. On January 16, 1813, he announced his departure for Naples and issued orders giving the army to Eugène, who was not even at headquarters. With difficulty Berthier (the chief of staff) persuaded him to wait until Eugène arrived, and the viceroy, when he appeared, protested that only the emperor could relieve Murat. But the king, his carriages waiting, would not be detained. At 4:00 A.M. on January 17 he galloped away, leaving the ever-dependable Eugène no choice but to assume command.

EUGÈNE TO THE ELBE

The emperor was grateful. "My son," he wrote Eugène, "take command of the Grande Armée. It pains me that I did not give it to you when I departed." But the father seemed determined to guide his son's every step. On January 22, in addition to the letter quoted, Napoleon sent the viceroy no less than *twelve* more, full of orders, instructions, and advice. And the flood continued: three on January 23, five on January 24, six on January 25, five on January 26.

In fact, Napoleon could do little but keep Eugène informed on the situation of other French forces and funnel him replacements. Only the viceroy could control operations, and he did so with superb skill and coolness, interpreting the emperor's orders as he saw fit. Against great odds, worsened in March when Prussia formally joined Russia, he fought a delaying action which proved him one of Europe's "Great Captains," as Napoleon in 1800 had predicted he would be. In the process he bought the emperor the time he needed to rebuild his army. With barely 14,000 men, he held Posen for twenty days, then withdrew in good order to the Oder, and finally the line of the Elbe and Saale. En route the army was reinforced steadily by divisions stationed in Germany and from France. In March his strength reached 50,000, enough to stop the allied advance. Napoleon, as usual, had his complaints. Eugène had evacuated Berlin too soon, encouraging Prussia to defect; his execution of orders was inexact; his reports were not detailed enough. The viceroy replied that he was doing his best; perhaps the emperor should replace him? "Men of war are becoming rare," wrote Napoleon testily to Berthier; sustained gratitude was not among his virtues. He could not admit that but for Eugène the enemy might have been on the Rhine.

JÉRÔME'S CONTRIBUTION

A key point of the viceroy's defense of the Elbe-Saale line was the fortress of Magdeburg, eastern outpost of Westphalia, provisioned for him by Jérôme. After his return to Cassel, the king had devoted himself to raising men and money to support Napoleon. He sent 1,500 replacements to the Grande Armée before it reached Borodino; by the end of 1812 he had dispatched 3,500 more, bringing his total contribution to 22,000 (not counting a 2,400-man garrison at Danzig). At the beginning of the retreat from Moscow, only 6,000 of these remained; in January 1813, only 760. Napoleon reported truthfully to Jérôme: "There exists no more Westphalian army with the Grande Armée." He ordered the king to raise a new army of 20,000 and provision Magdeburg for 15,000 French. Jérôme, who had foreseen the need, could promptly comply. In mid-February he reported that Magdeburg was ready and that the three Westphalian infantry regiments still with the Grande Armée had been brought up to strength. By May 1813 his army totaled 22,800. Meanwhile, however, Eugène's movement had flooded Magdeburg with French troops, who had quickly drained it of supplies and food. But Jérôme found more, despite the increasing recalcitrance of his population, and his own reluctance to rob his people further. Through intermediaries Jérôme began to beg the emperor for a command, but he got none. The king had left the army without permission in 1812, wrote Napoleon; he would employ no officer who could not obey orders.

THE EMPEROR RETURNS

On April 30, at Naumburg, Eugène welcomed Napoleon, who was ready to launch a new campaign with the reborn Grande Armée, now at 170,000 (including 60,000 under the viceroy). Striking across the Saale, the emperor won victories at Lützen (May 2) and Bautzen (May 21), then agreed to an armistice until 20 July. After the initial battle Eugène was sent back to the Kingdom of Italy, home to Augusta, as he well deserved. But he was also needed there to watch Murat, in Naples, and to raise troops for service in Germany. Further, Italy's defenses had to be readied for a possible Austrian attack. If Austria joined the allies, she was sure to try to recover her Italian possessions.

For the time being, Austria pursued a policy of "armed mediation," while Metternich tried to assess the extent of Napoleon's recovery. At Lützen and Bautzen the emperor had appeared frighteningly like the fighter of 1805 and 1809, but his agreement to an armistice had signaled weakness, and his enemies had multiplied during 1813. In March Sweden (allied with Russia since August 1812) had accepted a British subsidy, and Prussia had declared war on France. Alexander had won over the Poles by promising to restore their kingdom. Though the states of the

Rheinbund clung to the French alliance, all were nervously watching developments, and Saxony and Bavaria were clearly wavering.

Spain: 1812

JOSEPH TAKES COMMAND

Considering his long fight to recover authority, Joseph behaved poorly when it was restored. "Act with vigor and make yourself obeyed," Napoleon wrote him in April 1812.[7] But instead of seizing control of his armies, the king temporized and plagued Berthier for instructions. He frequently confined himself, officially ill, at Casa del Campo, and until late June seemed unable to adjust to his new responsibilities. Thereafter he did not perform badly, but the fates punished him for the time he had squandered. The operations of his five armies, totaling almost 300,000 men, had continued uncoordinated—the Army of the South (Soult) in Andalusia; of Portugal (Marmont), near Salamanca; of the North (Caffarelli), in Asturias, Galicia, and Navarre; of Catalonia (Dacaen); and his own Army of the Center, at Madrid.

Wellington, meanwhile, was not idle. In early 1812 he took Ciudad Rodrigo and Badajoz, key fortresses on the Spanish-Portuguese border. In June he marched on Salamanca with an army of 60,000 British, Anglo-Portuguese, and Spanish. Marmont (Army of Portugal) withdrew before him, drawing in garrisons and troops spread for provisioning, called on Caffarelli (Army of the North) for reinforcements, and informed Joseph of the situation. Buying time, the marshal crossed the Tórmes, then the Duero. (See Map 10, p. 284.) His strength, less sick in hospital, was only 50,000, however, and Caffarelli, hard pressed by guerrillas and the amphibious raids of Sir Home Riggs Popham's British marines, could give little help.

DECISION AT SALAMANCA

Joseph could not make up his mind whether to join Marmont with the Army of the Center (17,000) or remain in Madrid. His chief of staff, Marshal Jourdan, advised him to march. But what

7. In his own hand at the end of a letter from Maret (the foreign minister) to Joseph, dated April 16, 1812.

if he lost Madrid, as in 1809? His minister of war, O'Farrill, and a swarm of courtiers and their ladies begged him to stay. After three weeks of agonizing, terminated by three days of conferences during which both Joseph and Jourdan were reported "ill" and away from court, the king decided to march. He and the Army of the Center departed on July 20.

While Joseph deliberated, Marmont had decided to risk a war of maneuver. Familiar with Wellington's deliberate style, and underestimating his enemy's flexibility, he planned to move south of Salamanca, threaten the allied supply line to Ciudad Rodrigo, and drive Wellington into retreat. If Marmont had not become too bold, his plan would have worked, as Wellington himself later admitted. On July 15 and 16 he crossed the Duero and for four days, by brilliant (and exhausting) marching and countermarching, flanked every position that Wellington took. By July 21 he had forced the allied army to recross the Tórmes, where Wellington resumed the position he had held on June 27—on the hills south of Salamanca, in the vicinity of the village of Arapiles.

Marmont, now overconfident, followed. On the morning of July 22 the French moved rapidly around Wellington's right flank, seized the southernmost of two hills called "Arapiles," which overlooked the allied position, and sent cavalry toward the Ciudad Rodrigo road. (See Map 11, p. 284.) At the same time, however, some of Marmont's troops were still crossing the Tórmes, many were concentrated in the forests above the crossings, and the advance elements were strung out across the south "Arapile" and off toward the Ciudad Rodrigo road. Marmont's army, with only a few units facing the allies, was extended over a distance of ten miles, and extremely vulnerable. Declining to retreat as Marmont expected, Wellington faced his army south and attacked.

Suddenly Marmont found his center under concentrated assault, his right floundering in the forests, and his left (advance units) cut off from the main body. The French fought furiously, but as divisions or lesser units, not as a whole. Marmont, riding between his right and center in a desperate effort to organize his army, was shot from his horse, his arm so mangled that it had to be amputated. Clausel assumed command of the army, but only to watch it stream in rout across the Tórmes, where he directed the remnants toward Valladolid. In reasonable order, the Army of Portugal crossed the Duero on July 30, but under unrelenting pursuit by British cavalry, continued the retreat toward the Ebro.

On July 24, two days after the battle, Joseph appeared at Blasco Sancho, fifty miles east of Salamanca. Ignorant of Marmont's defeat, he would have been in extreme danger had Wellington known of his presence. He was preparing to move west, into the very lion's mouth, when a peasant informed him of the French retreat. Stunned, he started slowly for Madrid, then halted at Segovia, where Clausel had belatedly signaled they could join forces. The British, however, pushed Clausel north, and when the fact was confirmed (July 31), Joseph marched for Madrid at all speed. Wellington left General Clinton, with 12,000 men, to watch Clausel, and followed Joseph.

RETREAT TO VALENCIA

Joseph arrived in Madrid on August 3, roundly damning Marmont for glory-seeking, and blaming the Salamanca defeat on the marshal's failure to wait for him. From Segovia Joseph had ordered Soult to send him 10,000 troops immediately, then evacuate Andalusia and join him at Madrid with the entire Army of the South. Soult sent not a man, just letters arguing that the king should join *him*. It would be safer, said the marshal, to join forces in Andalusia, where Wellington could not follow without endangering his forces in northern Spain, and where food and supplies were plentiful. Plans to counter Wellington could be laid at leisure. Though Soult was influenced by a desire to remain in his "kingdom," his arguments made sense. Wellington had passed through Segovia only eight days after Joseph left, and was closing rapidly on Madrid. The vicinity of the capital was no place to join forces. The king, however, was ruled by the frantic fear of losing Madrid, which had some political basis, though the capital lacked the importance it had possessed in 1808. He repeated his orders to Soult, and when the marshal stood pat, decided that if Madrid must fall, he would withdraw to Valencia and consolidate all his forces there. He feared and detested Soult; Suchet, though hardly a docile subordinate either, was a more sympathetic personality.

On August 9–10 Joseph evacuated Madrid, he and the Army

of the Center covering while his civilian supporters went ahead to Ocaña. French and Spanish members of the government and civil service, their families and those of military officers, moved in a column of over three hundred carriages, wagons, buggies, surreys, carts—(says Miot) ". . . *voitures de tout gendre.*" Some rode horseback, or walked if they could do no better, carrying such possessions as they could on their backs.

On August 15 they set out across the parched plains of La Mancha, with hardly a tree to give shade, and bitterly cold at night. Joseph, with his army, rode a route parallel to the convoy, trying to give protection. Guerrillas hung on the flanks, seldom attacking, but preying on the nerves of the travelers. Large numbers of the king's Spanish troops, and even some of the royal guard, discouraged and taunted by the guerrillas, deserted. The civilians complained and heaped curses on the head of the king, when he was not in earshot, or directly on his officers and men. The French courtiers and their ladies, especially, says La Forest, created problems. They fainted in the heat, complained of the cold at night, carped at the soldiers and their servants, went to great lengths to demonstrate their lack of familiarity with sweat, dirt, and discomfort. They took up the use of the latest sobriquet of the unfortunate king, "*Le Roi Errant,*" originated by one of the guerrilla leaders following the retreat. They were a colony apart, thinking only of themselves, acting as though the whole Spanish affair had been arranged for their aggrandizement and comfort and was not producing as promised; "*centaines de vampires français,*" La Forest called them. Despite real and imagined difficulties, however, Joseph on August 31 reached Valencia, where Suchet was firmly in charge. Soult, exposed to attack from Madrid and Cádiz, reluctantly evacuated Andalusia and on October 2 reached Valencia also. Joseph, who had referred the matter of the marshal's disobedience to Napoleon, merely asked for his cooperation.

Of all that had happened on the retreat, the king had been most deeply hurt by the desertion of 3,500 of his 5,000 Spanish troops. For four years he had defended their employment against Napoleon and others, like the coarse-tongued Marshal Lefebvre, who had advised him to hire Alsatians and send "*vos f—— Espagnols à tous les diables!*" A Spanish king needed a Spanish army,

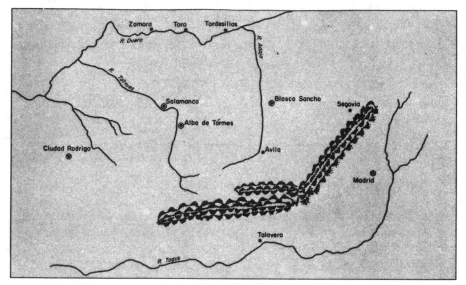

Map 10. Central Spain

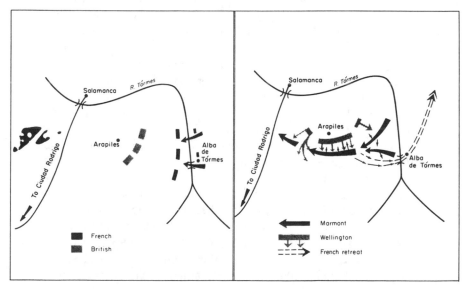

a. Initial positions   b. Battle positions

Map 11. The Battle of Salamanca, July 22, 1812

he had argued; he must show faith in his people; they would return it. Despite his Spanish soldiers' frequent desertions and chronic disloyalty, he had steadily tried to add to their numbers. In doing so he had displayed a certain brand of courage, but it was not a little mixed with personal vanity, the desire to be loved, to be king-on-his-own, and a well-developed penchant for self-deception. In August 1812 he had to face the truth, but being Joseph, he might have returned to his old attitudes if time had allowed.

WELLINGTON AT MADRID

Meanwhile, on August 12, 1812, Wellington entered Madrid, allowing Spanish guerrilla bands to precede him, and receiving wilder cheers for the gesture. He shortly had to take stern measures to quell disorders, caused partly by the *guerrilleros,* and his popularity dwindled somewhat. But the townsmen and peasants of the center supplied his army, more or less cheerfully, before he marched north again on September 1. His departure was prompted by the news that Clausel had reassembled 22,000 of the Army of Portugal and recaptured Valladolid. Since Joseph might soon return from Valencia with as many as 115,000 troops, Madrid had become too dangerous.

AGAIN SALAMANCA

Leaving Suchet's army in Valencia, Joseph, with the Armies of the South and Center, marched almost unopposed to Madrid, where on November 2 the populace resignedly welcomed him. His palaces and art treasures were intact, protected by his gentlemanly foe, which made him happy. He was shocked to learn, however, that some of his favorite hostesses had entertained the British instead of retiring to the country, as they had vowed to do. Retribution was due these society rebels! But there was not time. Driven on by Soult's impatience, the king marched after two days to Peñaaranda. There on November 9 he was joined by the Army of Portugal and part of the Army of the North.

Joseph reorganized his force into two corps, one under Soult and the other under General Drouet, count d'Erlon, an arrangement which insulted the marshal, who had hoped to replace Jourdan as chief of staff, and who hated Drouet. Soult considered Jourdan a military relic, and Drouet a palace politician; the latter he consistently addressed as "count" rather than "general." In fact, Drouet had been picked by the king over Souham, now commander (vice Clausel) of the Army of Portugal, for no better reason than friendship. Soult's disgruntlement was intense, which may explain his behavior during the ensuing action. The king's army, now at 97,000, marched for Salamanca, where Wellington had already taken up positions on the familiar hills of Arapiles. The allied army, meantime, had received British and Spanish reenforcements which brought its numbers to 70,000.

On November 14–16 the French crossed the Tórmes and arrayed opposite Wellington's positions—but they did not attack. Their royal commander kept to his tent, and Marshal Jourdan, suffering from the cold, was also inactive. In the evening Wellington saw that Soult had sent cavalry toward the Ciudad Rodrigo road—as Marmont had done the previous July. This time, however, the odds were against Wellington, and he knew it. He ordered the retreat Marmont had vainly expected—on Ciudad Rodrigo—and Wellington's army, for a few hours, was extended and vulnerable to flank assault, as Marmont's had been. Observers on both sides agree that if Soult had attacked results could have been disastrous for the allies, but he did not. Wellington slipped away and made good his retreat to Ciudad Rodrigo, where he took up winter quarters.

Exactly why Soult did not attack will never be known. Officially he stated that he considered Drouet too far away to support him. But whatever Soult's reason, Joseph, ultimately, was responsible for Wellington's escape. *He* was in command; no subordinate can be blamed for failing to put his superior's army in motion. Once more, as in 1809, he had lost an opportunity to crush the British-led allied army. He was not to have another.

JOSEPH CLINGS TO MADRID

Within a few days, taking 50,000 of his troops along, Joseph returned to the comforts of Madrid. As after Talavera (1809) he saw himself as victor in the campaign. Had not Wellington withdrawn before him? He had, but under his leadership the allies, in

1812, had forced the French out of Andalusia, and seized the frontier fortresses of Ciudad Rodrigo and Badajoz, from which they could strike into Spain at will. The French were still stronger than the allies, but dependent on Joseph's leadership, and the events at Salamanca proved that he had not learned to command. Nor did he seem interested in learning; at the end of 1812 he was trying to restore a peacetime routine at his court, despite the unanimous opinion of his military advisers that Wellington would attack again at the first sign of spring.

In early 1813 Napoleon withdrew some troops from Spain, but left the Army of Spain 200,000 strong. It could not be weakened too much in the face of Anglo-Portuguese-Spanish forces on the peninsula—one jaw of a vise the Allies were trying to close on France. Until the empire was safe, Joseph was expected to position his armies so as to protect southern France. Accordingly, he was ordered to establish his headquarters at Valladolid (between Wellington, at Ciudad Rodrigo, and the major routes to France), and occupy Madrid only as "one of the extremities of the line." For the time being the king's headquarters was to be his capital.

Joseph, however, in violation of orders and defiance of common sense, clung to Madrid. If he moved it would look like a retreat, he told La Forest. Napoleon had Clarke, the minister of war, reiterate the order in blunter terms. But February passed and the king was still in his capital, though he had shifted part of his forces northward. His courtiers and most of his ministers encouraged him to stay. If he "abandoned" Madrid, they argued, he would lose what Spanish support he had left—as if this would matter if he lost the war. Only on March 17, after Napoleon's orders had been repeated a third time, did he depart for Valladolid.

During 1812–1813 the fortunes of Napoleon and Joseph had followed the same cycle. In the spring of 1813 both came to grips with the allies again. We followed the emperor to the time of his truce with the enemy. Before it was out the Eagles in his brother's care would fall.

*Adieu, mes enfants! Would that I could press
you all to my heart; at least I embrace your
banner!*

*. . . General Petit, seizing the Eagle, came for-
ward. Napoleon . . . kissed the flag. The silence
. . . was broken only by the sobs of the
soldiers.*[1]

chapter nine
THE END OF THE EAGLES

Spain

*I*n March 1813 Joseph was accompanied to
Valladolid by some of his ministers and
courtiers. He was followed within weeks by thousands of *afrancesados*. The king's headquarters quickly took on the appearance
of a court. Civilians jammed available housing, caused a local food
shortage, and interfered with military activity. Joseph's generals
urged him to order them all off to France, but he declined. He
already felt guilty over abandoning Madrid. How could he send
"his people" away?

Napoleon, his eye on Spain as well as Germany, urged Joseph
to maintain contact with Wellington's army, so that he would not
be surprised. Jourdan recommended that the king concentrate his
armies to meet a major allied attack, sure to come soon. Joseph
took the advice of neither. Still thinking in terms of occupying as
much territory as possible, he left his armies dispersed. It was not
until May 18 that he ordered Madrid evacuated. By then the main
elements of the Army of the South (Gazan) and the Army of
Portugal (Reille)[2] were in the Valladolid area, but their units were
fanned out westward along the Duero, and south to Salamanca,

1. Napoleon's farewell to the Old Guard, April 20, 1814, at Fontainebleau.
Correspondance impériale, 21561.
2. Soult and Souham had been called to the Grande Armée.

some as much as seventy miles from their headquarters. The Army of the Center was scattered between Valladolid and Madrid, the Army of the North (Clausel) along the routes to France, the bulk of it in Biscay and Navarre, one hundred fifty to two hundred miles away.[3]

Joseph used every excuse for delay, even rumors that the Spanish rebels were turning against their British allies. He steadily predicted that Napoleon would soon make peace with Russia and turn his attention to Spain. On hearing of the emperor's "new concordat" with Pius VII he dispatched a delegation asking the Pope to recognize him as king of Spain, hoping that the response would paralyze the Spanish rebels' initiative. (No answer came; the Holy Father had repudiated the agreement, never really a concordat.)

Meanwhile in early May Wellington sent General Graham, with 40,000 Anglo-Portuguese, across the Duero in northern Portugal. On the north bank he was joined by Castaños with 25,000 Spanish, and the two turned eastward. (See Map 12, p. 290.) Joseph's positions on the Duero were outflanked. This done, Wellington himself, with 30,000 British, forced the Tórmes and Duero, and on June 4 linked up with Graham and Castaños, bringing his army to 95,000, not counting a horde of guerrillas who marched with him. The chiefs Sanchez, Polier, Barcena, Salazar, Monzo, and others, each on his own terms, accepted Wellington's leadership. Others cooperated independently, like Empecinado, who was giving his full attention to French convoys leaving Madrid.

Joseph sent out frantic orders for his armies to concentrate on Burgos, eighty miles to the northeast. He sent Jourdan to examine Burgos castle, only to have him report that it was wrecked and indefensible. But Reille (Army of Portugal) was already on the Burgos road, having retreated through Toro, so Joseph evacuated Valladolid and marched on Burgos with the Armies of the Center and South. The Army of the North, spread over the northern provinces, had difficulty in assembling. Clausel put 14,000 on the

3. Clausel had replaced Caffarelli, who was with the Grande Armée. The Army of Catalonia was, as always, engaged in Catalonia. The army of Aragon (Suchet) still held Aragon and Valencia.

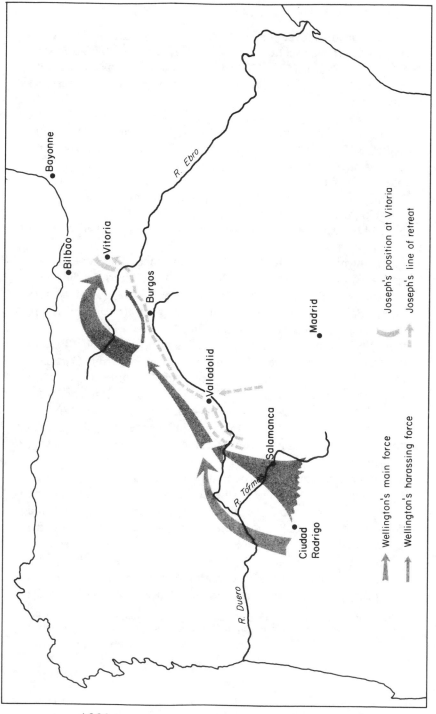

Bayonne

●Bilbao

●Vitoria

R. Ebro

●Burgos

Madrid
●

Valladolid
●

Salamanca
●

R. Tórmes

Ciudad
Rodrigo
●

R. Duero

Wellington's main force

Wellington's harassing force

Joseph's position at Vitoria

Joseph's line of retreat

Map 12. The Vitoria Campaign

march, but before he could join Joseph, the king had engaged Wellington.

Reaching Burgos on June 9 Joseph ordered the depots and artillery parks moved to Vitoria, seventy miles farther northeast. Toward the same place went the mass of civilian refugees coming from Madrid, jamming the roads and adding confusion to an already chaotic retreat. On June 12–13 the armies followed, the king with the advance elements, the rear guard fighting off British cavalry while engineers blew up the arsenal of Burgos fortress—prematurely, killing three hundred French soldiers.

The king was already beaten, but he did not know it. The months spent in Madrid, which should have been devoted to planning the coming campaign, could not be recovered. When his army should have been a solid, coordinated mass, it was scattered, and there was no plan either for attack or withdrawal. The paraphernalia of government, families, and plunder, which should have been abandoned, now added to his troubles. Madrid had been evacuated too late. Since no staff work had been done, the generals vied with each other for routes of retreat. Units of armies and corps became mixed on the roads and orders were carried out in a haphazard fashion or not at all.

Detaching units to keep pressure on the French rear, Wellington swung the bulk of the allied army north and sent it across the Ebro at points forty to sixty miles west of Joseph's line of march. By June 15 his units were marching east by parallel routes on Vitoria. The king was outflanked, but he determined to fight at Vitoria.

In numbers, the French were strong enough to fight, and perhaps win. Joseph allowed two whole divisions to march for France with convoys, but he still had a homogeneous force of 70,000. Wellington had over 100,000, but of these only the 30,000 British and 40,000 Anglo-Portuguese were completely dependable. Moreover, the French were better supplied—neither infantry nor cavalry lacked anything—the artillery had a surplus of two hundred cannon. The personal equipment of the French soldiers was first class, and there was plenty of food and ammunition.

The French in fact had everything except what they needed most—a commander. In the days before the battle Joseph allowed the generals to make most of their own dispositions. Jourdan did persuade the king to put Reille on the Bilbao road, but the other forces arranged themselves loosely on the heights west of the city, behind the Zadora River, leaving wide gaps between corps. At headquarters all was confusion and lethargy. A convoy carrying civilians (including Madame Nancy Derrieux, Joseph's latest love), which had arrived June 18, was "unaccountably" still in Vitoria on June 20; the city's streets were clogged with vehicles and baggage. The artillery park spilled over onto the major route to France. Says Miot of the day before the battle:

. . . 20 June passed in irresolution and inaction . . . No new disposition [of troops] was made, no order given which would have forecast the events of the next day; at such silence, at such immobility, one was given to suppose for a moment that the march of the enemy had been stopped, and one could believe that he was "dans la plus grande sécurité."

Marshal Jourdan, ill and moody, kept to his room. The king went nowhere near the lines until four the next morning, when it was much too late to shift troops.

On the morning of June 21, in fog and light rain, the allied army debouched into the hilly lowlands before Vitoria. General Graham struck southeast along the Bilbao road, General Hill northeast along that from Madrid, and Wellington east, commanding the main force (center) in person. As the allies drove in the French outposts they found that all the bridges over the Zadora were intact, and several neither defended nor covered by fire— red carpets into the French position, courtesy of Joseph.

The French fought well. Napier, who is not without prejudice, praises their courage again and again. Each corps did well as a unit, but all were outflanked and battered flank and rear by allied cavalry. Early in the day the undefended bridges played a key role. In the French center, British skirmishers went across the Tres Puentes bridge, then the whole Fifteenth Regiment of Hussars, all without losing a man or firing. Minutes later they had plunged through a gap between two French corps and were attacking from the rear.

A mighty French army, rudderless, floundered and milled in

confusion. At one o'clock in the afternoon Joseph, seeing that his center was crumbling, ordered his reserve to retreat on Vitoria. He then gave the order for the army to retreat by stages, depending on Reille to support the withdrawal by holding fast on the Bilbao road. It was the signal for the breakup. Still fighting well as individuals and in small units, the French forces withdrew in wild disorder toward cluttered Vitoria. Says Napier:

At six o'clock the French reached the last defensible height, one mile in front of Vittoria [sic]. Behind them was the plain in which the city stood, and beyond the houses thousands of carriages, animals and non-combatants, men, women, and children, huddling together in all the madness of terror; and as the English shot went booming overhead, the vast crowd started and swerved with a convulsive movement, while a dull and horrid sound of distress arose: but there was no hope, no stay for army or multitude. It was the wreck of a nation.

As the darkness fell, the allies reached Vitoria itself. Reille's rear was partially overrun. He was forced to withdraw and open a free passage across the Zadora in his sector, the only front which had held all day. In chaotic flood, the French mass took the roads to the north. British cavalary and the Spanish *guerrilleros* followed, wreaking havoc.

Joseph, barely evading capture by British hussars, fled north to Salvatierra, then joined the Army of the Center, retreating toward Saint-Jean de Luz, then took up with the Army of Portugal, which was making for the Bidassoa. On June 28 he retired impotently to Saint-Jean de Luz, where on July 12 Marshal Soult arrived with orders to take command of the Army of Spain.

Napoleon sent Joseph into "exile," first in southern France, then at his estate, Mortefontaine, near Paris. Though the Army of Spain would fight other battles, Spain was lost. Wellington shortly carried the war into southern France. In late 1813, Napoleon, in desperation, tried to thwart the British by restoring Ferdinand VII to the Spanish throne, but the Cádiz Cortes would not take the king as a French gift.[4]

Napoleon's enemies, declared and undeclared, took heart after the battle of Vitoria. Even if the battles of Lützen and Bautzen

4. In 1814 Ferdinand returned on his own terms.

had signaled the return of "the old Napoleon," he would be hard-pressed to win in Germany with Wellington attacking southern France. Austria shortly joined the allies. Catching the mood of Europe, Ludwig van Beethoven, at Vienna, produced "Wellington's Victory," a wild score cued for cannon fire and musket shots. The usually sedate master let himself go. One can almost see him, coattails flying, howling happily as this glorious piece of noise builds in his imagination.[5]

Germany

Napoleon doubtless erred in agreeing to a truce in the summer of 1813. It allowed him time to build up his forces in Germany (and Italy), rest his veterans, and shore up his supply services, but it was vastly more valuable to the allies. The armistice did not terminate on July 20, as originally agreed, but was extended to August 10, with hostilities to begin on or after August 17. Meanwhile Metternich played out the farce of "armed neutrality," Austria mobilized and declared war on France (August 12), and the allies agreed on strategy and over-all command.

Napoleon held the bulk of his army (250,000) near Dresden, with advance corps extended across Silesia.[6] With the cavalry was Murat, given a chance to redeem himself after repeated professions of devotion to the emperor. (We shall examine his motives later.) The allied armies were nominally commanded by the Austrian prince von Schwarzenberg, but he was accompanied by the monarchs of Russia, Austria, and Prussia, and actually controlled only the main army (240,000 Russians, Austrians, and Prussians). Operating almost independently were Bernadotte[7] (120,000 Swedes and Russians), Blücher (95,000 Prussians and Russians), and Bennigsen (60,000 Russians and Poles). The allied plan was a

5. Actually the piece was written to be performed on a machine invented by one Nepomuk Maelzel, but the mechanical monster choked on it, and it ended being played by orchestras, while Beethoven and Maelzel squabbled and sued each other over the profits from the concerts.
6. Oudinot had 70,000 opposite Bernadotte in the north, Wrede 30,000 Bavarians in the south. Other corps were assembling on the Rhine.
7. Former French marshal, since 1810 heir to the throne of Sweden.

variation of that which had broken Napoleon in Russia. No single army was to risk battle against Napoleon himself. Each was to retreat if challenged, making the French extend and exhaust their forces. Against Napoleon's earlier armies, such a scheme would probably have led to disaster, but not against his army of 1813, composed of raw recruits leavened with jaded veterans, led by weary and uninspired officers.

Blücher decoyed Napoleon into Silesia while Schwarzenberg struck at Dresden. But the allies' lack of coordination allowed Napoleon time to return to Dresden and win a battle (August 26–27). Again Napoleon went on the offensive from his Dresden base, but he was pulled three ways. Schwarzenberg and Bennigsen threatened from the south, Blücher from the east, and Bernadotte from the north. Retreating or advancing as French resistance allowed, all gradually closed on Dresden. The allies sustained larger losses than Napoleon, but his damaged him more. In addition, French troops, as the allies had hoped, were becoming exhausted, and their officers discouraged and lethargic.

In September Napoleon abandoned Dresden and withdrew to Leipzig, but within two weeks all the allied armies were again upon him, reinforced by the Bavarians, who had changed sides.[8] For three days (October 16–18) the "Battle of the Nations" raged. Despite furious efforts by the French, and occasional brilliant local victories, the allies slowly closed in, sealing off all but the western approaches to the city.

Before dawn on October 19, undefeated, Napoleon began an orderly withdrawal west. As his army left the city, however, movement became increasingly frantic and confused. In the dawn hours, Saxon and Badenese troops went over to the enemy and began firing on the French. Finally, the Lindenau Bridge was blown up prematurely, leaving some 60,000 French troops trapped in the city. Their commanders—MacDonald, Poniatowski, Reynier, and Lauriston—fought as long as they could. All hope lost, MacDonald swam the Elster River and escaped; Poniatowski, wounded and bleeding, drowned trying; the other two were captured.

Napoleon made for Frankfurt, then the Rhine, the size of his

8. Bavaria made an armistice with the allies on September 17, joined them on October 8.

army dwindling apace. Behind him, his German allies, led by Württemberg, joined the enemy one after another. Some of their troops, however, remained loyal to Napoleon, the Württembergers outstandingly so.

WESTPHALIA IN 1813

Almost in passing, without fanfare, the Kingdom of Westphalia was overrun and disappeared. Jérôme had continued to labor to strengthen Napoleon's forces, as we have noted, producing a new army—22,800 by May 1813, 26,000 by the fall—and provisioning Magdeburg. Napoleon showed his appreciation of Jérôme's efforts by canceling his debt to France and admitting a *French* debt to Westphalia (the amount to be negotiated).[9] Some French specie was actually sent to Magdeburg, though most of it went directly to supply and pay French troops. In retrospect, the financial operations have a fictional flavor; but if Napoleon had won the war, their results would have been real enough.

When Eugène withdrew to the Elbe (March 1813), Westphalia was separated from enemy territory only by the river, and the viceroy could not guard its whole length. In April General Chernyshëv, with 8,000 Cossacks, invaded Westphalia, guided by Dörnberg, leader of the 1809 uprising in Westphalia, now a general in Russian service. The Cossacks took Hanover and Brunswick, and made for Cassel. General Wintzingerode meanwhile captured Halle and sent his advance guard toward Cassel. For three days in mid-April Jérôme and General Hammerstein, with only 6,000 troops between them, managed to keep the enemy at bay until troops from the advance corps of the Grande Armée moved from Frankfurt to their relief. All the while the king scornfully rejected the pleas of panicky ministers that he abandon his capital. (The queen was already in residence in France.) Not only did he defend Cassel, but spent off-hours going about the streets, often on foot, reassuring the people, who remained calm throughout the crisis.

The king had again displayed coolness and leadership ability, and Napoleon let fall a few words of praise. But he would allow Jérôme no command or a place in the headquarters of the Grande

9. Figures from 1,800,000 to 3,700,000 francs were mentioned.

Armée. The memory of 1812 was too fresh, and the king was very useful in Cassel, where, with only occasional complaints, he continued to raise men, horses, and supplies for the imperial army. To his dismay, Napoleon broke up the Westphalian divisions he sent forward, assigning regiments and battalions to various French corps, where defection would be difficult, and if it occurred, not too damaging. Jérôme protested that such treatment destroyed his troops' sense of nationality and encouraged desertion, but was not heeded.

On a visit to the emperor at Dresden in June, Jérôme asked that a Westphalian corps be formed, under his command. Both he and his men, he argued, would show their mettle and loyalty in battle. Napoleon, however, refused to take a risk on either Jérôme or his Germans. He even insisted that the king accept a French guard—600 conscripts sent up from Mainz, mostly youngsters of the levy of 1814, whom he had to train.

Until August 1813 Westphalian troops stood loyally with the French, then two regiments of hussars deserted from Victor's corps. Most units, however, served well until Westphalia fell, and many fought on thereafter. One of the defecting regiments, however, was commanded by the brother of Westphalia's most-decorated hero, General Count Hans von Hammerstein, who had fought in Spain and won the Legion of Honor in Russia. On Napoleon's orders, Jérôme reluctantly had the general (his aide-de-camp) arrested on suspicion of conspiracy, together with several of his male relatives. The charges were proved to be totally false, and Hammerstein was paroled. His relatives, "rescued" by Chernyshëv's Cossacks when Cassel was overrun, protested loyalty to Jérôme and insisted on being made prisoners of war! Such extreme devotion was uncommon, but simple allegiance to Jérôme and Westphalia was not. He was right in saying that a national spirit had awakened in his kingdom.

THE COSSACKS AGAIN

On September 6 Bernadotte won a victory at Dennewitz and bared northern Westphalia to invasion. Bernadotte marched for Leipzig, but sent two columns into the kingdom, Chernyshëv's Cossacks (now 10,000) directly on Cassel. Jérôme, with less than

3,000 troops to defend his capital, called for help from the Mainz depot, but its elderly commander, Marshal Kellermann, feared to respond without Napoleon's authorization, and for two weeks sent none.

Meanwhile on September 27 Chernyshëv and his Cossacks appeared before Cassel. Through an officer under a flag of truce, the Russian general informed Jérôme that he saw no reason why "the czar's cousin" and the son-in-law of the king of Württemberg should leave his kingdom. If Westphalia would withdraw from the war, her territory would be respected. It is doubtful if Chernyshëv had specific authority to make this offer, but at the allied conferences at Prague, earlier, no consideration had been given to destroying the Kingdom of Westphalia. If Jérôme had accepted, therefore, the allies *might* have honored the terms. But the king would not turn his coat. Back went the proud answer: "King by the victories of France and for France, the Brother of the Emperor will not take advantage of his defeats."

The next day, with numerical odds of better than three to one, Chernyshëv attacked. During the morning Jérôme personally directed the defense of Cassel, apparently determined to fight to the end. But Reinhard, Napoleon's ambassador, finally persuaded him that his capture would turn a minor victory into an allied triumph. In the afternoon he put the defense under General Allix, French commandant of the city, and made for Frankfurt with his guard. Cossacks blocked the road, but the king cut his way through, hoping to meet reenforcements coming from Mainz, but none appeared. On reaching the border of his kingdom he turned his troops over to his aide-de-camp and went on to Coblenz with his ministers and members of the diplomatic corps.

On September 30 the townspeople of Cassel forced Allix to surrender. Seeing the situation was hopeless, they feared further resistance would only yield greater vengeance from the Cossacks and destruction of their property. By agreement Allix and his Westphalian troops marched away free, and Chernyshëv and his Cossacks marched in. The population was quiet, curious, but unenthusiastic. The city officials kept their heads during the few days of occupation which followed, and the national guard of Cassel helped to keep order. Chernyshëv, hoping to win recruits and promote good will, kept the depredations of his Cossacks at a minimum.

A week later (October 7), General Allix was back, reinforced, finally, from Mainz. The Cossacks withdrew without a fight and Allix turned viciously on those who had made him surrender, having some shot. On October 16 Jérôme returned, to the cheers of large crowds. Said he sadly ". . . they think I will deliver them from Allix." And in fact he did grant pardons freely, and dismiss the general (temporarily) for his brutality.

WESTPHALIA FALLS

Meanwhile the great battle of Leipzig was being fought. Shortly thereafter Napoleon ordered all troops evacuated from the area between the Elbe and the Rhine—Westphalia was doomed. Jérôme calmly prepared to leave, while Casselers, without disorder, sadly watched. In spite of his faults, they liked the king; Napoleon was the villain. On the evening of October 24, to applause, Jérôme appeared at the theater. Thirty-six hours later, at dawn on October 26, he called together the officers of his Westphalian guards at Napoleonshöhe and offered them the chance freely to leave his service. A good part of them chose instead to march with him. This settled, he set out, escorted by both Westphalian and French guards. Some of the Westphalians considered their duty done at the kingdom's border, but most were still with him when he reached Cologne on November 1.[10]

Jérôme's days of kingship were over. But the service of his Westphalians to the emperor was not. Some remained with the Grande Armée throughout the campaign in France. At the fortress of Küstrin, isolated in Prussian territory, General Füllgraff's Westphalians were the core of a garrison which held out until March 1814—six months after the fall of Westphalia and only ten days before the capitulation of Paris. Of the thousand who had entered in December 1812, only three hundred, two-thirds of them sick or wounded, were alive when Küstrin surrendered.

Westphalia reverted to her several former rulers without major disorders. In the provinces most of Jérôme's officials remained at

10. Admittedly, the Hessian tradition of keeping oaths, built during centuries of mercenary service, was a factor in the behavior of Jérôme's troops.

their posts, undisturbed, until replaced—evidence that there was not widespread hatred against those who had served the French. Desertions in the Westphalian army generally were not to the enemy. Soldiers, many underage and homesick, simply went home, abandoning their arms and uniforms with no intention of using them again for anyone's benefit. Most officers kept their oaths to Jérôme as long as he had a kingdom. Jérôme departed with dignity, escorted by a Westphalian guard. The king had done his duty to Napoleon first, and afterward his best for his kingdom. No one could have expected more.

MURAT WAVERS

After deserting the Grande Armée at Posen (January 1813), Murat made a beeline for Naples. In contact with the Austrians, he continued nevertheless to protest his devotion to Napoleon. Eugène, back in Milan in June 1813, had instructions to prepare Italy for probable assault by Austria, possibly aided by Naples. To test Murat, Napoleon ordered him to send a division to Eugène. With alacrity and florid professions of loyalty to the emperor, the king pledged to do so, but somehow his troops were never quite ready to march. Left on his own, the viceroy manned his defenses against Austria with 40,000 French and 20,000 Italian troops, holding back a reserve of 16,000 Italians for emergencies. (In addition, by summer's end, he had sent 28,000 Italians to Germany, replacing those lost in Russia; 10,000 were with the Army of Spain.)

Murat's behavior had importance much greater than was consonant with his actual power. If he cooperated with Eugène, Napoleonic Italy would probably be militarily safe, since Austria, fearful of being dominated in central Europe by Russia and Prussia, was bent on keeping most of her forces there. Moreover, the combined Italian and Neapolitan armies might threaten Austria's southern frontier sufficiently to incline her to peace in Germany, or allow Napoleon to win. If Murat defected, Eugène's forces would at least be neutralized, and Austria might be able to afford an attempt to recapture her Italian and Illyrian possesions while maintaining her interests in the north. The British, though committed to "free" Naples, were more anxious to keep a balance between Russo-Prussian and Austrian power in the north, and increasingly inclined toward a deal with Murat.

As early as December 1812 Murat's agent, Prince Cariati, had sounded out Metternich on the survival of Murat's kingdom independent of France, and found the Austrian minister willing to talk. In April 1813 the Austrian ambassador at Naples, Count Mier, signaled that Murat seemed ready to come to terms. In May, at Ponza, Murat's agents had discussed the problem with Lord Bentinck, since mid-1811 British ambassador to the Bourbon court at Palermo, commander of the British in Sicily, and virtual ruler of the island. Bentinck, however, had a dream of uniting Italy under a constitutional monarchy, and further (whatever the contradictions involved) felt himself committed to support the Neapolitan Bourbons. His attitude was much less flexible than that of the British government (Castlereagh), and no agreement was reached.

Before Murat's intrigues could proceed further, news came of Napoleon's victories at Lützen and Bautzen, and the king decided to postpone an open break with the emperor. His letters to Napoleon had been consistently submissive, and when Napoleon ordered him to join the Grande Armée, he responded, aware that he would give away his hand if he did not. From the first, he was a doom-singer. "He will sacrifice France and the army and kill you all . . ." he told Belliard. But at Dresden and Leipzig, catching the scent of battle, he led the imperial cavalry magnificently. Meanwhile Eugène pressed Caroline for Neapolitan troops, and was refused. She and Murat may have been inspired by Metternich's earlier "armed mediation" to think they could play the same role, but Leipzig dashed their hopes.

Caroline, surely, had decided to follow whatever policy would save her crown. Murat's case was different. The conscience of the simple, brave man was unquestionably troubled, as his emotional and sometimes incoherent letters to Napoleon show. He wanted to remain a king, but he hoped somehow to do so without attacking the Eagles of France, the sight of which moved him deeply.

Contacted at Dresden by Schinina, an agent of Metternich, Murat temporized. With Caroline, in Naples, Schinina got results. Aided by a personal message to the queen from Metternich, who years earlier had been her lover, he induced her to take a definite step toward treason. On October 17, while Murat fought at Leipzig, she called in Mier, the Austrian ambassador, and gave him a guarantee that until they negotiated an agreement no Neapolitan soldiers would leave the kingdom. "Thus without noise and smiling, she passed first to the enemy," says Fugier.

After Leipzig Napoleon allowed Murat to return to Naples, officially because he was needed there. The two publicly embraced as they parted at Erfurt (October 25). The emperor was aware of Murat's earlier contacts with the Austrians. Either he believed the king had repented, or, more probably, knew that precipitous action against him would drive Caroline into an immediate alliance with Austria. By letting Murat go, he could at least delay his defection, and if the war went well, perhaps prevent it. Unknown to Napoleon. Murat had sent his terms to Vienna: In return for Naples, Sicily, and the Papal States, he would join the allies with an army of 80,000.[11]

EUGÈNE AND MAX JOSEPH

In August and September Austrian troops under General Hiller, aided by local uprisings, took Illyria, then invaded the Kingdom of Italy. Eugène was forced back to the line of the Adige. Meanwhile his father-in-law, Maximilian Joseph of Bavaria, joined the allies (October 7), and "as a father" advised Eugène to desert Napoleon and receive in return the crown of Italy from the allies. Eugène replied that he feared for Augusta's health (she was again pregnant), but must do his duty. For her part Augusta honored Eugène's decision. "Our destinies are linked," she wrote him, and broke correspondence with her father, to whom she was very close. Max Joseph, eager to see his daughter queen of Italy, sent the prince of Taxis, in disguise, to try to make Eugène change his

11. By some accounts the emperor wrote a letter to the minister of police ordering that Murat be arrested if he entered Paris. If Napoleon wrote the letter, he doubtless had in mind preventing Murat's fomenting rebellion in France. There was no reason for him to go through France on his way to Naples. Probably no significance should be attached to the fact that Murat returned to his kingdom by way of Switzerland—this was the shortest route. It should be remembered also that at this juncture ex-kings Louis and Joseph were barred from Paris on penalty of arrest, and that after his expulsion from Westphalia so was Jérôme. Napoleon was sensitive to the mercurial temperament of the Paris population and wanted no one visiting the city whose presence might have an adverse effect on morale.

mind. The viceroy sent him away and reported his visit to Napoleon.

Italy

MURAT NEGOTIATES

All the while Murat was becoming more deeply involved in a double (or triple) game for not only the permanent possession of his kingdom, but the expansion of it. If, after all, he fought for Napoleon, he intended to get in return the Papal States, Tuscany, and perhaps part of the Kingdom of Italy. If he went over to the allies he hoped to gain the same mainland territory, plus Sicily. His most grandiose scheme was to unify all the states of the peninsula, in defiance of Napoleon *and* the allies. To gain support for the latter plan, he intended to cultivate the intelligentsia and secret societies, and test public sentiment with proclamations.

At Rome Murat paused to greet a crowd of proponents of Italian unity—freemasons, *Carbonari,* and others. Reaching Naples on November 5 he issued a proclamation to his army promising that it would never again fight in foreign climates, but in *Italy* and for *Italian* independence. Three days later he told the Austrian ambassador, Mier, that he was ready to help expel the French from Italy, but demanded specific commitments from the allies. At the same time his agents again approached Bentinck, and to please the British, Murat pointedly broke with the Continental System and opened Neapolitan ports to all flags. From Milan, en route to Naples, Murat had written Napoleon promising to march immediately with 30,000 troops to reinforce Eugène, but had questioned the viceroy's trustworthiness. He, Murat, should command the combined Neapolitan and Italian armies, the king wrote, since Eugène had been softened up by his father-in-law, and might be seduced by the allies at any moment.

"I have no more fear for Italy," wrote Napoleon to Eugène after receiving Murat's letter, referring to the latter's promise to lead troops to Italy. But after thus expressing his confidence in both rulers, he dispatched Joseph Fouché, the wily former minister of police, to Naples and Milan to ascertain how they really stood. The master ferret reported to Napoleon in December that Murat's defection seemed imminent, though the king had explained to him that he was protecting French interests by *pretending* to favor the allies. (Until the end, the king would allege to Napoleon that he was deceiving the Austrians and British.)

Meanwhile Murat asked Napoleon to abdicate as king of Italy, renounce Italian territory annexed to France, and divide the whole peninsula into two kingdoms—one for him (Murat) and one for Eugène, with the boundary at the Po. On Caulaincourt's recommendation Napoleon on December 25 accepted this proposal, but it was too late.

MURAT TURNS HIS COAT

Murat, still technically uncommitted, began moving troops north in late November. By early January the Neapolitans had occupied Rome, Tuscany, and the Papal States as far north as Bologna. The king himself had remained in Naples, concerned over the attitude of Bentinck, who not only seemed uninterested in an alliance, but refused him even an armistice. He was jubilant, therefore, when on December 31, 1813 Count Adam von Neipperg arrived from Vienna with a draft of an Austro-Neapolitan treaty approved by Lord Aberdeen, British ambassador to Vienna. Actually the British position was still unsettled, as Murat would soon learn. Aberdeen had instructions from Castlereagh to encourage Murat's anti-French acts without obligating Britain. The young ambassador, overawed by Metternich, had gone beyond his authority, but his action did not bind his government. The treaty guaranteed Naples to Murat; he, in return renounced his claim to Sicily and promised to support Austria (in Italy only) with 30,000 troops. Austria promised further to use her good offices to induce the other allies to guarantee Murat's throne, and at the general peace to support adding territory (unspecified) to Naples. On January 11, 1814 the king signed the treaty, formally betraying his emperor. Only a week before he had written Napoleon to expect ostensibly hostile acts, but to trust him. Why? Did he really think he could serve Napoleon in the enemy camp—or only hope to keep some credit with him—or could he not face himself if he admitted his treason? Chances are he did not know himself.

Really he was too simple and honest a man for treason, as Napoleon knew: "His wife made him defect, Caroline, my sister, has betrayed me!" The queen-spider, however, did not operate in the open. During her farewell reception for the French, most of whom now left Naples, a classic exchange occurred. Old Marshal Pérignon opined stiffly that she, surely, would soon leave also. "*Monsieur le maréchal,*" said Caroline demurely, "you must know that a wife's duty is to obey her husband."

On January 24, Murat, en route to join his army, entered Rome amid cheers and clamor—the legendary marshal, steed prancing, plumes flying—but now styling himself "Liberator of Italy." The Austrian generals were also trying to take advantage of Italian nationalism. Hiller had urged Italians to fight for independence, as had his replacement, Field Marshal Bellegarde. And the latter's subordinate, General Count Nugent, was freely flinging out promises of Italian freedom south of the Po. Murat, arriving at Bologna on January 31, immediately tried to upstage Nugent, but the result was disappointing. Only a small crowd gathered to see the king, and most stared blankly at the small paid claque which dutifully shouted "Viva Il Re d'Italia." His dream of winning popular support for Italian unity was deflated, but Murat at least had the satisfaction of taking under his command Nugent and his Austrians, as well as the Neapolitans, who, under Generals Carascosa and Coletta, were already facing Eugène's Italians along the Po and Enza Rivers. The cities and countryside were quiet, and the people seemingly interested only in avoiding the armies and safeguarding their property.

EUGÈNE AND MURAT

The emperor had advised Eugène in January to expect Murat's defection: "As soon as you have official notice it seems important to me that you gain the Alps with all your army." On February 8 the emperor informed Clarke (minister of war) that Eugène had orders to withdraw through the Alps to Lyons, and directed Clarke to reiterate the order and deliver copies to Eugène by telegraph, ordinary dispatch, and officer courier. Before the orders arrived, however, the viceroy, assuming that Napoleon's first letter left all decisions to him (it said "it seems important," not "withdraw," and the emperor was seldom imprecise), had committed himself to defend the kingdom. He was too deeply engaged to retreat without heavy losses. Moreover, he feared that his army, which was fighting well on Italian soil, would disintegrate if he marched for France. His Italians, after the enormous casualties of Russia and Spain, were in any case disinclined to foreign service, and many would surely desert if he abandoned their homeland. His "French" troops might disappear too, since they were mostly conscripts from Piedmont (annexed 1802), who would pass through their home province en route to France. For these reasons Eugène chose to defend the empire in Italy. If Napoleon disapproved, his correspondence gives no indication of it. Charges of disobedience to the emperor and self-seeking later leveled against the viceroy seem ridiculous in the light of his conduct in the fighting.[12]

Murat had ordered his generals to avoid engaging Eugène's troops and they had complied, not unhappily. Though personally courageous, most of them had not been bred to a military tradition and were more politicians than soldiers. The Austrian general Count Nugent was of another sort. Nominally under Murat, he quickly assessed the attitude of the Neapolitans and determined to carry the attack to the enemy, involving Murat's troops if possible and forcing them to fight.

Threatened from the east (Bellegarde) and south (Murat and Nugent), Eugène on February 3–4 withdrew from the Adige to the Mincio. (See Map 13, p. 308.) His defense hinged on the fortresses of Mantua and Peschiera, with his lightly guarded right flank along the Po from Borgoforte (guarded by Mantua) to Piacenza. Bellegarde followed Eugène to the Mincio, ready to give battle, but hoping Eugène would join the allies. He had already offered the viceroy promotion to king of Italy, his crown guaranteed by Austria, if he would turn coat. During Eugène's withdrawal to the Mincio, the offer was reiterated by a Bavarian general who urged Eugène to accept in the name of his father-in-law.

12. In his memoirs, Marshal Marmont, himself a traitor in 1814, made much of Eugène's orders to evacuate Italy. He alleged the viceroy had disobeyed the emperor, denied him an additional army with which to defend France, and doomed him to defeat. His accusations are disproved by Napoleon's correspondence after February 8, approving Eugène's conduct of the war in Italy, and later statements on the subject.

The viceroy's answer was no, and on February 8 he backed his words with action. Catching Bellegarde off balance, he slammed across the Mincio, and routed the Austrian army. Unhappily, Eugène's losses were so heavy and his own disorganization so great that he could not follow up on his victory, but his determination to fight was clear. Napoleon, elated, sent congratulations, and neither then nor afterward mentioned evacuating Italy.

In the south Nugent, on February 8, pushed through Carascosa's Neapolitans, crossed the Enza, took Parma, and marched on Piacenza, calling on Murat to support him. Bellegarde also demanded that Murat act, and simultaneously news came of Napoleon's setback at La Rothière (February 1, 1814). Murat, conscience-stricken, but seeing no alternative, sent word to Eugène that he would begin hostilities. Then within twenty-four hours news came of Napoleon's victories at Champaubert and Montmirail (March 10–11). Murat changed his mind, and withheld his troops, forcing Nugent to fall back on Parma. He then resumed correspondence with Eugène.

Nugent's successes, however, determined Eugène to strike to the south—to protect his Po front and further discourage Murat. On March 2 he sent Grenier, with 20,000 men, across the Po at Piacenza. Grenier seized Parma and Reggio (which he garrisoned), then turned north to Guastalla where he recrossed the Po. Eugène, meanwhile, had shifted his main army from Volta to Borgoforte, where he could lend support to Grenier, but it proved unnecessary. By March 4 Grenier was installed in Borgoforte, and the viceroy was back at Volta; his demonstration had been a total success.

Nugent, humiliated, struck immediately at the small garrison Grenier had planted at Reggio. With him was one brigade of Neapolitans, a token force which Murat had assumed would give him little help. To his astonishment, the king got word (March 7) that Nugent had the Franco-Italians surrounded. His men were attacking Eugène's! Riding up posthaste from Bologna, Murat arranged a truce, then allowed the French-Italian garrison to rejoin the viceroy's army. Nugent was beside himself with rage, as was Bellegarde when he got the news. The Austrians now dis-

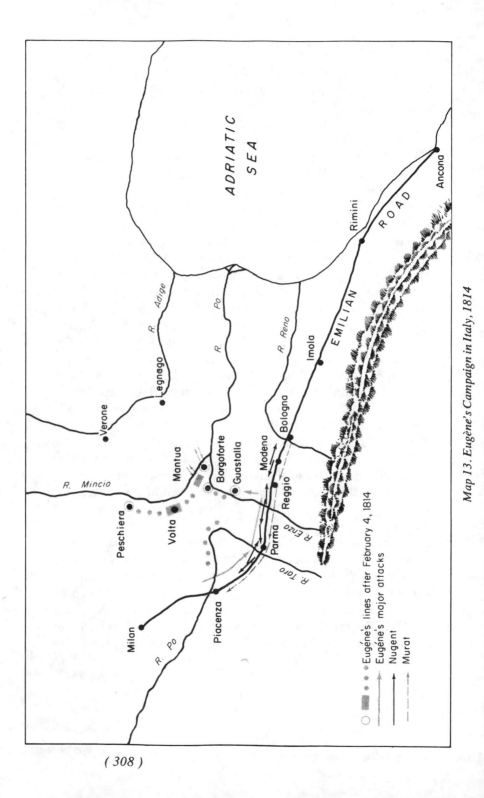

ADRIATIC SEA

Ancona

Rimini

EMILIAN ROAD

R. Adige

R. Po

R. Reno

Imola

Bologna

Legnago

Verone

R. Mincio

Mantua

Borgoforte

Guastalla

Modena

Reggio

R. Enza

Peschiera

Volta

Parma

R. Taro

Milan

R. Po

Piacenza

○ ● ● Eugène's lines after February 4, 1814

Eugène's major attacks

Nugent

Murat

Map 13. Eugène's Campaign in Italy, 1814

trusted Murat more than ever, but preferring not to drive him into joining Eugène, they let him play his game.

On March 14 the situation was complicated by the arrival of Lord Bentinck, who had just landed with an Anglo-Sicilian force at Livorno (Leghorn). The crusty soldier-diplomat was exercised over seeing Murat's flag flying in Tuscany (occupied en route to the front by the Neapolitans). He refused to address Murat as "Your Highness," since he recognized the Bourbon Ferdinand as the rightful king of Naples, preferring *Monseigneur,* which cut the sensitive Gascon to the quick. Insisting on mouthing what everyone else avoided saying, he accused Murat of not fulfilling his obligations to the allies. The king replied that he was unaware of a British treaty with his government, and would even evacuate Tuscany if one were signed. Lord Bentinck, losing his temper, threatened to invade Naples if Tuscany were not evacuated, and departed in high dudgeon.

Murat, much alarmed, turned to Eugène, whom Napoleon had recently authorized to make him a deal. Murat wants his kingdom expanded to the Po, the emperor had written—so be it. "Make a treaty in my name . . . [with that] extraordinary traitor." Promise him anything you like but Piedmont and Genoa; we need not feel bound by a treaty with him.[13] Eugène made an offer, but Murat hesitated before blandishments from all sides in the allied camp.

Bellegarde, who had sickness in his army, labored to ingratiate himself with the king. Mier assured him of Austria's good intentions. Caroline sent representatives begging him to keep his head. And finally Lord Bentinck reappeared with Sir Robert Wilson in trail. Instructed to hold his tongue by Castlereagh, Bentinck let the glib and charming Wilson deal with Murat, who was allowed to feel that the British government respected the Austrian treaty, but was made no promises. In the midst of these talks, news arrived that the allies were marching on Paris.

Murat, finally, committed himself fully. Moving his headquarters forward (April 14) he attacked Piacenza—his first calculated move against Eugène. But before the city fell, news came

13. In another desperation move, Napoleon returned the Pope to Rome, where the Pontiff, he said, would "lie like a bomb"—i.e., his status and the disposition of his former lands would have to be considered immediately by the allies.

that Napoleon had abdicated at Fontainebleau (April 11, 1814) and shortly that Eugène had signed an armistice with Bellegarde.

At the news of the emperor's fall, Murat cried unashamedly. Emotionally, he had never accepted that such a thing could happen, no matter what he did. In his bumbling way he had tried to qualify his treachery by not attacking Eugène, and in the process had half-betrayed his new allies. They did not love him. "I am here in the midst of strangers," he had written Napoleon in March. "I must hide my fears." Still the emperor's horseman, he wrote after the abdication: "Never doubt my heart, it is worth more than my head!" Yes. But Caroline had been his "head," and he had spoiled her schemes by listening too often to his heart.

There were, of course, rational sources for Murat's hesitancy to attack Eugène, primarily the British attitude. But also the Austrian approach to Italians suddenly changed in February 1814. Marshal Bellegarde, who had been talking loudly about Italian independence and freedom, suddenly announced that his emperor intended to restore the "antique edifice" of Europe. Would he honor his treaty with a parvenu king? Finally, face-to-face with Eugène's troops, Murat had to consider that if the viceroy were defeated he, Murat, would be at the mercy of the "strangers," who would no longer need him—unless he agreed to march on France, and what then? Still, as Caroline saw clearly, once their fortunes were cast with the allies, Murat should have supported them wholeheartedly. It was their only chance. The king's emotional management of affairs had all but ruined it.

THE FRUITS OF VICTORY

With Napoleon gone, Murat's one protection was the treaty with Austria. The other allies had made him no promises. He had hedged on his bargain with Austria, and moreover, the Austrian emperor had never formally ratified the document. Aware of his vulnerability, Murat raised no objection to the return of the old regime in northern Italy. In early May he withdrew to Naples. In addition to his normal territory, his troops occupied only part of the Papal Marches, a strip of the Adriatic coast extending north to Ancona. Naples herself was beset with internal troubles. The more reactionary clergy were recovering their influence, the secret societies were gaining strength, and contending, sometimes fighting, among themselves. The societies, and many of Murat's ministers and generals, pressed him to grant a new constitution, and their pleas were reinforced by exiles returning from Sicily, who were busily comparing Murat's government with Bentinck's dreams for a constitutional monarchy in Naples or united Italy. In this atmosphere Murat awaited the decisions of the powers, unsure that he would long be a king.

EUGÈNE, THE ITALIANS, AND THE ALLIES

The Convention of Schiarino Rizzino (April 16, 1814)—the armistice between Eugène and Field Marshal Bellegarde—required French troops to retire from Italy, but left fortresses in territory held by the viceroy in the hands of his Italian troops. Further, Eugène was allowed to send a delegation to the allied leaders at Paris. It seemed conceivable, therefore, that the kingdom would survive, and possible that Eugène would become king.

Eugène, at Mantua, realizing that advantages might accrue from moving quickly, appointed two of his generals delegates to the allies in Paris and sent them on their way. He then ordered his chancelor, Melzi, in Milan, to call the Italian senate into extraordinary session and ask it to appoint civilian delegates. Perhaps Eugène and his advisers moved too precipitously. At any rate, many Italians thought the activity of Melzi and his cohorts in Milan smacked of intrigue. There was objection also to having the senate, an appointive body, choose delegates, when the electoral college could have been assembled.

There were three major political factions in Milan: the French party, the Austrian party, and the "Pure Italian" party. The French party, which favored perpetuating the kingdom, intact, with Eugène as king, was led by Melzi and the ministers Paradisi, Vaccari, and Prina. It comprised those who would lose most by Eugène's departure, prominently officers, bureaucrats, judges, and businessmen dependent on French markets, plus not a few people, high and low, attached to the viceroy and/or the Napoleonic brand of liberalism. The Austrian party harbored the traditionalists—nobles of the old regime, a large segment of the clergy, former officials, and businessmen ruined by Italy's connection with

France. Surprisingly enough, many of the "Austrians" favored preserving the Kingdom of Italy rather than restoring petty states which had existed prior to 1796. They differed on candidates for the throne; some favored an Austrian archduke, others a lower ranking Hapsburg.

The most vociferous party, though not the largest, was the "Pure Italian" party. It comprised disgruntled military and civilian officials, ambitious aristocrats, and a swarm of intellectuals, especially those favoring the unification of (all) Italy. An important leader was General Pino, fired by Eugène after serving briefly as minister of war in 1805. Supporting the party on one basis or another were the Freemasons, the *Carbonari,* the Guelphs, and smaller similar organizations. The "Pure Italians" were divided in their aims. Men like Pino, Luini, the director of police, and the writer Ugo Foscolo were for putting Murat on the throne of a united Italy. Others supported an Austrian prince, or the third son of George III of England, had no candidate, or wanted a republic.

The public was for the most part attached to no faction. The masses were simply tired, in favor of nothing more than peace. It cannot be said that Eugène was loved, but he was generally respected by the people and though they had suffered greatly from the burdens of taxes and conscription, they blamed Napoleon, not Eugène, for their suffering.

The senate met on April 17, and after a whole day of wrangling, approved a resolution informing the allies that the senate "recognized the government" of Prince Eugène, and appointed three senators delegates to Paris. One delegate, Testi, protesting that the procedures had been irregular, refused to go, but the other two dutifully departed on April 18. The French party had won the first round.

On April 18 and 19, however, the Austrian and "Pure Italian" factions, momentarily allies, tried to negate the action of the senate by creating a public uproar. General Pino and the director of police, Luini, contrived to send virtually all troops out of the city and to reduce the police force to a minimum. Eugène's more affluent opponents hired gangs of men to foment disturbances. Spokesmen of the secret societies harangued crowds, accusing

Melzi of tricking the senators, alleging that they had elected Eugène king, and warning that if he were not expelled, taxes and conscription would remain at wartime levels. Prina, the minister of finance, unapproachable but hardly villainous, was pictured as grasping and venal. Liberty, independence, and religion were at stake!

When the senate met in regular session on April 20 a mob broke up the meeting and sacked the chamber. Then, as if on signal, the crowd marched to Prina's home, broke in, flung him from a second story window into the street, and dragged and beat him. Rescued but still pursued, Prina gave himself up to save his companions and was killed in the streets.

The disturbance in Milan gave Field Marshal Bellegarde an excuse to demand that Austrian troops be allowed to restore order. Eugène, whose troops had evacuated Milan on Pino's order, was unsure he could back up a refusal, and agreed. For the sake of order, he made the detested Pino commandant of Milan pending Bellegarde's arrival.

Though Eugène did not believe the game irrecoverably lost, he saw small possibility of winning, and none without further bloodshed and disorder. As weary of strife as his people, he was unwilling to bring more suffering down on them for what was probably a lost cause. On April 26, from Mantua, he issued a proclamation of farewell and ceded control of his army to Field Marshal Bellegarde. The next day he, Augusta, and their children (four girls, one boy) departed for Munich under escort of Austrian cavalry.

EUGÈNE AND AUGUSTA

Of the satellite rulers, no one had better served Napoleon than Eugène. Though his opportunities for successful and profitable defection had been good, he had stood by his emperor. Eminently successful as a governor, administrator, and soldier, he had received scant praise from his foster father except in times of crisis —1809, 1812, 1814. Asked to accept Napoleon's divorce from his mother, denied a crown, he nevertheless served faithfully to the end. Subjected to harsh and unjust criticism, he seldom answered, and if so mildly. When he disobeyed orders it was to the emperor's advantage, as he saw it, though in 1814 he did refuse flatly but politely to send Augusta to Paris. (She was pregnant and ill; her fifth child, a girl, was born at Mantua on April 13, three days before Eugène's truce with Bellegarde.) Augusta stood by Eugène throughout; in 1814 she refused her father's protection until after the empire fell. Early fearful that she would influence Eugène to follow Bavaria into the allied camp, Napoleon later repented of his suspicions. "Models of their sex," the emperor had called Eugène and Augusta the year of their marriage. They gave him proofs beyond his imagining.

THE END OF THE KINGDOM OF ITALY

Eugène's departure from Italy had the effect he had expected. Italian troops kept order in Milan until Bellegarde arrived. Austrian civil officials smoothly superceded those of the viceroy and began preparing the way for the return of the "ancient edifice" and its several hereditary rulers. "Italy" again became a geographic expression—but also a dream for something grander than Eugène's kingdom.

* 　 * 　 *

The satellite kingdoms had all disappeared. Naples remained, but as an independent state under King Gioacchino (I) Murat. He was no longer a Frenchman, and the fate of his kingdom depended upon the will of the allies and the decisions of the Congress of Vienna.

*Italians! The hour has arrived when great des-
tinies will be fulfilled. Providence finally calls
you to liberty; a cry which will make itself
heard from the Alps to the Strait of Scylla and
that cry is: The Independence of Italy!*
—MURAT AT RIMINI, MARCH 30, 1815

chapter ten

THE FIRST WAR OF ITALIAN INDEPENDENCE

Murat in the Hundred Days

THE EMPEROR RETURNS

*O*n February 26, 1815 Napoleon sailed blithely away from Elba. On March 1 the "Thunderer of the scene"[1] set foot on the coast of France and traveled north from Cannes to Grenoble, French troops joining him as he went. ("Where is the man who would fire upon his Emperor?") At Auxerre, Ney, who had vowed to put him in an iron cage, fell into Napoleon's arms. On March 20 he was in Paris, from whence the rotund and puffing Louis XVIII had precipitously fled.

Louis Bonaparte, busy at Rome suing for the annulment of his marriage, the custody of his children, and recovery of his property, declined to return. So did Eugène, rejecting the pleas of his sister Hortense. Prematurely aging, he was virtually captive in Bavaria, and for his children's sake he chose not to jeopardize the lands and incomes (as yet unspecified) guaranteed him by the Treaty of Fontainebleau.[2] But Joseph and Jérôme appeared in Paris, and the latter had first-hand news of Murat, whom he had visited at his headquarters near Rimini.

1. Lord Byron's words.
2. The treaty (April 11, 1814) promised him a "suitable establishment out-side of France," and contained similar vague commitments to the other Bona-partes except Napoleon and Marie Louise, who, respectively, got Elba and Parma.

What was he doing? asked Jérôme. Making war on Austria, Murat replied. Did he have an alliance with England? Was Napoleon going to cross the Alps with an army to help him? No. "Italy will rise en masse and give me an army of 150,000 men. . . . I will fear nothing . . .!" Jérôme, astounded, wished him well and went on his way.

MURAT AND THE NATIONALISTS

Murat was playing his trump card, and staking his crown on it. He had embarked on a crusade for the unification of Italy. He had "joined Napoleon," but in much the same way the United States had "joined Napoleon" by fighting the British during the War of 1812. The emperor had not asked that he attack the Austrians, but on the contrary, had sent Colonna d'Istria, chamberlain of Madame Mère, to ask Murat not to make any bellicose moves. Napoleon's plan was to notify the Congress of Vienna that he intended to rule France constitutionally, and would keep the peace. He hoped, since the allies had developed violent differences among themselves, they would let him be. He asked Murat to assure Austria and the congress that Naples also would keep the peace, and that he, Murat, had no military plans.[3]

But Murat did have plans, which, independent of Napoleon, he had been formulating for some time. His former minister of police, Maghella, sent on a mission to assess opinion in the Papal Marches, had told the king that Italians would flock to his banner. Others of the nationalist school, like Francesco Ricciardi, Antonio Nolli, Generals Colletta, Carascosa, Florestano Pepe, and Guglielmo Pepe, gave him encouragement. Writers of the "Italian School" outside the kingdom, like Foscolo, Monti, Manzoni, and Rossi, had long trumpeted the glories of unification. In Naples, the *Carbonari,* which propagandized for unification, had grown

3. Pauline Bonaparte and Madame Walewska had carried messages between Elba and Naples, and vessels of Napoleon's "navy" had frequently been in Neapolitan waters, but there is no evidence that Murat had coordinated any plans with Napoleon, or that he knew before the emperor's flight of the specific plan. Probably the king did know before Napoleon escaped that *something* was afoot on Elba, but then many others suspected something. For example, Cardinal Pacca, at Rome, had apprised the Congress of Vienna in mid-February that Napoleon probably planned to escape to Naples and even named the ship, the *Inconstant* on which he later escaped to France. (M. H. Weil, *Murat,* Vol. II, 353.)

immensely, and numbered among its leaders Maghella, Zurlo, the minister of the interior, and the marquis di Montrone, chamberlain of the king. The society fed Murat's ambitions, and assured him the support of *Carbonari* leaders in Florence, Bologna, Brescia, Milan, and elsewhere. Reports of British agents had also fallen into the king's hands which stated that particularly in Lombardy and Tuscany, men of education and talent refused employment because of their "Italian" sentiments, were spoiling to revolt against the Austrians, and would join any movement that had a reasonable chance of success. The powers feared such a movement, but not in connection with Murat. They saw the possibility that *Napoleon* might land in Italy, create a unified kingdom, and then move to recover France. Metternich, Talleyrand, and Castlereagh saw little danger of Italians flocking to Murat, but Napoleon —that was different. When the news of his flight from Elba came, the diplomats at Vienna were sure he was bound for Italy.

MURAT AND THE POWERS

Probably Murat would not have risked sponsoring an Italian unification movement, despite all encouragements, had not his support among the powers gradually eroded since April 1814. With Napoleon's fall the allies resembled the "Forces of Light" with the devil dead; evil vanquished, their swords cut empty air, and they looked for new devils in each other. For a while this tendency protected Murat. Austria, once in control of northern Italy, was most interested in wringing a favorable settlement in central Europe from Russia and Prussia, and cultivated Murat to avoid trouble in Italy. At the same time Russia, and to a lesser extent Prussia, were friendly to Murat since his army represented a counterpoise to Austria's in Italy. Further, Czar Alexander, a liberal-moralist of sorts, strongly objected to restoring the "Butcher King" Ferdinand to the Neapolitan throne. As he knew, however, the real villain of 1799 had been Ferdinand's queen, Marie Caroline, and she died in September 1814. The British, officially, sided with Austria, since they wanted the balance of power restored in Europe, and since they had agreed at Prague in 1813 to allow Austria to control the settlement in Italy. Personally, the British leaders, including Castlereagh and Wellington, who replaced him at Vienna (only) in February 1815, detested Murat as a turncoat. Wrote Talleyrand to Louis XVIII, "It is the *man* Murat they despise, more than the usurper."

It became apparent early that Bourbon France would also play a major role at the Vienna Congress. At a preliminary meeting in September Metternich used the term "allies," and Talleyrand shot back, smiling, "What allies? Against whom? Not against Napoleon: He is on the island of Elba. Surely not against the king of France: He is the guarantee of the duration of the peace." France and Bourbon Spain consistently opposed Murat and pressed for the restoration of Ferdinand IV, while under Talleyrand's direction France's influence grew steadily. A sure indication of new status was her treaty with Britain and Austria in January 1815 by which all agreed to prevent, by force if necessary, Russia from taking all of Poland, or Prussia all of Saxony. Shortly thereafter, the powers reached tentative agreements on Poland and Saxony and turned to the reorganization of Germany, already partly settled.

In early 1815, therefore, the balance of power was virtually restored in central Europe, and Murat lost the advantages deriving from the great powers' disputes. The British now charged openly that Murat had not fulfilled his obligation to the allies in 1814. Castlereagh and Wellington were irate over the king's attention to Whig visitors to Naples. To Murat they were just Englishmen, whom it seemed advantageous to cultivate—the duke of Bedford, Lord Sligo, Lord Holland, Lord Oxford. (He was captivated by their ladies, who seemed to be in love with him when they arrived. Lady Oxford had an affair with the cavalier-king, which she widely advertised, and the princess of Wales pursued him relentlessly —to the outrage of all parties.) The congress had come into possession of parts of Murat's correspondence with Eugène and Napoleon, some letters dating to within days of the end of hostilities. Prussia and Russia now had no need of Naples, and became indifferent to Murat's fate. Most crucial, Metternich had decided to sacrifice Murat to France and Britain in return for their support in the German settlement. The Austrian minister seemingly planned to provoke Murat by demanding that the Papal Marches be returned to the Pope, or if the king gave in, on some other matter, for example, the disposition of Ponte Corvo, ceded by Napoleon to the king's eldest son. But Murat himself provided a crisis which allowed Austria to act.

Unaware of the radical change in his position, Murat still counted Austria as an ally, Britain as a hostile neutral tied to Austria, Prussia and Russia as friendly neutrals, and France as his only important enemy. He decided to bully France into official friendship. In mid-February he instructed Campochiaro, at Vienna, to demand that Louis XVIII recognize him immediately or face war, and to ask that Austria grant free passage (through northern Italy) to the French border for Neapolitan troops. Campochiaro, abreast of the adverse developments at Vienna, except Austria's new position, declined to approach Talleyrand, but went to Metternich for advice. To his surprise, the minister gave him threats instead. If Naples disturbed the peace, Metternich said testily, Austria would put 150,000 troops on the Po, and to make his point clear, he delivered two notes (February 25 and 26) to Campochiaro. Murat's slim chance for survival, as Caroline told him insistently, was to keep the peace and cooperate with Austria, at whatever expense or humiliation. But the cavalier would not listen; he was bent on *doing something,* even if it was wrong.

DECISION-MAKING

Murat received the news of Napoleon's flight from Elba on March 4, and three days later word of Metternich's threats. During the next few days he agonized—out loud, striding about and gesticulating—"*Jésus! Marie!*"—over whether to attack Austria or wait for more news of Napoleon. Meanwhile he prepared for war. Caroline begged him to offer his aid *against* Napoleon—to improve their credit with the allies. If the emperor regained his power, she told Murat, he would destroy them—she knew him! Gallo, Murat's foreign minister, echoed her arguments, as did Agar, the finance minister, and of course Mier, the Austrian ambassador. The king was pressed to opt for war, however, by Maghella, Zurlo, the nationalists, and—the princess of Wales! Hopelessly in love with Murat, she vowed to follow him to the front. (That proved too much even for Murat, who was not a little relieved to get away from her.)

Murat decided finally (March 15) to fight. He reasoned that if he could strike quickly at the scattered Austrian armies in northern Italy he had a good chance of defeating them. If so, since Napoleon had again become the powers' major concern, the Austrians might make peace in Italy rather than withdraw troops from northern Europe. With all Italy under his rule, he would be in a strong position to bargain with the allies or Napoleon—whichever won—or both if there were a compromise settlement. If he did nothing, the winner, or both in cooperation, would likely crush him.[4]

Unquestionably Murat's conscience was eased by striking a blow which would disconcert the allies and might work in Napoleon's favor. "It is with irrepressible pleasure that I hear of the landing of Your Majesty on the shores of your Empire," he wrote on March 14. But Murat was fighting primarily for himself, and had catalogued all possible reasons to be optimistic, as he revealed to D'Ambrosio: "Venice is open and badly armed; the Piedmontese are already tired of the government of their inept King; the Milanese abhor Austrian domination; the Venetians have not lost the memory of their ancient glory; the Ligurians groan at what has been done to them; the bellicose populations of Romagna spoil with desire to serve under my flags. Austria is in no condition to fight on two fronts. I will beat them."

THE WAR

On paper Murat's army had reached almost 95,000, of which, sadly, he could deploy only 35,000 infantry and 5,000 cavalry, most of which had been moved north into the Papal Marches during February. Of the field army there remained at Naples only the Royal Guard—7,000 men under Pignatelli-Strongoli—the elite of Neapolitan regulars, their ranks strengthened with French

---

4. At the time of his decision, Murat knew that Napoleon had reached Grenoble, and was gaining strength. His grudge against the Austrians had been reinforced by the news that Pauline Bonaparte, a good friend who had spent much time in Naples, had been arrested in Tuscany by the Austrians. One of the most improbable reports circulated during the Hundred Days had it that the shapeliest of the Bonapartes had tried to escape *disguised as a boy*. She would have had a better chance as a giant mouse.

and German mercenaries. The troops in the Papal Marches, concentrated at Ancona and Macerata, were commanded by Carascosa, Lechi, D'Ambrosio, Pignatelli-Cerchiara, and Rossetti. Opposing Murat's forces, and not unaware of the enemy, was an Austrian army of 40,000, backed by garrisons of some 50,000 in the Quadrilateral fortresses. The Austrians, too, had made preparations in February. Schwarzenberg, now Austrian minister of war, had even consulted Wellington on the problem. Reserves had been set in motion toward Italy, and new commanders dispatched—General Baron Frimont from the army in Germany, and Field Marshal Lieutenant Baron Bianchi from the Aulic Council of War in Vienna.

On March 19 Murat's army began the campaign, the Royal Guard marching via Rome toward Florence, with Murat, on the opposite coast, advancing north along the Emilian Road. (See May 14, p. 322.) At Rimini, on March 30, he solemnly proclaimed the independence of Italy. Behind his lines recruiting stations opened and the people were bombarded with nationalist propaganda, but to little effect. Some segments of the intelligentsia were ready, produced tons of prepared appeals, and talked themselves hoarse, but the population displayed little more than curiosity. Eugène's former officers, whom Murat had been assured would desert the Austrians, remained with their troops. Probably a good many would have risked their careers if Napoleon had been present, but for Murat—no.

The king nevertheless was sure that quick victory would bring Italians to his banners by thousands (as indeed it might have). On April 2 he took Bologna without a fight. At the Panaro he won a minor victory over the Austrians and seized Modena. His army, however, increasingly showed signs of lethargy. The Neapolitans, never enthusiastic soldiers, were much discouraged not to be received as liberators, and could see that few volunteers were joining them. Their generals, perpetually away in conference, seemed more interested in forcing a new constitution on Murat than fighting the war. Moreover, some troops had not been paid in months, medical services were primitive, and food—never enough—came forward at irregular intervals. Then too, Murat, possessed with a frantic sense of urgency and responding to his cavalryman's re-

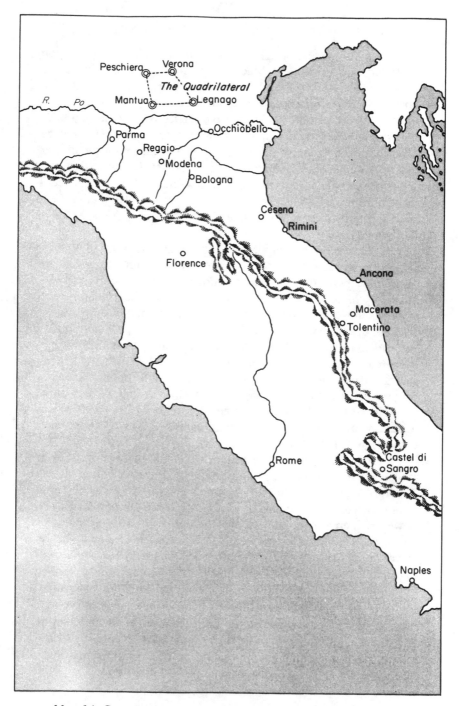

Map 14. Central and Northern Italy (Adapted from R. M. Johnston, The Napoleonic Empire in Southern Italy, Vol. I, The Macmillan Company [London], p. 285)

flexes, pushed his soldiers along at a killing pace. Malingering and desertion increased; discipline got progressively poorer. Nevertheless on April 8 the Neapolitans forced the Po at Occhiobello and established a bridgehead.

Frimont, now in command of Austrian forces, planned holding actions combined with small attacks to keep the Neapolitans off-balance while he regrouped and brought up reinforcements. On April 10, however, the first Austrian probing attack against Occhiobello sent the Neapolitans flying. Modena fell easily to another Austrian force the same day. Astonished, Frimont authorized his field commanders—Bianchi, Nugent, and Neipperg—to go over to the offensive.

Murat withdrew to Bologna and held a council of war, where his politically minded generals exercised their lungs interminably, talking constitution and war, but finally agreed on a plan—a retreat through Ancona. To give backbone to his army, the king ordered the Royal Guard, then near Florence, to reinforce him with all speed. Its commander, Pignatelli-Strongoli, menaced by a numerically superior Austrian force under General Count Nugent, was happy to comply, and marched rapidly southeast.

The Austrians, having fixed Murat's forces, moved in for the kill. Nugent marched on Naples via Rome; with Pignatelli gone there was little to stop him. Neipperg, with some 20,000 men, followed Murat's retreat, applying minimal pressure, while Baron Bianchi, with about 11,000 men, marched around Murat's flank —via Florence and Arezzo—to take him in the rear. Bianchi completed his march in thirteen days and on April 30 debouched from the mountains above Tolentino.

Murat meanwhile withdrew to Cesena, tried to negotiate with the Austrians, failed, and continued the retreat. At Ancona, on April 30, the royal guard joined him, but a few hours later he learned that an Austrian force was behind him. Leaving Carascosa's corps north of Ancona to hold Neipperg in check, the king hurried toward Tolentino with the guard and the divisions of D'Ambrosio and Lechi, a total of 15,000 men.

On May 2 Murat found Bianchi occupying the Monte Milone, highest ground near Tolentino. Attacking with the cavalry of the guards and D'Ambrosio's division, he managed to force Bianchi off the promontory. During the assault, however, the king had to dismount and rally his infantry on foot, a bad sign, and General D'Ambrosio, a good soldier, was wounded and had to be replaced by D'Aquino. Still, with Monte Milone as a starting point and artillery position, with 15,000 troops to Bianchi's 11,000, and Neipperg checked at Ancona, Murat's chances of success in the following day seemed good. But this did not take into account the indiscipline of his generals and the unsteadiness of his troops.

On May 3 the guard attacked before Murat gave the order. Furious, but unwilling to risk disengaging, he ordered D'Aquino to support the attack, only to find that many of his troops had scattered in search of food. Appalled, the king personally led forward what troops were ready, and called on Lechi to support him. But Lechi's division was near Macerata, more than a mile to the rear, and his troops too were scattered. Before Lechi could move up, D'Aquino's division was routed, and the guard forced to withdraw. Bianchi was stopped, however, by effective artillery fire from Monte Milone, and Murat began reorganizing.

Late the same day, however, word came that Count Nugent had passed through Rome and was approaching the frontier of Naples on the opposite coast. Murat, dumbfounded, ordered a general retreat, which quickly turned into a rout. Under forced march, the rear elements continually cut up by the cavalry of Neipperg and Bianchi, Murat's army veritably disappeared before his eyes. General Belliard, sent by Napoleon as French minister and adviser to Murat, arrived in the midst of the retreat, but could do little but keep Murat company. The king, with the remnants of his guard, reached Naples on May 18. Really, however, his reign had ended at Tolentino. Entering the palace he faced an irate Caroline, who thought he could have prevented the whole disaster by following her advice. "Do not be astonished to see me alive, Madame," said the first cavalier of Europe, "I have done my best to die."

THE KINGDOM FALLS

Before Murat arrived, Queen-Regent Caroline had in effect surrendered to the British. The king had foolishly expected them to observe the armistice of 1814 and give him three months notice before beginning hostilities, but even the British were not that legalistic. In early May a British fleet under Lord Campbell sailed into the harbor of Naples and placed the city under its guns. On May 13, on board the "Tremendous," Campbell's flagship, Cariati had signed an agreement in the queen's name under which she, her children, and staff, would be taken aboard when the Austrians arrived. Unable to occupy Naples, the British meanwhile left the maintenance of order to the queen, who did well. On May 15, when rioting seemed imminent, she toured the city in an open carriage, then mounted a horse and reviewed the civil guard, and all remained relatively quiet.

In the face of Murat's reverses and the presence of the British, his supporters deserted rapidly. Now that the old Bourbon queen was dead the *lazzaroni* could see no objection to the return of Ferdinand IV, especially if it would bring an end to the war. The middle class, whose profits had been swelled by trade with the British during the months of peace, then had dropped off drastically as Murat became more menacing and finally went to war, favored almost any sort of permanent peace settlement. Although for 1815 the king had eliminated the head tax and reduced personal taxes by one-quarter, the move was seen as a war morale measure, and it was generally thought that only a Bourbon restoration would bring permanent relief from heavy taxes and conscription. On May 12, when his army had all but disappeared, Murat had granted a constitution for Naples, a futile gesture toward his liberal following. They were busily scurrying underground or into exile. Only a small band of die-hards welcomed the king on May 18 when he returned to his capital.

On May 19, in civilian clothes, Murat, with a few of his staff, fled Naples. At a fishing village north of the capital the party hired two small fishing boats and set sail for Gaeta, which still flew Murat's flag (and would until August 8). But Gaeta's harbor was blocked by a British cruiser, and the king landed instead on the island of Ischia, where by sheer luck a vessel soon arrived bound for France and took him aboard.

Meanwhile Caroline (with her children) got aboard the *Tremendous* on May 21, proclaiming proudly to British officers on deck that Napoleon would restore her in four months. Campbell landed her at Trieste, from whence the Austrians took her to Vienna. On May 23 Field Marshal Lieutenant Bianchi and Prince-Regent Leopold of the Two Sicilies entered Naples. The Bourbons had returned—under Austrian escort.[5] Three days later Murat landed at Cannes, on the French Riviera, hoping again to find service with his emperor.

Communication between France and Naples had been difficult. The British controlled the sea, the Austrians northern Italy, and until April royalists held Marseilles. A letter of Napoleon's dispatched March 29 by couriers following two different land routes never got to Naples. (One rider was imprisoned in Switzerland, the other turned back at Turin.) After Marseilles raised the tricolor, allowing ships better able to run the British blockade to be dispatched, Murat was sent letters written him since March 20 and copies of the *Moniteur*.

On the same day (April 10) the emperor ordered General Belliard to Naples as minister of France, but could not tell him much of Murat. "He seems to have attacked the Austrians," said Napoleon. He had not intended him to, but would support him. Belliard could promise that Naples would be expanded—to the Po! The new French minister reached Naples on May 9, saw Caroline briefly, then hurried to join Murat, whom he found at Castel di Sangro on the evening of May 11. To his amazement he saw the king not with 80,000 men, as he had expected, but some 8,000 in a high state of disorganization. Belliard hastily wrote Napoleon to expect no help from Murat, but it was weeks before his dispatches reached Paris.

Jérôme brought Napoleon the first news of Murat's disaster on May 27. He had galloped ahead of Madame Mère and Cardinal Fesch, with whom he had left Gaeta on May 13 aboard the same ship which had brought Belliard. Almost simultaneously, a semaphore telegraph message from Marshal Brune, at Marseilles, revealed that Murat was in Cannes, and hard on its heels letters

5. Count Adam von Neipperg, leading his cavalry, had entered the preceding day. The constant companion of the ex-Empress Marie Louise, now duchess of Parma, Neipperg would become her second husband after the death of Napoleon.

came from Murat to the emperor and Fouché. The Gascon's sword was again at the service of France.

Napoleon did not care to use it. On first hearing that Murat had attacked the Austrians, he had been tolerant, since the allies seemed bent on war anyway, and might be discouraged by the king's action. But Murat had lost! Europe would see the disaster as an allied victory over Napoleon! There was no chance now the powers would accept his proffers of peace! Tell him, the agent Baudus was instructed ". . . that he doomed France in 1814; that in 1815 he compromised France and lost himself. . . ." Murat was ordered to retire to the country somewhere between Gap and Sisteron, there to await the emperor's pleasure.

Though furiously preparing for war, the emperor still held out the olive branch to the allies. "Inform the Congress [of Vienna]," he wrote Caulaincourt (foreign minister), "that when Murat attacked the Austrians . . . he absolutely ignored the position of the Emperor."[6] The powers, however, had declared Napoleon "outside the civil and social relations" and "an enemy and disturber of the peace of the world," and formed a new alliance. Their standing armies totaled almost 800,000 men. To meet them Napoleon had assembled 275,000, hoping to win a quick victory by crushing those nearest at hand—200,000, under Wellington and Blücher, in the Netherlands and the Rhineland.[7]

Desperate for commanders, Napoleon called Marshal Ney, despite his service to Louis XVIII and eleventh-hour defection in 1814, and let Masséna come out of retirement. Murat, who might have been extremely useful, was refused, and it was unlike Napoleon to reject useful persons. (He distrusted Fouché, but made him minister of police, knowing his talent and hoping to keep him under supervision.) Perhaps his decision on Murat was emotional. He was a traitor within the *family*—of deep significance to the Corsican emperor. His presence would have reminded Napoleon of another, more calculating traitor—his sister Caroline. The *Cahiers* of General Bertrand add another possible reason: Murat

6. In the *Correspondance impériale* this letter (item 21826) is dated April 19, 1815, but it was surely written between May 27 and June 2, 1815.
7. At Waterloo Napoleon would only have 72,000 present, however, and the allies 140,000 (after Blücher's arrival).

had denied Marie Walewska the property in Naples which Napoleon had given her. On three separate occasions the emperor stated that he had not called Murat to the army because of his mistreatment of the countess. Perhaps. It is not too difficult to believe that Napoleon bitterly resented this affront to a woman he had loved, who had borne him a son, and who came to him at Elba when all others had abandoned him.

For three weeks after landing Murat remained at Cannes, at the tavern Trois Pigeons, going out only at night. Depressed and bitter, he convinced himself that he had sacrificed all for Napoleon, and that Caroline had preferred the enemy camp to being with him (which was not altogether untrue). After receiving Napoleon's orders, he moved to the villa of Admiral Allemand, near Toulon, where he occupied himself with appeals to his friends—Fouché, Lucien Bonaparte, Madame Récamier, and others. His letters ran to a pattern: He had sacrificed his crown, family, reputation, everything but his honor for France and the emperor; he demanded justice, or at least the chance to fight again for the emperor. Fouché sent an agent to instruct him, in Napoleon's name (illegally), to wait near Lyons for orders to command an invasion of Italy. (Probably Fouché had political plans for him.) Murat wrote Napoleon directly that he would comply, but for reasons unknown, did not. He was still at Toulon when the news of Waterloo and Napoleon's second abdication (June 22) arrived.

Return to Pizzo

HOPES OF ASYLUM

The king resisted the requests of old companions that he take command of troops in the area and march on Marseilles. Instead, he began looking for safe haven. On July 5 he sent an emissary to Fouché, the apparent head of the French government, asking if the Commission of Government could return the French properties he had surrendered when he became king of Naples (1808). (Fouché might have done even more, but his own power was short-lived.) A plea for asylum in Austria was sent to Metternich. Passports to England were requested—from Wellington by an agent, from Castlereagh by message. Word was sent to Louis XVIII begging that he generously allow "Prince Joachim Murat" to retire in France. Getting no response to any of these tentatives, the king in mid-July sent General Rossetti to Lord Exmouth, whose fleet had put into Marseilles, to request transportation to England, but terms could not be agreed upon. Finally Murat's *valet-de-chambre* returned from a secret mission with the informal assurance that the Austrian emperor would give the king refuge—if he abdicated and took a modest title.

Before anything could be arranged, however, revenge-bent royalists put Murat's life in danger. He fled from Allemand's villa to another closer to Antibes, where he arranged to take ship for Le Havre. There he hoped to buy a passport to England by ordering Gaeta to surrender. (The fortress still held out.) At the last moment, however, the commandant of Toulon refused to allow him to depart, and the ship sailed with part of the king's staff, his baggage, and money, but not the king. To make matters worse he was outlawed, with a price of 24,000 francs on his head. For days he hid in the forests, sleeping in the open when some Bonapartist peasant would not give him a bed.

Then luckily he made contact with a group of men, including two young naval officers, who had determined to escape to Corsica. On August 23 they set out in a leaky little sailboat, and by prearrangement transferred at sea to the post boat for Corsica, although they came near sinking in high seas before they were picked up. On August 25 Murat landed at Bastia and pushed on to Vescovato, where he presented himself at the home of his former subordinate and good friend General Franceschetti.

ON CORSICA

Murat's next move smacked either of insanity, the most incredible bad judgment, or a determination to commit suicide. As Napoleon later observed, after having lost Naples while leading eighty thousand men, Murat decided to recover it with two hundred.

Corsicans were divided in their sentiments, but Bonapartists were in the majority, vocal, and savagely committed. Franceschetti and Murat put together a small expedition, paraded to Ajaccio, where the people cheered wildly, the civic guard turned out to render salute, and the Bourbon officials went into hiding. Murat, however, was interested only in debarking for Naples: "I can no longer live except among my people . . . Naples! . . . Naples!" Preparations for departure went forward; meanwhile, some of the king's men had changes of heart and disappeared, but ships could not be found for all of the remainder. In the end Murat's expedition had dropped from over six hundred to less than three hundred.

Just when almost all was in readiness, agents delivered to the king a letter from Metternich offering asylum in the Austrian empire, a passport, and an offer of safe passage to Trieste aboard a British ship which appeared in the harbor. He took the passport, perhaps planning to use it as a last resort, but refused to board the British ship. Instead, on September 28, he embarked with his little expedition for Naples, specifically Salerno, near the capital.

PIZZO

Murat's fleet comprised five Corsican "gondolas"—seaworthy but shallow draft—and one felucca—larger but also shallow, fitted out as a gunboat. The ships rose and fell with every ripple, prostrating half the men with seasickness within a few miles of the docks. At sea violent storms tossed them about, waves washed part of their food and water overboard, and finally, three of the gondolas became separated from the felucca (the king's flagship) and could not be located. Murat's captain asked to land at Pizzo, on the Calabrian coast, to pick up food and water before searching further. Murat not only consented, but decided to rally his people at Pizzo—one place was as good as another!

On Sunday morning, October 8, 1815, Murat stalked into the town square of Pizzo followed by Franceschetti and about thirty others. Sonorously, he announced himself to the few people abroad in the sleepy village. They knew him; he had been there in 1810, and arrayed in cavalry uniform, yellow boots, cape, and plumed cap, he was easily recognizable. But his former subjects seemed merely embarrassed, or frightened, and hung back, gawking. He approached a small group of coast guard soldiers parading in the square, and tried to inspect them—they ran. The crowd, meanwhile, had grown larger, found its voice, and become menacing.

Murat decided his chances were better in Monteleone, a few miles up the coast, and marched off. Behind him in Pizzo, however, the agent of police, Trentacapilli, two of whose brothers, both guerrillas, had been killed by Murat's troops, organized a small party, caught up with the king, and demanded his surrender. Murat made a half-hearted attempt to convince the policeman that he was traveling to Trieste, and produced his Austrian passport, but Trentacapilli insisted that he was under arrest. While they argued, more villagers came up, jeering and threatening. Seeing a chance, Murat and his party ran for the beach, only to find that their ships were a mile off shore. Pursued, they turned and tried to fight, but were overwhelmed; two men were killed, Franceschetti wounded. Murat was rolled in the sand, stripped of his clothes and valuables, and might have been killed had not the intendant of the largest local landowner, the duke d'Infantado, appeared and overawed the crowd. Trentacapilli shamefacedly marched the king off to prison in the castle at Pizzo.

King Ferdinand, at Naples, was notified by semaphore telegraph of the happenings at Pizzo. He ordered that a council of war try Murat and that its sentence be carried out within fifteen minutes after delivery. On the morning of October 13 the council, including several officers who had served Murat, convened. Its decision was foregone: The "French General" was declared a public enemy and sentenced to be shot. At 6:00 P.M. the sentence was carried out in the cramped courtyard of the castle.

Murat died like the soldier that he was. He declined to sit in a chair or allow himself to be blindfolded, and gave the commands to the firing squad himself. Vain to the end, he paused after the preliminary commands to motion to the soldiers to lower the muzzles of their muskets. "Shoot for the heart, spare the face," he said, then "Fire!"

At the time few mourned him. The Paris press wrote him off as a "turncoat" and "burlesque imitation" of a king. Napoleon said he had behaved like a fool and deserved what he got. Caroline was deep in an affair with the Neapolitan General Francesco Macdonald, whom she married within a year. Italians, engaged with their ancient enemies, hunger and poverty, barely raised their heads. But in later years they would erect monuments to Murat—the first ruler to strike a blow for Italian unification and independence—in Rome, Naples, . . . and in Pizzo and a hundred other places. Strangest of all, they would mark the path of his army to Tolentino with plaques and statues.

"*Povero fenno, povero fenno,*" Murat mused before his death, reverting to the Gascon dialect of his boyhood, remembering the dire predictions of his mother. "A poor head," Napoleon had said of him, but a sure instinct led him to Pizzo. "At least I shall die a King," he had told Franceschetti in Corsica. He was finished, so was his century, so was the Age of Glory and of the Gascon. Murat could have ridden with the lusty red-beard Henry IV, in the sixteenth century, as easily as he served Napoleon. But he did not belong to the nineteenth century, with its dreary parliamentary debates, industrialization, stagy immitations of the Great Revolution, and weapons that smashed the cavalry charge. It took a naïve soldier to fight for Italian independence in 1815; nineteenth-century men were needed to finish the job. The last of the satellite kings would be better remembered because, at the end, Murat behaved like a Gascon.

Organiser *est un mot de l'Empire.*
—BALZAC

chapter eleven
CONCLUSIONS

*A*fter many decades of controversy, scholars seem agreed that Napoleon had no fixed, unchanging, master plan for Europe. Georges Lefebvre saw him as a "man of the eighteenth century" possessed with a passion for rational organization and efficiency, who tightened and extended his control continually until his commitments exceeded his power.[1] André Fugier sees him as a creature of expedients (. . . *il garda l'esprit dégagé* . . .) whose design was a product of accumulating day-to-day decisions.[2] The history of the satellite kingdoms confirms that Napoleon progressively centralized control of his empire until he seemed bent on founding a European government in which national states had no part.

As First Consul Napoleon more than achieved the goals of the defunct Directory—a France of "natural frontiers" (the Rhine, the Jura, the Alps, and the Pyrenees) flanked by "sister republics."[3] His system might die with him, however, and the republics were too independent for his taste—even Italy, where he was president. To insure the perpetuation of his government, he made himself hereditary emperor, with the right to adopt heirs. He tightened his system by annexing the Ligurian Republic (Genoa) to France and converting the Italian and Batavian (Dutch) Re-

1. Georges Lefebvre, *Napoleon* (4th ed.; Paris: 1954), p. 66 and *passim*.
2. André Fugier, *Napoléon et l'Italie* (Paris: 1947), p. 332. Excellent summaries of the older theses on the Grand Design may be found in Pieter Geyl, *Napoleon, For and Against* (paperback ed.; New Haven: 1963).
3. He did not restore the short-lived Roman and Parthenopean (Neapolitan) Republics, but with the annexation of Piedmont (1802), France extended beyond the Alps.

publics into kingdoms, then expanded it to include Naples, West-phalia, and Spain.

His royal relatives were expected to provide adoptive heirs of suitable rank and serve as obedient viceroys and faithful allies. By 1810, however, Napoleon was convinced that he could father his own heir,[4] and had found a new bride. Moreover, clan loyalty and self-interest had not, as expected, kept the satellite rulers properly submissive. Murat and Louis had become nationalists; Jérôme, though guardedly, pled for his people; Joseph ignored the war that sapped the empire's strength to play the king and involve himself prematurely in progressive endeavors. Further, the national spirit developing in Italy and Westphalia, recovering in Naples and Holland, and evident in Spain among *afrancesados* as well as rebels, portended ill for the future. It seemed desirable to check its growth by fragmenting the kingdoms into French departments and/or military governments, as the situation dictated, centering all control in Paris and teaching the people loyalty to the empire.

During 1810 Holland was annexed to France, as was a fifth of Westphalia (most of Hanover and part of her original territories). Marshal Davout flaunted Jérôme's authority in what remained of his kingdom. The French garrison in Naples was strengthened, and Murat was systematically humiliated. Three-quarters of Spain was removed from Joseph's control and placed under French military governors, and the annexation of northern Spain was threatened. Napoleon seemed bent on forcing all three remaining kings to abdicate or on removing them.[5] As for Italy, Eugène's viceroyalty was ordered terminated twenty years after the anticipated birth of Napoleon's son. Already designated the "king of Rome," he would inherit the crowns of both the empire

4. As noted earlier, he had sired three illegitimate children. The last, born in 1809 to the Countess Walewska, he could be certain was his—and it was a boy.

5. As we know, "disciplinary" pressure on Jérôme continued into 1811, and on Murat until 1812. Joseph's authority was not restored until March 1812. Meanwhile in January 1812, the valley of the Aran, in northern Catalonia, was added to the French department of Haute Garonne and the rest of Catalonia divided into four departments for administration by French "intendants." La Forest was told to explain to Joseph that Catalonia was *not* annexed to France, however. *See* the *Correspondance du comte de la Forest,* 7 v. Edited by Geoffroy de Grandmaison. (Paris: 1905–1913), VI, 80 and footnote.

and Italy.[6] France meanwhile had been extended onto the Italian peninsula to include Rome (the "second city" of the empire), and into the Balkans (the Illyrian Provinces), and had absorbed the Hanse cities on the North Sea and western Baltic.[7] The empire seemed destined to become a highly centralized European state, a new "Roman Empire," governed from Paris, and ceremonially, Rome.[8]

NAPOLEON AND THE RULERS

To Napoleon, doing one's duty to France and to a subject state were the same thing. No empire; no kingdoms. At base, the states existed (and had been granted their constitutions) by right of conquest. Naturally the emperor responded with fury when his policies were questioned. Eugène, and to slightly lesser degree, Jérôme, understood his attitude. Louis, Joseph, and Murat accepted his basic proposition intellectually, as they told the emperor *ad nauseam* in their correspondence, but not emotionally. When it came down to cases, they resisted (as best they could) sacrificing national interests for the sake of the empire.

Arguments as to whether Napoleon or his rulers were "right" seem fruitless. The answer depends on one's viewpoint. If one accepts that the perpetuation of the empire was necessary and good, and that the emperor, even if not always right, had to be obeyed to maintain the discipline necessary for survival, then all Napoleon did was justified. If one takes a national viewpoint, then one can sympathize with Louis's view of the Continental System, Murat's outrage at having his invasion of Sicily sabotaged, or Joseph's complaint that the Spanish would never trust him if he were forced to violate his constitution.

6. Unless a second son were born, in which case he would assume the Italian crown, probably in title only. Eugène was compensated with the Grand Duchy of Frankfurt, and promised a principality in France. *See* the *Correspondance de Napoleon Ier*, 32 v. (Paris: 1858–1870), XX, pp. 84–85, 249–250.

7. Imperial fiefs dotted the states beyond, e.g., Berg, Frankfurt, and Erfurt in Germany, Neuchâtel in Switzerland, Ponte Corvo and Benevento in Naples, and Albufera in Spain. Elisa Bonaparte and her husband Prince Bacciocchi governed Piombino and Lucca (outside France) and Tuscany (part of France). The Grand Duchy of Warsaw, governed by the king of Saxony, remained at Napoleon's disposal.

8. *See* J.-Edouard Driault, *Napoléon en Italie* (Paris: 1906), pp. 676–677. He seems overenthusiastic over the "Roman" aspect of the empire, however.

To say that a ruler was more liberal or humane than Napoleon raises questions: Were imperial or national goals more worthy? Did the ends (in either case) justify the means? Would the emperor's (hopefully) short-term cruelties have brought Europe greater benefits than the rulers' more humane efforts? Was there any difference between Napoleon's liberalism and that of the rulers, or is it only that the latter disagreed as to implementation? Overall, would Europeans generally have had more liberty, equality, and prosperity (not to speak of unity and power) if they had sacrificed temporarily to allow Napoleon to achieve his vaunted "general peace?" Was the preservation of European national states and the production of new ones in the nineteenth century (which the success of Napoleon might have prevented) "good" or "bad"?

Napoleon, after all, wanted the Spanish rebellion ruthlessly crushed so that Spain, under an efficient, progressive government, could better serve both her people and the empire. ". . . I seized by the hair the chance fortune gave me to regenerate Spain . . ."[9] he said, and doubtless meant it. The Dutch sustained heavy casualties in an economic war, which, if won, would have netted them great benefits. (We shall not attempt to judge whether it *could* have been won.) Who was more humane? Napoleon, or Joseph and Louis?

The emperor granted (even helped to write) constitutions which called for representative bodies, then discouraged their use for fear of weakening the kingdoms and the empire. In installing the *Code Napoléon,* however, Joseph, Louis, and Murat all proved less zealous than the emperor. In Spain it was applied only in the military governments;[10] in Holland only after annexation to France; in Naples never, in its true spirit (though nominally in force after January 1, 1809). Though Napoleon tailored his policies to local conditions,[11] he was generally more forceful about

9. Emmanuel de Las Cases, *Mémorial de Saint Hélène,* 8 v. (Paris: 1823–1824), IV, 287.

10. And that part of Catalonia attached to the French department of Haute Garonne in 1812. See footnote 7.

11. In Germany, for example, he catered to the nobles, since they still had the loyalty of most of the peasants. In return for stomaching the abolition of feudalism they got priority for civil and military posts.

promoting social revolution than his rulers, surrounded as they were by members of the old ruling classes. And as Franklin Ford noted in discussing the period: "The most important change of all occurred in the social structure, and equally important, in the way men conceived the social structure."[12] Who was more liberal— Napoleon or the rulers?

Why discuss the relative merits of Napoleon and his rulers, one might ask. Were not all their governments "illegal"? But where does legality begin? Unhappily history answers: "Usually in force; popular consent comes afterward, often long afterward." Setting aside the question, the basic issues between Napoleon and his rulers are ageless. How much force is justified to make men "free"? Who is to decide whether they are free? At what governmental level are decisions to be made? If the people are to consent, how? What is the unit of popular consent? Where does enlightened authority end and tyranny begin? The answers depend on one's political faith.

Liberals in the satellites answered the questions we have posed differently. Liberal nationalists were divided for or against Bona-partist rulers, most clearly in Spain, where they had to choose sides in the war, elsewhere less openly. At one extreme old Jacobins opposed any monarchy, at the other, wishful thinkers hoped to liberalize legitimate rulers when they returned. As time passed pan-Germanism and pan-Italianism caught the emotions of increasing numbers. Others were alienated by the suppression of representative bodies and the tightening of censorship. Finally, in the last years, when the rulers had to concentrate almost solely on raising troops and money, the defection of idealists accelerated. Napoleon, who had begun as a Jacobin, seemed to have moved through phases as "enlightened dictator" and "enlightened monarch" to tyrant. The defectors ignored, however, that the liberal schoolmaster of Europe was compelled to abandon teaching to restore order in his class. Enraged by the rejection of his "enlightenment," he was more determined than ever to apply Rousseau's dictum to force men "to be free"—in all of Europe. Napoleon wore the imperial purple, but he no more "betrayed the Revolu-

12. Franklin L. Ford, "The Revolutionary-Napoleonic Era: How Much of a Watershed?" *American Historical Review*, LXIX, No. 1 (October 1963), 24.

tion" than did Robespierre. Those who allege he did judge by the history of France, not Europe.[13] Ultimately the emperor had not enough force to "free" Europe, and its nations, including France, were cast back into the maw of the Old Regime.

EUROPE

For a time, however, there had been a Europe and Europeans. "Men of practical bent and modern outlook," says R. R. Palmer, "freed from both popular demands and old-noble pretensions . . . protected by armed force, until 1813 . . . worked together at the liquidation of the Old Regime."[14] Among them were men who suppressed their sense of nationality to labor for the empire—for Europe. Reinhard, born a German, trained in the French bureaucracy, served Napoleon in Switzerland, Moldavia, and elsewhere, but also, without losing pride in his origins, maintained a purely imperial outlook as French ambassador to Westphalia. The Piedmontese Prina managed the finances of Italy. The Corsican-French Ferri-Pisani worked in Naples and later Spain. Pierre-Louis Roederer, the model of Frenchman turned imperial civil servant, reformed the finances of Naples and administered the Grand Duchy of Berg. All saw themselves as functionaries of a European government, at home anywhere in Europe. They were Europeans the like of whom would not be seen for a century. Between their time and the 1920's nationalism drowned others of their ilk, and until after World War II muffled the voices of most who saw Europe whole.

"Men of practical bent . . ." says Professor Palmer. True. The intellectuals mostly lost faith in Napoleon. In the earlier stages of his career reformers and literary lights of all nationalities had seen him both as tamer and protector of the Revolution—Goethe and Müller, Bilderdijk, Monti and Cuoco, Llorente and Jovellanos—but sooner or later they were disillusioned. In the last days a few suddenly saw that their choice lay between Napoleon and the return of the Old Regime, and made a gesture. The aging Ugo

13. Jacques Godechot, for all the depth of his erudition, feels that France was not a center of "revolutionary impulsion" from 1797 until 1830. (*La Grande Nation*, 2 v. [Paris: 1956], II, 696.)

14. R. R. Palmer, *The Age of Democratic Revolution*, 2 v. (Princeton: 1959–1964), II, 571.

Foscolo, for example, insisted upon joining Eugène's army. Generally, though, the intelligentsia had defected to the schools which would stir the mentality of the nineteenth century—liberal nationalism or pan-nationalism, romanticism, and conservatism, and for a few leftist Jacobins, socialism. Napoleon had driven them away, but he had not intended to.

The emperor's vision was larger. He planned an empire of departments directed from Paris, but as the number of non-French departments increased, a multinational, multilingual European state would have surely emerged. What began as a French empire would have become Europe, integrated in every respect. There were tariff barriers between France and the kingdoms, for example, but there would have been none, ultimately, between France and her new departments. A "common market"? Why not? The empire, in time, would have been no more French than the Grande Armée of 1812, which, as we know, was two-thirds "foreign." In 1812 Napoleon saw himself fleetingly as leading Europe's legions against those of the Orient.[15] Romantic and farfetched? His defeat destroyed all semblance of European unity and left a power balance which Russia (or the Soviet Union) has played to her advantage ever since. At Saint Helena Napoleon predicted that Russia and the United States would become great powers.[16] He said nothing regarding a unification of Germany and little about Italian national possibilities—perhaps because he still saw Europe whole.

THE LEGACY OF THE KINGDOMS

In 1814 Ferdinand VII of Spain returned to resume his traditional powers, reject the Constitution of 1812, and viciously smash the Cádiz leaders who had written it—all with the backing of the peasant masses. Westphalians, though remarkably quiet during the last days of the kingdom, cheered the return of their legitimate princes. The Dutch welcomed back the scion of the House of

15. On Napoleon's fixation for the East, see Émile Bourgeois, *Manuel historique de politique étrangère*, 4 v. (Paris: 1893–1926), and F. Prat, *Napoleone e l'oriente* (Milan: 1945).
16. André Fugier, *La Révolution française et l'empire napoléonien;* vol. IV of *Histoire des relations internationales.* Ed. by Pierre Renouvin. (Paris: 1954), p. 404.

Orange. Italy stood by Eugène until Napoleon fell, but thereafter the Old Regime was restored with minimal difficulty. Neapolitans, listlessly supporting Murat, proved unequal to his "Crusade of 1815," and afterward bent their backs again to the Bourbons.

In the stillness that followed Napoleon's disappearance, the masses of Europe manifested little interest in anything but repose and the reconstruction of their private lives. But the peoples were not unlike graduates who say they "learned nothing in college," but whose every utterance reflects attitudes and ideas acquired there. They had been deeply affected by the years of the empire, and not least the peoples of the satellite kingdoms. It is not remarkable, for example, that the cycle of nineteenth-century Italian revolutions began in Naples in 1820, or that in 1830 the first German rulers to be overthrown (if temporarily) were those of Brunswick and Hesse-Cassel (formerly part of Westphalia) and Saxony (long under close imperial supervision).

"The peoples of Germany, those of France, of Italy, of Spain, want equality and value liberal ideas," wrote Napoleon to Jérôme.[17] What he meant was that they *would* want enlightenment once they tasted its benefits. Unhappily the bulk of the people, who everywhere were peasants, either refused to sample the proffered advantages (as in Spain) or saw immediate benefits outweighed by new burdens of taxation and conscription. In all the kingdoms, nevertheless, feudalism was abolished (technically even in Spain), and serfdom wherever it existed, and, except in Spain, the peasants knew enough to challenge any tampering with these basic reforms.

In all the kingdoms constitutions had been granted, if not strictly applied; Westphalians remembered that even peasants had sat in the *Ständeversammlung;* legislative power over taxation had been practiced (Holland, Westphalia, Italy) or promised (Spain and Naples). The *Code Napoléon* had either been applied or held up as a model; equality before the law had become an established principle; jury trial had been introduced; civil and religious liberty had been guaranteed, and minority groups elevated to full, active citizenship (notably the Jews of Holland and Germany). Guilds

17. *Correspondance de Napoléon Ier*, 32 v. (Paris: 1858–1870), XV, 166 (November 15, 1807).

and other economically privileged groups had been suppressed, and internal tariffs condemned if not abolished. The political and economic power of the churches had been reduced, and the confiscated properties of nobles and churches pledged (if not always devoted) to public welfare and education.

Most important, perhaps, the kingdoms left behind a coterie of trained personnel—bureaucrats, judges, magistrates, soldiers— who were familiar with the most efficient systems extant for the administration of government, finances, the law, and armies. Not until the return of the restored rulers (absent five to eighteen years) did these men fully realize how much their attitudes had changed, and how truly careers had been "open to talent." They, together with liberals and intellectuals, both former enemies and former friends of Napoleonic government, constituted the core leadership of revolutionary movements of the early nineteenth century.

The idea persists that the satellite kingdoms were "robbed" for the benefit of France. One envisions wagons rolling toward Paris with coin for the imperial treasury and revered works of art for the Louvre. To dismiss the latter quickly, many of the paintings and objects were legitimately purchased, and still belong to the French government.[18] As to treasure wagons, many rolled from France into Spain; few indeed came from the kingdoms to France. The states contributed largely by supporting French troops within their borders; much of the money they supplied was spent locally, either by army buyers or the troops themselves, to the benefit of native merchants and producers. Because of the cost of the Spanish War, the French taxpayer's burden was *increased* by the holding of the satellite kingdoms. Moreover, the tax rate in France was always higher than in the kingdoms, which added to the general

18. Admittedly, so do many "stolen" works, however. Louis XVIII did not want to offend the French public by returning them all, and the allies were sympathetic. The conquerors, moreover, could not agree on which works had been "legally" seized. The czar set a precedent by ignoring the whole problem and buying hundreds of confiscated paintings and objects, most of which are now in the Hermitage, at Leningrad. *See* Dorothy Mackay Quynn, "The Art Confiscations of the Napoleonic Wars," *American Historical Review*, L, No. 1 (April 1945), 437–460. See also Cecil Gould, *Trophy of Conquest* (London: 1965); and Ferdinand Boyer, "Les responsabilités de Napoléon dans le transfert à Paris des oeuvres d'art de l'étranger," *Revue d'Histoire Moderne et Contemporaine*, XI (Octobre–Décembre 1964), 241–262.

fear of annexation. Trade agreements favored France, and the Continental System caused distress, but native merchants managed to make immense profits anyway, especially in Italy and Naples. Further, despite economic dislocations, there were some permanent gains—new industry, new crops, and much technological improvement.[19] Everywhere, the value of broad tariff-free trading areas was demonstrated, positively on a small scale (Italy, Westphalia, Naples), and negatively on a larger one.

The kingdoms (and the empire generally) also set precedents in problem-solving by legislation (decreed or voted), by which the governments asserted the right, in principle, to rearrange any and all areas of national life. In the long run this legacy, valued property of all contemporary governments, whatever their political systems, would overshadow all others. Napoleon did not originate the process, nor was it a French innovation, though Louis XIV and the Committee of Public Safety had used it most masterfully, and the latter immensely widened its scope. Napoleon and his rulers, however, demonstrated it more fully in more areas than had anyone else before. Aside from constitutions and mandatory administrative, legal, and judicial reform programs, there were laws requiring smallpox inoculation and land redistribution, ordering the establishment of public schools and new industries, granting specific guarantees to minorities, and a hundred other things. Not all were implemented, but success was sufficient to orient progressives toward reform from seats-of-power. Napoleon's answer to all ills—legislate, administer, enforce—has been echoed ever more widely and loudly by every generation since his time.

THE KINGDOMS AND THE FALL OF NAPOLEON

Explanations for Napoleon's fall are legion, and few are without some validity. Most emphasize some factor such as the impact of the Continental System on Russia, Austria's periodic diplomatic humiliations, or the exclusion of Prussia from Germany, which drove her into Austria's arms, all with the sustained opposition of Great Britain in the background. Some prefer to believe that Napoleon, driven by an insatiable will-to-power, ultimately provoked

19. To cite one of the newer books, *see* Rudolph Strauss, *Die Lage und die Bewegung der Chemnitzer Arbeiter in der ersten Hälfte des 19. Jahrhunderts* (Berlin: 1960), p. 8 and *passim*.

overwhelming opposition—from legitimate rulers, the Church
(both as religious force and power structure) and Christians generally, from liberals and conservatives, from nationalities, and the
uniformly oppressed peoples of Europe.[20] Whatever the attitudes
of rulers, diplomats, churchmen, and leaders of all political factions, however, peasant masses formed the armies which defeated
the emperor of the French. Why did they fight? Whether their
authors choose to recognize it or not, the evidence supporting all
theses reveals that the peoples were nonrationally, or emotionally,
motivated. They fought primarily neither because of the disadvantages of French government, nor to alleviate their suffering,
nor for concrete advantages expected from national independence
and/or unification. They fought for their ancient states or nations,
hereditary rulers, and established churches. They responded to
the call of tradition and conscience, or acted out of habit.
(Whether this was good or bad, right or wrong is not in question
here.)[21] During the "War of Liberation" in Germany, the illusion
of a vast popular uprising against the French was given by the
progressive defection of the princes (followed by their dutiful subjects) to the allies. Pan-German and liberal propaganda surely
contributed to the pervading spirit, but it incited to action only the
intellectuals and a few leaders (like Vom Stein's group), who generally favored restoring the major princes, reforming their governments, and linking them in loose confederation. In Westphalia
there was little movement until the old princes returned to point
the way. In Spain, the rebels, under noble and clerical leadership,
had fought desperately for Crown and Church, ignoring the aspira-
tions of the Cádiz liberals. East of the Niemen, the masses had
risen to defend "Mother Russia" and the monarchy. The nationalism of the peasants of Austria and Prussia was almost as
anachronistic. None could have produced arguments for sustaining

20. If one ignores or discounts Napoleon's worthy objectives, he fits beautifully
into Canetti's picture of the ruler as "survivor," i.e., one whose sense of power
requires that not only his enemies but his supporters die, in the last extremity *all*
of them. *See* Elias Canetti, *Crowds and Power.* Tr. by Carol Stewart (New York:
1962), pp. 231–234.)
21. I acknowledge my debt, which is obvious, to the scholarly anti-intellectuals,
of whom Professor Crane Brinton of Harvard is the chief exponent among historians. *See* his *Ideas and Men* (Englewood Cliffs, N.J.: 1950), pp. 503–526, and
the interpretive sections of *The Jacobins* (New York: 1930) and *A Decade of
Revolution* (New York: 1934).

or restoring the Old Regime. They did what they *felt* was "right." In Italy and Naples, despite widespread enthusiasm among native leaders for liberalism and pan-Italianism, the common man, reverting to traditional attitudes still common among Italians,[22] displayed a practiced indifference which allowed the restoration of the Old Regime.

One cannot view Murat's defection as an important factor in wrecking the empire; Italy and Westphalia both sacrificed heavily to sustain it. Only in Spain did developments contribute markedly to Napoleon's downfall. "C'est ce qui m'a perdu," he said at Saint Helena.[23] Clearly the immense cost of the Spanish venture in lives, money, and matériel had greatly weakened the empire before the Russian campaign began. If nothing else, as we know, 300,000 French troops were engaged in the peninsula in 1812, over 200,000 in 1813. One might argue that, considering Russian strategy, they would not have helped Napoleon in 1812, but later, surely, their presence in Germany could have been decisive.

In Spain, moreover, we have the prime example of a people moved by anachronistic nationalism. Unless one wishes to defend an Old Regime of the most medieval character extant (à la Henry Adams), or argue that Spanish self-determination on any terms was better than what Napoleon offered, then they were acting against their own interests. Nevertheless in five years of war (with British aid) they took 300,000 French casualties, cost France a billion francs in specie and probably an additional three billion otherwise, damaged the prestige of French arms and the morale of French soldiery, and inspired other Europeans to resist.

The Spanish war debilitated the empire as did nothing else, and Joseph, in command of French forces at critical times, bears heavy responsibility for its continuance and the eventual loss of Spain. Napoleon's success in 1808–1809 seems to show that Spain could have been conquered if the French armies had been properly

22. Says Luigi Barzini, Jr.: "The tenacity and eagerness with which the individual pursues his private interests and defends himself against society, his mistrust of noble ideals and motives, the splendid show, the all-pervading indulgence for man's foibles make Italian life pleasant and bearable in spite of poverty, tyranny, and injustice. They also waste the efforts and the sacrifices of the best Italians and make poverty, tyranny, and injustice very difficult to defeat." (*The Italians* [New York: 1964], p. 376.)

23. Las Cases, *Mémorial,* IV, 285.

directed. Joseph's good intentions, liberalism, personal magnetism, and—yes—goodness arc not in question. He loved his people, forgave their rebellion, betrayals, and insults, wept for them, and labored for their welfare. But he lost the war. He was not of the stuff of warrior-kings; he was not a Napoleon. Can we blame him for that? No. We do not. We simply say he lost Spain.

Moreover, Napoleon, ultimately, must be held accountable for the disaster. Aware of Joseph's military incapacity, surely after 1809, he would neither give anyone else overall command in Spain, or come there again himself. Instead he tried to direct the war from Paris, and matters went badly (though largely because the marshals would not cooperate in his absence). In 1810 or 1811 his presence might have spelled victory in Spain. But in 1810 he was busy reorganizing the empire for the benefit of his anticipated son, and so happy with his new bride that he could not bear to leave her. (Genius can ill afford happiness.) In 1811 he was preparing for war on Russia, which, tragically, he considered more important than completing he conquest of the peninsula. In 1812, fearing to trust anyone else, he again gave Joseph the army of Spain. The results were catastrophic, and probably could have been otherwise if Joseph had simply obeyed Napoleon's orders. In the final analysis, however, Napoleon was responsible.

AND FINALLY

For all their conflicts, Joseph never ceased to defend Napoleon. "The war, prolonged by the enemies of France, forced extreme measures," he wrote testily in 1833 to madame de Saint-Ouen, whose book on the empire offended him. The emperor had defended the people of Europe against the "oligarchy," as they now knew, because ". . . the masses, who judge only by instinct . . . sense truth and justice. . . ."[24] Perhaps not, but Napoleon still holds the fascination of men a century and a half after his fall. He was much more than a conquerer.

The emperor's satellite rulers, except for Eugène given derisive treatment by the architects of the Napoleonic legend, still get

24. Joseph Bonaparte, *Lettres d'exil inédites (Amérique—Angleterre—Italie), 1825–1844.* Ed. by Hector Fleischmann. (Paris: 1912), pp. 196–197.

short shrift in the histories of the era. Yet they were all extraordinary men, who, each in his own way, tried to serve his people. Louis was remembered with affection and Eugène with respect from the time of their departure. Jérôme's scandalous reputation has endured to this day, though it was temporarily eclipsed by the behavior of the restored duke of Brunswick and elector of Hesse. Nevertheless his government's constructive work was admitted, if grudgingly, even by the nationalistic German historians of the nineteenth century, and more fully by later ones.[25] Murat's disastrous campaign of 1815 netted him a place in the pantheon of Italian unification.[26] Joseph, wrote the former rebel Toreño, ". . . would have captivated the Spanish if they had not already been so gravely wounded as to honor and pride," and gave him credit for his progressive efforts.[27] The more reputable Spanish historians have consistently elaborated on this theme. In all the former kingdoms some nostalgia was generated for the Napoleonic regimes, the more where the restored rulers were arbitrary and oppressive, as in Spain. When Joseph died, in 1844, men who had earlier been his bitterest enemies, including former guerrilla chiefs, sent their respects.

In a sense, Murat's fate was symbolic of that of the empire—a tragic reward for attempting too much, if heroically. Why did it have to be so? No answer we can support with evidence is satisfactory, for the deep causes of history, the forces that move the players and shape the stage, remain hidden. The philosophers of the craft may guess at them, but we might be wiser to say with Homer:[28]

. . . many a strong soul went down to Hades, and left the heroes themselves prey to dogs and carrion birds, while the will of the gods marched on to fulfillment.

25. *See* Rudolf Göcke und Theodor Ilgen, *Das Königreich Westfalen* (Düsseldorf: 1888), p. 272; Arthur Kleinschmidt, *Geschichte des Königreichs Westfalen* (Gotha: 1893), pp. 142–154 and *passim;* and Friedrich Meinecke, *Das Zeitalter des deutschen Erhebung* (Göttingen: 1957), p. 62 and *passim.*
26. *See* especially the documents and commentary of M.-H. Weil, *Joachim Murat, roi de Naples,* 5 v. (Paris: 1909–1910), V, 584 and *passim.*
27. José-Maria, Conde Toreño, *Histoire du soulèvement de la guerre et de la révolution d'Espagne,* 4 v. (Paris: 1835–1836), I, 357.
28. From the first lines of the *Iliad.*

SELECT BIBLIOGRAPHY

Documents (Napoleon)

Bertrand, Général, *Cahiers de Sainte-Hélène, 1815–1819*, 2 v. Ed. by Paul Fleuriot de Langle (1949–1959).

Bonaparte, Napoléon, *Correspondance de Napoléon Ier; publiée par ordre de l'empereur Napoléon III*, 32 v. (1858–1870). *Supplément*. Ed. by A. du Casse (1887).

————, *Correspondance inédite de Napoléon Ier, conservée aux Archives de la Guerre*, 5 v. Ed. by E. Picard and L. Tuetey (1912–1925).

————, *Dernières lettres inédites de Napoléon Ier*, 2 v. Ed. by Léonce Brotonne (1903).

————, *Inédites Napoléoniens*. Ed. by A. Chuquet (1913).

————, *Lettres de Napoléon à Joséphine*, 2 v. Ed. by Mme. de Faverolles (1833).

————, *Lettres de Napoléon à Joséphine et lettres de Joséphine à Napoléon* (1959).

————, *Lettres de Napoléon Ier à Marie-Louise écrites de 1810 à 1814* (1960).

————, *Lettres inédites de Napoléon Ier*, 2 v. Ed. by L. Lecestre (1897).

————, *Lettres inédites de Napoléon Ier*. Ed. by L. de Brotonne (1898).

————, *Mémoires pour servir à l'Histoire de France sous Napoléon, écrits a Sainte-Hélène, sous la dictée de l'Empereur, par les généraux qui ont partagé sa captivité et publiés sur les manuscrits entièrement corrigés de sa main*, 9 v. (1829–1830).

————, *Memoirs*: dictated by the Emperor at St. Helena to the generals who shared his captivity. Edited by Somerset de Chair with a preface by Michael Foot (1986).

————, *Ordres et apostilles de Napoléon (1799–1815)*, 4 v. Ed. by A. Chuquet (1911–1912).

————, *Oeurves littéraires et écrits militaires*. 3 v. Ed. Jean Tulard (1969).

————, *Proclamations, ordres du jour et bulletins de la Grande Armée*. Ed. by Jean Tulard (1964).

————, Lettres, decisions et actes de Napoléon à Pont de Briques et au Camp de Boulogne, An VI/1798-An XII/1804. Ed. F. Beaucour (1979–1984).

Bourdon, Jean, *Napoléon au Conseil d'Etat, notes et procès-verbaux inédits de Jean-Guillaume Locré* (1963).

Gourgaud, Gaspard, Baron, *Sainte-Hélène: journal inédit*. 2 v. Ed. by E. H. de Grouchy and A. Guillois (1899).

Las Casas, Emmanuel, *Mémorial de Sainte-Hélène*. 8 v. (1823–1824).

Montholon, C.-J.-T. de, *Récits de la captivité de l'Empereur Napoléon*. 2 v. (1847). First pub. in London as *History of the Captivity of Napoleon at Saint Helena* (1846).

O'Meara, B. E., *Napoleon in Exile*, 2 v. (1822).

Warden, W., *Letters Written on Board His Majesty's Ship The Northumberland, and at Saint Helena (1816)*.

Documents, General

Bonaparte, Lucien, *Mémoires* (1818).

Bourrienne, Louis A., *Mémoires de M. de Bourrienne, Ministre d'Etat, sur Napoléon, le Directoire, le Consulat, l'Empire et la Restauration*, 10 v. (1830).

Broglie, A. Ch. L. V., Duc de, *Personal Relations 1785–1820*, 2 v. (1887).

Buonaparte, Letizia, *Lettere di . . .* [in Italian] Ed. by Piero Mosciatelli (1936).

Carnot, Lazare, *Correspondance général de Carnot*, 4 v. (1892–1907).

Caulaincourt, A.-A.-L. de, *Mémoires*, 3 v. Ed. J. Hanoteau (1933).

———, *Mémoires: la campagne de Russie, l'agonie de Fontainebleau*. Ed. by André Castelot. (1986).

Chaboulon, Fleury de, *Mémoires de Fleury de Chaboulon, ex-secrétaire de l'Empereur Napoléon et de son cabinet*, 3 v. (1901).

Chateaubriand, François A. R., *De Bonaparte et des Bourbons, et de la necessité de se raillier à nos princes légitimes pour le bonheur de la France et celui de l'Europe* (1814).

Chaulanges, M., Maury, A. G., and Sèves, R., *Textes historiques, l'époque de la Révolution, 1789–1799*, ID., *L'époque impériale, 1800–1815*, 2 v. (1960).

Damas, R. de, *Mémoires*, 2 v. (1912–1914).

Dumas, Mathieu, Comte, *Précis des événements militaires . . . sur les campagnes de 1799 à 1814*, 19 v. (1817–1826).

———, *Souvenirs du Lieutenant Général Comte Mathieu Dumas, de 1770 à 1836 . . .*, 3v. (1839).

Durand, Mme, *Mémoires sur Napoléon, l'Impératrice Marie Louise et la cour des Tuileries* (1828).

Fain, Baron, *Mémoires du baron Fain, premier secrétaire du Cabinet de l'Empereur* (1808).

Fouché, J., *Mémoires de J. Fouché, Duc d'Otrante, ministre de la Police générale*, 2 v. (1824).

Gentz, Friedrich von, *Tägebucher, 1800–1828* (1861).

Grouchy, Emmanuel, Marquis de, *Mémoires du Maréchal de Grouchy*, 5 v. (1873–1874).

Hauterive, Ernest d', *La police secrète du premier empire: bulletins quotidiens adressés par Fouché à l'Empereur, 1808–1809* (1963).

Hugo, Joseph Léopold Sigebert Cte, *Le Général Hugo, 1773–1828, lettres et documents inédits* (1926).

————, *Mémoires de Général Hugo*, 3 v. (1823).

Iung (or Jung), Théodore, *Lucien Bonaparte et ses mémoires, 1775–1840*, 3 v. (1882–1883).

Jaucourt, Comte de, *Correspondance du Comte de Jaucourt, ministre des affaires etrangères, avec le prince de Talleyrand pendant le Congrès de Vienne* (1905).

Junot, Laure, Duchesse d'Abrantès, *Mémoires*, 2 v. (1934).

Laplace, Mme de, *Lettres a Elisa Napoléon, princesse de Lucques et de Piombino, réunies et annotés par Paul Marmottan* (1897).

Maistre, Joseph de, *Mémoires* (1863).

Maret, Hugues Bernard, Duc de Bassano, *Souvenirs intimes de la Révolution et de l'Empire*. Ed. by C. de Sor (1843).

Masséna, André, Prince D'Essling, *Mémoires de Masséna*, 7 v. (1848–1850).

Méneval, Claude-François de, Baron, *Mémoires pour servir à l'histoire de Napoléon Ier . . . 1802 . . . 1815*, 3 v. (1894).

Metternich-Winneburg, Clemens Lothar Wenzel, Fürst von, *Aus Metternich's nachgelassenen Papieren*, 8 v. Ed. by Prince Richard Metternich (1880–1884).

Mollien, François N., *Mémoires d'un ministre de trésor public, 1780–1815*, 3 v. (1845). New ed. (1898).

Ney, Michel, Duc d'Elchingen, Prince de la Moskowa, *Mémoires*, 2 v. (1883).

Österreich, Karl von, *Ausgewählte Schriften*. Ed. by F. von Malcher (1893).

Rémusat, Claire E.-J.-G. de Vergennes, comtesse de, *Mémoires, 1802–1808*, 3 v. (1870–1880).

Savary, Anne-Jean-Marie-René, *Mémoires du Duc de Rovigo, pour servir à l'histoire de l'Empereur Napoléon*, 8 v. (1829).

Ségur, Philippe P., Comte de, *Histoire et Mémoires*, 7 v. (1873).

Stein, Freiherr vom, *Briefe und amtliche Schriften*, 3 v. in 4 (1957–1961).

————, *Reden und Aufsätze* (1961).

Talleyrand-Périgord, Charles Maurice de, Prince de Benevent, *Correspondance inédite du Prince de Talleyrand, et du roi Louis XVIII . . . 1814–1815* (1881).

————, *Lettres inédites à Napoléon, 1800–1809* (1889).

————, *Memoirs of the Prince de Talleyrand*, 5 v. (1891).

Thibaudeau, Antoine Claire, Comte, *Mémoires . . . 1799–1815* (1913).

Thiébault, Paul Charles, *Mémoires du général baron Thiébault, 1792–1820*. Ed. by Robert Lacour-Gayet (1962).

Wellington, Arthur, *The Dispatches of Field Marshal the Duke of Wellington*, 12 v. Ed. by Lt. Col. Gurwood (1834–1838).

Napoleon and His Era

Andreas, Willy, *Napoleon* (1962).

Aubrey, O., *Sainte-Hélène*, 2 v. (1935).

Aziz, Philippe, *L'Europe sous la botte francaise* (1983).

Bainville, Jacques, *Napoléon*. New ed. (1962).

Bertaud, Jean Paul, *La France de Napoléon*, 1799–1815 (1987).

Bignon, Baron, *Histoire de France sous Napoléon*, 12 v. (1838).

Biver, Comtesse Marie-Louise, *Le Paris de Napoléon* (1963).

Bouhler, Philipp, *Napoleon, Kometenbahn eines genies* (1942).

Brunn, Geoffrey, *Europe and the French Imperium*. PB Ed. (1963).

Chandler, David, *Waterloo: The Hundred Days* (1980).

Christophe, Robert, *Napoléon, empereur de l'Ile d'Elbe* (1959). Tr. as *Napoleon on Elba* (1963).

Connelly, Owen, *The Epoch of Napoleon* (1972 & 1978).

Cooper, Leonard, *The Age of Wellington* (1964).

Cubberly, R. E., *The Role of Fouché during the Hundred Days*. (1969).

Driault, E., *La vraie figure de Napoléon*, 3 v. (1928–1930).

Duhamel, Jean, *Les cinquante jours de Waterloo à Plymouth* (1963).

Dunan, Marcel, ed., *Napoléon et l'Europe* (1961).

Fisher, H. A. L., *Napoleon* (1912).

Fugier, André, *La révolution française et l'empire napoléonienne*, v. IV of *Histoire des relations internationales*. Ed. by Pierre Renouvin (1954).

Ganière, Paul, *Napoléon à Sainte-Hélène; La lutte contre Hudson Lowe* (1960).

Godlewski, G., *Trois cents jours d'exil: Napoléon à l'Ile d'Elbe* (1961).

Göhring, Martin, *Napoléon, von alten zum neuen Europa* (1959).

Groen, J. J., *La dernière maladie et la cause de mort de Napoléon* (196_).

Guerrini, Maurice, *Napoléon devant Dieu, profil réligieux de l'empereur* (1960).

Guillemin, Henri, *Madame de Staël, Benjamin Constant et Napoléon* (1959).

Hales, E. E. Y., *Napoleon and the Pope* (1962).

Holtman, Robert B., *The Napoleonic Revolution* (1967).

Horne, Alistair, *Napoleon, Master of Europe, 1805–1807* (1979).

Hubert, Emmanuelle, *Les cent jours* (1966).

Kircheisen, Friedrich M., *Napoleon I, sein Leben und seine Z· 't*, 9 v. (1911–1934).

Lachouque, Henri, *Napoléon en 1814* (1959).

Lefebvre, Georges, *Napoléon*. 4th ed. (1953).

Lovie, J., and Palluel, A., *L'Episode Napoléonien: Aspects Extérieurs* (1972).

MacKenzie, Norman, *Escape from Elba: The Fall and Flight of Napoleon, 1814–1815* (1985).

Madelin, Louis, *Le consulat et l'empire*, 16 v. (1937–1954); 2 v. cd. (1932–1934).

Manfred, Albert Zakharovich. *Napoléon Bonaparte*. Trans. (Russian to French) by Patricia Champie et Genevieve Dupond (1980).

Markham, Felix M., *Napoleon* (1963).

Markov, Walter M., *Die Napoleonzeit: Geschichte und Kultur des Grand Empire*. (1985).

Martineau, Gilbert, *Le roi de Rome* (1982).

Masson, Frédéric, *Napoléon et sa famille*, 13 v. (1900–1919).

———, *Napoléon à Sainte-Hélène* (1912).

Melchior-Bonnet, Bernardine, *La conspiration du général Malet* (1963).

Mistler, Jean (ed.), *Napoléon et l'Empire*, 2 v. (1968).

Ollivier, Albert, *Le dix-huit Brumaire* (1959).

Oman, C., *Britain Against Napoleon* (1942).

Palmer, R. R., *The Age of Democratic Revolution*, 2 v. (1954–1959).

Poisson, G., *Napoléon et Paris* (1964).

Prat, F., *Napoleone e l'Oriente* (1945).

Presser, Jacob, *Napoleon, die Entschlusselung einer Legende*. Trans. aus dem Niederlandischen von Christian Zinsser. (1979).

Ramsey, Matthew, *Professional and Popular Medicine in France, 1770–1830* (1988).

Ravignant, Patrick, *Napoleon* (1985).

Rose, J. Holland, *Life of Napoleon I* (1901).

Rosebery, Archibald Philip Primrose, Earl of, *Napoleon, The Last Phase* (1900).

Sewell, William H., Jr., *Work and Revolution in France: The Language of Labor from the Old Regime to 1848* (1980).

Schreiber, Hermann, *Das Volk steht auf: Europas Befriedungskampf gegen Napoleon* (1982).

Sieburg, Friedrich, *Napoleon: die hundert tage* (1962).

Stirling, Monica, *Madame Letizia* (1961).

Stoeckl, Agnes de, *Four Years an Empress* (1961).

Sutherland, Christine, *Marie Walewska* (1979).

Tarlé, E., *Napoléon* (1937).

Tersen, Emile, *Napoléon* (1959).

Thiers, Louis Adolphe, *Histoire du consulat et de l'empire*, 21 v. (1845–1869).

Thompson, J. M., *Napoleon Bonaparte* (1952).

Tulard, Jean, *Le Grand Empire, 1804–1815* (1982).

Vallotton, Henry, *Marie-Thérèse, Impératrice* (1963).

Wast, T. du Nicole, *Laure Junot, duchesse d'Abrantès* (1985).

Welschinger, H., *Le divorce de Napoléon* (1889).

Zeeden, Ernst Walter, *Europe im Umbruch: von 1776 bis zum Wiener Kongress* (1982)
Zierer, Otto, *Kaiser Europas: Napoleon und seine Zeit*. (1981).

Diplomacy; Napoleon and Europe

Askenazy, S., *Napoléon et la Pologne* (1925).
Belvederi, Raffaele, *Il, papato di fronte alla rivoluzione ed alle conseguenze del Congresso di Vienna, 1775–1846* (1961).
Bertier de Sauvigny, G. de, *Metternich et son temps* (1959).
Bourgeois, E., *Manuel historique de politique étrangère*, 4 v. (1892–1926).
Buckland, G., *Metternich and the British Government from 1809 to 1813* (1932).
Butterfield, H., *The Peace Tactics of Napoleon 1806–1808* (1929).
Deutsch, H. C., *Genesis of Napoleonic Imperialism* (1938).
Driault, Edouard, *Napoléon et l'Europe*, 5 v. (1910–1927).
Dundulis, Bronius, *Napoléon et la Lituanie en 1812* (1940).
Fournier, A., *Gentz und Cobenzl, Geschichte der österreichen Diplomatie 1801–1805* (1880).
Goldmann, K., *Die preussisch-brittischen Beziehungen in den Jahren 1812–1815* (1934).
Guillon, E., *Napoléon et les suisses, 1803–1815* (1910).
Hales, E. E. Y., *Napoleon and the Pope* (1961).
Handelsmann, M., *Napoléon et la Pologne* (1909).
Heymann, E., *Napoleon und die grossen Machte im Fruhjahr 1806* (1910).
Kraehe, Enno E., *Metternich's German Policy*. Vol. I: *The Contest with Napoleon, 1799–1814* (1964).
Kissinger, Henry A., *A World Restored: Metternich, Castlereagh and the Problems of the Peace, 1812–1822* (1957).
Latreille, A., *Napoléon et la Saint-Siège, 1800–1808, l'ambassade du cardinal Fesch à Rome* (1935).
Lebel, G., *La France et les principautés danubiennes* (1955).
Lefebvre, A., *Histoire des cabinets de l'Europe pendant le consulat et l'empire*, 3 v. (1847).
Lumbroso, A., *Napoleone e il Mediterraneo* (1934).
Mowat, R. B., *The Diplomacy of Napoleon* (1924).
Nasalli Rocca, S., *Giuseppe de Maistre* (1933).
Niven, Alexander C., *Napoleon and Alexander: A Study in Franco-Russian Relations, 1807–1812* (1986).
Omodèo, A., *Un reazionario, il conte J. de Maistre* (1939).
Pingaud, A., *Bernadotte, Napoléon et les Bourbons 1797–1844* (1901).
Pradt, D. de, *Histoire de l'ambassade dans le Grand Duché de Varsovie en 1812* (1815).

Puryear, V. J., *Napoleon and the Dardenelles* (1951).

Ross, Steven T., *European Diplomatic History, 1789–1815: France Against Europe* (1969).

Rössler, Hellmuth, *Graf Johann Philipp Stadion, Napoleons Deutscher Gegenspeiler* (1966).

Ragsdale, Hugh, *Detente in the Napoleonic Era: Bonaparte and the Russians* (1980).

Rudolfin, Freiin von Oer, *Der Friede von Pressburg, ein Betrag zur Diplomatiegeschichte des napoleonischen Zeitalters* (1965).

Sorel, Albert, *L'Europe et la révolution française*, 8 v. (1885–1904).

Ursel, Vicomte J. d', *La défection de l'Autriche* (1912).

Vandal, A., *Napoléon et Alexandre Ier*, 3 v. (1891–1896).

Vercesi, E., *Pio VII, Napoleone e la Restaurazione* (1933).

Webster, C. K., *British Diplomacy, 1812–1815* (1921).

————, *The Congress of Vienna* (1937).

War

Arthur, Charles B. *The Remaking of the British Navy by Admiral St. Vincent: Key to the Victory over Napoleon . . . 1795–1805* (1986).

Batty, Robert, *Campaign of the Left Wing of the Allied Army, in the Western Pyrenees and South of France, 1813–1814* (1823).

Belis, Roger, *La campagne de Russie, 1812* (1966).

Blond, Georges, *La Grande Armée, 1804–1815* (1979).

Bond, Gordon C., *The Grand Expedition: The British Invasion of Holland in 1809* (1979).

Bonnel, Ulane, *La France, les Etats-Unis et la guerre de course, 1797–1815* (1961).

Burton, R. J., *From Boulogne to Austerlitz: Napoleon's Campaign of 1805* (1912).

Cate, Curtis, *The War of the Two Emperors: The Duel between Napoleon and Alexander: Russia, 1812*. New York, 1985.

Chandler, David G., *The Campaigns of Napoleon: The Mind and Method of History's Greatest Soldier* (1966).

Choury, Maurice, *Les grognards de Napoléon* (1968).

Desbrière, E., *Projets et tentatives de débarquement aux iles britanniques 1793–1805*, 3 v. (1901).

Dodge, T. A., *Napoleon: A History of the Art of War*, 4 v. (1907).

Duffy, Christopher J., *Austerlitz, 1805* (1977).

————, *Borodino* (1972).

Dupont, M., *Napoléon et la trahison des maréchaux, 1814* (1970).

Elting, John R., *Swords around a Throne: Napoleon's Grande Armée* (1987).

Epstein, Robert M., *Prince Eugene at War, 1809* (1984).

Esposito, V., and Elting, J. R., *A Military History and Atlas of the Napoleonic Wars* (1964).

Farrère, Claude, *Histoire de la marine française* (1962).

Gachot, E., *La troisième campaigne d'Italie, 1805* (1911).

Gallaher, John G., *The Iron Marshal: A Biography of Louis N. Davout* (1976).

Glover, Richard, *Britain at Bay . . . 1803–1814* (1973).

―――, *Peninsular Preparation: The Reform of the British Army, 1795–1809* (1963).

―――, "The French Fleet, 1807–1814; Britain's Problem; Madison's Opportunity," *Journal of Modern History* (1967).

Gourgaud, Gaspard, Baron, *Napoléon et la grande armée en Russie*. 2 v. (1825).

Howarth, David, *Waterloo: Day of Battle* (1968).

Kramer, Hans, *Erzherzog Johann und Tirol* (1959).

Labaume, Eugène, *A Circumstantial Narrative of the Campaign in Russia, Embellished with Plans of the Battles of Moskwa and Malo-Jaroslavitz* (1815).

Lachouque, Henry, *Napoléon: 20 ans de campagnes* (1964). Trans. as *Napoleon's Battles: A History of His Campaignes* (1967).

―――, *Napoléon et la garde impériale* (1957). Adapted by Anne S. K. Brown as *The Anatomy of Glory* (1961).

―――, *Waterloo, la fin d'un monde* (1958).

―――, *Les derniers jours de l'empire* (1965). English translation by Lovett F. Edwards (1967).

Lawford, J. P., *Napoleon: The Last Campaigns, 1813–1815* (1977).

Liddell Hart, B. H., *The Ghost of Napoleon* (1933).

Low, E. G., *With Napoleon at Waterloo* (1911).

Lynn, John A., *Bayonets of the Republic: Motivation and Tactics of the Army of Revolutionary France* (1984).

Mahan, A. T., *The Influence of Sea Power Upon the French Revolution and Empire, 1793–1812*, 2 v. 14th ed. (1919).

Maine, R., *Trafalgar* (1957).

Makers of Modern Strategy. Ed. by Peter Paret, with Gordon Craig & Felix Gilbert. Princeton, NJ, 1986.

Marshall-Cornwall, James, *Napoleon as Military Commander* (1968).

Marcus, G. J., *The Royal Navy in the Age of Nelson, 1793–1815* (1971).

Marshall-Cornwall, James, *Napoleon as Military Commander* (1968).

Morriss, Roger, *The [British] Royal Dockyards during the Revolutionary and Napoleonic Wars* (Leicester, 1983).

Nafziger, George F., *Napoleon's Invasion of Russia* (1988).

Naylor, John, *Waterloo* (1960).

Nicolson, Nigel, *Napoleon 1812* (1985).

Oman, Carola, *Britain Against Napoleon* (1942).

Oman, Sir Charles W. C., *Studies in the Napoleonic Wars* (1930).
Palmer, Alan W., *Napoleon in Russia* (1967).
Parker, H. T., *Three Napoleonic Battles* (1944).
Petre, F. L., *Napoleon at War*. Ed. A. A. Nofi. NY, 1984.
Phipps, Ramsey W., *The Armies of the First Republic and the Rise of Napoleon's Marshals*. 5 v. (1926–29). Reprint 1985.
Porter, Sir Robert Ker, *A Narrative of the Campaign in Russia, During the Year 1812*. 2d Ed. (1814).
Quennevat, J. C., *Atlas de la grande armée: Napoléon et ses campagnes, 1803–1815* (1966).
Quimby, Robert S., *The Background of Napoleonic Warfare. The Theory of Military Tactics in 18th Century France* (1957).
Rogers, Hugh C. B., *Napoleon's Army* (1974).
Ross, Steven T., *From Flintlock to Rifle Infantry: Tactics, 1740–1866* (1979).
Rothenberg, Gunther E., *The Art of Warfare in the Age of Napoleon* (1978).
———, *Napoleon's Great Adversaries: The Archduke Charles and the Austrian Army, 1792–1814* (1982).
———, *The Military Border in Croatia, 1740–1882* (1974).
Scott, Samuel F., *Response of the Royal Army to the French Revolution* (1978)
Ségur, Philippe Paul, Comte de, *Histoire de Napoléon et de la grande-armée pendant l'année 1812*, 2 v. (1825). New Ed. (1960). Tr. and abr. by J. D. Townsend as *Napoleon's Russian Campaign* (1958).
Tarlé, E., *Napoleon's Invasion of Russia*, tr. (1942).
Theiss, Viktor, *Leben und Wirken Erzherzog Johanns* (1960).
Thiry, Jean, *Iéna* (1964).
Thiry, Jean, *Ulm, Trafalgar, Austerlitz* (1963).
Thomazi, A., *Napoléon et ses marins* (1950).
Tranie, Jean, *Les Polonaise de Napoléon*, Paris, 1982.
Tranie, Jean, & Carmigniani, J.-C., *Napoleon et l'Allemagne: La Prusse, 1806; Napoleon el la Russie, 1805–1807*. Paris, 1984.
———, *Napoléon, 1813: La campagne d'Allemagne* (1987).
Wheeler, Harold Felix and Broadley, A. M., *Napoleon and the Invasion of England*. 2 v. (1908).
Woloch, Isser, *The French Veteran from the Revolution to the Restoration* (1979).

Economic History

Bergeron, Louis, *Banquiers, négociants et manufacturiers parisiens du Directoire à l'Empire* (1975).
Blanchard, M., *Les routes des Alpes occidentales à l'époque napoléonienne* (1920).

Bockenheiwer, K., *Mainzer Handel: Der Zoll und Binnenhafen zu Mainz, 1648–1831* (1887).

Crouzet, F., *L'économie britannique et le blocus continental, 1806–1813* (1958).

Dornic, François, *L'évolution de l'industrie textile au XVIIIe et au XIXe siècle: l'activité de la famille Cohin* (1956).

Dunan, Marcel, *Napoléon et l'Allemagne: Le système continental et les débuts du royaume de Bavière* (1942).

Ellis, Geoffrey, *Napoleon's Continental Blockade* (1981).

Fohlen, Claude, *Naissance d'une civilisation industrielle* (1961).

Geiger, Reed G., *The Anzin Coal Company, 1800–1883: Big Business in the Early States of the French Industrial Revolution* (1974).

Huillier, F. L., *Le blocus continental dans le grand-duché de Bade* (1951).

Jouvenel, B. de, *Napoléon et l'economie dirigée: le blocus continental* (1942).

Latour, François, *Le grand argentier de Napoléon* (1962).

Lumbroso, A., *Napoleone e il Mediterraneo* (1934).

Mousnier, Roland, *Progrès scientifique et technique au XVIIIe siècle* (1958).

Olson, Mancur, Jr., *Economics of the Wartime Shortage: A History of British Food Supplies in the Napoleonic Wars and in World Wars I and II* (1963).

Pernoud, R., *Histoire de la Bourgeoisie en France*, 2 v. (1962).

Pivec-Stelè, M., *La vie économique des provinces Illyriennes, 1809–1813* (1931).

Strauss, Rudolph, *Die lage und die Bewegung der Chemnitzer Arbeiter in der ersten hälfte des 19e jahrhundert* (1960).

Tarlé, E., *La vita economica dell' Italia nell' età napoleonica* (1950).

Viennet, Odette, *Napoléon et l'industrie française. La crise de 1810–1811* (1947).

Italian Peninsula (geographic) and Minor States

Auréas, Henri, *Un général de Napoléon: Miollis* (1961).

Balboa, Cesare, *Della Storia d'Italia, dalle origini fino ai tempi nostri.* New ed. (1962).

Boyer, Ferdinand, *Les artistes italiens et Napoléon* (1954).

Butera, Maria Maddalena, *Campagne italiane nell' eta napoleonica: la prima inchiesta dell Italia moderna* (1981).

Capra, Carlo, *L'eta rivoluzionaria e napoleonica in Italia, 1796–1815* (Torino, 1978).

Corsini, Andrea, *I Bonaparte a Firenze* (1961).

Driault, E., *Napoléon en Italie 1800–1812* (1906).

Fugier, A., *Napoléon et l'Italie* (1947).

Hériot, Angus, *Les Français en Italie, 1796–1799* (1961).

Hirn, J., *Tirols Erhebung im Jahren 1809* (1909).
Lemmi, Francesco, *L'età napoleonica* (1938).
Lensi, A., *Napoleone a Firenze* (1936).
Luchaire, J., *L'evolution intellectuelle de l'Italie de 1815 à 1830* (1906).
Lumbroso, A., *Ai Tempi di Napoléone* (1913).
McClellan, G. B., *Venice and Bonaparte* (1931).
Madelin, L., *Rome sous Napoléon* (1906).
Natali, Giovanni, *L'Italia durante il regime Napoleonico* (1955).
Noether, Emiliana P., *Seeds of Italian Nationalism, 1700–1815* (1951).
Pane, Luigi dal, *Storia del lavoro in Italia dagli inizi del secolo XVIII al 1815* (1958).
Pingaud, A., "La politique italienne de Napoléon Ier," *Revue Historique* (1927).
[*Il*] *Principato napoleonico dei Baciocchi (1805–1814): Riforma dello stato e società*. Atti del convegno internazionale, Lucca 1984. A cura di Vito Tirelli. (1986).
Ramm, Agatha, *The Risorgimento* (1962).
Reumont, A. von, *Geschichte Toscanas* (1877).
Rodocanacchi, E., *Elisa Bacciocchi en Italie* (1900).
Salvatorelli, L., *Il pensiero politico italiano dal 1700 al 1870* (1941).
[*Il*] *Sistema museale dell' arcipelago toscano*. A cura del Centro nazionale di studi napoleonici e di storia dell'Elba, Portoferraio (Pisa, 1985).
Solmi, A., *L'idea dell' unità italiana nell' età napoleonica* (1934).
Soriga, R., *L'idèa nazionale italiana* (1941).
Tavera, Nedo, *Elisa Bonaparte Baciocchi principesse di Piombino.* (Firenze, 1982).
Villani, Pasquale, *Italia napoleonica* (Napoli, 1978).
Zaghi, Carlo, *Potere, chiesa e societa: studi e ricerche sull'Italia giacobina e napoleonica* (Napoli, 1984).

Central and Northern Europe

Arnold, Raymond, *L'université en Allemagne de l'ouest: Histoire, structure et caractères* (1962).
Baxa, J., *Adam Müller* (1921).
Beaulieu-Marconnay, K. von, *Karl von Dalberg und seine Zeit*, 2 v. (1879).
Biro, Sidney, *The German Policy of Revolutionary France*, 2 v. (1957).
Bitterauf, Th., *Geschichte des Rheinbundes* (1905).
Bruford, W. H., *Culture and Society in Classical Weimar, 1775–1806* (1962).
Buschleb, Hermann, *Westfalen und die preussischen Truppen, 1795–1802: Ein Kapitel Militarpolitik und Landesgeschichte* (1987).

Carsten, F. L., *Princes and Parliaments in Germany, from the Fifteenth to the Eighteenth Century* (1959).

Courvoisier, Jean, *Le maréchal Berthier et sa principauté de Neuchâtel, 1806–1814* (1959).

Dänhardt, H., *Joseph Görres politische Frühentwicklung* (1926).

Droz, J., *Le romantisme allemand et l'état: Resistance et collaboration dans l'Allemagne napoléonienne* (1966).

Ergang, Robert R., *Herder and the Foundations of German Nationalism* (1931).

Fisher, Herbert A. L., *Studies in Napoleonic Statesmanship: Germany* (1903).

Gentz, Friedrich v., *Österreichische Manifeste von 1809* (n.d.)

Gibelin, J., *L'esthétique de Schelling et l'Allemagne de Madame de Staël* (1934).

Gooch, G. P., *Germany and the French Revolution* (1920).

Hamerow, Theodore, *Restoration, Revolution, and Reaction: Economics and Politics in Germany* (1958).

Hantsch, Hugo, *Die Geschichte österreichs*, 2 v. (1962).

Haussonville, Comte d', *Madame de Staël et l'Allemagne* (1928).

Heller, H., *Hegel und der nationale Machtstaatsgedanke in Deutschland* (1921).

Höltzle, E., *Das alte Recht und die Revolution. Eine politische Geschichte Württembergs in der Revolutionszeit, 1789–1815* (1931).

Junkelmann, Marcus, *Napoleon und Bayern: von den Anfanger des Konigreiches* (1985).

Kaehler, Siegfried A., *Studien zur deutschen Geschichte des 19. und 20. Jahrhunderts* (1961).

Kann, Robert A., *A Study in Austrian Intellectual History, from Late Baroque to Romanticism* (1960).

Kircheisen, Friedrich M. (ed.), *Fürstenbriefe an Napoleon I*, 2 v. (1929).

Kohn, Hans, *Prelude to the Nation States: The French and German Experience, 1789–1815* (1967).

Krieger, Leonard, *The German Idea of Freedom: History of a Political Tradition* (1957).

Langsam, W. C., *The Napoleonic Wars and German Nationalism in Austria* (1930).

Leroux, R., *La théorie du despotisme éclairé chez Karl Theodor von Dalberg* (1932).

Lysiak, Waldemar, *Cesarski poker* (Warszawa, 1978).

Meinecke, Friedrich, *Das Zeitalter der deutschen Erhebung, 1795–1815*. 6th ed. (1957). Trans. by Peter Paret as *The Age of German Liberation* (1959).

———, *Weltbürgertum und Nationalstaat*. 5th ed. (1919).

Nabholz, H., *Die Schweiz unter Fremdherrschaft 1798–1815* (1921).

Paret, Peter, *Yorck and the Era of Prussian Reform 1807–1814*. (1966).

———, *Clausewitz and the State*. 2nd Ed. (1985).

Pivka, Otto von, *Napoleon's German Allies* (1978).

Raack, Richard C., *The Fall of Stein* (1965).
Rambaud, A., *La Domination française en Allemagne*, 2 v. 4th ed. (1897).
Rambow, G., *L. von der Marwitz und die Anfänge der konservativer Politik und Staatsanschauung in Preussen* (1930).
Ritter, Joachim, *Hegel und die französische Revolution* (1957).
Robert, André, *L'idée national autrichienne et les guerres de Napoléon* (1933).
Rosenberg, Hans, *Bureaucracy, Aristocracy, and Autocracy: The Prussian Experience, 1660–1815* (1958).
Sauzin, L., *Adam-Heinrich Müller, 1779–1829. Sa vie et son oeuvre* (1937).
Schmidt, Ch., *Le grand-duché de Berg, 1806–1813* (1905).
Schnepel, H., *Die Reichstadt Bremen und Frankreich von 1789 bis 1813* (1935).
Schubert, Freidrich von, *Unter dem Doppeladler. Erinnerungen eines Deutschen im russischen Offiziersdienst 1789–1814* (1962).
Senkowska-Gluck, Monika, *Donacji napoleonski w Ksieswie Warszawskim* (1968).
Simon, Walter M., *The Failure of the Prussian Reform Movement, 1807–1819* (1955).
Shanahan, William O., *Prussian Military Reforms, 1786–1813* (1954).
Srbik, Heinrich Ritter von, *Deutsche Einheit: Die Idee und Wirklichkeit vom Heiligen Reich bis Königgratz*, 4 v. (1935–1942).
Streisand, Joachim, *Deutschland 1789–1815* (1959).
Treue, Wilhelm, *Deutsche Geschichte von 1807 bis 1890* (1961).
Uhlmann, J., *Joseph Goerres und die deutsche Einheits-und Verfassungsfrage bis zum Jahre 1824* (1912).
Weis, E., *Die begrundung des modernen Bayerischen Staates unter Max. Ier* (1974).
White, Charles E., *The Enlightened Soldier: Scharnhorst and the Militarische Gesellschaft in Berlin* (1988).
Winter, C., *Die Reorganisation des preussischen Staates unter Stein und Hardenberg* (1931).
Wohlfiel, Rainier, *Spanien und die deutsche Erhebung, 1808–1814* (1965).
Zöllner, Erich, *Geschichte Österreichs, von den Anfängen bis zur Gegenwart* (1961).

Kingdom of Italy

Adalbert, Prinz von Bayern, *Eugen Beauharnais, der Stiefsohn Napoleons* (1940).
Anglini, Werther, *La municipalità de Ancona e il suo tentativo d'annessione alla Cislapina* (1964).
Beauharnais, Eugène de, Prince, *Mémoires et Correspondance politique et militaire du Prince Eugène*, 10 v. Ed. by A. du Casse (1858–1860).

Blanchard, M., *Les routes des Alpes occidentales à l'époque napoléonienne, 1796–1815* (1920).

Bressan, Edoardo, *Poverta e assistenza in Lombardia nell'eta napoleonica.* (Milano, 1985).

Bucci, Sante, *La Scuola Italiana Nell'Eta Napoleonica: Il Sistema Educativo e Scholastico nel Regno d'Italia* (Roma, 1976).

Camponetto, Salvatore, *Il giacobinismo nelle Marche, Pesaro nel Triennio rivoluzionario, 1796–1799* (1962).

Challois, Léonard, *Histoire de Prince Eugène de Beauharnais, Prince d'Eichstätt, Duc de Leuchtenberg par G—, exofficier d'infanterie* (1821).

Colletta, Pietro, *Memoria militare sulla campagna d'Italia del 1815* (1820) in *Opera inédite e rare*, 2 v. (1861–1862).

Como, Ugo da, *I Comizi Nazionali in Lione per la Costituzione della Repubblica italiana*, 3 v. (1934–1938).

Darnay, Baron, *Notices historiques sur S. A. R. le prince Eugène, vice-roi d'Italie* (1830).

Deutsch-Italienisches Historikertreffen (1975 : Mainz), *Deutschland und Italien im Zeitalter Napoleons*. Hrsg. von Armgard von Reden-Dohna (Wiesbaden, 1979).

Faye, Planat de la, *Le Prince Eugène en 1814* (1857). [Documents]

Foscolo, Ugo, *Poesie, lettere e prose letteraire* (1964).

Fourmestraux, *Le Prince Eugène*, 2d ed. (1867).

Hanoteau, Jean, *Le ménage Beauharnais, Joséphine avant Napoléon* (1935).

———, *Les Beauharnais et l'Empereur, lettres de l'Impératrice Joséphine et de la Reine Hortense au Prince Eugène* (1936).

Ivray, J. d', *La Lombardie au temps de Bonaparte* (1919).

Lavalette, Comte de, *Mémoires et souvenirs du Comte de Lavalette* (1831).

Malzi d'Eril, Duca di Lodi, *Memorie, documenti e lettere inedite di Napoleone I e Beauharnais*, 2 v. Ed. by Giovanni Malzi (1865).

Melzi d'Eril, Francesco, *I carteggi di Francesco Melzi d'Eril, Duca di Lodi*. Ed. by Carlo Zaghi (1965).

———, *Ricordo di Monaco. Eugenio Beauharnais e Augusta di Baviera, Documenti inedite* (1987).

Morandi, C., *Idee e formazione politiche in Lombardia 1748–1815* (1927).

Naselli, Carmelo Amedeo, *La soppressione napoleonica della corporazioni religiose . . . 1808–1814* (Roma, 1986).

Natali, Giovanni, *L'Italia durante il regime Napoleonico* (1955).

Oman, Carola, *Napoleon's Viceroy: Eugène de Beauharnais* (1966).

Pieri, Piero, *Storia militare del risorgimento: Guerre e insurrezioni* (1962).

Pingaud, A., *La domination française dans l'Italie du nord, 1796–1805: Bonaparte, president de la république italienne*, 2v. (1914).

———, "La politique italienne de Napoléon Ier," *Revue Historique* (1927).

———, "Le premier royaume d'Italie," *Revue des Etudes Napoléoniennes* (1923 and 1925). [5 Articles]

———, "Le premier royaume d'Italie," *Revue Historique Diplomatique* (1926–1930; 1932–1934). [4 Articles]

———, *Les hommes d'état de la république italienne, 1802–1805, notices et documents biographiques* (1919).

———, "Les Italiens dans la campagne de Russie et la campagne de 1813 vue par les Italiens," *Monde Slave* (1926–1927).

[*La*] *proprieta fondiaria in Lombardia dal catasto teresiano all' eta napoleonica*. A cura di Sergio Zaninelli (Milano, 1986).

Rath, R. John, *The Fall of the Napoleonic Kingdom of Italy* (1941).

———, *The Provisional Austrian Regime in Lombardy-Venetia, 1814–1815* (1969).

Schneidawind, Franz, *Prinz Eugen, Herzog von Leuchtenberg, Fürst von Eichstätt und vormals Vicekönig von Italien* (1857).

Scrittori e architetti nella Milano napoleonica. Toti Celona, Elisa e Leonardo Mariani Travi. Ed. by Renato Rigamonti (1983).

Seel, Henrich, *Erinnerungen zus den Zeiten und dem Leben Eugens Herzog von Leuchtenberg nach authentischen Quellen* (1827).

Tarlé, E., *Le Blocus continental et le royaume d'Italie* (1931).

Tascher de la Pagerie, Comte, *Le Prince Eugène. Réfutation des memoires du Duc de Raguse en ce qui concerne le Prince Eugène* (1857).

Tessadri, Elena S., *Il vicere Eugenio di Beauharnais* (1982).

Vaudoncourt, Général de, *Histoire politique et militaire du Prince Eugène Napoléon, Vice-Roi d'Italie* (1828).

Weil, M. H., *Le prince Eugène et Murat*, 5 v. (1902). [Documents]

Zaghi, Carlo, *L'Italia di Napoleone della Cisalpina al Regio* (1988).

Zangheri, Renato, *La pròprieta terriera e le origini de Risorgimento nel Bolognese*. I: *1789–1804* (1961).

Kingdom of Naples

Acton, Harold, *The Bourbons of Naples* (1956).

Auriol, Charles, *La France, l'Angleterre et Naples de 1803 à 1806*, 2 v. (1904–1905).

Bechu, M.-E. [Marcel Dupont], *Murat: cavalier, maréchal de France, prince et roi* (1980).

Bertaut, J., *Le ménage Murat* (1958).

Bonaparte, Joseph, *Lettres d'exil inédites (Amérique—Angleterre—Italie 1825–1844*. Publiées . . . par Hector Fleischmann (1912).

———, *Lettres inédites ou éparses de Joseph Bonaparte à Naples 1806–1808*. Ed. by Jacques Rambaud (1911).

————, *Mémoires et correspondance du roi Joseph*, 10 v. Ed. by A. du Casse. 2d ed. (1854).

Bourbon, Marie Caroline de, Reine, *Correspondance inédite de Marie-Caroline, reine de Naples et de Sicile, avec le Marquis de Gallo*, 2 v. (1911).

Caldora, Umberto, *Calabria napoleonica 1806–1815* (1960).

Convegno di studi sul Risorgimento in Puglia (2nd 1979: Bari, Italy), *Il decennio francese in Puglia, 1806–1815* (Bari, 1981).

Colletta, Pietro, *Histoire du royaume de Naples* (1835).

Colletta, Pietro (1775–1831), *La campagna d'Italia di Gioacchino Murat*. A cura di Carlo Zaghi (Torino, 1982).

Croce, B., *Storia del regno di Napoli* (1925).

Damas, Roger de, comte, *Mémoires*, 2 v. Ed. by J. Rambaud (1914).

Dufourcq, Albert, *Murat et la question de l'unité italienne en 1815* (1898).

Dupont, Marcel, *Murat* (1934).

Fiore, Enzo, *Un re al bivio: Il tradimento di Murat* (1972).

Franceschetti, Général D.-C., *Mémoires sur les événements qui ont précédé la mort de Joachim Ier, Roi des Deux-Siciles . . . suivi de la correspondance privée de* [Franceschetti] *. . . avec la Reine* [Caroline Bonaparte] (1826).

————, *Supplément aux mémoires sur les événements qui ont précédé la mort de Joachim Ier, roi de Naples* (1829).

Galvani, Charles, *Mémoires sur les événements qui ont précédé la mort de Joachim-Napoléon, roi des Deux-Siciles* (1843).

Garnier, J. P., *Murat, roi de Naples* (1959).

Garofalo, L., *Giuseppe Zurlo* (1932).

Helfert, Baron von, *Joachim Murat, seine letzten Kämpfe und sein Ende* (1878).

Johnston, R. M., *The Napoleonic Empire in Southern Italy and the Rise of the Secret Societies*, 2 v. (1904).

La Volpe, G., *Gioacchino Murat . . . amministrazione e riforme economiche* (1931).

Lumbroso, A., *L'agonia di un regno* (1904).

Macirone, Francis, *Interesting Facts Relating to the Fall and Death of Joachim Murat*. 3d ed. (1817).

Miot de Melito, Andre François, Comte, *Mémoires du comte Miot de Melito*, 3 v. Ed. by Gen. Hector Fleischmann (1858).

Murat, Joachim, *Lettres et documents pour servir à l'histoire de Joachim Murat*, 8 v. Ed. by Paul Le Brethon (1908–1914).

————, "Lettres inédites," *Revue des Études Napoléoniennes*. Ed. by Morgulis (1936).

Pignatelli-Strongoli, Francesco, *Memorie intorno alla storia del Regno di Napoli dell' anno 1805 al 1815* (1820).

Prieur, Jean, *Murat et Caroline* (1985).

Rambaud, Jacques, *Naples sous Joseph Bonaparte 1806–1808* (1911).

Roederer, Pierre L., Comte, *Oeuvres du Comte Pierre Louis Roederer*, 8 v. (1853–1859).

Rosselli, John, *Lord William Bentinck and the British Occupation of Sicily* (1956).

Spandoni, D., *Per la prima guerra d'indipendenza italiana nel 1815* (1929).

Spinosa, Antonio, *Murat: da stalliere a re di Napoli* (1984).

Tulard, Jean, *Murat, ou. L'Eveil des nations* (1983).

Valente, Angela, *Gioacchino Murat e l'Italia meridionale* (1941).

Weil, M. H. [Documents and Commentary], *Joachim Murat, roi de Naples*, 5 v. (1909–1910). *Le Prince Eugène et Murat*, 5 v. (1902). *Le Revirement de la politique autrichienne à l'égard de Joachim Murat et les négociations secrètes entre Paris et Vienne* (1908). *Les Négociations secrètes entre Joachim Murat et le Prince Eugène, 1814* (1906).

Wilson, General Sir Robert, *Private Diary* (1861).

Valente, Angela, *Gioacchino Murat e l'Italia meridionale* (1965).

Villani, Pasquale, *La vendita dei beni dello Stato nel Regno di Napoli, 1806–1815* (1964).

Kingdom of Holland

Arjuzon, C. d', *Hortense de Beauharnais* (1897).

Baasch, E., *Holländische Wirtschaftsgeschichte* (1925).

Billy, André, *Hortense et ses amants, Chateaubriand, Sainte-Beuve* (1961).

Bonaparte, Hortense de Beauharnais, Reine de Hollande, *Mémoires*, 3 v. 12th ed. (1927).

Bonaparte, Louis, *Gedenkschriften Lodewijk Napoleon, Koning van Holland. Gekozen, vertaald en met getuigenissen van tijdgenoten vermeerderd door Wim Zaal* (Amsterdam, 1983).

Bonaparte, Louis, *Documents historiques et réflexions sur la gouvernement de la Hollande*, 3 v. (1820).

Bonaparte, Louis, Cte de Saint-Leu, *Réponse à Sir Walter Scott sur son histoire de Napoléon* (1831).

Castries, Rene de La Croix, duc de, *La Reine Hortense: fille d'Impéritrice et mère d'empereur.* (1984).

Caumont La Force, Marquis de, *L'architrésorier Lebrun, gouverneur de la Hollande, 1810–1813* (1907).

Colenbrander, H. T., *Konig Lodewijk 1806–1810*, 2 parts (1909–1910). Vol. 5 of *Gedenkstukken der Algemeene Geschiedenis van Nederland 1795–1840*, 10 v. (1905–1922).

———, *Schimmelpenninck en Konig Lodewijk* (1911).

Duboscq, A., *Louis Bonaparte en Hollande, d'après ses lettres* (1911).

Falck, A. R., *Brieven van A. R. Falck, 1795–1832*. Ed. by O. W. Hora Siccama (1861).

Grovestins, C. F. Sirtema van, *Gedenkschriften van graaf van der Duyn van Maasdam en van den baron van der Capellen* (1857).

Hogendorp, G. K. van, *Brieven en Gedenkschriften, 1788–1813*, 7 v. (1866–1903).

Houtte, J. A. van (ed.), *Algemene geschiedenis der Nederlanden*, 12 v. (1949–1956). Vol. IX, 1795–1840.

Jorissen, Theodorus, *De omwenteling van 1813* (1867).

———, *De ondergang van het koninkrijk Holland . . .* (1871).

———, *Napoléon Ier et le roi de Hollande* (1868).

Kikkert, J. G., *Koning van Holland, Louis Bonaparte* (1981).

Kluit, M. E., *Cornelis Felix van Maanen tot het herstel der onafhankelijkheid. 9 Sept. 1769–6 Dec. 1813* (1953).

Kraijenhoff, K. R. T., *Levensbijzonderseden van . . .* Ed. by H. W. Tydeman (1844).

Lacretelle, P. de, *Secrets et malheurs de la reine Hortense* (1936).

Legrand, *La révolution française en Hollande; La république Batave* (1894).

Manger, J. B., *Recherches sur les relations économiques de la France et de la Hollande pendant la Révolution française* (1923).

Mendels, I., *Herman Willem Daendels, vóór zijne benoeming tot Goeverneur Generaal van Oost-Indië 1762–1807* (1890).

Raillicourt, D. Labarre de, *Louis Bonaparte, roi de Holland* (1963).

Rocquain, F., *Napoléon Ier et le roi Louis* (1875).

Roëll, W. F., *Verslag van hetgeen ter gelegenheid van het verbliff des Konings van Holland te Parijs in 1809 en 1810 is voorgevallen, benevens aanhangsel en bescheiden over eene eventueele verdediging der hoofdstad in 1810* (1837).

Shama, Simon, *Patriots and Liberators: Revolution in the Netherlands, 1780–1813* (1977).

Sillem, J. A., *De politieke en staathuishoudkundige werkzaamheid van Issac Jan Alexander Gogel* (1864).

Sneller, Zeger W., *Geschiedenis van de Nederlandse landbouw, 1795–1940*. 2d Ed. (1951).

Stapel, F. W., *Geschiedenis van Nederlands-Indië* (1943).

Turquan, J., *Le Reine Hortense (1783–1837) d'après les temoignages des contemporains* (1896).

Verberne, L. G. J., *Gogel en de uniteit* (1948).

Vries, Theun de, *Rutger Jan Schimmelpenninck. (1941)*.

Wichers, L., De regeering van Koning Lodewijk Napoleon 1806–1810 (1892).

Wiskerke, C., *De afschaffing der gilden in Nederland* (1932).

Wit, C. H. E. de, *Het Ontstaan van Het Moderne Nederland, 1780–1848* (1978).
Wright, C., *Daughter to Napoleon* (1961).

Kingdom of Westphalia

Amelunxen, Clemens, *König und Senator: Jerôme und Lucien, zwei Bruder Napoleons* 1980).
Berding, Helmut, *Napoleonische Herrschafts- und Gesellschafts-politik im Königsreich Westfalen, 1807–1813* (1973).
Beugnot, Jacques Claude, *Mémoires*, 2 v. 2d ed. (1868).
Bonaparte, Catérine et Jérome de Westphalie, *Briefwechsel*, 3 v. (1886–1887).
Bonaparte, Jérome, roi de Westphalie, *Mémoires, avec la correspondance de la reine Catherine et la correspondance du roi avec Napoléon*, 7 v. Ed. by A. du Casse (1861–1868).
Casse, A. du, "Correspondance de Reinhard," *Revue Historique* (1879).
———, *Le général Vandamme et sa correspondance*, 2 v. (1890).
———, *Mémoires pour servir à l'histoire de la campagne de 1812 en Russie, suivis des lettres de Napoléon au roi de Westphalie pendant la guerre de 1813* (1852).
———, (ed.) *Souvenirs d'un aide-de-camp du roi Jérome* (1890).
Cathérine de Westphalie, *Correspondance inédite avec sa famille et celle du roi Jérome*. Ed. by A. du Casse (1893).
Fisher, H. A. L., *Studies in Napoleonic Statesmanship: Germany* (1903).
Göcke, Rudolf & Ilgen, Theodor, *Das Königreich Westfalen* (1888).
Handelsmann, Marcel, *Napoleon et la Pologne* (1909).
Henking, K., *Johannes von Müller* (1928).
Holzapfel, Rudolphi, *Das Königreich Westfalen* (1895).
Kircheisen, F. M., *Jovial King* (1932).
Klcinschmidt, A., *Geschichte des Königreichs Westfalen* (1893).
Kohl, W., *Die Verwaltung der östlichen Departments des Königreichs Westphalen, 1807–1814* (1937).
Lang, W., *Graf Reinhard* (1896).
Les rois frères de Napoléon Ier. Ed. by A. du Casse (1883). [Documents: Two thirds on Jérôme. Heavy on Reinhard's letters.]
Mansuy, Abel, *Jérôme Napoléon et la Pologne en 1812* (1930).
Martinct, André, *Jérôme Napoléon, roi de Westphalie* (1863).
Melchior-Bonnet, Bernardine, *Jerôme Bonaparte ou l'inverse de l'epopée* (1979).
Reinhard, Madame K. F. von, *Une femme de diplomat, Lettres de Mme. Reinhard à sa Mère*. Tr. from Ger. by Baronne von Wimpffen [n.d.]
Schib, Karl, "Die Gründung der Universität Berlin und Johannes von Müllers

unfreiwellige Rücktritt aus dem Dienste Preussens,'' *Revue suisse d'histoire* (1963).

Schlossberger, Graf von, *Briefwechsel der Königin Katarina und der Königs Jérôme von Westfalen, sowie des Kaisers Napoleon mit Friedrich von Württemberg*, 3 v. (1886–1887).

Senfft, Graf von (comte de), *Mémoires du comte de Senfft* (1863).

Stählin, F., *Napoleons Glanz und Fall in Deutschen Urteil* (1952).

Thimme, F., *Die inneren Zustände des Kurfürstentums Hannover unter der französisch-westfälischen Heerschaft*, 2 v. (1893–1895).

Wagener, W., *Westphalen und die Franzosen* (1813).

Wegener, Hélène, *Die Relationen Napoleons I mit dem Königreich Westfalen* (1905).

Kingdom of Spain

Alexander, Don W., *Rod of Iron: French Counterinsurgency Policy in Aragon during the Peninsular War* (1985).

Alcazar Molina, Cayetano, *El Madrid del dos de mayo* (1952).

Arteche y Moro, José Gomez de, *Guerra de la independencia; historia militar de España de 1808 à 1814*, 4 v. (1868–1903).

Artola Gallego, Miguel, *Los Afrancesados* (1953).

———, *La España de Fernando VII* (Madrid, 1968).

Aymes, Jean-René, *La deportation sous le Premier Empire: Les espagnols en France, 1808–1814* (1983).

Aymes, J. R., *La guerre d'independance espagnole* (1973).

Bigarré, Auguste Julien, Baron, *Mémoires du général Bigarré, aide-de-camp du roi Joseph, 1775–1813* (1899).

Bonaparte, Joseph, *Mémoires et correspondance*. Ed. by A. du Casse, 10 v. 2d ed. (1854).

Cambronero y Martinez, Carlos, *El Rey Intruso; apuntes históricos referentes à José Bonaparte* (1909).

Chastenet, J., *Godoy, Master of Spain, 1792–1808* (1953).

Clermont-Tonnerre, A.-M.-G., duc de (1779–1865), *L'Expedition d'Espagne, 1808–1810*. Ed. by Catherine Desportes (1983).

Conard, Pierre, *La constitution de Bayonne, essai d'édition critique* (1910).

———, *Napoléon et la Catalogne, 1808–1814*, 2 v. (1910).

Connelly, Owen, *The Gentle Bonaparte: A Biography of Joseph, Napoleon's Elder Brother* (1968).

Davies, D. W., *Sir John Moore's Peninsular Campaign* (1974).

Defourneaux, Marcelin, *Pablo de Olavide ou l'Afrancesado, 1725–1803* (1959).

Demerson, Georges, *Don Juan Meléndez Valdés et son temps, 1759–1817* (1962).

Desdevises du Dezert, G., *L'Espagne de l'ancien régime*, 3 v. (1897–1904).

Dumas, Mathicu, *Souvenirs du Lieutenant Général Comte Mathieu Dumas, de 1770 à 1836*, 3 v. (1839).

Foy, Maximilien Sébastien, *History of the War in the Peninsula* (1827).

Fugier, André, *Le junte supérieure des Asturies et l'invasion Francaise, 1810–1811* (1930).

———, *Napoléon et l'Espagne, 1799–1808*, 2 v. (1930).

Garcia-Rodriguez, José María, *Guerra de la independencia* (1945).

Gates, David, *"The Spanish Ulcer": A History of the Peninsular War* (1986).

Glover, Michael, *Wellington's Peninsular Victories* (1963).

Godoy y Alvarez de Faria, Manuel de, Principe de La Paz, *Memoirs of Don Manuel de Godoy* (1836).

Gouvion de Saint-Cyr, Marquis de, *Journal des opérations de l'armée de la Catalogne en 1808 et 1809* (1821).

Grandmaison, Geoffrey de, *La France et l'Espagne pendant le Ier Empire* (1899).

———, *L'Espagne et Napoléon, 1804–1814*, 3 v. 3d ed. (1908–1931).

Glover, Michael, *Wellington as Military Commander* (1968).

Grasset, A., *La guerre d'Espagne, 1807–1813*, 3 v. (1914–1932).

Hamilton, Earl J., *War and Prices in Spain, 1651–1800* (1947).

Herr, Richard, *The Eighteenth Century Revolution in Spain* (1958).

Hibbert, Christopher, *Corunna* (1961).

Horward, Donald D., *The Battle of Bussaco: Masséna vs. Wellington* (1965).

———, *Napoleon and Iberia: The Twin Sieges of Ciudad Rodrigo and Almeida, 1810* (1988).

Hugo, Joseph Léopold Sigebert, *Le général Hugo, 1773–1828, lettres et documents inédits* (1926).

Jourdan, Jean Baptiste, *Mémoires militaires (Guerre d'Espagne)*. Ed. by Vicomte de Grouchy (1899).

Jovellanos, Gaspar Melchor de, *Mémoires politiques de Gaspar de Jovellanos . . .* (1825).

Junot, Laure, Duchesse d'Abrantès, *Souvenirs d'une ambassade et d'un sejour en Espagne et Portugal de 1808 à 1811*, 2 v. (1837).

La Forest, Antoine René Charles Mathurin, Comte de, *Correspondance du Comte de La Forest, ambassadeur de France en Espagne 1808–1813*, 7 v. (1905–1913).

Longford, Elizabeth, *Wellington: The Years of the Sword* (1969).

Lovett, Gabriel H., *Napoleon and the Birth of Modern Spain*, 2 v. (1965).

Marmont, Auguste Frédéric Louis Viesse de, Duc de Raguse, *Mémoires du Maréchal Marmont, duc de Raguse de 1792–1841*, 9 v. 2nd ed. (1857).

Masséna, André, Maréchal Prince d'Essling, *Mémoires*. 7 v. 1849–1850). New Ed. 1966.

Memorias para la historia de la revolucion española. Con documentos justifi-cativos. Recogidas y compiladas por Juan Nellerto. (Paris, 1814–1816).

Mercader-Riba, Juan, *Barcelona durante la occupación francesca 1808–1814* (1949).

——, *José Bonaparte, Rey de Espana (1808–1813): Estructura del estado es-panol bonapartista* (Madrid, 1983).

Miot de Melito, Andre François, Comte, *Mémoires du comte Miot de Melito*, 3 v. Ed. by général de Fleischmann (1858).

Moore, Sir John, *The Diary of Sir John Moore.* Ed. by Major Gen. Sir J. F. Maurice (1904).

Murat, Joachim, *Lettres et documents pour servir à l' histoire de Joachim Murat*, 8 v. Ed. by Paul le Brethon (1908–1914).

Myatt, Frederick, *British Sieges of the Peninsular War* (1987).

Les Espagnols et Napoleon. Actes du colloque international d'Aix-en-Provence . . . 1983 (1984).

Nabonne, B., *Joseph Boneparte, le roi philosophie* (1949).

Napier, Sir William Francis Patrick, *History of the War in the Peninsula*, 6 v. (1827–1840).

Neves, Jose Acursio das (1766–1834), *Historia general da invasio em Portugal e da restauracao deste reino* (Porto, 1984).

Oman, Sir Charles W. C., *A History of the Peninsular War*, 7 v. (1902–1930).

Oman, Carola, *Sir John Moore* (1953).

Pelet, J. J., *The French Campaign in Portugal, 1810–1811.* Trans. & Ed. by Donald D. Horward (1973).

Pla y Cargol, Joaquin, *La guerra de la independencia en Gerona y sus Comarcas* (1953).

Pouzerewsky, *La charge de la cavalerie de Somo-Sierra (Espagne), le 30 nov-embre 1808* (1900).

Roux, Georges, *Napoléon et le guepier espagnole.* Paris, 1970.

——, *La guerra napoleonica de Espana.* Trans. from French by Felipe Xim-enez de Sandoval (1971).

Shafer, Robert Jones, *The Economic Societies in the Spanish World 1763–1821* (1958).

Suchet, Louis Gabriel, Duc d'Albufera, *Memoirs of the War in Spain from 1808 to 1814*, 2 v. (1829).

Thiébault, Paul Charles, *Mémoires du général baron Thiébault, 1792–1820.* Ed. by R. Lacour-Gayet (1962).

Toreño, José María, Conde de, *Histoire du soulèvement de la guerre et de la révo-lution d'Espagne*, 4 v. (1835–1836).

Tranie, J. & Carmigniani, *Napoleon's War in Spain: The French Peninsular Campaigns, 1807–1814.* From the notes and manuscripts of Commandant

Henry Lachouque. Translated by Janet S. Mallender and John R. Clements (1982).

Villa-Urrutia, W. R. de, *El Rey José Napoléon* (1927).

———, *Relaciones entre España e Inglaterra durante la Guerra de la Independencia: Apuntes para la historia diplomatica de España de 1808 a 1814.* (Madrid, 1911–1914).

Ward, S. P. G., *Wellington* (1963).

———, *Wellington's Headquarters . . . 1809–1814* (1957).

Weller, Jac, *Wellington in the Peninsula, 1808–1814* (1962).

Wellington, Arthur, *The Dispatches of Field Marshal, The Duke of Wellington,* 12 v. Ed. by Lt. Col. Gurwood (1834–1838).

Wojciechowski, Kajetan, *Pamietniki moje w Hiszpanii.* Wstepem i przypisami opatrzyl oraz wyboru ilustracji dokonal Waldemar Lysiak (Warsaw, 1978).

Background and Reference

Barzini, Luigi, Jr., *The Italians* (1964).

Bertier de Sauvigny, G. de, *La restauration* (1963).

Bonaparte, Joseph. France. Archives Nationales. *Archives de Joseph Bonaparte.* Inventory by Chantal de Tourtier-Bonazzi (1982).

Bonaparte, Louis. France. Archives nationales. *Archives du cabinet de Louis Bonaparte, roi d'Hollande.* Inventory by S. de Dainville-Barbiche (1984).

Bonaparte, Napoleon, France. Archives Nationales. *Archives Napoléon: état sommaire.* Inventory by Chantal de Tourtier-Bonazzi (1979).

Boyer, Ferdinand, "Les responsabilites de Napoléon dans le transfert à Paris des oeuvres d'art de l'étranger," *Revue d'Histoire Moderne et Contemporaine* (1964).

Canetti, Elias, *Crowds and Power* (1962).

Chandler, David G., *Dictionary of the Napoleonic Wars* (1979).

Connelly, Owen, *Dictionary of Napoleonic France* (1985).

Charles-Roux, F., *Bonaparte, Governor of Egypt* (1937).

Churchill, Winston S., *The Age of Revolution* (1957).

Davois, Gustave, *Les Bonapartes littérateurs* (1909).

Fayet, Joseph, *La révolution française et la science* (1959).

Ford, Franklin L., "The Revolutionary-Napoleonic Era: How Much of a Watershed?" *American Historical Review* (1963).

Godechot, Jacques, *La Grande Nation: L'Expansion révolutionnaire de la France dans le monde, 1789 à 1799.* New Ed. (1983).

———, *L'Europe et l'Amerique à l'epoque Napoleonienne.* Vol. 37, *Nouvelle Clio* [bibliography]. (1967).

———, *Les Institutions de la France sous la Révolution et l'Empire* (1968).

Horward, Donald D., *Napoleonic Military History: A Bibliography.* (1986).

Labarre de Raillicourt, Dominique, *Les généraux des Cent Jours et du gouvernement provisoire, mars-juil. 1815. Dictionaire biographique* . . . (1963).

Meyer, Jack A., *An Annotated Bibliography of the Napoleonic Era: Recent Publications, 1945–1985*. Westport, CT, 1987.

Palmer, R. R., *The Age of Democratic Revolution*. 2 v. (1959–64).

Quynn, Dorothy M., "The Art Confiscations of the Napoleonic Wars," *American Historical Review* (1945).

Tulard, Jean, *Bibliographie critique des mémoires sur le Consulat et l'Empire*. Geneva, 1971.

Villat, Jean, *La Révolution et l'Empire, 1789–1815*. 2 v. Paris, 1947. [*Clio*; bibliography.]

INDEX